D0915582

Scottish Weapons and Fortifications
1100-1800

Frontispiece. Map of Scotland showing the principal places mentioned in the text

Scottish Weapons and Fortifications 1100-1800

Edited by
DAVID H. CALDWELL
National Museum of Antiquities
of Scotland

JOHN DONALD PUBLISHERS LTD
EDINBURGH

ISBN 0 85976 047 2

Phototypesetting by Burns & Harris Limited, Dundee
Printed in Great Britain by Bell & Bain Ltd, Glasgow

Preface

This book grew out of two conferences held in Edinburgh, the first under the auspices of the Society of Antiquaries of Scotland and both with the backing of the Extra-Mural Studies Department of Edinburgh University. The first conference in December 1976 was on the theme of *Scottish Weapons* and the second in the spring of 1978 on *Weapons and Fortifications*. Owing to the great interest in the work presented on both occasions it has been thought desirable to bring it together here, along with other material suggested by discussion at the conferences, and some work by other scholars in related fields.

As our title suggests, the book is primarily aimed at elucidating the history of weapons and fortifications in Scotland in the Medieval Period and afterwards; but the contents have not just narrowly been confined to matters purely relating to Scotland. Rather the intention has been to show how many of these things in Scotland relate to similar phenomena elsewhere. In some of the papers the relationship between fortifications and weapons is also explored. The book as a whole gives an indication of current thought and achievements in a vast field but cannot pretend to a complete coverage of all aspects of it. There is still much work needing to be done.

D.H.C.

NOTES ON THE CONTRIBUTORS

Claude Blair is Keeper of the Department of Metalwork in the Victoria and Albert Museum, London. He is a leading authority on European arms and armour and has taken a particular interest in Scottish weapons.

Geoffrey Boothroyd has written profusely on firearms of all sorts and is a regular contributor to *The Shooting Times*. He has for long been deeply interested in Scottish pistols.

David H. Caldwell is a Research Assistant in the National Museum of Antiquities of Scotland, Edinburgh. He is mainly interested in the Medieval Period and is currently working on early Scottish artillery.

George Good is an archaeologist with Bristol City Museums and concentrates his researches in the Medieval Period.

Iain MacIvor is an Inspector of Ancient Monuments for Scotland. He has published important works on artillery fortifications, including Berwick, Fort George and Craignethan.

Stuart Maxwell is Deputy Keeper of the National Museum of Antiquities of Scotland. Apart from Scottish weapons, his interests include costume and silver and he has written authoritatively on all of these.

William Reid is Director of the National Army Museum, London, and has long been interested in Scottish weapons. He has written several articles about them in the *Scottish Arms Review* and the *Connoisseur*.

Jack G. Scott was until recently Keeper of the Department of Archaeology, History and Ethnography in Glasgow Art Galleries and Museums. Among his many interests are prehistoric chambered tombs and Scottish weapons.

Robert B. K. Stevenson, recently retired from his position as Keeper of the National Museum of Antiquities of Scotland, keeps up a lively interest in Scottish history and antiquities. He has made numerous contributions to our knowledge of Scotland's past.

Sara Stevenson is a Research Assistant in the Scottish National Portrait Gallery, Edinburgh. She is doing work on some aspects of the history of ideas and has been involved in the planning and mounting of several highly successful Edinburgh Festival exhibitions.

Geoffrey Stell is an Investigator with the Royal Commission on Ancient and Historical Monuments of Scotland. He is especially interested in the architecture and society of medieval Scotland and Northern England.

Christopher J. Tabraham is an Inspector of Ancient Monuments for Scotland. He has carried out excavations at Threave Castle and Kelso Abbey and has also done survey work in the South-West.

Eric J. Talbot is a lecturer in the Department of Archaeology, Glasgow University. He is particularly interested in mottes and other early castles in Scotland and elsewhere and has carried out excavations on several of them.

Gerard L'E. Turner is Senior Assistant Curator of the Museum of the History of Science, University of Oxford. He has published extensively on the history of scientific instruments, including *Descriptive Catalogue of Van Marum's Scientific Instruments in Teyler's Museum* (Leyden, 1973).

NOTE ON BIBLIOGRAPHICAL REFERENCES

The titles of several periodicals and journals in the notes in this volume have been abbreviated but it is hoped in such a way that there can be little doubt as to their full titles. For example, *Proceedings, Society* and *Journal* have been rendered as *Proc., Soc.* and *Journ.* respectively. Certain other works of importance relating to Scotland are abbreviated as follows:

Aberdeen-Banff Coll.	*Collections for a History of the Shires of Aberdeen and Banff* (Spalding Club, 1843).
Aberdeen Council Register	*Extracts from the Council Register of the Burgh of Aberdeen* (Spalding Club, 1844-8).
Accts Masters of Works	*Accounts of the Masters of Works I, 1529-1615*, ed. H. M. Paton (Edinburgh, 1957).
Acts of Council	*The Acts of the Lords of Council in Civil Causes*, edd. T. Thomson et al. (Edinburgh, 1839, 1918-).
Acts of Council (Public Affairs)	*Acts of the Lords of Council in Public Affairs 1501-1554: Selections from Acta Dominorum Concilii*, ed. R. K. Hannay (Edinburgh, 1932).
Acts Parl. Scot.	*The Acts of the Parliaments of Scotland*, edd. T. Thomson & C. Innes (Edinburgh, 1814-75).
Balcarres Papers	*Foreign Correspondence with Marie de Lorraine Queen of Scotland, from the Originals in the Balcarres Papers* (Scot. Hist. Soc., 1923-5).
Barbour, *Bruce*	J. Barbour, *The Bruce* (Scot. Text. Soc., 1894).
Brosse Missions	*Two Missions of Jacques de la Brosse*, ed. G. Dickinson (Scot. Hist. Soc., 1942).
Buchanan, *History*	G. Buchanan, *The History of Scotland*, translated J. Aikman (Glasgow & Edinburgh, 1827-9).
Cal. Docs. Scot.	*Calendar of Documents relating to Scotland*, ed. J. Bain (Edinburgh, 1881-8).
Cal. State Papers (Thorpe)	*Calendar of the State Papers relating to Scotland 1509-1603*, ed. M. J. Thorpe (London, 1858).
Cal. State Papers Scot.	*Calendar of the State Papers relating to Scotland and Mary, Queen of Scots 1547-1603*, edd. J. Bain et al. (Edinburgh, 1898-).
Cal. State Papers Venetian	*Calendar of State Papers and Manuscripts, relating to English Affairs, existing in the archives and collections of Venice, and in*

	other libraries of Northern Italy, edd. R. Brown et al. (London, 1864-).
Cawdor Bk	*The Book of the Thanes of Cawdor* (Spalding Club, 1859).
Chron. Auchinleck	*The Auchinleck Chronicle, ane Schort Memoriale of the Scottis Croniklis for Addicioun*, ed. T. Thomson (Edinburgh, 1819/1877).
Chron. Bower	*Johannis de Fordun Scotichronicon cum Supplementis et Continuatione Walteri Boweri*, ed. W. Goudall (Edinburgh, 1759).
Chron. Fordun	*Johannis de Fordun, Chronica Gentis Scotorum*, ed. W. F. Skene (Edinburgh, 1871-2).
Chron. Lanercost	*Chronicon de Lanercost* (Maitland Club, 1839).
Dalrymple, *Historie*	*The Historie of Scotland, wrytten first in Latin by the most reverend and worthy Jhone Leslie, Bishop of Rosse, and translated in Scottish by Father James Dalrymple 1596* (Scot. Text. Soc., 1888-95).
Dalyell, *Fragments*	*Fragments of Scottish History*, ed. J. G. Dalyell (Edinburgh, 1798).
Diurnal of Occurrents	*A Diurnal of Remarkable Occurrents that have passed within the country of Scotland, since the death of King James the Fourth till the year 1575* (Bannatyne & Maitland Clubs, 1833).
Dundas Papers	*Royal letters and other Historical Documents selected from the Family Papers of Dundas of Dundas*, ed. W. Macleod (Edinburgh, 1897).
Edinburgh Burgesses	*Roll of Edinburgh Burgesses and Guild-Brethren 1406-1700*, ed. C. B. B. Watson (Scot. Records Soc., 1929).
Edinburgh Burgh Accts	*Edinburgh Records: The Burgh Accounts*, ed. R. Adam (Edinburgh, 1899).
Edinburgh Burgh Recs.	*Extracts from the Records of the Burgh of Edinburgh* (Scot. Burgh Records Soc., 1869-92).

Exch. Rolls	*The Exchequer Rolls of Scotland,* edd. J. Stuart et al. (Edinburgh, 1878-).
Fraser, *Melville*	W. Fraser, *The Melvilles Earls of Melville and the Leslies Earls of Leven* (Edinburgh, 1890).
Fraser, *Pollock*	W. Fraser, *Memoirs of the Maxwells of Pollock* (Edinburgh, 1863).
Hamilton Papers	*The Hamilton Papers,* ed. J. Bain (Edinburgh, 1890-2).
Henry VIII Letters & Papers	*Letters and Papers, Foreign and Domestic, of the reign of Henry VIII,* edd. J. S. Brewer et al. (London, 1862-1932).
Hist. MSS. Comm.	*Reports of the Royal Commission on Historical Manuscripts* (London, 1870-).
James V Letters	*The Letters of James V,* edd. R. K. Hannay & D. Hay (Edinburgh, 1954).
Major, *History*	J. Major, *A History of Greater Britain* (Scot. Hist. Soc., 1892).
Pinkerton, *History*	J. Pinkerton, *The History of Scotland from the Accession of the House of Stuart to that of Mary with Appendices of Original Papers* (London, 1797).
Pitcairn, *Trials*	*Criminal Trials in Scotland from 1488 to 1624,* ed. R. Pitcairn (Edinburgh, 1833; also Bannatyne & Maitland Clubs).
Pitscottie, *Historie*	R. Lindesay of Pitscottie, *The Historie and Cronicles of Scotland* (Scot. Text Soc., 1899-1911).
Prot. Bk Grote	*Protocol Book of Mr. Gilbert Grote 1552-73* (Scot. Rec. Soc., 1914).
Reg. Mag. Sig.	*Registrum Magni Sigilli Regum Scotorum,* edd. J. M. Thomson et al. (Edinburgh, 1882-).
Reg. Privy Council	*The Register of the Privy Council of Scotland,* edd. J. H. Burton et al. (Edinburgh, 1877-).
Reg. Sec. Sig.	*Registrum Secreti Sigilli Regum Scotorum,* edd. M. Livingstone et al. (Edinburgh, 1908-).

State Papers (Ireland) Henry VIII	State Papers published under the Authority of His Majesty's Commission, vols. II-III, King Henry the Eighth Part III (London, 1834).
Stirling Recs.	Extracts from the Records of the Royal Burgh of Stirling, ed. R. Renwick (Glasgow, 1887-9).
Treasurer Accts	Accounts of the Lord High Treasurer of Scotland, edd. T. Dickson et al. (Edinburgh, 1877-).
Wardrobe Inventories	A Collection of Inventories and other Records of the Royal Wardrobe and Jewel-house, and of the Artillery and Munition in some of the Royal Castles 1488-1606, ed. T. Thomson (Edinburgh, 1815).

A fuller list of abbreviated titles of works relative to Scottish History to 1560 may be consulted in a supplement to the *Scottish Historical Review*, xlii (1963).

Acknowledgements

The authors and publishers are grateful to the following for supplying illustrations and allowing them to be reproduced:

Bibliothèque royale Albert Ier, figs 67, 68, copyright; Claude Blair, fig 166; The British Museum, fig 83; The Duke of Buccleuch, figs 210, 211; Chandler's of Exeter, fig 95; A. C. Cooper, fig 77; The Master and Fellows of Corpus Christi College, Cambridge, figs 39-40; The Courtauld Institute, London, figs 72, 79; John Dewar Studios, figs 7, 41, 52, reproduced by permission of the Secretary of State for Scotland; The Department of the Environment, figs 38, 55-57, 59, 92-93, 105-106, 123, 165, 192; Dundee Art Gallery and Museum, fig 143; Glasgow Art Galleries and Museums, figs 3, 34, 217, 223-224; Haermuseet, fig 131; The Duke of Hamilton, figs 209, 213; The Marquess of Lothian, figs 205, 208; The Museum of London, figs 97-98, 128; The National Gallery of Canada, Ottawa, fig 76; The National Galleries of Scotland, fig 8; The National Monuments Record of Scotland, figs 46, 48-49, 51, 137, 149; The National Museum of Antiquities of Scotland, figs 36-37, 65-66, 89, 124-125, 136, 141-142, 147, 154, 156-158, 161-164, 194, 228-233; The National Museum of Ireland, figs 121-122; The National Portrait Gallery, London, figs 207, 215; Nederlands Legeren Wapenmuseum, fig 119; Norsk Folkmuseum, fig 91; Perth Museum and Art Gallery, fig 144; Her Majesty the Queen, figs 71, 102, 159, 193, 216; Reading Museum, fig 126; The Duke of Rothes, fig 195; The Royal Commission on Ancient and Historical Monuments of Scotland, figs 6, 10-11, 235-236; Lord Saltoun, fig 212; The Scottish Development Department, figs 9, 16-19, 21-23, 25, 27-31, 52; The Scottish National Portrait Gallery, figs 191, 197-200, 202, 206; The Scottish United Services Museum, fig 134; Miss Smythe of Methven, fig 196; The Tate Gallery, London, fig 190; The Victoria and Albert Museum, London, figs 71, 133; Wallis and Wallis, Lewes, Sussex, fig 130.

Sincere thanks are due also to the following for making drawings for reproduction:

Tom Borthwick, figs 44, 47, 58, 64; Colin Hendry, figs 78, 80, 82, 94, 103, and fig 116 from an idea by W. Reid; Mrs A. V. B. Norman, fig 87; Mr and Mrs A. V. B. Norman, fig 88; Bend Petersen, fig 50.

List of Figures

Contents

1 The Defences of Earth and Timber Castles

Eric J. Talbot

Because of the very nature of earth and timber castles it is not possible to make accurate observations about their contemporary defences (except for their mounds and ramparts) without recourse to excavation. Few examples have been excavated and the results have shown little consistency. The aim of this paper, therefore, will be to look at the characteristics of these monuments as they survive and to comment upon their origins and evolution.

Much controversy has raged recently over the origin of the castle in England.[1] The generally accepted view of archaeologists and historians alike was that William the Conqueror, and his followers, introduced the motte-and-bailey castle of earth and timber into England in 1066 and that this was the normal form of fortification constructed then and for many years to come. The situation has, however, proved on closer examination to be much more complex. It does not appear that this form of castle, with its earthen mound and attached enclosure, was common in Normandy before 1066. In fact, only seven castles of the motte form, and documented before 1066, can be seen on the ground today in the area of the Duchy of Normandy.[2] In southern Italy, the mottes of the Norman settlement, of the early eleventh century, have not yet been studied in enough detail to see if any pre-date Norman involvement in England.[3]

The Anglo-Saxon Chronicle records that the Norman followers of Edward the Confessor had castles on land granted to them but although mottes are present at three of the four places suggested (Canfield or Clavering in Essex and Richard's Castle and Ewyas Harold in Herefordshire — the motte at Hereford, the fourth site, was destroyed many years ago), it cannot be certain that the mounds present are primary. No evidence of a pre-1066 date for the motte at Richard's Castle was forthcoming in excavations in the 1960s.[4]

Ordericus Vitalis, the great chronicler of the Conquest period, states that one of the major reasons for English failure in 1066 was the absence of castles in England. Saxon defences can be seen, in the main, as communal — walled towns like Wareham and Winchester — but there have been recent attempts made to show that there were defended thegnly residences at the time of the Norman Conquest. At Sulgrave, in Northamptonshire, the excavator[5] showed that a stone gate tower had been engulfed by a later Norman ringbank. The interior of the site had been occupied by a late Saxon residence. At Goltho, in Lincolnshire, a ringbank was actually revealed to be a contemporary defence around a Saxon thegnly residence and after the Conquest became a castle site.[6] It has been suggested,[7] that at Earl's Barton, in Northamptonshire, the late Saxon church may have been part of a thegnly complex, delimited by a crescentic bank possibly strengthened in the Norman period, and that here again there might have been a situation where '. . . if a ceorl throve so that he had fully five hides (600 acres) of his own land, church and kitchen bellhouse and burh-gate, seat and special duty in the king's hall, then was he hence-forth of thegnright worthy'.[8]

On balance, it is generally felt that outside a feudal context, it is not permissible to use the term 'castle' and that we should continue to regard the coming of the Normans to England as an event which saw the introduction of castles for the use of feudal lords of all ranks.

The depiction of motte castles in the Bayeux Tapestry has led scholars to believe that this was *the* castle of the Conquest, but a more systematic study of remains in the field has shown that the earliest castles in England were, in all probability, of a simple enclosure form. At William's landing point — Pevensey — a ditch was dug and a bank thrown up in a corner of the Roman fortifications.[9] The Bayeux Tapestry shows a motte under construction at Hastings but excavation[10] has not confirmed a Conquest date for the motte, and the adjacent earthwork enclosure may well prove to be the primary defence.

According to Ordericus Vitalis a castle was built in London whilst William was away at Barking for a few days shortly after his coronation. This again is believed, from the results of archaeological excavations, to be an enclosure castle of earth and timber, L-shaped and sited within a corner of the Roman defences of London.[11]

There would appear to be two basic reasons for the relatively slow appearance of the motte in England after the Conquest — its novelty, seemingly, as a defence work in the duchy of Normandy and the need during and after the Conquest campaigns to defend quickly men and equipment. The creation of a more sophisticated defence site by the addition of a motte came often, it can be surmised, only later, and this is witnessed by the results of archaeological research at Castle Neroche, Somerset.[12] Here an ostensibly straight-forward motte-and-bailey castle (situated at the end of a spur) showed two phases of enclosure defence before the addition of a motte.

Some Norman castles of earth and timber never contained a motte element and have come to be known by the unfortunate archaeological term of 'ringwork'. Earthworks with enclosing bank and ditch are exceedingly basic forms of defence, but medieval examples, however, can often be characterised by a relatively massive bank which encloses a somewhat small area — an average diameter of c. 30 metres is quite common but in the case of Old Sarum — a royal castle — the diameter is c. 120 metres. In some instances only excavation (in the absence of other evidence) is likely to show whether such an earthwork is Norman or not. A puzzling group of 'ringworks' in the area of the Danelaw[13] have some features which could indicate Danish construction, but with the absence of firm documentation (a recurring aspect of many medieval earthworks) field observation cannot be a substitute for excavation. This group, if shown to be Danish, would further complicate the issue concerning the origin of the castle in England. In Scotland, a couple of northern ring-works may be of Norse origin: Cubbie Roos's Castle on Wyre, in Orkney, has an encircling earthwork which may be primary;[14] Castlehill in Caithness may be a Scottish campaign castle or possibly a fortification of the Norse Earls of Orkney.[15]

Ringworks are to be found in Normandy,[16] and similar earthworks occur in neighbouring areas, for example, Belgium.[17] It is now felt, especially where concentrations of ringworks are to be found (e.g., Glamorgan, Shropshire and Wessex),[18] that the occurrence and continued use of ringworks in certain parts of Britain shows a preference for this form of earthwork castle rather than an early and restricted use. Crookston Castle, near Glasgow, may well have functioned as an earthen ringwork castle from the later twelfth to the early fifteenth century.[19]

After c. 1068, mottes were more commonly constructed in England (one of the first was at York), and in Wales they mark the areas of Norman conquest and settlement although ringworks are to be found too. Not all of these castles can be regarded as permanent bases, for some, by their very remote situation, can only be regarded as campaign castles (e.g., Tomen-y-Mur in Merionethshire). Earth and timber (and also stone) castles were built by the Welsh in imitation of those of their hostile Norman neighbours. It is significant that there was no strong tradition of fortification in Wales before the Norman campaigns of conquest began.[20]

Norman settlement in Scotland was peaceful and was at the invitation of the Scottish kings in order to bolster and extend their authority. Throughout the twelfth century these settlers came and built castles as the strong-points of their landholdings.[21] Many were of the motte-and-bailey form (although large mottes, without a bailey, were built to house all the buildings of the castle — e.g., Boreland of Borgue) with the principal and most strongly concentrated distribution in the southwest of the country — in Dumfriesshire and Galloway. Recently, a few ringworks have been identified in Scotland.[22] Those near Glasgow, on the lands of Walter fitzAlan, steward to Malcolm IV, were built perhaps as late as the 1180s.

Many of these Scottish earth and timber castles could well have been lived in throughout the Middle Ages — see Crookston (above). At Huntly, in Aberdeenshire, and at Edzell, in Angus, for example, there are no structural remains between the motte phase and the tower houses of the late Middle Ages. A sixteenth century plan shows the motte at Castle-milk in Dumfriesshire still with a keep on its summit.[23] The motte at Lumphanan, in Aberdeenshire, continued to contain the castle buildings until modern times.[24]

Stone castles were relatively common in the second half of the twelfth century and yet the castle of the Anglo-Norman invasion of Ireland was the motte castle. An enclosing earthwork of the ringwork principle is to be seen at Baginbun — one of the first landing points of the Anglo-Normans. A bank and ditch cuts off a promontory at this site near Wexford. Professor M. J. O'Kelly has excavated at Beal Boru, Co. Clare, a pre-Norman ringfort and has shown that a re-defence took place in the period of Anglo-Norman campaigns.[25] Very many thousands of ringforts exist in Ireland and in such varying degrees of survival and regularity that it is difficult without excavation to determine the date of con-struction and length of use.[26] The excavated mound of Lismahon, Co. Down, is of interest in that it is the result of in-filling and heightening the interior of a ringfort — a situation to be considered below elsewhere in Ireland and Britain.[27]

The strategic value of an elevated earthen mound for defence purposes may have occurred to one person or a number of people in the eleventh century — or before? There are earlier precedents (e.g., Roman signal stations),[28] for this concept and the example may have been learned by later strategists. There is a strong possibility that the motte 'emerged' from existing forms of fortification — although one must perhaps allow for a number of independent origins. At Der Husterknupp in the North Rhineland the excavation of the castle mound emphasises the dilemma which faces the archaeologist concerned with the development of the motte.[29] The motte of Der Husterknupp may well have been an alien imposition of independent origin and built upon an existing earthwork enclosure or it may have been the result of a realisation that in-filling and heightening the existing defence not only made it more defensible but also obviated the effects of flooding.

This latter consideration may also have a long ancestry: the *turpen* and *wurten* of the Low Countries and coastal northern Germany are settlement mounds of the Migration Period which may have had some influence upon military ideas in later centuries. Federsen Wierde, between the Elbe and Weser, is a classic example of this kind of settle-ment.[30] There are mottes in England which because of their siting and relatively low height lead one to think that the prime concern of elevation was not military, but a desire to raise the buildings of the castle above the level of flooding. An example of this may be suggested at Howton in Herefordshire, for here a low mound is in evidence close to a tributary of the River Monnow — one of a number of similar mounds recognised in the Wye/Severn Basin. Usually the motte is a part of a castle and can be regarded as a defence element only occupied during an attack although some large mottes (often royal or baronial) had permanent residences on the summit. There are contemporary accounts of such situations — e.g., at Sycharth in Denbighshire[31] and at Merchem near Dixmüde.[32] The mound, in some instances, would have required a considerable period of time for construction and a large number of men to carry out the work. In the first phases of Norman conquest and settlement in Britain and Ireland it would appear unlikely that the motte would have been a primary undertaking in the building of an earth and timber castle. Many a bailey may well prove, on excavation, to represent the first phase of construction (e.g., at Castle Neroche) and be, in effect, a ringwork with the motte an additional defence feature when circumstances allowed its construction. The value of a motte dominating a bailey (where the residential buildings of most castles were situated) comes out very effectively in the siege of Llandovery Castle by the Welsh in 1113: '. . . Gruffydd ap Rhys . . . went to Llandovery . . . and tried to breach it and set it on fire, but he failed; for the keepers of the castle . . . resisted him. Nevertheless, he burned the outer castle. After he had been shot at from the tower and many of his men had been wounded by arrows and others killed, he turned back again'.[33]

Some baileys may prove to be secondary and to be the second enclosure earthwork on the site. A few mottes examined archaeologically in Britain and Ireland have shown evidence for their construction up from an existing enclosure earthwork. The Bayeux Tapestry representation of Hastings motte shows a team of men digging a ditch and throwing up the layers of soil into a regular reversed stratigraphic sequence. This kind of constructional aspect may have arisen when experimenting with this relatively new form of defence but it must have become obvious that instability would result from horizontal layering. A timber keep, let alone a stone one, unless built up from the original ground surface, could be endangered by soil slip. In the case of Clifford's Tower, York, flooding weakened the motte and caused cracking in the quatrefoil tower of stone. It would be necessary to section a large number of mottes in areas of differing soil conditions in order to generalise, but it is to be noted that methods other than that shown at Hastings can be witnessed in the archaeological record for the throwing-up of castle mounds. At Aldingham, on the Lancashire coast,[34] the section of the motte shows three constructional phases: 1 — ringwork; 2 — infilled ringwork with low motte created; 3 — heightened mound. It is not known if the change represents differing preferences for defences or the response to a prevailing local situation.

At Alstoe in Rutland,[35] St Weonard's Tump in Herefordshire,[36] and Lorrha in Co. Tipperary,[37] however, a progression from ringwork to motte is witnessed in the sectional evidence but as a feature of the whole constructional process and not as a cultural or strategical development. Tip-lines at these sites show that a ring bank was created, in-filled and heightened to form a motte and thus ensured a greater stability than by layering horizontally material obtained by ditch digging. At the Peel of Lumphanan in Aberdeenshire the glacial drumlin had been heightened to form a motte, the upcast being revetted with turf[38] (fig. 1).

Figure 1. Lumphanan. Excavation in progress. Results show an approach to the motte by way of a causeway across the ditch and a cobbled path leading to the summit

The utilisation of pre-existing fortification lines has already been discussed but excavation has also shown that motte builders used existing eminences (artificial or natural) either as a core for the motte (e.g., a Bronze Age barrow at Tre-Oda, Cardiff[39] (fig. 2) and a burial mound again — around which the ring bank was thrown up — at St Weonard's Tump) or, by scarping them, turned them into a motte form — e.g., Macharioch, Kintyre (Argyll).

Occasionally a promontory would be cut off by a curving ditch so that the end of the spur became an almost circular isolated area level with

Figure 2. Tre-Oda. Motte under excavation prior to complete destruction. Bronze Age barrow at core

(e.g., Kilninver, south of Oban, Argyll) the ground beyond or perhaps elevated to form a motte.

It has become apparent from archaeological endeavour at a number of widely separated sites that not always was the motte a primary feature and that a defensive and free-standing tower came first and was subsequently surrounded by an earthen mound. The Bayeux Tapestry shows a timber castle in the process of construction (in that only the palisade is in evidence) on the top of a motte but recent work at the motte at South Mimms, Middlesex, has shown that a wooden tower came first and that the motte was a secondary feature. This was a castle of the Anarchy and is tentatively dated 1141-2.

The motte section shows that it was constructed by first creating a ring bank and then in-filling to form a mound as has been described above. In order, in all probability, to protect the base of the round keep, a motte was created as a secondary defence at Skenfrith in Monmouthshire. It can thus be seen that two separate functions can be witnessed for mottes — to create an elevated position for a building, and to protect the base of an existing structure. Recent excavations at Doué-la-Fontaine, in Normandy, reveal that at an early date at this hall-keep the latter consideration was one adopted by strategists and was not one which necessarily developed as a response to developments in siege warfare. The most spectacular example of a sequence of stone tower to motte encompassed tower is to be witnessed at Farnham in Surrey.[40] During the Anglo-Norman campaigns in Ireland, there was an interesting occurrence of the surrounding of a tower with an earthen mound. The tower was not a keep, but the church tower of Meelich on the Shannon.[41]

Earth and timber defences were adequate for the warfare of the time. They could be used as instruments of siege like the ringworks at Faringdon[42] and Corfe[43] and, seemingly, a motte at Hereford.[44]

NOTES

1. R. A. Brown, 'The Norman Conquest and the Genesis of English Castles', *Château Gaillard*, iii (1969), 1-14.
2. B. K. Davison, 'Early Earthwork Castles: A New Model', *Château Gaillard*, iii (1969), 37-47.
3. A. J. Taylor, 'Three Early Castle Sites in Sicily', *Château Gaillard*, vii (1975), 209-14.
4. P. E. Curnow & M. W. Thomson, 'Excavations at Richard's Castle, Herefordshire'. *Journ. Brit. Archaeol. Assoc.*, xxxi (1969), 105-27.
5. B. K. Davison, 'Three Eleventh Century Earthworks in England', *Château Gaillard*, ii (1967), 45-8.
6. M. Beresford, 'Goltho: A deserted medieval village and its manor house', *Current Archaeol.*, lvi (1976), 262-70.
7. B. K. Davison, 'The Origins of the Castle in England', *Archaeol. Journ.*, cxxiv (1967), 208-10.
8. Ibid., 204.
9. D. Renn, *Norman Castles in Britain* (London, 1973), 276, 279.
10. P. Barker, *The Techniques of Archaeological Excavation* (London, 1977), 38.
11. Davison, 'Three Eleventh Century Earthworks', 40-43.
12. B. K. Davison, 'Castle Neroche: An Abandoned Norman Fortress in South Somerset', *Proc. Somerset Archaeol. Nat. Hist. Soc.*, cxvi (1972), 16-58.
13. J. Dyer, 'Earthworks of the Danelaw Frontier' in *Archaeology and the Landscape*, ed. P. J. Fowler (London, 1972), 222-36.
14. E. J. Talbot, 'Scandinavian Fortification in the British Isles', *Scot. Archaeol. Forum*, vi (1974), 39-40.
15. Idem, 'Castlehill, Caithness: A Viking Fortification?', *Proc. Soc. Antiq. Scot.*, cviii (1976-7), 378-9.
16. M. de Bouard, 'Les Petites enceintes circulaires d'origine mediévale en Normandie', *Château Gaillard*, i (1964), 2-135.
17. R. Borremans, 'Fouille d'une motte féodale a Kontich', *Château Gaillard*, i (1964), 20.
18. D. J. C. King & L. Alcock, 'Ringworks of England and Wales', *Château Gaillard*, iii (1969), 90-127.
19. E. J. Talbot, in 'Medieval Britain in 1974', *Med. Archaeol.*, xix (1975), 242.
20. L. Alcock, 'Pottery and Settlements in Wales and the March, A.D. 400-700' in *Culture and Environment*, ed. I. L. Foster & L. Alcock (London, 1963), 281-302.
21. G. W. S. Barrow, 'The Earliest Stewarts and their lands' in *The Kingdom of the Scots*, 337-61; G. G. Simpson & B. Webster, 'Charter Evidence and the distribution of mottes in Scotland', *Château Gaillard*, v (1972), 175-92.
22. E. J. Talbot, 'Early Scottish Castles of Earth and Timber: Recent Fieldwork and Excavation', *Scot. Archaeol. Forum*, vi (1974), 48-57.
23. W. M. Mackenzie, *The Medieval Castle in Scotland* (London, 1927), 33.
24. E. J. Talbot (forthcoming).
25. M. J. O'Kelly, 'Beal Boru. Co. Clare', *Journ. Cork Hist. & Archaeol. Soc.*, lxvii (1962), 1-27.

26. C. J. Lynn, 'The Medieval Ringfort — An Archaeological Chimera?', *Irish Archaeol. Research Forum*, II, i (1975), 29-36; T. E. McNeill, 'Medieval Raths? An Anglo-Norman Comment', *Irish Archaeol. Research Forum*, II, i (1975), 37-39.
27. D. M. Waterman, 'Excavations at Lismahon, Co. Down', *Med. Archaeol.*, iii (1959), 139-76.
28. B. Hope-Taylor, 'The Norman Motte at Abinger, Surrey' in *Recent Archaeological Excavations in Britain*, ed. R. L. S. Bruce-Mitford (London, 1956), 244-46.
29. A. Herrnbrodt, *Der Husterknupp* (Köln, 1958).
30. W. Haarnagel, 'Die Wurtensiedlung Feddersen Wierde Im Nordsee-Küstengebiet', *Ausgrabungen in Deutchland Gefördert von der Deutschen Forschungsgemeinschaft 1950-1975*, ii (1975), 10-29.
31. D. B. Hague & C. Warhurst, 'Excavations at Sycharth Castle, Denbighshire', *Archaeologia Cambrensis*, cxv (1966), 108-27.
32. S. Cruden, *The Scottish Castle* (Edinburgh, 1963), 8.
33. Brut y Tywysogion (Red Book of Hergest Version) in *The Text of the Bruts*, ed. T. Jones & J. G. Evans (Cardiff, 1955), 87.
34. *Current Archaeol.*, xi (1968), 23.
35. G. C. Dunning, 'Alstoe Mount, Burley, Rutland', *Antiq. Journ.* xvi (1936), 396-411.
36. T. Wright, 'Treago and the Large Tumulus at St Weonard's', *Archaeol. Cambrensis*, x (1855), 168-174.
37. E. J. Talbot, 'Lorrha Motte, County Tipperary', *N. Munster Antiq. Journ.*, xv (1972), 8-12.
38. Idem, in Medieval Britain in 1975', *Med. Archaeol.*, xx (1976), 185-6.
39. J. Knight & E. J. Talbot, 'The Excavation of a Castle Mound and Round Barrow at Tre-Oda, Whitchurch', *Trans. Cardiff Nat. Soc.*, xcv (1968-70), 9-23.
40. Renn, *Norman Castles*, 187-9.
41. J. O. Ruthven, *A History of Medieval Ireland* (London, 1968), 76.
42. *Gesta Stephani*, ed. K. R. Potter & R. H. C. Davis (Oxford, 1976), 181-3.
43. Renn, *Norman Castles*, 159.
44. *Gesta Stephani*, 109-11.

2 Three Medieval Swords from Scotland

Jack G. Scott

The construction of the M74 motorway near Hamilton, in Lanarkshire, a few years ago, led to the remarkable discovery of a very unusual medieval sword, now in Glasgow Art Gallery and Museum.[1] Between Hamilton and Motherwell the motorway runs along sandy flats, known as Low Parks, close to the south bank of the River Clyde. In this area a local fisherman, looking for bait, was passing along a deep cutting made in the sand by a mechanical excavator when he saw protruding from the side of the cutting, about 12 ft. (3.65 m.) below the surface, what appeared to be a small iron rod. He pulled at this, and found himself, to his astonishment, holding by the tang a medieval sword with cross, but lacking pommel and grip (fig. 3). No doubt because of the dryness of the sand the sword is in very good condition; indeed, it may be surmised that the mechanical excavator which exposed it may have also torn off the pommel. How the sword came to be where it was is a matter for speculation, since the finder was unable to place the find spot precisely. It may have been lost in a former meander of the river; it might even have come from the ditch of a motte which has been cut through by the road.[2]

The sword is 3 ft. 8¼ in. (1.122 m.) in length, of which the tapering tang, rectangular in section, takes up 7¾ in. (197 mm.); the bend in the tang may well indicate where it was struck by the mechanical excavator. The thrusting blade is straight and tapering, diamond-shaped in section for most of its length, and terminates in a sharp point. Below the cross there is a well-marked ricasso, grooved at each edge, 4¼ in. (107 mm.) long. Set into the ricasso, and piercing the blade, is a series of three inserts, in brass or latten, possibly consecration marks, recalling the Holy Trinity. Each mark is built up from seven separate pieces — an outer ring and an inner ring, between which five U-shaped pieces have been fitted, to give the appearance of a five-spoked wheel. Below the ricasso, on each side, there runs a central groove, 6⅛ in. (155 mm.) and 6⁷⁄₁₆ in. (163 mm.) long respectively. Stamped approximately centrally in each groove is an armourer's mark (fig. 4). It somewhat resembles a capital letter 'K'.

The cross, 10½ in. (267 mm.) long, is elaborate, consisting of a rectangular central block with short curved tongues (fig. 4). Straight arms, oval in section and ending in spatulate tips, emerge from each side of the block. Each face of the block, and parts of the arms, have traces of engraved designs, whilst specks of gold, still surviving, show that the whole was once gilt.

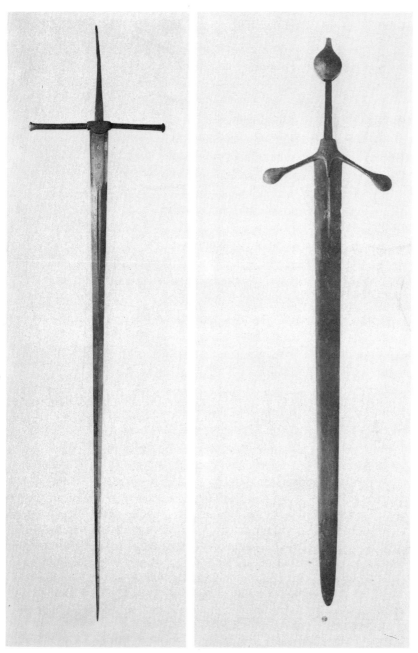

Figure 3. *Left:* hand-and-a-half sword found near Hamilton, blade early 15th cent; *right:* hand-and-a-half sword, probably Scottish, 15th cent. *Glasgow Art Gallery and Museum*

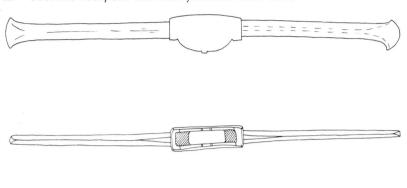

Figure 4. *Above:* lateral and underside views of the cross, probably 17th cent., associated with the early 15th-cent. sword found near Hamilton. Half size. *Below, left:* armourer's mark stamped on the blade of the early 15th-cent. sword found near Hamilton. *Below, right:* armourer's mark, inlaid in gold in the blade of the 15th-cent. sword in Glasgow Museum. Both marks actual size

Clearly the blade is of the type developed in the later fourteenth century, capable of being wielded in both hands if necessary, and designed to search out gaps in plate armour, which was giving ever increasing protection against the cutting edge. These thrusting swords, as Sir James Mann has pointed out, suited the battle tactics of the time, when knights would dismount from their horses before joining battle, and would advance upon each other with shortened lances grasped in both hands, or with two-hand swords held before them.[3] The length of the ricasso on the Hamilton sword is sufficient to enable the blade to be grasped by the left hand below the cross, which such fighting would require, as pointed out by Oakeshott.[4] At Aarau in Switzerland, as is well known, the tombs of two knights who fell at the Battle of Sempach, fought in 1386, were found to contain such swords.[5] By analogy with these swords it might be deduced that the Hamilton sword had a pommel of Oakeshott's 'scent-stopper' form, Type T2.[6]

Despite these general comparisons, it is not easy to find close parallels for the sword. Oakeshott illustrates a sword, now in the Castel San Angelo at Rome, which he classifies as of his Type XVII, assigned to the second half of the fourteenth century.[7] This has the grooved ricasso merging into the diamond-shaped blade seen on the Hamilton sword, but with the central groove of the blade prolonged as far as the cross. The correspondence is sufficiently close for the Hamilton sword to · be classified as of Type XVII also. A sword with somewhat similar blade, in the Tower of London, has a ricasso 6$\frac{1}{16}$ in. (154 mm.) long, and is dated by Blair as early fifteenth century.[8]

An extensive though incomplete search of the literature has failed to produce a medieval parallel for the cross. So far as its form is concerned, its distinctive feature is the development of the écusson, or block, as a distinct element, originally enhanced by an engraved design which, though not now obvious, was certainly the same on each side. Mr A. V. B. Norman, Master of the Armouries at the Tower of London, has examined the sword, and suggests a seventeenth century date for the cross. This being so, and since there is no doubt about the association of blade and cross, one must assume that a valued surviving medieval blade had been remounted in the seventeenth century.

Strongly contrasting with the Hamilton sword, and surely representing a very different fighting tradition, is a hand-and-a-half sword (figs. 3, 5) acquired in 1973 by Glasgow Art Gallery and Museum.[9] Although recently brought from Northern Ireland, the sword is said to have been discovered in Scotland, and it may be regarded as Scottish in origin. Much of the blade and tang are covered with a thin brown patina such as can form on iron which has lain for a long period in fresh water under relatively oxygen-free conditions. The pommel and cross are rather more corroded. It may be suggested that corrosion of the blade and tang have been inhibited by scabbard and grip, though these do not now survive, and that the sword is a river or bog find. Some credibility is lent to this suggestion by the discovery of grains of sand embedded in the corrosion of the hilt. The sword is, in fact, said to have had a scabbard when first recovered.

The sword is 3 ft. 5$\frac{7}{8}$ in. (1.14 m.) in length, the blade 3 ft. 0$\frac{3}{16}$ in. (0.92 m.). The blade is double-edged, tapering slightly to a rather blunt tip, and plain with slightly bevelled edges. A shallow groove, which starts in the base of the tang, runs out only some 6 in. (150 mm.) below the cross. Inlaid in gold in the groove on either side of the blade, near the hilt, is what was probably intended to be a running wolf (fig. 4). If so, it is of the earlier short stocky type, and not the elongated form of the later fifteenth and sixteenth centuries, which was to become the mark of Passau or Solingen.[10] On one side of the tang are two grooves, almost meeting in V-shaped form, which might be a bladesmith's mark. The pommel is a variation of the wheel form. It is hollow, made up of two bossed out iron plates, connected at the sides by separate iron strips, the joints run in

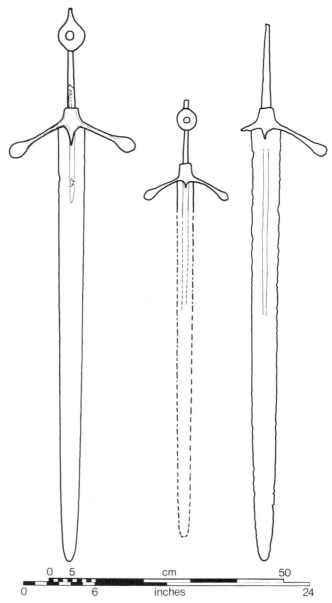

Figure 5. *Left:* hand-and-a-half sword, probably Scottish, 15th cent. *Glasgow Art Gallery and Museum. Centre:* right-hand sword, probably Scottish, 15th cent. *Kretzschmar von Kienbusch Collection. Right:* hand-and-a-half sword, from the River Ayr. *Kyle and Carrick District Museums*

with brass. A distinctive feature is that the plates and sides are prolonged to the tip of the tang, thus imitating and at the same time dispensing with a tang button.

But it is the cross which gives the sword its especial — and particularly Scottish — appearance. The cross consists of a central block extending up the tang and furnished with short pointed tongues below, the arms sloping downwards and expanding to form spatulate terminals.

The opportunity is taken here to publish a closely related sword, now on loan to Glasgow Art Gallery and Museum from Kyle and Carrick District Museums.[11] The sword (fig. 5) is believed to have been found in the River Ayr, perhaps in Ayr itself, some years ago. It is greatly corroded, and one arm of the cross is lost. The tang is better preserved, perhaps because the grip for a time protected it from corrosion. Nevertheless, the general resemblance to each other of the Glasgow and Ayr swords is remarkable.

The Ayr sword is 3 ft. 7$\frac{13}{16}$ in. (1.113 m.) in length, with a straight, double-edged blade, 2 ft. 11$\frac{1}{8}$ in. (0.892 m.) long, 2$\frac{1}{2}$ in. (64 mm.) wide at the cross, without a ricasso and tapering gradually to a blunt tip. On each side a shallow groove runs out some 16 in. (406 mm.) below the cross. The tang is rectangular in section, and tapering; pommel and grip are missing. The cross is of iron; it consists of a shallow central socket extending about 1 in. (25 mm.) up the tang, with two tongues of similar size extending below down the blade. One arm survives, sloping downwards to end in a spatulate tip. The cross is still held in place by an iron wedge driven down between tang and socket.

There is now considerable evidence to show that the sword with downward sloping spatulate-terminal cross is of Scottish origin, though as will appear, known in Ireland too. In a recent study of the late medieval monumental sculpture of the West Highlands Steer points out that swords with hilts of this type are first depicted perhaps as early as the third quarter of the fourteenth century, and continue to be represented throughout the fifteenth century.[12] He suggests that the term 'claymore', applied by Mann, and later by Hayes-McCoy, to certain of these swords,[13] should be reserved for the true 'claymore' of the sixteenth century, the quillons of which have quatrefoil terminals.[14] This view is accepted, though no such single convenient alternative name is offered for describing the swords under discussion here.

Four swords of the type are now known. Besides the two described in this paper there is one from Ireland, though the locality is not recorded.[15] The fourth again has no locality, and is in the Kretzschmar von Kienbusch collection in the U.S.A.[16] This is a right-hand sword, and a drawing of it, based upon published descriptions and measurements, is given here for comparison (fig. 5). A right-hand sword from Perthshire, in the National Museum of Antiquities of Scotland, and a cross found near the Bank of England, published by Laking, are not discussed here since, though related in some respects, their crosses do not have spatulate terminals.[17] It is possible that another unlocalised sword from Ireland, in the National Museum of Ireland, may be a member of the group, but unfortunately its cross terminals are missing.[18]

Three of the group may be described as hand-and-a-half, and agree closely in size, their blade lengths ranging from 2 ft. 11⅛ in. (0.892 m.) for the Ayrshire sword to 3 ft. 0½ in. (0.927 m.) for the Irish sword. Tang lengths vary from 6⅞ in. (175 mm.) to 8 1/16 in. (204 mm.). The Irish sword has the longest cross, with arms 6 in. (152 mm.) long, but also the narrowest blade. The smaller proportions but general correspondence of the Kienbusch sword show clearly that it is a right-hand version of the same type.

All the blades have definite but not prominent central grooves. The two surviving pommels are of the wheel type, though with the prolongation to the tip of the tang for the Glasgow sword, as described above. The Kienbusch sword is described as having 'a tall rectangular button on top', but since it is an excavated piece it remains possible that its configuration may parallel that of the Glasgow sword, for the description also states that the pommel 'is made of comparatively thin metal and must have been brazed together, although corrosion hides the joins'. The further suggestion that the pommel was once filled with lead can hardly be right.[19] It is much more likely that the filler in both this and the Glasgow sword pommels was clay, which could well disappear with time in a buried weapon.[20]

Oakeshott describes the Kienbusch sword as vaguely of his Type XVIII,[21] but the three hand-and-a-half swords seem to have blades more appropriate to swords of his Type XIII or, more specifically, XIIIA, which he suggests belongs to the period 1240-1350.[22] As already pointed out, the mark on the blade of the Glasgow sword may be compared with that inlaid in the blade of the sword found in the river Thames near Dowgate Street in London, and assigned by Mann to the fourteenth century.[23] The Irish sword blade has a punched lion rampant within a shield which Hayes-McCoy, following Mann, suggests may be a German mark, possibly of Lüneburg.[24] It might rather imply a Scottish origin, but however this may be is perhaps more likely to be fifteenth century in date than earlier. The two surviving pommels are perhaps not closely datable, but it may be noted that the tang button was a prominent feature of many claymores of the sixteenth century.

So much for the dating features of the swords themselves: as for monumental evidence, the closest parallel by far to the sword hilts of this group is to be found upon the tomb slab of Gilbert de Greenlau, at

Kinkell, in Aberdeenshire (fig. 6), which is dated 1411.[25] Gilbert's sword is clearly hand-and-a-half in size, and has all the characteristics of the hilts of the group, even to the prolongation of the tang beyond the wheel pommel. The detail of the scabbard and sword belt is also of interest.

Figure 6. *Left:* effigy of Bricius MacKinnon, third quarter of the 14th cent. *Iona Museum. Right:* tomb slab of Gilbert de Greenlau, dated 1411, Kinkell

In West Highland monuments swords with spatulate-terminal crosses are frequently portrayed, but most have lobated pommels of ultimately Viking derivation, though it is a curious fact, as Steer points out, that no late medieval sword with such a pommel appears to have survived.[26] Steer does refer to portrayals of two swords with spatulate-terminal crosses and disc pommels (with tang buttons or pommel prolongations) on slabs which he considers as probably fifteenth century in date; both are right-hand swords.[27] On the effigy of Brice MacKinnon (fig. 6), which Steer dates as probably third quarter of the fourteenth century, the sword has a lobated pommel and a long cross with tongues and very slightly spatulate terminals.[28] This may illustrate the emergence of the sword with spatulate-terminal cross, a type which, except as an archaic survival, Steer considers had gone out of use by the end of the fifteenth century.[29]

All these facts, taken together, suggest that the sword with spatulate-terminal cross may have begun to develop in Scotland about 1375, was fully developed by 1400 and had ceased to be used some years before 1500. There seems to be no reason to assume that the right-hand was earlier than the hand-and-a half version: the two were in all likelihood contemporary, serving different purposes. It is possible that such swords were latterly more popular in West than in other parts of Scotland, and that it was from Scotland that the sword was introduced into Ireland.

There is little doubt that the evolution of such a sword at such a time will appear strange when viewed against the trends of sword development in mainland Europe, or even in England, in the fifteenth century. The sword belongs firmly to Oakeshott's Group I (1050-1350), designed primarily for cutting, which almost everywhere else in western Europe gave way to swords with blades of stiffer section, effective for thrusting, and designed to cope with the plate armour prevalent after 1350.[30] The reason must be that the sword continued to be successful against the armour to which it was opposed. If the evidence of the West Highland effigies is to be taken at face value, the type of armour worn by Brice MacKinnon in the second half of the fourteenth century underwent little development for most of the following century (fig. 6). It consisted of a basnet, a mail coif or aventail, a quilted aketon, gauntlets, sabatons and possibly greaves.[31] A small, heater-shaped shield also appears, but this may simply be a heraldic device. Such armour was certainly outmoded by general European standards, and hence the cutting sword may have remained effective.

Nevertheless, it will be admitted that there is no sign of arrestment in the development of the sword hilt. The design of the écusson, or central block, as a separate element, with tongues, and the downward sloping arms, evolved when the rest of Europe was for the most part content

with the simplest of straight crosses. The wheel pommel with tang prolongation is again entirely new. Thus, as surviving examples now show,
the sword with spatulate-terminal cross was no mere survival, but underwent a vigorous evolution: it is worthy of consideration in its own right
among the works of the late medieval swordsmith.

NOTES

1. Reg. no. A737.
2. National Grid reference NS 727566: the find was briefly reported in *Discovery and Excavation in Scotland* (1973), 38.
3. J. Mann, 'A fourteenth century sword found in the river Thames near Dowgate Street', *Antiq. Journ.*, xxxix (1959), 288.
4. R. E. Oakeshott, *The Sword in the Age of Chivalry* (London, 1964), 60.
5. E. A. Gessler, 'Die Ritterlicher Bewaffnung von 1386', *Zeitschrift für Historische Waffen- und Kostum-Kunde*, vi (1912-14), 203-8; Oakeshott, *The Sword in the Age of Chivalry*, 66, 105; C. R. Beard, 'On the Date of Certain Swords', *Connoisseur* (June 1923), 78-81.
6. Oakeshott, *The Sword in the Age of Chivalry*, 105.
7. Ibid., pl. 30A.
8. C. Blair, *European and American Arms, c. 1100-1850* (London, 1962), no. 34.
9. Reg. no. A7311.
10. Mann, 'A 14th cent. sword', 287, pl. XLIV.
11. Reg. no. LA7719. I am indebted to my colleague, Mr B. J. Hayton, for drawing my attention to the sword, and to Mr M. Bailey, of the Maclaurin Gallery, Rozelle Estate, Ayr, for information as to the origin of the sword.
12. K. A. Steer and J. W. M. Bannerman, *Late Medieval Monumental Sculpture in the West Highlands* (Edinburgh, 1977), 169.
13. G. A. Hayes-McCoy, 'Sixteenth Century Swords Found in Ireland', *Journ. Roy. Soc. Antiq. Ireland*, lxxviii (1948), 66; Mann, 'A Late Medieval Sword from Ireland', *Antiq. Journ.*, xxiv (1944), 96.
14. Steer and Bannerman, *Sculpture in the W. Highlands*, 169.
15. Hayes-McCoy, '16th cent. Swords', pl. IV; Mann, 'A Late Medieval Sword', pl. XIVc: in the National Museum of Ireland.
16. *The Kretzschmar von Kienbusch Collection of Armor and Arms* (Princeton, N.J., 1963), ed. J. F. Hayward, et al., pl. XCIV, no. 316; Oakeshott, *The Sword in the Age of Chivalry*, pl. 26D; J. Wallace, *Scottish Swords and Dirks* (London, 1970), pl. 2.
17. Wallace, *Swords and Dirks*, pl. 4; Sir Guy Laking, *A Record of European Armour and Arms through Seven Centuries* (London, 1920), ii, 308-9, fig. 686.
18. Hayes-McCoy, '16th cent. Swords', 66 and pl. V.
19. *Kienbusch Collection*, 152.
20. For proof of baked clay inside the pommel of a sword of about 1300 cf. H. L. Peterson, 'A Note on a Medieval Sword', *Journ. Arms & Armour Soc.*, vii (1971), 56-57.
21. Oakeshott, *The Sword in the Age of Chivalry*, pl. 26D.
22. Ibid., 41-47.
23. Mann, 'A 14th cent. Sword', 287-8.
24. Hayes-McCoy, '16th cent. Swords', 66, 68, n. 13.

25. F. A. Greenhill, 'Notes on Scottish Incised Slabs (II)', *Proc. Soc. Antiq. Scot.*, lxxx (1945-6), 43-46; noted also in *Kienbusch Collection*, Oakeshott, *The Sword in the Age of Chivalry*, and Wallace, *Swords & Dirks*.
26. Steer and Bannerman, *Sculpture in the W. Highlands*, 169.
27. Ibid., 168-9.
28. Ibid., 169, pl. 8A. I am indebted to the National Monuments Record of Scotland for permission to use this photograph.
29. Ibid., 169.
30. Oakeshott, *The Sword in the Age of Chivalry*, 53.
31. Steer and Bannerman, *Sculpture in the W. Highlands*, 24-25.

3 Late Medieval Defences in Scotland[1]

Geoffrey Stell

Introduction

The term 'late medieval' is very elastic, and depending upon what aspect of Scottish culture or what part of the country is being considered, its meaning can be stretched to cover a period extending from the later thirteenth century to the seventeenth century.[2] Its use here, however, is confined to the period of early Stewart Scotland from the accession of Robert II in 1371 to the death of James IV at Flodden in 1513.

The first of these dates has no particular significance from a purely architectural standpoint, but the period as a whole is marked by a relatively high and widespread level of good quality stone building when compared with what is generally assumed to have been the case in the preceding and succeeding decades. The period has a dynastic and political unity insofar as it witnessed the establishment and continuance of the royal house of Stewart. It has also, like contemporary England, by tradition been specially marked out by some historians as the age of the overmighty subject who was congenitally prone to take issue with his peers or with the Crown at the least provocation, and who was assisted by unruly private armies of retainers; and the loyalty of these retainers, because (on English analogies) it was allegedly based upon money rather than upon land, was considered to be ever doubtful. According to this view,[3] turbulence and civil discord lay never very far from the surface of Scottish social and political life, and frequently erupted into open violence and anarchy, especially during royal minorities and regencies. However, the elements of political faction and military conflict appear to have been overemphasised, and this simplistic and misinformed picture of conditions in late medieval Scotland has recently received some much-needed historical correctives.[4]

Even so, the traditional account continues to exert an influence, either overtly or tacitly, on our interpretation of the design and purpose of the many fine secular buildings in Scotland that date from this period. Although architectural historians have clearly demonstrated their awareness of some of the more obvious fallacies in the historical argument, the older view still tends to prevail when late medieval buildings are being analysed and classified.[5] This is perhaps partly a legacy from the work of the late Dr W. Douglas Simpson, whose prodigious output on late medieval monuments included *inter alia* three important general papers that were published around the years of World War II.[6] In these articles he set out to demonstrate that the system of so-called 'bastard feudalism' was responsible for the design and layout of a particular type of keep-gatehouse castle in which the builder is supposed to have taken as much defensive precaution against his own retainers within as against potential attackers without. This thesis, and the military thinking that lay behind it, was applied equally to British and continental castles, and was subsequently written into almost everything else that he composed on the subject. The result has been that some otherwise valuable architectural descriptions have been marred by historical preconceptions, and his popular and influential guidebooks, for example, are larded with emotive references to the 'rampant ruffianism among the old Scottish baronage' and to the potential treachery and fickle behaviour of the 'jackmen' or 'bullies' in their employ.[7]

In view of the traditions that have grown up around the subject, and in the light of current historical reappraisals, there seems to be good reason for scrutinising afresh the architectural evidence of permanent defensive features in Scottish buildings of the later Middle Ages. Earlier generations of architectural scholars have set the descriptive and analytical guide-lines for such a study,[8] which might now be discussed within a wider historical context. For, ever since Renaissance ideas concerning architecture first filtered into Scotland in the sixteenth and seventeenth centuries, we have gradually become conditioned to accepting what a private house, on the one hand, and a fortress, on the other, should look like, and how each should be furnished and equipped. Secular buildings which date from an age prior to this 'civilising' domestic tradition tend to combine these two elements to a considerable degree, and in appearance and character do seem to be products of an essentially martial society, relatively speaking. But, accepting that feudal society had an ethos different from our own in a number of important respects, it is relevant to ask whether, in architectural terms at least, the differences have not been all too frequently overstated, and whether a misleading impression has not been given of a society and building industry that is totally alien from those of later ages. In the process, might not a defensive cast have been given to features of building construction that originally could have been innocent of warlike purpose? Moreover, for an age that was allegedly rife with disturbance, a surprising amount of superior quality architecture, not to mention sculpture and other notable artistic achievements,[9] was produced as a result of fairly widespread patronage. So it might further be asked whether, having to a large extent created this social paradox themselves, architectural historians have been justified in explaining away the building activity simply as the typical accompaniment to a period of ferment, and as the natural and immediate response to conditions of civil and foreign war. In order to set the purely military aspects of Scottish late medieval architecture into some form of broad historical perspective, therefore, it is necessary to assess briefly the importance of those considerations other than the pressing needs of defence which governed the construction and shaping of these buildings.

Domestic Architecture of the later Middle Ages

As has been pointed out elsewhere,[10] the ubiquitous late medieval tower-house in all its variant forms probably owed its popularity to its equal adaptability both for use as a place of strength and as a domestic residence. But the really significant changes in their design and fittings that took place before 1513 are for the most part attributable to domestic and public needs:[11] the more widespread practice of glazing window-openings; the more generous provision of fireplaces; increased and better private household accommodation; and more closely integrated service facilities. Where prestige, status and wealth permitted, a great hall was erected for ceremonial and public affairs in much the same way as kings and great magnates had done since the very beginnings of the feudal castle, and as lesser men were to continue to do in the sixteenth century. There is nothing intrinsically sinister about the appearance of these traditional buildings in this period, although the means to build, staff and use them was evidently given to rather more families than had previously been the case, and, in these respects, they may give some indication of changing family fortunes and comparative sizes of households and retinues.

The hall block in stone or timber was a feature of domestic planning throughout the Middle Ages, and there is no *prima facie* reason for assuming that all stone-built structures of this type that stand independently of other major buildings should necessarily be ascribed on typological grounds to the thirteeenth or early fourteenth centuries.[12] Some recognised examples of these 'hall-houses' or fortified manor-houses with their minimum amount of defensive equipment may, on further study, be found to belong to the mid or late fourteenth century at least, since the art-historical and typological criteria that have so far been applied to their dating still allow much latitude for debate. First brought together by MacGibbon and Ross as a group of anomalous structures in different parts of the country which have some points in common with each other, these 'hall-houses' have since tended to be placed in typological isolation, whilst comparison with stone-built halls in enclosure-castles and the influence of neighbouring major building-works have tended to be understated.[13] In any case, the first phases of Kindrochit in Mar, the first stone-built portion of Linlithgow Palace as rebuilt by James I after 1424, the second phase of Craigie Castle (whatever date can confidently be placed on the primary work), and possibly Dalquharran Castle, for instance, may equally belong to this manor-house category and fall within the period under review.[14] Moreover, the precise distinction between a hall and a tower becomes much less easy to define when one examines the proportions of plan-form, function, and the numbers of storeys of some of the elongated hall-like towers of later fourteenth- and early fifteenth-century date, good cases in point being the Stewart family residence of Dundonald, Carrick Castle in Cowal, and the main block of Crookston Castle.[15]

In addition to the continued sequence of 'hall-houses' into this period, there are other types of contemporary secular building which appear to be predominantly domestic in conception and character. The splendid little fifteenth-century tower at Mauchline, for example, which probably served as the centre of a monastic grange of Melrose Abbey, shows little apparent concern for defence apart from its parapeted wall-head which has been subsequently rebuilt.[16] And the only visible concession to the need for security at the principal MacDonald residence at Finlaggan on Islay lies in the fact that it occupies an insular site.[17]

Castle building, the social and economic background[18]

Quite apart from these particular building-types which appear primarily residential in purpose, other important practical and pacific considerations entered into the general process of stone castle building and applied as much to this age as to any other. It is possible and reasonable to regard the majority of earthworks such as ringworks, mottes and later artillery outworks as direct products of military conditions that could be thrown up relatively quickly and cheaply, perhaps utilising resources of unskilled labour.[19] But, because of the specialised work involved, castle-building in stone and lime required a good deal more careful preparation, expense, time and effort. The pace and intense concentration of national resources on the part of earlier royal castle builders such as Edward I of England cannot by any means be taken as the norm, and the critical decision to build or rebuild a major stone castle or tower was not one that could be lightly embarked upon, speedily carried through or indulged in every now and again by a baronial family of average means, or at least no more so than their country-mansion building successors.[20] Much remains to be known in detail about the incomes and expenses of Scottish noble and baronial families in the later medieval period, but it can be reasonably assumed that major building works of this kind, just as later, probably involved an investment or diversion of a substantial proportion of estate revenues over perhaps a decade or more. Most paradoxically of all, of course, a potential private builder would at the outset have to enjoy fairly settled conditions and some degree of physical and legal security of tenure if he was to be reasonably confident that the building he was erecting would in fact materialise, and that it would not be unduly vandalised, contested or taken over during the course of the works. It is thus worth pondering whether anyone but the crown, the richest noble or a fool would deliberately set their sophisticated and expensive stone structures at risk by building speculatively either in very disturbed conditions, or on land to which they had no good title. But, as with a number of thirteenth-century strongholds, it is not always possible to determine easily or precisely whether a particular building phase of a castle was royal or baronial. It is equally difficult to distinguish the amount of direct or indirect royal assistance in building operations that can be suspected in those castles where royal and private authority was clearly interdependent and which were staffed with royal officials or royal garrisons in times of need.[21]

Whether royal, quasi-royal or noble, however, the builders who had more resources at their command and greater prestige to maintain, might in certain cases be expected to build towers, halls and defences on a scale and in a manner that went quite beyond their immediate functional requirements. This age, like any other, possessed a high degree of status-consciousness that was reflected not only in the patronage of most aspects of architecture and sculpture, but also in sumptuary legislation and later on, for example, in pieces of legislation like the one about food which regulated the number of dishes at table according to rank and the presence of impressionable foreigners![22] Within the accepted framework of contemporary architectural fashion, status-building that was simply calculated to impress applied just as much to proud medieval castle-builders as it obviously did to the mansion-builders of later centuries. The relatively uneventful history of some of those monuments whose defences have remained virtually intact can perhaps be taken as one measure of their success in this respect, although conversely in some cases such as Tantallon Castle[23] their sheer massive scale might equally present an irresistible challenge to later developed techniques of siege warfare (fig. 7). Furthermore, within localities dominated by royal or greater noble castles certain of their more impressive features and styles seem to have been borrowed and to have percolated through the social scale, perhaps even persisting for a number of generations.

Against this background can be set the appearance of increasing numbers of baronial families in the stone-building class from about the last quarter of the fourteenth century onwards. If we make the reasonable assumptions that house-building was generally accorded a high priority by the individuals concerned, and that over this period there was

Figure 7. Tantallon Castle, aerial view. Earthwork rampart and ditch centre, at the top extremity the tower and traverse wall probably built c.1523x8

no discernible reduction in the real cost of high-quality stone-building, then the general character, size and probable dates of these residences may thus give us some crude measure of the relative wealth, tenurial status, and the point in time at which their builders 'arrived', so to speak, into a higher socio-economic category. Several local groups of buildings up and down the country illustrate this general point, and on the western seaboard, for example, there is a very fine series of tower-houses erected during this period by the MacLeans of Duart, the MacLeods of Dunvegan, the MacLeans of Coll, the MacNeills of Barra, and the MacLaines of Lochbuie.[24]

In summary, therefore, these are a few of the general social, economic and architectural factors which lay behind the late medieval castle-building industry, and may cause us to hesitate a little in accepting all of what we see today at its apparent face value. These factors may go some way towards explaining an inbuilt conservatism and an adherence to established principles of fortification and domestic planning in the later Middle Ages. They may also help to correct an involuntary and fairly widespread tendency on our part to assume a builder's or occupant's immediate willingness and ability to adapt his defences and his life-style to suit the changing dictates in siege warfare or to follow every changing breeze in the political and social climate.

Siting and strategy

All this is not to deny that the need for security and defence was an important element in late medieval architectural design, and there are a number of ways of demonstrating a continued demand for defensive strongholds. The actual siting of many late medieval buildings in naturally defensible, commanding and often remote positions is the most obvious manifestation of a desire to gain maximum tactical advantages, or at least physically to dominate, confound, and keep at a distance potential intruders. Some parts of the country offered numerous rocky eminences and promontories that were taken advantage of, and many of these sites demanded considerable and spectacular feats of building construction. Coastal promontary-sites were also much in favour, especially along the eastern seaboard, and, if circumscribed by precipitous cliffs, these sites had the advantage of permitting man-made defences to be almost wholly concentrated on the landward field. Peninsulas and tongues of land formed in freshwater lochs or by confluences of rivers could also be screened in much the same manner, but many castles in these positions seem to have been constructed in such a way as not entirely to prevent, but rather to restrict access to the flanks and rear of the site. There are a few well-known offshore castles and fortified islands, and the insular traditions of earlier generations were also perpetuated by the known or suspected use in this period of small, frequently causewayed island-refuges that are particularly numerous in the Western Isles and parts of Galloway.[25] Throughout the country, in fact, the continued occupation or rebuilding of what were obviously the best sites with a previous history of fortification was not unexpectedly a relatively common phenomenon. Such a practice might involve reshaping or strengthening an existing stone structure such as the royal castles of Edinburgh and Stirling, or overlaying, encircling or adding to an older earthwork, as in the case of Urquhart Castle.[26]

However, the choice of site is by no means always clearly explicable in military terms, and appears to have been tempered by more pacific considerations. The availability of a reliable water-supply was a prerequisite in war and peace, and the proximity of suitable boat-landings, anchorages, and overland routes for convenient access by sea and land was also necessary at all times. However, a remarkably high proportion of castles, like their sub-medieval and modern successors, simply stood in

Figure 8.   Breachacha Old and New Castles. Watercolour by Poole, *National Galleries of Scotland*

close proximity to the fertile and valuable demesne lands that provided their main means of economic support, and in these instances, we shall probably search in vain for any strictly military purpose in their setting. Innumerable late medieval buildings survive encapsulated within or adjacent to later mansions on sites which lack obvious defensive advantages and were considered desirable by succeeding generations of 'civilised' builders. Among the group of West Highland towers mentioned above, for example, the siting of Moy Castle, Lochbuie, Mull, and Breachacha Castle, Coll (fig. 8), is particularly significant in relation to their eighteenth-century successors.

Nevertheless, as centres of royal, noble, ecclesiastical or baronial authority, virtually all late medieval castles and towers can be reckoned to have served a variety of political and administrative purposes within their localities, including, when necessary, matters of defence. The siting or re-occupation of buildings in some areas also received tacit or positive encouragement from the Crown, as can be witnessed by James I's famous injunction of 1426 requesting all landowners north of the Mounth to build, reconstruct or repair their 'castellis, fortalyces and maner places . . . duell in thame be thaimself or be ane of thare frendis for the gracious governall of thair landis be gude polising and to expend the froyte of the landis in the cuntre quhare the landis lyis'.[27] The 'increase of policy within the kingdom', that is, the civilising effect of estate improvement, also came to be written into some feu charters and licences to crenellate issued during the reign of James I.[28]

Notions of overall defensive strategy on a regional, if not a national scale were probably never entirely absent in the later medieval period, but the building or garrisoning of strategically linked strongpoints only began to find clear public expression in contemporary historical record in about the last quarter of the fifteenth century. In 1476, for example, the revocation of grants made during James III's minority acknowledged that certain castles were 'the keys to the kingdom'.[29] And in 1481, faced with the prospect of war with England, the Scottish parliament announced James III's intention to repair the royal castles of Dunbar and Lochmaben, charging the lords spiritual and temporal to follow suit so 'that hes Castelles neire the Bordoures and on the Sea coaste, sik as Saint-Andrewes, Aberdene, Temptallon, Hume, Douglas, Halis, Adringtowne, and specially the Hermitage, that is in maist danger, and sik vther Castelles and strengthes, that may be keiped and defended fra our enemies of England: That ilk Lord stuff his awin house (that is, supply munitions), and strength them with victualles, men and artailzierie, and to amend and reparrell them quhair it misters'.[30]

The problem of littoral defence, and especially the intermittent threat to shipping and property in the Forth estuary, had for some time been a matter of local and private concern. Again, however, the issue became more acutely pressing and public in the later fifteenth and early sixteenth centuries when the construction of a number of strategically positioned private strongholds was actively promoted and encouraged by the Crown.[31] The effectiveness of this local network for coastal defence must also have been considerably enhanced by buildings like Ravenscraig Castle, Fife (fig. 9), and the lofty seven-storeyed and loop-holed tower at the neighbouring church of St Serf's, Dysart.[32]

Figure 9. Ravenscraig Castle

Licences to crenellate and the elements of defence

Royal licences granting permission to build fortifications or to fortify private dwellings to some degree reflect the Crown's direct concern for local and national defence, but known licences are few, especially when compared with the actual or surviving numbers of contemporary fortified structures.[33] Unlike England,[34] however, the practice of issuing special written licences may have been a matter of proper legal conveyance in particular circumstances, and the unlicensed remainder do not appear to have been regarded as being in any way adulterine. Whatever their precise political and legal significance, these licences do usefully provide some indications of the elements of defence that seemed especially significant to contemporaries.

The licence granted to James Dundas in 1424, for instance, referred to crenelles, other defensive features 'below and above', and walls and ditches 'as is usual in a fortalice of this kind according to the manner of the kingdom of Scotland'. In 1449 Herbert, Lord Maxwell, was also empowered to fortify his tower at Mearns 'with walls and ditches', whilst the Cawdor Castle licence of 1454 enabled the structure to be strengthened likewise 'with walls and ditches . . . and the summit of the same with small turrets and means of defence' *(turriculis et ornamentis defensionis ac apparatibus et fortitudinibus bellicis)*.[35] Among a later group of licences dating from the reign of James IV, specific mention is made of 'iron bars' in the case of Inchgarvie in 1491, 'irn yettis, machcolyn' at Esslemont in 1500, 'irn zettis, barmkin, portculis, battaling, corbald-sailzie' at Carnock in 1511-12, and the right to construct outer defences *(antemurali sive propugnaculo)* at Urquhart Castle in 1508.[36]

On the basis of this documentary evidence alone, therefore, it is clear that particular attention was paid to the wall-heads, the protection of all entrances, and the creation of enclosures and earthworks. Other features such as narrow newel stairs, thick walls, stone vaults, slit-windows and iron window-grilles remained largely undocumented in this period and may simply have been taken for granted. Although some of these might later be found to possess defensive capabilities in certain circumstances, in origin they might simply have been attributable to current notions of building construction and semi-domestic purposes. In this particular respect, for example, the history, incidence and purpose of stone-vaulted construction in (or its absence from) medieval and later monuments in Scotland deserves further study, especially in relation to the availability of building-materials and to the need for fireproofing. Even purposely defensive apparatus cannot always be assumed unequivocally to have been features of true warlike intent rather than symbols of prestige, since it is questionable whether the occupant would make regular or even occasional use of all the fixed defensive gadgetry on his premises.

Wall-head defences. The parapets dating from the earlier part of this period are generally carried on oversailing courses of modest projection formed by continuous or individually moulded corbels, or they are simply carried up flush with the main wall-surface. Despite the processes of ruin, later alterations to upperworks, and the heavy hand of restoration, traces of authentic late medieval battlements are not altogether rare, but detailed studies have not yet been published in sufficient quantity to allow us to demonstrate, for example, whether there are any significant variations in type,[37] and whether or not the proportions of late medieval crenelles and merlons are respectively less deep and broad than their thirteenth-century predecessors. The parapets, standing originally to average man-height, are generally backed by open wall-walks that are paved and drained by a series of transverse runnels and weepers.

Older forms of wall-head defence employing overhanging galleries or platforms of timber also persisted into the later Middle Ages, although clear unambiguous evidence of continuous types of all-wooden hourds is not easy to come by. The triple series of apertures or putlog-holes that run around three sides of the fourteenth-century tower at Threave may be the most complete vestige of this kind of arrangement that still survives (fig. 28). However, the details are somewhat baffling and are capable of other, but perhaps rather less convincing explanations.[38]

Judging from the amount of extant wall-head corbelling of bold projection and multiple coursing, stone continued to be commonly combined with timber in the formation of bratticed platforms, known as bartizans or *bretasches*. However, the surviving evidence does not always indicate clearly whether the now-vanished superstructure was invariably of timber. This feature came to be translated wholly into stone-built machicolated parapets, perhaps from the early fifteenth century in better quality buildings but became more widespread by 1500 and later. As has previously been suggested, late medieval builders were probably not unaware of the purely decorative effect of this treatment, and the machicolated crown added to the south-east or 'Douglas Tower' at Bothwell Castle has fancy arcuated openings, in southern French style.[39] The smaller box-machicolation or *bretasche*, placed usually within dropping distance of an entry, generally has an altogether more direct and purposeful air, and slots also came to be formed in the bases of oversailing angle-rounds. With or without machicolations, in fact, open turrets or rounds of this kind had become a fairly standard parapet feature by the beginning of the sixteenth century, although the chronology of its appearance, like so much else relating to the wall-head, is extremely difficult to chart precisely.

Finally in this section, mention should also be made of the fact that what have been interpreted as internal, as opposed to external machicolation-slots were not unknown in Scotland before this period, and at Cardoness Castle, for instance, there is a hatch above the entrance-lobby which bears a superficial resemblance to the so-called 'murder-holes' of some Irish castles.[40] Like them, however, the opening may equally have performed a rather less dramatic function in the lifting and lowering of goods.

Protection of entrances. Special protective measures continued to be made at the entrances themselves, both at the larger gate, where one existed, and at smaller doorways, such as the postern and sea-gate, and those giving access to the tower and wall-walks. Following the pattern of some fortified manor-houses, the principal entrance to the late medieval tower was in many cases placed at an upper floor level, and by inference appears to have been approached by a timber forestair or retractable ladder which has often left little archaeological trace. The doors were, in accordance with long-established tradition, secured by sliding wooden draw-bars that were of a length and thickness commensurate with the size of the door, and were housed in slots behind the door-jambs. As evidenced by overhead slots and chases in the side-walls, some of the smaller entrances in late fourteenth- or early fifteenth-century work were also equipped with a miniature portcullis which was presumably worked by windlass from a chamber above.

Surviving remains of two pairs of rebates and two sets of crook-hinges usually point to the former existence of a double-door arrangement, and this period marks the earliest recorded appearance of the iron gate or 'yett'.[41] Hinged and hung in conventional manner and placed normally, but not invariably, behind the main door, these cross-barred wrought-iron gates were of a very strong, fairly standard, and, it has been claimed, peculiarly Scottish construction. The known provenance of a sizeable proportion of the fifty or so extant specimens suggests a genuine late medieval date, although some of these may represent subsequent adaptations of existing entrance-arrangements. Moreover, at least two of the yetts — those from Balveny and Doune Castles — are of a larger, two-leaved variety, and, unlike the others, were more clearly associated with the arrangements of the main outer gateway.

The gatehouse layout of a major late medieval castle usually consisted of a vaulted passage (also known as a 'transe' or pend) of variable length, which often had an arch-pointed exterior and was flanked by guard-chambers and janitor's lodge, with a prison somewhere in the vicinity. In general purpose and effect they were not wholly unlike the great four-teenth-century gatehouses that gave access to the monastic precincts of Arbroath Abbey and St Andrews Cathedral-Priory.[42] The castle gate-ways were generally equipped with a series of folding doors, and were associated with at least one portcullis which might be placed near the front, or at the rear, or about two-thirds of the way down the length of the entrance-passage. In contrast to its disappearance from the smaller doorways where it was superseded by the less cumbersome yett, the portcullis continued to put up a brave show at most of the major gate-houses where it could be more easily installed and operated from a purpose-built chamber above. In view of its occurrence in royal works of early sixteenth-century date, however, it is not yet clear whether any dating or functional significance can be attached to the absence of evidence of portcullises from sites where they might otherwise have been expected. No late medieval portcullis has survived intact, but the few de-

scriptive references to them include, for example, the 'enormous portcullis of massy iron' which was in position at Spynie Palace in 1795.[43]

The longer entrance-passages generally possessed three folding gates
or doors, and the innermost in the series was usually hung in such a
manner as to open outwards, rather than inwards like the others. It is
now almost impossible to state dogmatically whether this was a matter
of practical structural convenience, custom, or military necessity. In
strictly military terms, it was certainly a method of isolating the gate-
house-passage and of effectively shutting off the courtyard for a time if it
were entered by a besieging party, or if, as one authority has seriously
suggested,[44] it were filled by the lord's own mercenaries running amok,
perhaps as a result of a lack of pay or an excess of alcohol! Alternatively,
this arrangement, which does not seem to be confined to any particular
type of castle, better suited formal and ceremonial exits from the courtyard, and it was also a simple means of tying back the opened gates
against the side walls of the passage.

The gatehouse either stood independently at some appropriate
position in the curtain wall, or was structurally integrated with the
principal residential block. The combined tower-gatehouse design was
partly borrowed from earlier Edwardian-style castles, but in the later
examples the gatehouse salient was not thrust quite so far forward and
was not usually towered in the same way. This fashion held sway for a
time in the fourteenth and early fifteenth centuries, but, apart from commanding a good centrally placed view, the arrangement offered few
special military advantages other than the rather dubious facility of
working the portcullis from one of the lord's private rooms above the
entry.

By the middle decades of the fifteenth century a few royal buildings
were being designed with the main entrance-passage placed underneath
the hall range, a trend which, in some parts of the country, took very
firm hold during the sixteenth century. The changeover is perhaps nowhere better illustrated than at the episcopal castle of St Andrews.[45]
There, the multi-period fourteenth-century keep-gatehouse was finally
rendered redundant as an entry in the sixteenth century when an existing
gate was converted into the principal entrance beneath the hall, an
alteration which involved a sideways shift of only a few metres in the
position of the main gate. At Linlithgow Palace this hall-gatehouse
arrangement meant that the portcullis was operated from passages that
ran beside the great hall whilst the drawbridge cables were evidently
worked from the hall itself. But, as in the case of the keep-gatehouse, it
might be a mistake to infer that thinking of a predominantly military
nature lay behind these changes.

Where there was a ditch or a moat, the main gate was often fronted by

Figure 10. Dalhousie Castle, from Grose's *Antiquities*

an outward extension of the gatehouse, and a number of earlier gate-
houses (and some towers) received secondary additions of foreworks or
barbicans in the later Middle Ages. The ditch was usually spanned by a
defensive bridge, and by this period bridges with timber-decked super-
structures resting on stone piers and stone abutments may have been
commoner than those constructed wholly of timber or wholly of stone.[46]
Most major bridges incorporated a mobile section, which was either of
the retractable roller or of the lifting variety. Surviving physical evidence
of late medieval drawbridges is, however, largely confined to the shapes
of the masonry features built to accommodate them: the drawbridge-pit;
the apertures for the hoisting mechanism; and the recess in the gate-
house-façade which the drawbridge occupied when in a raised position
(fig. 10). Judging from this limited evidence, one bascule type of bridge
appears to have had a pair of wooden arms from which chains were suspended at the extremities, and which were housed in vertical slots in the
gatehouse wall. Extended slots would also be required if chains alone
were used, the height of the slot being determined by the height and
position of the windlass in relation to the point on the bridge to which
the chain was affixed.

Studies of drawbridge design and operation, like so many other
features of medieval military architecture, have tended to be greatly in-

fluenced by the work of Viollet-le-Duc, and especially by the lively and detailed illustrations that support his text.[47] There may well be major discrepancies in the typology and dating of French and Scottish examples in this period, and the archaeological reliability of some of his more complex devices can probably be impugned. Until Scottish bridges have been examined in detail on their own terms, therefore, it would be imprudent to generalise too widely on trends in their size, design, efficiency and use in the later Middle Ages. However, preliminary observation suggests, firstly, that fewer, if any, of the smaller footbridge types attached directly to a hall or tower-block were built in this period; secondly, that there are some late (that is, early sixteenth-century) examples in which the bridge and/or drawbridge is set some distance forward of the main mass of the gatehouse and barbican; and thirdly, that the creation of alternative access arrangements in cases like Tantallon Castle hints at a realisation of the lifting bridge's relative inconvenience and inefficiency, particularly on dry-ditched, as opposed to wet-moated, sites.

Earthworks and enclosures. The evidence of the licences demonstrates that much importance was still attached to earthwork defences, and most late medieval stone castles have an association with surviving earthworks of some kind, even if it is only a short stretch of rock-cut ditch. The relationship of the length of ditch or the full line of circumvallation to the layout of the stone-built structure may often be close enough to suggest contemporaneity, and the same may be true of outer wards that are likewise circumscribed by banks and ditches. In any case, moated sites and cognate types of structure that were wholly or predominantly of earth and timber construction appear to have continued in occupation, if they were not actually still being built in the later Middle Ages.[48]

However, judging the date, type and purpose of medieval earthworks purely on the basis of their surface remains is a difficult task, and serious problems of interpretation arise in those cases, not only where late medieval buildings stand on sites of known earlier occupation, but also where sixteenth- and seventeenth-century artillery defences have led to the adaptation or creation of outworks, often on a fairly extensive scale (fig. 11). These later artillery fortifications usually have certain readily identifiable technical characteristics, but where they occur in conjunction with one or more earlier earthwork phases, the surface evidence presents a confused picture that can only properly be tested by archaeological excavation. Even where parts of the outworks are known to conceal wall-foundations as at Torthorwald and Cessford Castles, the character and alignment of the enclosure or barmkin-wall can often be detected only by judicious use of aerial photography and excavation.[49]

The curtain-wall of a major late medieval castle might stand to a full height of anything up to fifteen or sixteen metres inclusive of parapet.

Figure 11. Hermitage Castle, aerial view

Taken in conjunction with a frontal ditch, such a height was generally considered to be beyond the reach of scaling-ladders and towers of the most sanguine siege-engineer. Barmkin-walls associated with the majority of towers were generally somewhat lower than that, ranging from one to two storeys in height. In those cases where the walls have no longer survived, a rough indication of the former level of a parapet wall-walk is sometimes provided by the tusking and the vertical position of the door in the tower that formerly gave access on to it, although of course some allowance has to be made for the possibility of a stepped approach.

The thickness of late medieval curtains varies widely from about one to four metres, and this dimension would be determined as much by height, structural stability, and the need for intra-mural chambers, as by its potential capacity for defensive resistance and the accommodation of a wall-walk. Thus, whilst some curtains, like, for instance, the forework at Lochmaben,[50] were solid throughout, others were of cellular construction containing a labyrinth of stairs, passages and mural chambers. Some also served as the outer load-bearing walls of courtyard buildings, and are found equipped with all the usual domestic accoutrements like water-inlets, slop-sinks, garderobe-chutes and large windows lighting the main apartments on the upper floors.

Depending in large measure on the nature of the site, the curtain-wall might be laid out as a screen-type forework, which at its most regular and symmetrical would include a centrally placed gatehouse, a pair of terminal towers, and possibly a couple of interval towers. The towers themselves might be D-shaped, circular or oblong in plan externally, and one species of drum-tower was oblong within. Similar towers might also be attached to a curtain-wall which formed a complete enclosure or *enceinte,* and in this type of layout, the principal residential block could be either free-standing within or integrated with the outer circuit. At its most irregular, a polygonal enclosure of this kind would tend to be made up of varying lengths of straight and curved stretches of walling and to incorporate a number of salients. They are often distinguishable from their thirteenth-century predecessors only in relatively small points of architectural detail, and for this reason it is still possible and understandable for expert opinion to differ to the extent of more than two centuries on their dating.[51]

Gunpowder Artillery Fortifications

The components of defence that have been analysed show few major changes from the principles of stone fortification that were well established in Britain before 1371. If a castle failed to impress a would-be assailant by reason of its position, height, bulk and apparent impregnability, its inbuilt defences seemed to be designed to provide no more than close-range stalling manoeuvres, whilst its main strength, if required, lay in its capacity for passive resistance over a long period. This is not to under-estimate the effectiveness of all the devices and lockerfuls of conventional weaponry at the disposal of the castle occupants, as long as these were simply required to resist arms of a like kind.

The increasing use of gunpowder siege artillery and firearms, mainly by royal armies in the earliest stages, introduced a novel element into this state of affairs in the fifteenth century. The character of these early gunpowder weapons is discussed elsewhere in this volume, but three related questions remain to be considered here in fairly general terms: how effective were conventional forms of defence against the new weaponry, what changes did it induce in contemporary architectural design, and approximately when did these changes occur in Scotland in the period before 1513?

Siege warfare. Unlike, for instance, some of the well-documented and publicised Scottish activities of Edward I of England, historical accounts of late medieval sieges in Scotland vary considerably in their fullness of content and accuracy. A terse entry in a chronicle account might refer to the fact that a siege or assault had taken place, occasionally perhaps commenting on the extent of the damage that had been sustained. Fuller, but indirect and mostly retrospective evidence, is provided by official government accounts of expenses laid out for royal sieges. However, any further details on the duration, the methods and conduct of any particular siege, the precise reasons for its occurrence in the first place, and the way in which its final outcome was settled are not often available or even apparent. Historical inferences on these matters have thus to take careful account of a multiplicity of relatively indeterminate factors, each of which, singly or in combination, might have a profound bearing on the siege operations: the amount of resources, priority and preparation applied to the task by besiegers and besieged; problems of timing and logistics; personal and political affiliations; and questions of local topography. In the absence of corroborative evidence, then, it would clearly be a mistake to assume that the length and result of a siege was necessarily attributable to the use of developing artillery weapons, or to the inherent defensive strength or weakness of the castle concerned.

Sieges that were relatively protracted, desultory, and inconclusive, and those that appear to have been settled primarily by diplomatic or political, rather than by military means, took place throughout this period, irrespective of whether bombards or other firearms are known to have been used or not. They include, for example, the attempts on the town and castle of Berwick-on-Tweed in 1417 and 1482; James I's half-hearted and abortive assault on Roxburgh in 1436; a reputedly nine-month siege of Edinburgh Castle in 1445; rather shorter sieges by James II against Blackness and Threave Castles in 1453 and 1455, both of which appear to have been settled by agreement; sporadic efforts at removing an English garrison from Dunbar Castle in 1483-5; James IV's attempts against the disaffected rebels who held Dumbarton Castle in the latter half of 1489; and his short tilt at Norham Castle in 1497. However, one of the most illuminating detailed comments on the practical difficulties of taking a traditionally built stronghold even with the assistance of firearms falls slightly outside this period. The English commander's report on his attack of Cessford Castle in 1523 stated that if the defence had been continued and if agreement had not been reached with the owner he did not see how the castle could have been taken.[52]

On the other hand, there is an almost equal number of successful and relatively rapid sieges known or presumed to have been achieved largely by the actual or threatened use of gunpowder artillery. During James IV's reign, Crookston and Duchall Castles appear to have capitulated fairly quickly to the threat of bombards, and artillery may have played an important part in the later successful campaign against the Islanders.[53] However, credit for the earliest successful blitzkrieg-type siege operations involving the use of artillery goes to King James II.[54] Whether or not he used cannon in his attacks on all the Douglas strongholds is not absolutely clear, but they were certainly used at Hatton Castle in 1452 and then in 1455 at the famous sieges of Threave and Abercorn Castles.[55] Abercorn was later described as 'by far the most strongly fortified of the whole' (of the Douglas castles), and a contemporary chronicle account referred to the fact that 'the king remanit at the sege and gart strek mony of the towris doun with the gret gun, the quhilk a Francheman schot right wele, and failyeit na shot within a faldome quhar it was chargit him to hit'.[56] In his own account of the one-month siege James reported shortly afterwards to King Charles VII of France that the towers of the curtain *(turribus eiusdem castri per circuitum)* had collapsed as a result of the continual blows of the 'machines'.[57]

Although of limited military value, these sieges seem to have attracted a kind of showpiece publicity, perpetrated partly by James himself. On this demonstration it would be easy to exaggerate the importance and effect of the firearms, and correspondingly to overstate the vulnerability of existing defences. Nevertheless, the experience of some of James II's more devastating domestic activities must have been somewhat traumatic, and, with the benefit of hindsight, historians might view his attack on the Douglases as marking the beginnings of a long process of erosion, or at least a shaking-up of established and perhaps slightly smug attitudes towards private security and defence. To most noble and baronial families in this period, however, the threat of gunpowder artillery probably remained fairly remote, and could be expected to come mainly from the king himself or from foreign invaders.

Effects on architectural design. Descriptions of sieges in Scotland rarely supply specific indications of how the besieged, as opposed to the besiegers, defended themselves with and against firearms. There is also a notable absence of the technical terms that were later attached to the component parts of artillery fortifications. Narrative accounts of building works in the early sixteenth century continued to refer to defences *(munitiones)* with much the same terminology as before, and one of the earliest recorded uses of the term, 'gun-hole', for example, is dated 1532.[58] In these respects, therefore, the documentary sources provide only circumstantial evidence on phases of building, or on the possession and use of firearms, and the earliest stages in the development and spread of artillery fortifications have thus to be assessed almost unilaterally by archaeological and architectural criteria.

The most elementary manifestation of the real or pretended use of firearms was the device of the gun-loop, and the most common early type was the simple vertical slit incorporating a rounded aperture at base. Loops of this 'inverted keyhole' kind vary in size, and several early variations were worked out on its basic vertical shape, including the double-ended or 'dumb-bell' loop and a curiously archaic-looking crosslet-headed type.[59] They are generally associated with conventional splayed embrasures, but the actual form of the opening is of questionable efficiency both for the purposes of sighting and ventilation. These loops were evidently designed for use with handguns or mounted pieces, but their arrangements and operation are discussed below in more detail by Iain MacIvor in a separate chapter.

Placed singly or in series, the loops provided a frontal battery of sorts, and from the outset there appears to have been a genuine attempt to position them in such a way as to gain enfilading cover. Buildings of L-shaped or kindred plan-forms had an inbuilt salient that could be utilised, and extruded rounded towers of traditional model came to be much favoured for this purpose. The layout of Ravenscraig Castle in Fife, for example (fig. 12), comprises a converted central hall block with flanking towers of D-shaped plan and oblong interiors, built along the lines of thick-walled terminal towers of earlier castles such as Tantallon (fig. 13). At Ravenscraig the hall and towers were embellished in up-to-date fashion with large 'inverted keyhole' loops, two at least of which cover the ditch in front of the main entrance. It is generally assumed that, apart from the later gun-platform and outbuildings, Ravenscraig was completed within the period of documented royal building operations between 1460 and 1463, but there is cause for doubting the complete homogeneity of its original design as an artillery fortress. Some of the architectural features, particularly of the more prominent west tower, have the appearance of late fifteenth- or sixteenth-century work, and the Sinclairs, into whose possession the castle had by that time passed, appear to have had more than a casual interest in artillery.[60]

Drum-towers of this more massive thick-walled variety were occasionally adapted or introduced into curtain-walls for defence by firearms, but the majority of towers were miniature and generally more boldly projecting versions of their predecessors. They were usually round-chambered within, and rose to a height of three or four storeys through walls of no exceptional thickness. They were positioned at suitable points in the curtain, usually at an angle or covering an entry, but where they occur in series there is not always a discernible consistency in their spacing. Not every site could provide a straight uninterrupted view across adjacent lengths of wall, and there is a noticeable trend towards ironing out stretches of curtain that were covered by these tower proto-bastions. At its most regular and complete, a newly constructed or re-built curtain might form an overall quadrangular layout, whilst the traditional screen-type forework, which in most cases already comprised straight and regular lengths of walling with flanking cover, required little modification for this conception of artillery defence. It is thus not sur-

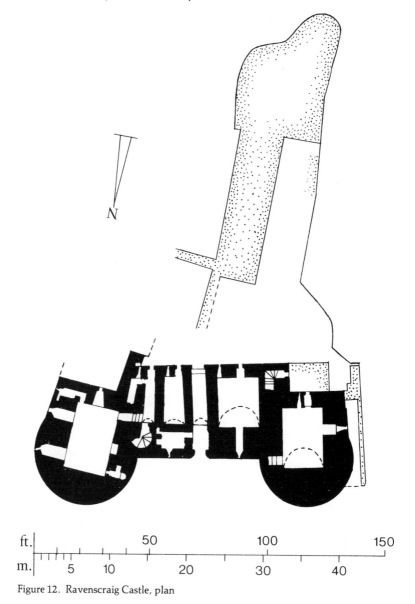

Figure 12. Ravenscraig Castle, plan

prising that the forework at Stirling Castle, which was rebuilt between
about 1500 and 1510 (fig. 14), may have followed an earlier alignment.
In fact, apart from some features of the gatehouse and an increased
ascertainable thickness of the curtain in relation to its height, there is not

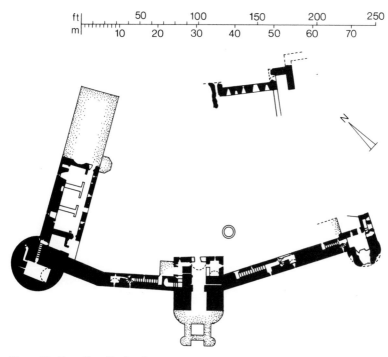

Figure 13. Tantallon Castle, plan

a great deal to distinguish the traditional lines of this forework (fig. 15) from its fourteenth-century predecessors elsewhere in Scotland.[61]

Being a royal work and being reasonably closely dateable, the Stirling Castle forework is one measure of the stage which artillery fortifications in Scotland had reached by about 1513. From about the middle of the *quattrocento* the pace of thinking and writing about, as well as actually constructing gunpowder fortifications, was set by groups of artists and engineers in various parts of the European continent, and especially in the Italian peninsula. By the early years of the sixteenth century there had evolved in central Italy a sophisticated type of fortress which had solid and massive but relatively low curtain-walls capable of mounting and resisting cannon. More revolutionary still, these artillery fortresses possessed solid pointed angle-bastions capable of providing cannon fire in virtually all directions.[62] Conditions in contemporary Scotland were not sufficiently propitious for such technological developments, and, although Ravenscraig Castle (Fife) may have come close to the European forefront at an early stage in this process, the fortifications in Scotland

Figure 14. Stirling Castle, forework: gatehouse and west curtain-wall

generally by comparison appear to be based on traditional models, improvised, adventitious, and limited in their potential use of heavy firearms.

Chronology. Except for Stirling Castle forework and the first phase of Ravenscraig Castle, there has so far been no attempt to ascribe dates to these various early artillery features, although the circumstantial evidence of sieges would favour a greater likelihood of their occurrence in or after the reign of James II (1437-60).

Unfortunately, so far as Scottish medieval architecture in general is concerned, methods of dating architectural features and their reliability have not been discussed in print as openly and as fully as the subject would seem to merit. As has already been indicated, a number of social, economic, geographical and functional considerations would tend to determine how and when a particular building fashion took hold and how long it endured. It is thus not always possible to determine a fixed point of departure or termination for any feature, and establishing even an approximate date (that is, within a decade) for a late medieval secular building by comparative dating methods is often not as easy as we may have been led to believe. The special problems of using the 'inverted keyhole' loop as a dating signature are also compounded by the fact that it

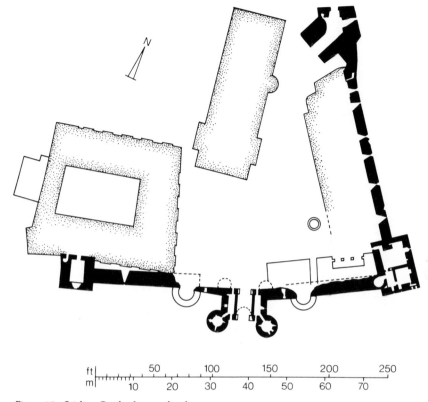

Figure 15. Stirling Castle, forework, plan

could be improvised from existing slits without too much difficulty. Making all due allowances, however, the earliest well-authenticated appearance of this type of loop in Scotland is in 1460-3 work at Ravens-craig Castle (Fife), whilst its supersession by horizontal wide-mouthed types probably took place gradually over two or more decades after about 1520.[63]

Among Scottish fortifications that possess some form of artillery defence there are two principal claimants for a date earlier than 1460: the inner curtain-wall at Craigmillar Castle (fig. 16), and the curtain-wall at Threave Castle. At Craigmillar, the angle-towers and some, but not all, of the associated gun-loops are integral features of the curtain (fig. 17), but the generally accepted dating of the curtain itself is based on Nisbet's mis-reading of an inscription surrounding the large armorial panel above the main gate. 'Below (the armorial),' he wrote, 'on the stone is the year of God 1427', and from the rest of his description it seems reasonably

Figure 16. Craigmillar Castle, aerial view

clear that the 'stone' in question is the extant panel and not one that has otherwise disappeared since Nisbet's time.[64] The lower border of the existing panel contains an orthographical variant of the name 'Craigmillar', whilst the much-worn upper border has subsequently been deciphered as a sequence comprising 'a coronet, a wreath and a saltire flanked by two roundels'.[65]

The inner curtain at Craigmillar is one of the classic Scottish statements of the quadrangular angle-towered layout of late medieval date, but the apparently two-sided or L-shaped main curtain at Threave is of equally regular and perhaps even more purposeful design so far as it goes. The Threave curtain, which probably originally rose to a height of two storeys, has a pronounced batter and a closely spaced series of slits and emplacements. This casemated wall of mortared rubble construction is further protected by the remains of three cylindrical angle-towers and a ditch, and the masonry impress of the hoisted drawbridge can still be seen in the gatehouse in the east curtain. The overall layout and individual features of the wall, towers and gatehouse could almost be described as *sui generis* and are not in themselves precisely dateable; the closest parallels for the towers at least, however, indicate a balance of

Figure 17. Craigmillar Castle, north curtain-wall

probabilities that is weighted in favour of a date later than 1500, a verdict which remained uncontested until a few years ago.[66]

Following recent archaeological excavations at the site, it has now been suggested that the greater part of this gun-looped wall was built by the Douglas family and was in existence prior to the famous siege of 1455.[67] Whilst the archaeological dating evidence for the drystone riparian curtain and harbour is above question, it does perhaps remain a matter of opinion whether the published findings are sufficient to provide a convincing *terminus ante quem* date for the completion of the upstanding portions of the south and east curtains in their existing form. For the architectural evidence does appear to correspond much more happily with a date in the period following a royal visit to the castle in 1501 and during the tenure of either the Dunbars of Mochrum or the Lords Maxwell as custodians of the royal castle and Stewards of Kirkcudbright.[68] Threave undoubtedly had an association with artillery that is clearly reflected in its recorded possession of at least two great guns in 1512, in the record of repairs to an 'artillery house' there in 1458, and, rather more ambiguously, in the payments to Sir John Dunbar, who was said to be 'in' the castle at the time it capitulated in 1455 and shortly afterwards appeared as the maker and repairer of military engines.[69] But none of this circumstantial historical evidence necessarily points to a curtain-wall of relatively sophisticated design, as opposed to a more makeshift and hurried artillery defence of drystone or earthwork construction having been put up by the Douglases.

Some Conclusions

Enough has already been written above to indicate a number of qualifications that might be made to the purely military and conventionally accepted views of late medieval castles and their defences. The buildings themselves are not so much physical reminders of political disorder as tangible illustration of contemporary social and economic trends. It is perhaps a little premature to say whether architectural priorities and styles differed markedly from region to region and whether, on the showing of the architectural evidence alone, one period or one area such as the Borders or the West Highlands was intrinsically more turbulent or more pacific than another.[70] The preliminary indications are that the incidence of the majority of late medieval buildings mainly reflects the pattern of landowning and wealth, and that, as in earlier and later ages, particular types of building occurred in particular areas at a particular time according to the current state of patronage, fashion and finance. Firm conclusions on all these aspects of medieval secular building have, of course, to rest upon a solid foundation, and these final remarks are thus confined to the broad but fundamental questions of chronology and typological classification.

Identifying a building-type or feature and establishing its earliest appearance are among the more rewarding aspects of medieval architectural research. So far as Scottish castles in particular are concerned, it is well known that one of the acknowledged doyens of the subject, the late Dr W. MacKay Mackenzie, accepted only grudgingly that there could be early stone castles and thereby apparently post-dated a number of major monuments.[71] Partly reacting to this rare error of judgment and aided by more recent developments in the scope and techniques of medieval archaeology, students of Scottish military architecture have since tended on the whole to become more pre-disposed towards accepting the earliest possible date for any building or type. Thus the pendulum has now swung almost as far in the opposite direction from Mackenzie, and contemporary attitudes sometimes appear to have almost reached a stage whereat 'earlier' has become synonymous with 'more interesting'.

But the general problem occasionally penetrates a little deeper than that. For once certain building-types have been established as 'early' or 'late', according to present-day opinion, there is a natural tendency to bring together all examples of these identified types into the same and often fairly narrow date-range. There is an equally natural corollary to think in terms of building 'evolution' or 'development' as a simple line progression through the centuries, usually seen in this period as the 'decline' of the castle from a predominantly military to a domestic status.[72] 'Early' (that is, thirteenth-century) period-types in Scotland are generally taken to include, for instance, hall-houses and enclosure-castles, especially simple straight-sided enceintes of a recognisable geometrical layout, whilst tower-houses are regarded as a 'late' phenomenon.[73] Further research may indeed confirm the balance of emphasis suggested by this pattern, but, even assuming that the system of classification would have conveyed some meaning to the medieval builder, the social and archaeological truth may be rather more complex than we assume at present. Whilst our rigid type-classifications and the process of ascribing dates on purely typological grounds may thus be distorting a strong element of continuity in Scottish medieval society, the categorisation of monuments into 'ecclesiastical', 'fortified' and 'domestic' groups, although convenient for the purposes of analysis, may also be of questionable assistance to our fuller understanding of the structure and organisation of that society. It would not be too tendentious to re-state that an overall concern for the appearance, transmission and endurance of architectural fashions, coupled with a much closer integration of social and building history are among the chief *desiderata* of medieval architectural studies in Scotland today. Nowhere, perhaps, is this approach more essential and demanding than in relation to the architecture of the later Middle Ages, and especially to that of the fourteenth century, a period for which clear terms of dating reference have yet to be achieved.

Acknowledgments

The author wishes to thank Dr Jennifer M. Wormald of the Department of Scottish History, University of Glasgow, and Mr Geoffrey D. Hay of the Royal Commission on the Ancient and Historical Monuments of Scotland for reading and offering comments upon a draft of this article. A part of the material on which this survey is based was gathered in the course of official duties on behalf of the Royal Commission on the Ancient and Historical Monuments of Scotland, and is included here by courtesy of the Commissioners. The opinions expressed in this essay are, of course, personal. Illustrations are Crown Copyright, Royal Commission on Ancient Monuments, Scotland.

NOTES

1. This essay is concerned principally with the standing remains of castles, towers, and, where appropriate, churches and their precincts. Some of the general remarks may have relevance for the study of burgh defences before 1513, but treatment of this subject can best await further publication of a growing body of archaeological information, e.g. J. Schofield *et al.*, 'Excavations south of Edinburgh High Street, 1973-4', *Proc. Soc. Antiq. Scot.*, cvii (1975-6), 155-241.

   Reference is normally given to the most recent and fullest available architectural description of the majority of individual monuments mentioned in the main text of this paper. The descriptions are generally contained in either D. MacGibbon & T. Ross, *The Castellated and Domestic Architecture of Scotland*, 5 vols. (Edinburgh, 1887-92) [*Cast. & Dom. Arch.*], the relevant *Inventory* volume of the Roy. Comm. Anc. Hist. Monuments Scot. [RCAHMS], or in article literature; q.v. also J. R. Kenyon, *Castles, town defences and artillery fortifications in Britain: a bibliography 1945-74* (CBA Research Report no. 25, 1978), 55-65, 74.

2. I. A. Crawford, 'The Divide between Medieval and Post-Medieval in Scotland', *Post-Med. Archaeol.*, i (1967), 84-89.

3. Discussed by J. M. Brown (ed), *Scottish Society in the Fifteenth Century* (London, 1977), 1-9, and cf. *infra*, n. 6.

4. Ibid., 10-65, and J. M. Brown, 'Taming the Magnates?' in *The Scottish Nation*, ed. G. Menzies (London, 1972), 46-59. Cf. also R. G. Nicholson, *Scotland: the later Middle Ages* (Edinburgh, 1974).

5. E.g., S. H. Cruden, *The Scottish Castle* (Edinburgh, 1960), 83-91, 129-30. Cf. Also A. Emery, 'The Development of Raglan Castle and Keeps in Late Medieval England', *Archaeol. Journ.*, cxxxii (1975), 151-86, at 173, 181 and refs. cited.

6. W. D. Simpson, 'Doune Castle', *Proc. Soc. Antiq. Scot.*, lxxii (1937-8), 73-83; 'Castles of "Livery and Maintenance"', *Journ. Brit. Archaeol. Assoc.*, iv (1939), 39-54; and '"Bastard Feudalism" and the Later Castles', *Antiquaries Journ.*, xxvi (1946), 145-71.

7. W. D. Simpson, *Crichton Castle* (HMSO, 1957, official guide), 3; *Doune Castle* (1966), at pp. 14-18; '"Bastard Feudalism" and the Later Castles', 154.

8. *Cast. & Dom. Arch.*, and W. M. Mackenzie, *The Medieval Castle in Scotland* (Edinburgh, 1927).

9. J. S. Richardson, *The Medieval Stone Carver in Scotland* (Edinburgh, 1964), 35-58; K. A. Steer & J. W. M. Bannerman, *Late Medieval Monumental Sculpture in the West Highlands* (Edinburgh, 1977), *passim*.

10. Cruden, *The Scottish Castle*, 100-43; W. D. Simpson, 'The Tower-Houses of Scotland' in *Studies in Building History*, ed. E. M. Jope (London, 1961), 229-42; J. G. Dunbar, *The Historic Architecture of Scotland* (London, 1966), 36-46.

11. G. Stell, 'Architecture: the changing needs of society' in *Scottish Society in the Fifteenth Century*, ed. J. M. Brown (London, 1977), 153-83, at pp. 156-9.

12. Cf. Cruden, *The Scottish Castle*, 91-99; Dunbar, *Historic Architecture*, 33-36; *Inventory of Argyll* (RCAHMS), ii, 27-28, and nos. 282, 290. Cf. also the restricted date-range that has been applied to 'hall-houses' in Ireland and Northern England, D. E. Waterman, 'Moylough Castle, Co. Galway', *Journ. Roy. Soc. Antiq. Ireland*, lxxxvi (1956), 73-76; 'Rectangular Keeps of the Thirteenth Century at Grenan (Kilkenny) and Clanworth (Cork)', ibid., xcviii (1968), 67-73; P. W. Dixon, *Fortified Houses on the Anglo-Scottish Border* (Unpublished Oxford D.Phil. thesis, 1976), i, 21-27. The present line of argument does not of course deny that some Scottish examples are demonstrably of 13th-century date, e.g. R. C. Graham & W. G. Collingwood, 'Skipness Castle', *Proc. Soc. Antiq. Scot.*, lvii (1922-3), 266-87, and *Inventory of Argyll* (RCAHMS), i, no. 314.

13. Cf. *Cast. & Dom. Arch.*, i, 545-61; *Inventory of Dumfries* (RCAHMS), no. 510; *Inventory of Fife*, no. 529; W. D. Simpson, 'Morton Castle, Dumfriesshire, *Trans. Dumfries & Galloway Archaeol. Soc.*, 3rd series, xxii (1938-9), 26-35; 'Rait Castle and Barevan Church, Nairnshire', *Proc. Soc. Antiq. Scot.*, lxxi (1936-7), 98-114; and 'The Castles of Duffus, Rait and Morton Reconsidered', *Proc. Soc. Antiq. Scot.*, xci, (1958-9), 10-14, for the gradual shift in opinion on the architectural dating evidence. For halls in enclosure-castles see Kildrummy and Urquhart Castles, and for the local contexts, cf. Rait Castle and Barevan Church (*supra*); the second phases of Craigie and Dundonald Castles; Tulliallan Castle and Dunfermline Abbey; and Morton Castle, whose details can be compared with Caerlaverock and Hermitage Castles among others.

14. W. D. Simpson, *The Earldom of Mar* (Aberdeen, 1949), 44, fig. 21; *Inventory of West Lothian* (RCAHMS), no. 356; *Cast. & Dom. Arch.*, iii, 296-301, 344-8. The earlier phase of Craigie is ascribed to c. 1200 largely on the proportions of the immured crenelles, Cruden, *The Scottish Castle*, 94.

15. W. D. Simpson, 'Dundonald Castle', *Ayrshire Coll.*, i (1947-9), 42-51; *Cast. & Dom. Arch.*, iii, 186-92; W. D. Simpson, 'Crookston Castle, *Trans. Glasgow Archaeol. Soc.*, n.s. xii (1953), 1-14.

16. *Cast. & Dom. Arch.*, iii, 202-4; R. C. Reid, 'Mauchline Castle', *Trans. Dumfries & Galloway Archaeol. Soc.*, 3rd series, xvi (1929-30), 166-71. Late medieval bishops' palaces and lodgings of monastic dignitaries can also be included in this category, e.g. the Bishop's Palace, Kirkwall, *Inventory of Orkney and Shetland* (RCAHMS), ii, no. 402, and the 'Commendator's House', Melrose Abbey, *Inventory of Roxburgh*, ii, no. 567, at pp. 287-8.

17. See descriptions in *Chron. Fordun*, ii, 43, and Monro's *Western Isles of Scotland*, ed. R. W. Monro (Edinburgh & London, 1961), 56-57.

18. This section incorporates some summary conclusions from current research into the baronial castles of Scotland and Northern England; it is proposed to set out these findings in more detail in due course.

19. G. G. Simpson & A. B. Webster, 'Charter evidence and the distribution of mottes in Scotland', *Château Gaillard*, v (1970), 175-92, and cf. A. A. M. Duncan, *Scotland: the Making of the Kingdom* (Edinburgh, 1975), 434-8.

20. J. G. Edwards, 'Edward I's Castle Building in Wales', *Proc. British Academy*, xxxii (1946), 15-81; A. J. Taylor, 'Castle-building in Wales in the later thirteenth century: the prelude to construction' in *Studies in Building History*, ed. Jope, 104-33; *The History of the King's Works*, ed. H. M. Colvin, i (London, 1963), 293-422. For the cost and duration of some Scottish royal works that can be matched against a known or roughly ascertainable amount of late medieval architecture, see, e.g., *Exch. Rolls*, iv, pp. cxxxvi-cxxxix and refs. cited for James I's work at Linlithgow, and ibid., vii, pp. l-liv, and refs. cited for Queen Mary's operations at Ravenscraig Castle and the former Trinity College, Edinburgh.

21. Cf. C. L. H. Coulson, 'Rendability and castellation in medieval France', *Château Gaillard*, vi (1972), 59-67. For royal and baronial co-operation in the matter of building and staffing castles see below n. 28-29, and *Reg. Sec. Sig.* [*RSS*], i, nos. 722, 1668. *Acts of Council (Public Affairs)*, 13, 104, 388, 589-91, and *Reg. Privy Council* [*RPC*], i, 18, are later examples cited by T. I. Rae, *The Administration of the Scottish Frontier 1513-1603* (Edinburgh, 1966), 45, 68.

22. *Acts Parl. Scot.* [*APS*], ii, 18, 49 and 488. I am much indebted to Dr Jennifer M. Wormald for these references, and for the references to *RSS*, see n. 21.

23. *Inventory of East Lothian* (RCAHMS), no. 106; W. D. Simpson, 'Tantallon Castle', *Trans. E. Lothian Archaeol. Soc.*, vii (1958), 18-26.

24. *Inventory of the Outer Hebrides* (RCAHMS), nos. 439, 504; *Inventory of Argyll*, iii,

for Duart, Moy, Kinlochaline and Breachacha Castles (nos. 339, 346, 343, 334). See also W. D. Simpson, ' Breachacha Castle in the Isle of Coll', *Trans. Glasgow Archaeol. Soc.*, n.s. x (1941), 26-54; and D. J. Turner & J. G. Dunbar, 'Breachacha Castle, Coll: Excavations and Field Survey, 1965-8', *Proc. Soc. Antiq. Scot.*, cii (1969-70), 155-87.

25. E.g. *Inventory of Wigtown* (RCAHMS), nos. 11, 98, 226, 390; *Inventory of the Outer Hebrides*, nos. 211, 213, 215, 380-1; E. Beveridge, *Coll and Tiree* (Edinburgh, 1903), 23-26; A. Fairbairn, 'Excavation of a medieval site on Donald's Isle, Loch Doon, Ayrshire', *Proc. Soc. Antiq. Scot.*, lxxi (1936-7), 323-33; H. Fairhurst, 'A medieval island settlement in Loch Glashan, Argyll', *Glasgow Arch. Journ.*, i (1969), 47-67. See also *RPC*, viii, 737 for the famous instruction to royal Commissioners to obtain delivery of the houses of defence and 'crannakis' of the rebellious Islesmen in 1608.

26. *Inventory of Edinburgh* (RCAHMS), no. 1; *Inventory of Stirling*, no. 192; W. D. Simpson, 'Urquhart Castle', *Trans. Gaelic Soc. of Inverness*, xxxv (1929-30), 51-82, and 'Glen Urquhart and its Castle: a study in environment' in *Aspects of Archaeology in Britain and abroad: essays presented to O. G. S. Crawford*, ed. W. F. Grimes (London, 1951), 316-31.

27. *APS*, ii, 13, cited by Mackenzie, *The Medieval Castle*, 139. Cf. above, n. 21, *RSS*, i, nos. 722, 1668.

28. Mackenzie, *The Medieval Castle*, 138-9 citing *Aberdeen-Banff Coll.*, iii, 524-5, and *Reg. Mag. Sig.* [*RMS*], ii, nos. 3390, 3880.

29. *APS*, ii, 113 refers to 'omnes donaciones et concessiones custodie castrorum ad longos terminos et specialiter castrorum que sunt claves Regni'.

30. Ibid., 133.

31. *Chron. Bower.*, ii, 467; *RMS*, ii, nos. 2038, 2040; *RSS*, i, no. 453; and *Dundas Papers*, lxxiii.

32. *Inventory of Fife* (RCAHMS), nos. 224, 364. See n. 60.

33. Mackenzie, *The Medieval Castle*, 215-29 and refs. cited. See also Fraser, *Melville*, iii, 46, no. 49; *Aberdeen-Banff Coll.*, iii, 524-5, and less well authenticated traditions of licences in e.g. *The Statistical Account of Scotland*, ed. J. Sinclair (Edinburgh, 1791-9), xix, 474-5 (Castle Huntly), and A. Jervise, *The Land of the Lindsays* (Edinburgh, 1882 edn.), 346 (Inverquharity Castle).

34. T. H. Turner & J. H. Parker, *Domestic Architecture of the Middle Ages*, vol. 4 (Oxford, 1859), 401-22, and refs. cited.

35. *RMS*, ii, no. 1; Fraser, *Pollok*, i, 167-8, no. 39; *Cawdor Bk.*, 20-1.

36. *RMS*, ii, nos. 2038, 3390; *RSS*, i, nos. 552, 2360, cited by Mackenzie, *The Medieval Castle*, 225-7.

37. For stepped merlons, see *Inventory of Fife* (RCAHMS), no. 588.

38. Cf. *Cast. & Dom. Arch.*, i, 164; *Inventory of Kirkcudbright* (RCAHMS), no. 41; Mackenzie, *The Medieval Castle*, 88-89, 186-7; and W. D. Simpson, *Threave Castle* (Official guide, 1947), 6. Sockets for hourds also exist at Kissimul Castle, and there is evidence of a continuous wooden platform or gallery at Hermitage Castle, *Inventory of Roxburgh* (RCAHMS), i, no. 63.

39. Mackenzie, *The Medieval Castle*, 89-91. For Bothwell Castle see W. D. Simpson, 'The architectural history of Bothwell Castle', *Proc. Soc. Antiq. Scot.*, lix (1924-5), 165-93, and 'Bothwell Castle reconsidered', *Trans. Glasgow Archaeol. Soc.*, xi (1947), 97-116.

40. *Inventory of East Lothian* (RCAHMS), no. 27; *Inventory of Kirkcudbright*, no. 8; *An Archaeological Survey of County Down* (Belfast, 1966), 125, 223, 225, 232, 241, 244-5, 247-8, 251, 254. Cf. Mackenzie, *The Medieval Castle*, 99.

41. D. Christison, 'On the grated iron doors of Scottish Castles', *Proc. Soc. Antiq. Scot.*, xvii (1882-3), 98-135, and 'Additional notices of yetts or grated iron doors', *Proc. Soc. Antiq. Scot.*, xxii (1887-8), 286-320. Cf. also the references to yetts in the licences in n. 36.

42. D. MacGibbon & T. Ross, *Ecclesiastical Architecture of Scotland* (Edinburgh, 1896), ii, 30-52; *Inventory of Fife* (RCAHMS), no. 460.

43. C. Cordiner, *Remarkable Ruins and Romantic Prospects of North Britain with Ancient Monuments* (London, 1795), not paginated.

44. See above, n. 6-7.

45. *Inventory of Fife* (RCAHMS), no. 465.

46. For castle bridges of timber, see S. E. Rigold, 'Structural aspects of Medieval Timber Bridges', *Med. Archaeol.*, xix (1975), 48-91, and for defensible bridges of stone in Scotland, see e.g. *Inventory of Midlothian* (RCAHMS), no. 140, and H. R. G. Inglis, 'The Ancient Bridges in Scotland, and their relation to the Roman and Medieval Bridges in Europe', *Proc. Soc. Antiq. Scot.*, xlvi (1911-12), 168-9 where the defensive aspects of medieval bridge design may have been exaggerated. 'Pontibus veheticis videlicet le drawbriggis' are specifically referred to in *Aberdeen-Banff Coll.*, iii, 524-5.

47. E. Viollet-le-Duc, *Dictionnaire de l' Architecture*, vii (Paris, 1864), 220-59, especially 253-9.

48. A. H. Allcroft, *Earthwork in England* (London, 1908), 400 ff, and Mackenzie, *The Medieval Castle*, 97, for castle earthworks in general, and for moated sites in Scotland, see *Inventory of Roxburgh* (RCAHMS), i, 47-48, and E. F. Burdon Davies, 'The Moated Manor at Dunrod, Kirkcudbrightshire', *Trans. Dumfries & Galloway Archaeol. Soc.*, 3rd series, xliii (1966), 121-36.

49. Allcroft, *Earthwork in England*, 603-10; B. H. St J. O'Neil, *Castles and Cannon* (Oxford, 1960), 80-115; *Newark on Trent: the Civil War Siegeworks* (Roy. Comm. Hist. Monuments, 1964), for artillery earthworks. *Inventory of Dumfries* (RCAHMS), no. 590, and *Inventory of Roxburgh*, i, no. 207, for Torthorwald and Cessford Castles.

50. *Inventory of Dumfries* (RCAHMS), no. 445 (2); A. D. S. Macdonald & L. R. Laing, 'Excavations at Lochmaben Castle, Dumfriesshire', *Proc. Soc. Antiq. Scot.*, cvi (1974-5), 124-57.

51. E.g., *Inventory of the Outer Hebrides* (RCAHMS), no. 439, and Cruden, *The Scottish Castle*, 42-45.

52. *Calendar of Letters and Papers, Foreign and Domestic, Henry VIII*, III, ii, no. 3039. Cf. also the ineffectiveness of James V's famous siege of Tantallon Castle in 1528 as recounted in Fraser, *Douglas*, iv, 137-8, no. 122.

53. *APS*, ii, 214-15; *Treasurer Accts.*, i, 109-17 for the Crookston and Duchall campaign. For the expeditions to the Western Highlands and Islands, see R. L. Mackie, *King James IV of Scotland* (Edinburgh, 1958), 72-78, 188-99, and refs. cited.

54. M. Toynbee, 'King James II of Scotland: Artillery and Fortification', *The Stewarts*, xi (1962), 157-62.

55. *Exch. Rolls*, v, 606-8, for the siege of Hatton Castle; ibid., vi, 4, 12, 92, *Chron. Auchinleck*, 12, 54, Pinkerton, *History*, i, 486-8 (Abercorn); and *Exch. Rolls*, vi, 119, 199-209, and *Cal. Docs. Scot.*, iv, no. 1272 (Threave). Gunpowder ordnance was probably used to 'cast down' Inveravon Tower (*Chron. Auchinleck*, 12; *Exch. Rolls*, vi, 12; and *Inventory of West Lothian* (RCAHMS), no. 299), but details of the action taken against Douglas and Strathavon Castles are evidently not known; see *APS*, ii, 76.

56. Buchanan, *History*, ii, 159; *Chron. Auchinleck*, 54. For the results of the archaeological excavation on the site of Abercorn Castle, cf. *Med. Archaeol.*, viii (1964), 261, and *Discovery and Excavation in Scotland 1963* (Council for British Archaeology, Scottish Regional Group, 1963), 51.

57. Pinkerton, *History*, i, 486-8.

58. *A Dictionary of the Older Scottish Tongue*, ii, 745. See also the reference of 1519 to

what were described as 'grete murdour holes' designed for use with great bombards at Wark Castle, cited by C. J. Bates, *The Border Holds of Northumberland* (Newcastle-upon-Tyne, 1891), 342, and discussed by J. R. Kenyon, 'Wark Castle and its Artillery Defences in the Reign of Henry VIII', *Post-Med. Archaeol.*, xi (1977), 50-60. Details of Wark Castle are not included in the calendared entry in *Cal. State Papers* (Thorpe), i, 7, no. 57.

59. Cruden, *The Scottish Castle*, 215-18, and A. M. T. Maxwell-Irving, 'Early Firearms and their influence on the Military and Domestic Architecture of the Borders', *Proc. Soc. Antiq. Scot.*, ciii (1970-71), 192-223.

60. See above, n. 20, 32; and cf. W. D. Simpson, *Ravenscraig Castle* (Aberdeen, 1938), 7-8, 29-30, and refs. cited.

61. *Inventory of Stirling* (RCAHMS), i, no. 192, at pp. 183, 193-6.

62. J. R. Hale, 'The Origins of the Bastion', in *Europe in the Late Middle Ages*, ed. J. R. Hale, J. R. L. Highfield & B. Smalley (London, 1965), 466-94; and J. R. Hale, *Renaissance Fortification, Art or Engineering?* (London, 1978).

63. Cf. Cruden, *The Scottish Castle*, 215-24. For the dating and typology of the earliest gun-ports in England cf. O'Neil, *Castles and Cannon*, 1-40; D. F. Renn, 'The Southampton Arcade', *Med. Archaeol.*, viii (1964), 226-8; 'The Earliest Gunports in Britain?', *Archaeol. Journ.*, cxxv (1968), 301-3; and J. R. Kenyon, 'Wark Castle and its Artillery Defences'.

64. A. Nisbet, *A System of Heraldry*, i (Edinburgh, 1722), 312.

65. *Inventory of Midlothian* (RCAHMS), no. 156, and Cruden, *The Scottish Castle*, 115, 118, 216. This inscription has also been interpreted as a coronet and a roundel flanking the date 1504; see the marginalia in the late W. D. Simpson's personal annotated copy of the *Inventory of Midlothian* which is now deposited in the National Monuments Record of Scotland.

66. For the standard descriptions of Threave see n. 38, and cf. Cruden, *The Scottish Castle*, 115-19, 217. For the angle-towers, see Craigmillar curtain-wall, Stirling Castle Forework (c. 1500-10), and the 'Bulwerk', Linlithgow Palace (early 16th cent.).

67. *Med. Archaeol.*, xxi (1977), 238-9. See also ibid., xix (1975), 242; and xx (1976), 185. Interim reports are also contained in *Discovery and Excavation in Scotland 1974*, 76-77; *1975*, 28; *1976*, 38-9; and *1977*, 20.

68. *Treasurer Accts.*, ii, 113; *RSS*, i, nos. 873, 2697.

69. *Treasurer Accts.*, ii, 350; *Exch. Rolls*, vi, 199, 293, 456.

70. Cf. the use of architectural evidence in e.g. Duncan, *The Making of the Kingdom*, 441-2, and in *Scottish Society*, ed. Brown, 237-8.

71. Mackenzie, *The Medieval Castle*, 1-72; 'Clay castle-building in Scotland', *Proc. Soc. Antiq. Scot.*, lxviii (1933-4), 117-27; and cf., e.g. *Inventory of Dumfries* (RCAHMS), nos. 33 (1) and (2), 510.

72. Cf. A. H. Thompson, *Military Architecture in England in the Middle Ages* (Oxford, 1912), 287 ff; R. A. Brown, *English Castles* (London, 1976 edn.), 128-53.

73. For 'hall-houses' and tower-houses, see n. 10-14. For castles of enclosure as an early period-type, *Cast. & Dom. Arch.*, i, 65-142; iii, 42-113; Cruden, *The Scottish Castle*, 22-56; Dunbar, *Historic Architecture*, 23-25; J. G. Dunbar & A. A. M. Duncan, 'Tarbert Castle', *Scot. Hist. Rev.*, l (1971), 1-17. Cf. the inferential early dating of what may equally be 14th cent. works at, for example, Hailes and Ardrossan Castles.

4 The Artillery Fortification at Threave Castle, Galloway

Christopher J. Tabraham & George L. Good

Summary

Between the years 1974 and 1978 archaeological excavations were carried out at Threave Castle, situated a little over a kilometre to the west of the burgh of Castle Douglas in the heart of Galloway. These excavations have produced, amongst other things, evidence to demonstrate that the artillery wall, wrapped around the forbidding tower-house of Archibald 'The Grim', third Earl of Douglas, was erected by either the eighth or ninth (and last) earl prior to the overthrow of this once-powerful Scottish family in 1455. If this is so it makes the wall the earliest artillery work recorded in Scotland and one of the earliest surviving in Europe.

Historical introduction

The Castle of Threave stands upon an island bearing that name on the River Dee some 14 km. upstream from the burgh and port of Kirkcudbright (fig. 18). Though it has long been suspected that there was a residence here before the medieval period, the archaeological record has produced little which indicates activity on the island earlier than the arrival of the Black Douglas family in the latter half of the fourteenth century. It was then that Archibald 'The Grim', following his elevation to the Lordship of Galloway in 1369, chose Threave Island as his place of residence within Galloway and had the five-storey tower-house that now dominates the island erected.[1]

The Douglases continued as Lords of Galloway for the following eighty years until their premature disappearance from the stage of Scottish politics in 1455 at the hand of the young King James II (1437-1460), who had resolved to rid himself of this potential threat to the Stewarts' hold on the throne.[2] The final scene in this drama was enacted on the island with a famous siege that lasted well over three months and demanded the best piece of ordnance the king possessed in his arsenal at Linlithgow. Even this failed to batter down the doors and walls of the castle and a more ancient weapon — bribery — was employed by the Royal Exchequer in order to effect a successful outcome. Threave then became the property of the Crown and a succession of temporary keepers replaced the Douglases as residents. Together with the castles at

Figure 18. Threave Castle and island from the north-east. Only the furthest part of the island was habitable, the remainder being under water for most of the year

Caerlaverock and Lochmaben, both in the sheriffdom of Dumfries, Threave was an integral part of the West March defences of the Scottish kingdom.

The death of James IV and the crushing defeat of his army on Flodden Field in 1513 rocked the nation. Hasty measures had to be taken by his widow and one such action was the transfer of Threave into the keepership of the Lords Maxwell, an influential Dumfriess-shire family. The keepership became hereditary in 1523 and it was to remain in that family's hands for the following 117 years at which time (1640) Lieutenant Colonel John Hume's Covenanting Army successfully besieged the island fortress and supervised its dismantling (fig. 19). The siege was motivated by religious considerations, Threave for the last hundred years having taken no significant part in the defence of the realm.

The artillery wall

The artillery wall that encloses the Douglas tower-house has now been completely excavated and its exact form ascertained[3] (fig. 20). The excavations showed that there was no masonry wall along the north side of the tower-house and only a small exploratory trench was hand-dug in

Figure 19. Threave in 1789 as seen by Captain Grose. Portions of the artillery work, now collapsed, were still standing at the time of his visit

this area, which has an abundance of organic material surviving in the wet conditions. The clay-bonded curtain-wall along the river-bank on the west has had to be totally dismantled stone by stone and rebuilt in the same position using a mortar mix to protect it from the fast-flowing waters of the Dee.

The work has three characteristics and these will be described separately. The principal feature of the work, and the one which has survived almost intact since its erection, is the masonry curtain-wall built along the east and south sides of the tower-house, the whole surrounded by a rock-cut moat. It comprises two stoutly built mortared walls with a circular three-storeyed tower at the south-east corner and two similar towers, one at the end of each of the walls (fig. 21).

The walls themselves, built from the local Silurian shale, are 1.5 m. in breadth at ground-level and are constructed with a continuous external batter, thereby giving them greater strength against the more horizontal trajectory of cannon. In their present state the walls attain a height of almost 3.5 m., though it is clear that the wall-head had at one time been furnished with a parapet and wall-walk that is sadly missing today but which would have raised the overall height of the wall to nearer 6 m. Both walls are liberally provided with slits for use either with hand-held

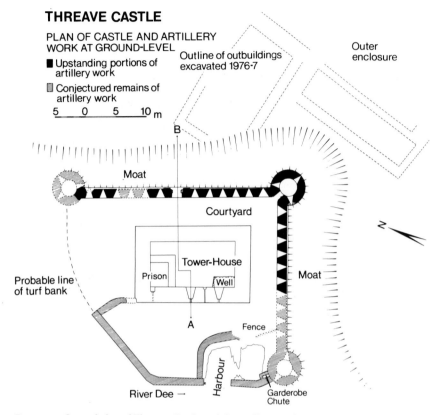

Figure 20. Ground plan of Threave Castle and the artillery work

gun-pieces or, more likely, cross-bows and long-bows (fig. 22). The slits do not conform to a uniform pattern. There are idiosyncrasies in their design such as the different treatment of their ceilings, some being arched, others flat-lintelled. This is probably little more than accidental, the result perhaps of more than one squad of stone-masons working upon its construction. More significant would seem to be the treatment of the slits either side of the entrance into the south-east tower. Here they are more widely splayed though the reason for this is not readily apparent to the writers, for the increased splays still did not allow the defender to protect the curving wall of the south-east tower.

   The entrance through this work was centrally situated along the east wall. Though the stone-robbing activities following the 1640 siege have denuded it somewhat, it is still a most prepossessing feature (fig. 23). It lacks the continuous external batter of the adjoining walls, rising per-pendicularly from the bedrock to a height of almost 8 m. The principal

Figure 21. The artillery work at Threave from the south-east. The oak drawbridge is a modern replica

feature is the gateway itself, the lowest of the three storeys in the gate-house. The opening is 2.4 m. high and 1.3 m. wide and there is evidence to indicate the existence of three barriers. The first was the drawbridge itself which, when raised, was housed within the gatehouse and effectively became the outermost barrier. There are the vestiges of creuk-and-band hinges on both the internal and external faces of the door jambs indicating the existence of two further doors, one of wood, the other (more likely the interior one) possibly an iron 'yett' for strengthen-ing. Immediately above this innermost door was an arch which sup-ported the winch mechanism for the raising and lowering of the bridge (fig. 24). A single vertical slit in the wall above the entrance indicates that the bridge may have been moved quite simply by means of a single rope. The third storey above the winch house was merely a platform from which the defenders could protect the entrance below. It was entered through a doorway in the west wall which communicated with the ground by means of a ladder or some other form of timber staging.

It should be noted here that the artillery work was little more than a curtain wrapped around the tower-house. As originally conceived there would have been an elaborate timber structure consisting chiefly of

Figure 22. The rear of the artillery work at Threave. The wall-head and towers were reached by a series of timber ladders and staging placed against the stonework

ladders and a wall-walk butted up against the inner face of both walls, the gatehouse and the three circular towers. This has now totally disappeared and only the faintest traces of joist-holes survive in the walls, none making much sense. With the eye of faith one can perhaps see the vestigial traces of a stair climbing up to the wall-head at the very northern end of the east wall immediately before the entrance into the north-east tower. Also the raggle cut into the south wall of the tower-house indicates that the courtyard here was covered over.

It is now impossible to tell whether there was ever a direct link between the gatehouse and the tower-house behind. There are three corbels, now cloured away flush with the wall-face, immediately above the entrance into the tower-house, which at one time were thought to have supported timbers carrying a walkway from the door in the east wall of the main hall (the third storey within the tower) over the courtyard and on to the topmost level of the gatehouse. This would have meant a most awkward and steeply inclined descent through a gradient of three in four and it must be extremely doubtful whether such an access

Figure 23. The gatehouse in the east curtain-wall at Threave

ever existed. The doorway in the tower-house and the three corbels below might therefore be primary features in the building associated with the lifting and lowering of the moveable outside stair to the tower's only entrance at first floor level.

Of the three circular towers that are associated with the two curtain walls, only the south-east example survives almost intact bar its timber floors. The north-east and south-west towers were heavily damaged during the 1640 siege and subsequently fell into the moat. The excavation of the fallen masonry of the south-west tower has shown that, in almost every detail, with the exception of one important difference, this tower had been of the same design. From the little that remains of the north-east tower it is possible to assume that this too was of the same form though sharing with the south-west tower that one basic difference — no entry into the tower at ground-floor level.

The towers (fig. 25) are all of three storeys in height, each flight having an internal diameter of between 2.6 and 2.8 m. They are furnished with gun-loops in the lower two storeys — three at each level — whilst the topmost level, which was open to the elements, had a tall parapet punctured by three crenelles. The gun-loops take two distinct forms.

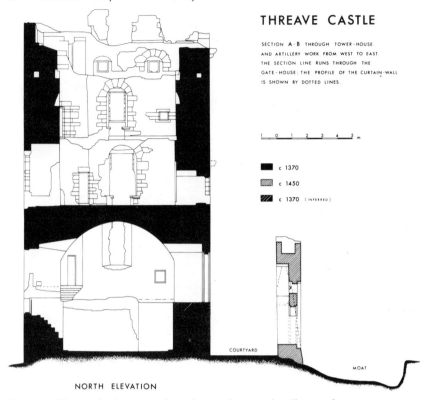

THREAVE CASTLE

SECTION A-B THROUGH TOWER-HOUSE
AND ARTILLERY WORK FROM WEST TO EAST.
THE SECTION LINE RUNS THROUGH THE
GATE-HOUSE; THE PROFILE OF THE CURTAIN-WALL
IS SHOWN BY DOTTED LINES.

c 1370

c 1450

c 1370 (INFERRED)

COURTYARD

MOAT

NORTH ELEVATION

Figure 24. Threave Castle, section through tower-house and artillery work

Those within the ground-floor chambers are of the dumb-bell variety with internal splays only and apertures measuring 270 mm. in diameter (fig. 26). The reasoning behind this design is still a matter of conjecture. The loops within the first-floor chambers are of the more common inverted keyhole pattern with apertures 280 mm. in diameter and the vertical slits 610 mm. long and 80 mm. wide. A notable feature of some of the loops is the check in their sills which housed a cross timber on which the small guns that penetrated the loops were mounted.[4] This feature is not peculiar to one form of loop and its non-existence at certain loops may only be the result of indifferent consolidation work carried out at the monument in the 1910s.

The whole of this artillery work was surrounded by a rock-cut moat which effectively diverted the course of the River Dee around the east and south sides of the tower-house to form an island within an island. The average width of the moat from the curtain-wall to the upper lip of

Figure 25. Threave Castle, the south-east tower

the counter scarp was 8 m. and the original depth some 2 m. The moat completed the artillery defence of the tower-house along its most vulnerable flanks — the island itself and the high ground to the east known as Little Wood Hill (fig. 27). To the west and north of the tower-house the topography was far kinder to the islanders, for the fortunate absence of high ground (from which an artillery assault could be mounted) was augmented by the extremely boggy nature of the west bank of the river. For this reason, then, the artillery wall along the west and north was constructed in a fashion markedly different from that described above.

The west face of the tower-house and its north-west corner were protected by a masonry wall 36 m. in overall length and with a breadth at ground level of 1.15 m. The wall stood little more than 500 mm. in height upon excavation and as a consequence little can be said about its form. It

THREAVE CASTLE

GUN - LOOPS   IN   SOUTH - EAST   TOWER

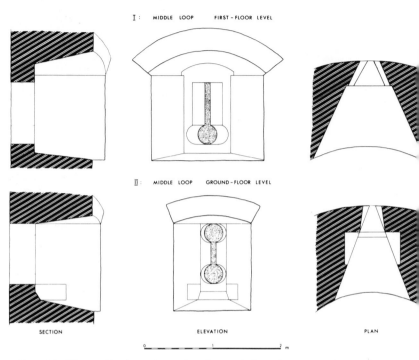

Figure 26. Threave Castle, sections, elevations and plans of representative gun-loops in the south-east tower

was constructed of the same material as the main work — namely the local Silurian shale — though the stones were not lime-mortared but simply set in a soft yellow clay. There was the faintest trace that the outer face had been battered in a manner similar to the main walls on the east and south. The approximate height of the wall can be estimated by referring to the north-west corner of the tower-house into which the wall was tailed. The robbed-out quoins here attain a height of 2.3 m.

A function of this west wall was to enclose — and so protect — the small rock-cut harbour lying immediately north of the south-west circular tower (fig. 28). The entrance was '4 m. wide and had an oak door, traces of which were found during excavation within the harbour. The tower-house wall immediately behind the entrance was given added protection by the extension of the west wall round the inner edge of the harbour. The remaining gap between this wall extension and the south curtain-wall was filled by a small fence, the post-holes of which were found during excavation in 1975.

Figure 27. Threave Castle and artillery work from the west. Little Wood Hill is at the top right-hand corner of the picture

In the south-west corner of the harbour at the junction of the west curtain with the south-west tower exist the footings of a garderobe chute that was added to the tower at a later date. The stones of the west wall were robbed out at this point to allow the garderobe contents to outflow through the wall and into the river (fig. 29). This addition represents an unfortunate disturbance at a crucial point in the wall's circuit, for it could be argued that the west wall was built at a period earlier than the principal east and south walls. Nevertheless upon excavation, it would seem that the stones of the west wall originally butted up against the sloping face of the south-west tower indicating, if anything, that the west wall was constructed at a later date.

Finally, the north flank of the tower-house never appears to have been considered pregnable by the keepers of the castle and a simple turf rampart was constructed between the west wall and the north-east tower, thereby completing the circuit of the artillery defence.

The dating evidence

Flodden Field saw the demise of many a Scottish knight and one of

Figure 28. Threave Castle, harbour and artillery work from the south-west

them was Sir John Dunbar, keeper of Threave Castle on behalf of the Crown. His untimely death necessitated his office being hastily transferred upon Robert, fifth Lord Maxwell, and at that time a report on the condition of the castle described it as being 'falty, ruinois and fallin doun in divers partis'. Lord Maxwell was directed to attend to its 'uphald, bigging and reparatioun' and the building activity that is thought to have taken place on the island fortress as a consequence of this order was the construction of the artillery work. Elsewhere in this volume it is argued that the architectural evidence for the towers at least supports this early sixteenth-century date, though it has been stated previously that 'the dumb-bell or key-hole patterns . . . came into fashion in Scotland during the second half of the fifteenth century'.[5]

Another possible date for its construction could have been the period of direct Crown involvement on the island between the 1455 siege and its

Figure 29. The garderobe chute within the harbour at Threave during excavation. The relationship between the west curtain-wall and the south-west tower has been destroyed by the construction of the outflow for the garderobe

transfer into the Maxwell family's hands in 1513. There is no evidence to support this suggestion either, other than that it agrees with the architectural dating for the gun-loop forms mentioned above.[6]

A third alternative has been suggested in recent years by Cruden.[7] He argued that the curtain may have represented the measures the last Douglas took to 'strengthen his position in the prevailing atmosphere of royal suspicion in 1454'.

This uncertainty as to the date of construction of the work persuaded the writers that archaeological excavation might be of some assistance. The immediate results were inconclusive. Sections cut across the moat revealed nothing in the way of datable material and the slight traces of construction trench within which the west wall had been founded proved sterile also. An indication that the work might have belonged to the fifteenth, and not the sixteenth, century came from the discovery of a jetton, or gaming-counter, found amongst other debris upon the floor of the south-west tower. It was in excellent condition and has been identified as emanating from Burgundy. Its date of minting is uncertain though the last quarter of the fifteenth century would seem the most likely.[8]

Figure 30. The oak gate-post at the northern side of the harbour entrance at Threave.
The tree from which it was fashioned was felled in the winter of 1446/7

The consolidation work upon the west wall, however, produced a fortunate clue. Set in the heart of the wall, some 9 m. north of the harbour entrance and little more than 200 mm. from the base, was found a much worn and very rare silver penny minted towards the end of Robert III's reign (died 1406). The numismatist reported that it could be considered as being in circulation no later than the early 1460s.[9] This statement received surprising confirmation soon after, following dendro-chronological work upon a number of oaks found during the excavations (fig. 30). The two oak sections of most relevance were taken from the timber post that was found set into a pit at the entrance to the harbour on its northern side (and presumably the post that supported the harbour gate) and a large timber found lying horizontally across the harbour mouth (and considered to belong to the gate itself). The sections were complete from their hearts out to the sapwood and bark and the pro-visional dates for the felling of the tree(s) from which they came is the same — namely the winter of the year 1446.[10] This would give a building date for the west wall of 1447, given that there is little evidence of trees being seasoned for any length of time in the medieval period.

The crucial question to be answered at this point is: Was the west wall built contemporaneously with the principal artillery work? A categorical

Figure 31. Stone foundations to the south-east of Threave Castle during excavation. The furthermost building has been cut by the moat

answer cannot be given. It has been demonstrated above (page 65) that the crucial point of contact between the west wall and the south-west tower had been disturbed prior to excavation and, though it is felt by the excavators that the west wall, if anything, is later than the tower, this cannot be asserted with absolute conviction. As yet there is no secure independent dating for the construction of the main curtain. Excavations in 1977 to the east of the moat, however, have revealed the stone footings of two buildings, both built towards the end of the fourteenth century to provide extra accommodation for the island's residents. They had been demolished principally because they were an encumbrance to the efficient working of the artillery work. Indeed the more northerly of the two buildings had been partially destroyed by the cutting of the rock-cut moat (fig. 31). Upon excavation the destruction-levels in both buildings were located and both, fortunately, contained datable material. The more northerly of the two produced a coin considerably alloyed and barely identifiable,[11] the other a jetton, similar to that found within the south-west tower. Both pieces tend to confirm the mid-fifteenth-century date.

Should the whole work prove to be a product of the Douglases, then two references in the written material immediately begin to take on a greater significance. On 9 June 1455, at a meeting of the Scottish Parliament in Edinburgh, the ninth Earl of Douglas was accused of treason by James II 'pro proditoriis munitionibus et fortificationibus turrium et fortaliciorum de Treve'.[12] The records do not elaborate further, but in the Exchequer Rolls for the year 1458, auditing for work carried out in the previous year, the sum of £40 13s 4d is reimbursed to the then keeper, William Edmonstone, for repairs to the 'domus artilerie'.[13] Was this 'artillery house' the artillery work described above? That such a work was built for no other purpose than for artillery defence cannot be doubted and it is logical to think that, during times of peace, the three circular towers would have housed the ordnance pieces, gunpowder and other accoutrements. There can be no doubt that the building of the artillery work was within the financial capabilities of the Douglases, but can it be reasonably demonstrated that it was within their technological capabilities also? A further search of the written material suggests this could have been so.

The siege of 1455 was a long and protracted affair. All the might of the warlike James II's arsenal was brought to bear on the castle walls — without success. Soon after the flight of James, ninth Earl of Douglas, to England and his transfer of the castle into King Henry VI's hands on 15 July 1455,[14] James II bribed the besieged into surrendering up the stronghold. The Douglas' custodian, Sir John Fraser, received £5 13s 6d; another, John Whiting, a further £5, but the excessively generous sum of £50 was given to John of Dunbar and others who were with him in the castle at the time.[15] Nor was money the only medium of bribery. Lands that had been annexed by James at the outset of the siege were returned. John Fraser received back his estates at Dunrodsannock, John Whiting his at Kildarach, both in the Stewartry. John of Dunbar, however, not only got back his manor at Duchrae, a little to the north of Threave Island, but received in addition estates at Kelton, Lochdougan, Kirkbride, Carlingwark and 'Slewyndaw', all to the south of the island.[16] John of Dunbar's good treatment by a monarch against whom he was fighting just months before is puzzling, particularly as he was not even head of the defending garrison. His career after the downfall of the Douglas family, however, explains the thinking behind James II's largesse.

The Exchequer Rolls for the year 1457 record the reimbursement of £20 to John of Dunbar 'pro fabrica et reparacione certorum instrumentorum bellicorum'.[17] The Rolls for the following year record a payment to him of £6 for repairs carried out to the great bombard and other instruments in the arsenal at Linlithgow.[18] Other payments to him about the same time record his journeys to Flanders, the centre of ordnance manufacture, to supervise the purchasing and transporting back to Scotland of articles (e.g. saltpetre) connected with cannon.[19]

John of Dunbar's period within the king's arsenals at Linlithgow and Edinburgh was limited to the three years following the island siege. His last recorded payment for work done (the drying of gunpowder) is in the Rolls for the year 1459.[20] It can hardly be a coincidence that this period bridges the gap between the death of the king's gunner, John of Moray, in 1455[21] and the arrival of a new gunner, Dedrik the Dutchman, in 1457.[22] It would seem that John of Dunbar was considered by the king a suitable temporary substitute for the post, though there is an indication that John himself was too well advanced in years to be considered for a permanent appointment. Soon after entering the service of the king he received a grant of land at Crimond in Buchan.[23] It was to here, and not the Stewartry, that he repaired about 1460 to live with his daughter, Beatrice, until his death in 1478.[24] He had been knighted prior to his death, and the reason for this honour has been handed down to us in the documents relating to the transfer of the Crimond estates from Beatrice to her husband, Gilbert Hay. It was James III, eldest son of James II, who bestowed the honour 'pro eius servitio regi et projenitori suo diversis vicibus in guerris suis, et specialiter ad conquestum et recuperationem castri de Roxburgh impenso'.[25] Roxburgh, it will be remembered, was the place where James II was killed, dying from the wounds incurred from the explosion of one of his own cannon. It is to be hoped that this was not the one repaired by Sir John three years before!

The latter half of the fifteenth century was a pioneering age where the design and use of ordnance was concerned and, considering that Sir John's trade was gun-smithing, there must be a strong possibility that it was he who was the designer of the artillery work that stands today as one of the most sophisticated and significant achievements of its age. It has been shown that John was in the castle at the ending of the siege; he was also there in 1447, the year the wall was built according to the dendrochronological evidence. In that year, Princess Margaret, widow of the fourth Earl and daughter of Robert III, in her capacity as Lady of Galloway, confirmed a grant of land near Whithorn.[26] The document was dated at Threave on 6 August 1447 and one of the witnesses was John of Dunbar, squire ('armigeris').

NOTES

1. For descriptions of the castle see: D. MacGibbon & T. Ross, *The Castellated and Domestic Architecture of Scotland* (Edinburgh, 1887), i, 157-67; *Kirkcudbright Inventory* (Roy. Comm. Anc. Hist. Monuments Scot., 1914), 28-34, no. 41., W. D. Simpson, *Threave Castle* (H.M.S.O., 1967. Official Guide).
2. For a recent reassessment of this confrontation see R. Nicholson, *Scotland: The Later Middle Ages* (Edinburgh, 1974), 354-66, 369-73.

3. See note in *Med. Archaeol.*, xxi (1977), 238-9. Also ibid., xix (1975), 242; and xx (1976), 185.

4. An examination of the probable form of the guns themselves is contained elsewhere in this volume by Iain MacIvor.

5. Simpson, *Threave Castle*, 5.

6. The absence of any reference to large-scale building activity at Threave during this period in an otherwise detailed account of expenditure in the Exchequer Rolls leads one to doubt the plausibility of this second suggestion.

7. S. H. Cruden, *The Scottish Castle* (Edinburgh, 1960), 115-119.

8. The writers are grateful to the late Mr S. E. Rigold of the Inspectorate of Ancient Monuments, England for his analysis of the jetton. A full report is appearing in the excavation report in *Med. Archaeol.* (forthcoming).

9. The writers are grateful to Mr R. B. K. Stevenson, until recently Keeper of the National Museum of Antiquities of Scotland, for his identification and assessment of the coin.

10. The writers are grateful to Dr M. G. L. Baillie of the Palaeoecology Laboratory, The Queen's University of Belfast, for the dendrochronological work on the oaks.

11. Mr R. B. K. Stevenson suggests, with reservations, that the coin may be a penny of James I (1406-37).

12. *Acts Parl. Scot.*, ii, 76a.

13. *Exch. Rolls*, vi, 459.

14. *Pell's Issue Rolls*, 15 July 1455, in *Cal. Docs. Scot.*, iv, 259.

15. *Exch. Rolls*, vi, 203, 204 and 199.

16. Ibid., vi, 199 and 202.

17. Ibid., vi, 293.

18. Ibid., vi, 385.

19. Ibid., vi, 308-10.

20. Ibid., vi, 495

21. Ibid., vi, 116.

22. Ibid., vi, 385.

23. Ibid., vi, 265.

24. Ibid., viii, 524.

25. *Reg. Mag. Sig.*, ii, no. 1437.

26. Ibid., ii, no. 383.

5 Royal Patronage of Arms and Armour Making in Fifteenth and Sixteenth-Century Scotland

David H. Caldwell

In the fifteenth and sixteenth centuries the Scottish army was composed principally of the male population of the country between the ages of sixteen and sixty whose duty it was to turn out 'weill bodin in feir of weir' to serve the king. This service was to be for a maximum of forty days in any one year and to be at each individual's own expense. Acts of parliament at regular intervals laid down the minimum requirements in arms and armour and ordered the holding of 'wapinschawings' by sheriffs, baillies and other officers, so that those who were insufficiently armed could be punished and made to conform.

This form of military organisation could provide the Scottish kings with a large army at very little cost. The Spanish ambassador to James IV, Don Pedro de Ayala, was impressed both by its size and quality,[1] and English sources[2] record that the Scots were well provided with armour at Flodden Field in 1513, at a time when the system was at a peak of efficiency. The mechanisms for arming and calling out the Scottish host were, however, of themselves not enough to ensure an adequate fighting force. The proscription of golf and football in favour of archery[3] tells us something of the difficulty in training men in the use of weapons, and various enactments to increase the importation of munitions from the continent[4] and the payments made for weapons bought there[5] suggest there was a problem in supplying enough of the right sort of arms. Here we are concerned only with this latter problem, the supply of arms and armour, and a particular approach adopted by succeeding kings and governors of encouraging their production in this country. This patronage took three main forms. Firstly, the importation of craftsmen from the continent; secondly, the establishment of royal workshops with paid craftsmen; and thirdly, the encouragement of craftsmen, normally burgesses of Edinburgh, by official titles and fees. The aim was first and foremost to supply the king with arms and armour for himself and his retainers, but this policy had the wider effect of improving the supply of munitions in the country in general. Foreign craftsmen introduced skills not readily available beforehand, the royal workshops produced the artillery necessary for the army, fortresses and ships, and craftsmen were given greater freedom to work.

The foreigners in royal service were presumably found lodgings in Edinburgh but do not seem to have become burgesses or members of the hammermen's craft. By working in the castle and palace they may have been saved from friction with the burgesses and guilds. At the same time their work was better able to be supervised by the king or his officials. While foreign craftsmen certainly had greater freedom of work than the native, so also did the latter when in royal service. To give some examples: in an instrument drawn up in April 1569 as a result of a dispute within the hammermen's craft between the blacksmiths and locksmiths over the respective areas of their work, the king's work is specifically excepted from the restrictions pertaining to both crafts.[6] In 1553 three masters of the gunnery establishment — the master gunner, melter and smith — were given power to trade in wine, wax, silk and all other merchandise[7] — a right normally reserved only for those who had renounced their craft. Robert Selkirk, royal cutler at the beginning of the sixteenth century, did work on armour and guns as well as swords and daggers.[8]

Royal attention was focussed particularly on the manufacture of artillery and if we give more consideration to this here it is because of its importance in the military organisation of the time.

The significance of guns was not slow to dawn on the Scots and they are known to have been using them in the fourteenth century, certainly in the 1380s and probably much earlier.[9] The first clear evidence that guns were being made in Scotland comes in 1473 (see below), but given the simple wrought iron structure and small size of the earliest guns it would be unlikely if they were not being made earlier than that.[10] The royal guns were sufficiently important by the 1450s to warrant the appointment of a master of the artillery — William Bonar — who was such by 1458.[11] Large bombards — guns made for battering down walls — played a significant role in James II's vigorous policy of crushing the Black Douglases and recovering lost ground from the English. Some or all of these, like the redoubtable Mons Meg, were products of workshops in the Low Countries.[12]

Royal interest in artillery was not limited to large siege guns. James II was well aware of the value of smaller guns for use in the field, but in this case he thought it incumbent upon his subjects to supply them. 'Certane of the gret baronys' were asked to supply 'cartis of weir' in the parliament of October 1455[13] and James III was also to ask for them several years later.[14] It is doubtful if these two kings met with an enthusiastic response. Turning up to the royal hosts armed to the back teeth was one thing, dragging a cart of guns along was another that the barons were not going to have imposed on them lightly, and although we know that by the sixteenth century the nobility and burghs were often well equipped with artillery, there is little evidence that they fielded it on behalf of the king.[15] Acts of parliament of 1535 and 1540[16] enjoined the nobility, prelates and burghs to supply themselves with hagbuts of crok — small pieces of artillery, that is — but there is no mention that these should be taken to the host or used on royal raids.

Sometime before his death in 1488 James III had been given by the French some of the new, sophisticated cast bronze guns which first made their appearance in the second half of the fifteenth century[17] and which made a great impact on the warfare of the day. Such guns were more reliable and easier to transport than the cumbersome wrought iron bombards, and packed a much greater punch, firing iron shot in place of stone. To James III must go the credit for first attempting the manufacture of these guns in Scotland. The one surviving treasury account for his reign, covering the period from 3 August 1473 to 1 December 1474, records the expenditure of no less than £780 6s. 5d. on the artillery and workmen, a vast sum of money.[18] The evidence is extremely scanty but it does seem that gun founding was being done in a house in the grounds of the Blackfriars priory in Edinburgh, not altogether successfully, as a payment had to be made for mending and roofing it after the casting of a gun, presumably because the mould had exploded.[19] William the Goldsmyth, an Edinburgh burgess, was already making a gun for James in the April of 1473, but it was a Frenchman called Rannald the Gunner who was rewarded for making the same or another in the following February.[20] A little more information can be gleaned from the Exchequer Rolls. There is a payment made a decade later for charcoal for making a bombard mould in Edinburgh Castle,[21] so that it is not inconceivable that the Edinburgh foundry was productive for a good number of years. The gunmaking in Stirling Castle at this time[22] may only have been of wrought iron guns, the making of which continued in Scotland until late in the sixteenth century. Some bits and pieces of wrought iron guns survive, notably four breech blocks and a small breech loading gun in the National Museum in Edinburgh (fig. 32).

The Treasurer's Accounts are fortunately much more complete for the reign of James IV, but it was only in 1507 that the making of bronze guns was taken up again from whenever it was left off by James III. In that year metal to cast the first gun was allowed for in the accounts.[23] Stirling figures as the centre of operations now, the actual casting being done in the castle, though there is some evidence of gun casting in Edinburgh too. The expertise of a great number of people was drawn upon, especially potters for their knowledge of clay and casting.[24] The man in charge of the actual casting, however, was a French gunner who may possibly be identified with a certain John Veilnaif who first turns up in 1505.[25] Possibly this enterprise was not too successful. We do not hear of any

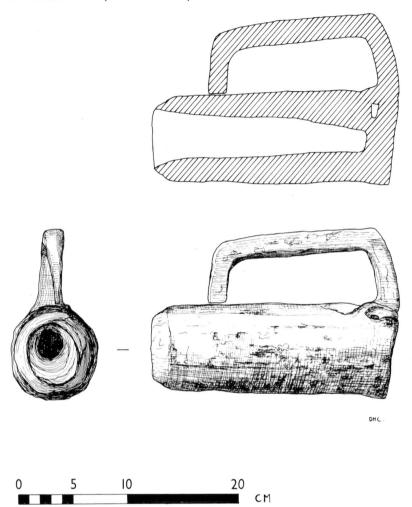

DHC.

0   5   10   20
                              CM

Figure 32. Chamber of a breech-loading gun from Fife. *National Museum of Antiquities of Scotland*

guns being finished, although there is another unfortunate gap in the records.

By 1511 the centre of operations had been transferred to Edinburgh Castle where it was to remain permanently, and in the same year a group of French gunners, under the leadership of a certain Gerwez, was brought into the country and immediately set to work in the castle.[26] A Scotsman, Robert Borthwick, was then, or was soon to become, the master melter of the king's guns. Borthwick was to retain this post until

Figure 33. Bell by Robert Borthwick, 1528. *Kirkwall Cathedral*

his death in 1531-2, and is well remembered as the maker of the semi-legendary 'seven sisters'.[27] The Scots were well equipped with bronze artillery by the time of the Battle of Flodden in 1513, some French, supplied as late as December 1512,[28] some bought from the Dutch founder Hans Popenruyter;[29] but some of the captured guns which so impressed the English must surely have been the work of Borthwick and his colleagues.[30]

The aftermath of the bitter defeat of Flodden saw the Scots at the weary task of re-arming, and Borthwick was soon back in business casting guns.[31] Although there are no surviving guns which can be ascribed to him with any confidence there are two examples of his work-manship dating to 1528 preserved in St. Magnus' Cathedral, Kirkwall — two bells, and a third which has been recast — which boast that they were made by him in Edinburgh Castle, and give a good indication of the quality of his work (fig. 33).[32]

Borthwick was succeeded as master melter by a French servant of his, Peris of Rowane,[33] i.e. Piers de Rouen, who in turn was succeeded by his son David in 1548.[34] Both of them kept up some sort of contacts with their homeland, the latter being apprenticed in France.[35] The work of the royal foundry was probably never very prolific, largely because making guns was a very costly business. Almost all the guns have long since been melted down, lost or destroyed. A fine exception to this sorry tale is a falconet, or small falcon, with the royal arms and James V's initials, preserved in Glasgow Art Gallery and Museum (fig. 34).[36]

A remarkable group of small bronze guns surviving mostly in private collections are probably some of the 'grete hakbuttis of found' and/or 'doubill hagbuttis of funde' that David Rowan was casting in 1552 and 1552/3.[37] Of these at least seven can be claimed with some reason to be Scottish, five being inscribed with the date 1553 and five with the Hamilton arms and the initials IH for James Hamilton, Earl of Arran and Governor of the realm (fig. 35).[38] Guns such as these were used primarily in the field, mounted on trestles, and were taken on campaign stowed in carts along with the necessary shot, powder and accessories. Two further pieces of David Rowan's work can be identified: firstly, the standard choppin measure of Edinburgh, dated 1555 and bearing a shield with the monogram DR, which is probably his mark (fig. 36). He was paid by the burgh in 1556 for making brass weights for the Over Tron, and this may have been made by him at that time.[39] Secondly, the pint measure of the burgh of St Andrews is stamped with the same mark and bears the date 1574.

The larger Scottish artillery apart from Mons Meg has now all passed away, but we can gain a fair impression of it from the documents and also, fortunately, from two carved panels that once graced the Barrier gateway of Edinburgh Castle dating to the early seventeenth century.[40]

All this royal enterprise in gunfounding, we may suppose, encouraged metal workers in the burghs to meet the needs of the nobility and lairds. Four small guns dated 1588, bearing the initials and arms of William Forbes of Tolquhoun, show that there were some very competent founders at work. These guns no doubt formed part of the defences of Tolquhoun Castle, completed at that time. The royal foundry, however, seems to have ceased casting guns long before this. The latest records we have relating to gun casting are in 1558, and ten years later the Regent Moray was to ask Cecil if he could arrange for 20,000 weight of metal to be cast with the English ordnance, as there was no good 'meltary' at that time.[41]

James IV's interest in guns did not end with the artillery but naturally

Figure 34. Small falcon with arms and initials of James V, on modern carriage. *Glasgow Art Gallery and Museum*

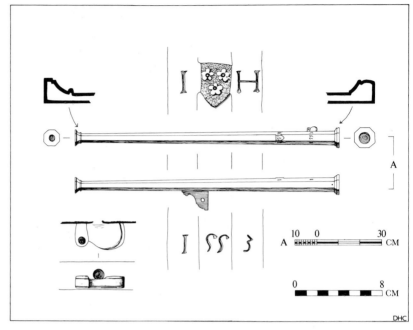

Figure 35. Great hagbut of found, 1553, with arms and initials of the Earl of Arran. Probably made by David Rowan

extended to cover hand firearms. Handguns, called culverins,[42] appear in our records in the late fifteenth century and James apparently first started taking a real interest in 1507.[43] In that and the immediately succeeding years the treasurer paid out several sums of money for embellishing James' guns and to his successful competitors in shooting matches. He also attempted to shoot birds and hunt deer with them.[44] Just as many pieces of artillery had to be imported from abroad; so did many handguns,[45] and efforts had to be taken to stop their export.[46] All the same, firearms were a sufficient threat from 1540 onwards for numerous writs to be issued forbidding the shooting of birds and wild animals.[47]

The making of firearms in Scotland dates to the beginning of the sixteenth century. Sir James Pettigrew, who was connected with the gun casting at Stirling, and who was also to be one of the chief searchers for gold in Crawfordmuir, was paid £10 for making a culverin for the king in 1508.[48] That he made it himself does not seem in doubt, as in 1502 he was paid for devising a clock for Stirling,[49] and the skills involved in making a gun were no greater than this task. Pettigrew was unlikely to be unique in having sufficient metal working knowledge to make guns. In the same

Figure 36.   David Rowan's mark on the standard choppin of Edinburgh. *Huntly House Museum*

year a lorimer, George Bell, was paid for supplying two locks for a culverin of the king's — possibly the gun locks themselves.[50]

No more is heard of the gunmaking talents of these two gentlemen. Instead, we find a certain George Keppin, Dutchman, and his servant Kasper Lepus, culverin makers, installed in Edinburgh Castle from October 1510, and receiving regular payments at least until September 1515.[51] It would seem that James IV had set the making of firearms on a similar basis to the production of artillery. Keppin was succeeded as culverin maker by others: James Hannay[52] and John Bickerton,[53] though their task was largely one of maintaining and restoring the royal arsenal of firearms, mostly got from abroad. The gunners entered in the royal establishment as smiths in the 1560s and later were probably often gunsmiths in our sense of the word.

Firearms makers thus worked under royal control, but despite the obvious advantages of encouraging the manufacture of firearms in the burghs there is little evidence of even indirect royal encouragement at this time. The acts of parliament of 1535 and 1540 which demanded the procurement of hagbuts also ordered those with land of a value of forty pounds to have one culverin and those with land worth a hundred marks to have two.[54] The demand for guns grew more with the increasing reliance on mercenary troops in warfare who were mostly armed with them, and by the status that handguns acquired as instruments of prestige to be worn with civilian clothing.[55] Pistols were already in use before 1550[56] and inevitably craftsmen came to the fore to help supply the market. By the end of the sixteenth century there were numerous craftsmen mostly describing themselves as dagmakers, working principally in Edinburgh, Canongate and Dundee. Charles Whitelaw's *Dictionary of Scottish Arms Makers* lists thirty, fifteen and eighteen for each place respectively and the numbers increase during the seventeenth century. According to an English spy report of August 1575 the 'gun forgers' of Edinburgh had promised to furnish at all times when commanded fifty calivers a week, and others powder for the same, and the regent had 'six fair muskets got from Flanders' to serve as patterns. The same report also claims that the gunsmiths had furnished 'the most part' of the gentlemen and horsemen of the realm with 'dagges' otherwise called 'snaphaunces',[57] and this is important evidence for the early production of this type of gun mechanism in Scotland.

A few late sixteenth-century gun barrels decorated with inlaid metals survive,[58] no doubt of much finer quality than the calivers the Edinburgh gunsmiths intended to mass produce with the encouragement of the regent, and also several pistols dating from the very end of the century and the beginning of the next, more fully described here in the paper by Mr Boothroyd.

Edged weapons of all sorts were mounted and sold by cutlers, armourers and blacksmiths, but unlike for the gunmakers and makers of armour, there was never a royal workshop for the production of blades, and the majority of surviving Scottish sword blades are of continental manufacture. Our documentary sources provide us with no references to Scottish blade smiths. Sword blades are not, however, included in the various lists of munitions imported for the royal use and it seems most likely that the various craftsmen working in the burghs had sufficiently organised their own supplies to make this unnecessary.[59] Knife and dagger blades, on the other hand, were probably mostly manufactured locally, as also the heads for Scottish long-shafted weapons.

Robert Selkirk, a burgess of Edinburgh and deacon of the Hammermen from 1501-4, was feed as the royal cutler from 1497 until his death in

1512. It appears that he was a skilled craftsman who was especially able at decorating armour and weapons of all sorts with gilding, and he supplied James IV with gilt daggers at regular intervals, probably to be distributed as gifts.[60] William Rae, one of a notable dynasty of Edinburgh cutlers, succeeded Selkirk and was in turn followed by his son William in 1565[61] and James Young in 1578.[62] Cutlering was a flourishing business in Scotland and in the course of the sixteenth century we have knowledge of no fewer than twenty-five cutlers working in Edinburgh alone.[63]

We can do little more than imagine the appearance of the swords and daggers supplied to James IV and V from the descriptions in the Treasurer's accounts. The sword and dagger in the Herald's College in London, said to have been taken from the body of James IV at Flodden, are later in date.[64] Some two-handed swords survive which give some idea of what the utilitarian types of sword were like, mounted with distinctively Scottish hilts (fig. 37).[65] By the beginning of the seventeenth century we have evidence of a distinctive type of ballock knife being made in Scotland, the blades richly gilt (fig. 38).[66] One wonders how different these are from the gilt daggers being made earlier in the sixteenth century? A ballock knife of about 1500 has been found at Coldingham Priory and is now in the National Museum, and the supposed representation of James V on the palace facade at Stirling Castle shows him with one at the waist.[67]

A certain Nicholas Pannaile[68] was feed as early as 1472 as the royal bowyer, and Nicholas Montgomery[69] turns up in the Exchequer Rolls as bowyer from 1489 until 1495. These bowmakers not only made bows but shafts for spears and other weapons. It is interesting, however, that English bows were reckoned of greater value[70] and we find an English bowyer in Edinburgh and being used in the 1530s.[71]

Crossbows were also of great importance from an early date. In Scotland they may principally have been used in siege-work rather than in field campaigns, and for hunting. James IV took great joy in shooting with one until he discovered the potential of a hand-gun.[72] The first official appointment of a crossbow maker that we can trace is of Adrian Abell in 1537.[73] John Tesart, a Frenchman, was feed in 1539.[74] Crossbows were used at this time on the royal ships, as in 1540 Tesart was paid for servicing the twenty-two crossbows on the *Sallamander*.[75] No early bows have come down to us, and only fragments of crossbows.[76]

A thick cloud of darkness obscures the history of the early Scottish armourers. Notices of their activities are few enough, and practically nothing of their work, actual or in representation, has come down to us. It may indeed be the case that until late in the fifteenth century very little plate armour was made in Scotland and that most of it in use was

Figure 37. Two-handed sword of 'Lowland type', late 16th cent. *National Museum of Antiquities of Scotland*

imported from the continent. James II was sent a German suit of armour immediately prior to his death.[77] James IV had armour bought in France in readiness for his marriage,[78] and James V bought stands of harness of the fashion of King Francis and of the Dauphin's fashion while he was wooing his first French bride in France in 1536.[79] Besides these show-pieces, large quantities of munition armour were got in the sixteenth century, mostly from France and the Low Countries for the use of the king's men.[80] Before this the injunctions to the lieges of what equipment they should wear at the wapinschawings, with the emphasis on the wearing of 'jacks' — that is canvas jackets reinforced internally with plates of iron or horn — suggests the unavailability of plate armour.[81]

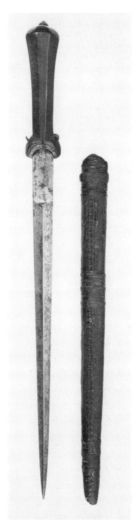

Figure 38. Ballock knife or dudgeon dagger, early 17th cent. *Tower of London Armouries*

On the other hand, the Scots nobility seem deliberately to have discarded plate armour during the sixteenth century, after their defeat at Flodden.

David II had an armourer on his pay role in 1364[82] but from then until the 1440s evidence is completely lacking for royal interest in armour. In the 1440s and '50s, however, there was a John Moncur, armour maker, working in Dundee, who supplied armour to James II.[83] He was followed in the second half of the century by a William Moncur and another John, possibly all related. John was given a royal fee in 1472-3.[84] Moncur of

Dundee was a regular supplier of pieces of armour to James IV in the period 1495-1497.[85] Yet another Moncur patronised by James IV was Andrew, working in Edinburgh with his house on the Castlehill. He was already a master of his craft by 1494, was a deacon in 1497 and 1500 and was a town councillor in 1516.[86]

From 1475 to 1499 a certain John Tait, of Leith (?), was freed as the royal armourer, at first for ten merks a year, then ten pounds,[87] and he was succeeded in this office by Allan Cochran, an Edinburgh master, capable not only of supplying individual pieces of armour but complete stands for the king and Christopher, the heir apparent to the Danish throne.[88] The next royal armourer, another Edinburgh master, William Smeithberd, was appointed in 1526[89] and he was joined by another Edinburgh armourer, Thomas Softlaw, in 1538.[90] Much of the work they did was in the nature of restoring and repairing the munitions imported from abroad, and apart from Allan Cochran, the only other armourers in Scotland whose services were utilised in the first half of the sixteenth century were foreigners sponsored by James IV and V.

The first of these we can trace is Lawrence, 'the French armourer', who came to Scotland in 1495 in the train of Perkin Warbeck, the pretender to the English throne, and he stayed on until he was discharged in September 1503.[91] The harness mill being built in 1496, perhaps at Stirling, was probably for him.[92] In 1502 James IV arranged for Passing and some other French armourers to come across and set them to work in Edinburgh.[93] Much of the equipment to erect their armour mill was shipped across from France and there are numerous sums allowed for in the Treasurer's Accounts for its erection. It was already complete enough by 5 April 1503 to require a horse to drive it,[94] and Passing had made a harness for Pat Sinclair, the master of the wardrobe, by the following Christmas.[95] Passing, unfortunately, died a couple of months later, though the work of finishing the armour mill was completed by two of his men.[96] An armourer was then sent to France to bring back another armourer but one does not seem to have arrived until sometime in 1507.[97]

The next development in this field did not take place until 1531 when work was started on refurbishing the arminghouse at Holyrood Palace, and work was done on the armourers' chamber and house. The building of a new horse mill to turn the great grind-stones and leather-covered polishers was under the supervision of Ewo, a French wright stationed at Dunbar Castle. There is mention also of the forging and the smelting house.[98] A French armourer had come to Scotland with a servant of the Duke of Albany in 1530,[99] and we have the names of two armourers who were probably amongst those employed at the palace: Guillame Haymont, who returned to France in 1532,[100] and John Counseill who

Figure 39. The arrival of Scotia in Scotland, from the *Scotichronicon,* early 15th cent.
Corpus Christi College, Cambridge, MS 171, fol. 146

hurt his hand and apparently died as a result in 1533.[101] Yet another
French armourer was sent for by James V's new wife, Mary of Guise, in
1538.[102] Whether or not he turned up we do not know, but already there
was in Scotland another Frenchman, Jacques Leschender — entered first
as a gunner in March 1537/8 — who remained to work as an armourer
until the death of James V in 1542. He supplied the king with a light suit
of armour with double teslettis (tassets or thigh defences) and a steel
bonnet, along with other bits and pieces.[103]

Thereafter royal attempts to keep up an armourer's shop seem to have
ceased, although care was taken to keep up the supplies of armour. There
were several armourers working in Scotland by the end of the century,
not only in Edinburgh, but in other towns like Elgin and Glasgow. Most
of those, however, may only have mounted and repaired swords.[104]

There are practically no surviving pieces of armour from Scotland.[105]
Of interest is a fifteenth-century manuscript of Fordun's *Scotichronicon*
with battle scenes,[106] (figs. 39, 40) and also some fifteenth-century
sepulchral monuments which depict armour, generally similar to that
shown on English monuments, with perhaps a greater conservatism —
hip belts being shown even on the latest, but no tassets.[107] There are no
royal tomb effigies of the period and the great seal, which shows the king
mounted and armed, changed little in design from the reign of Robert II

Figure 40. The Battle of Bannockburn, from the *Scotichronicon. Corpus Christi College, Cambridge*, MS 171, fol. 265

to James V. The armour on the latter's seal is that appropriate to the second half of the fourteenth century.[108]

We cannot omit to mention the makers of brigantines and jacks in this very brief survey. A Frenchman called Ligier was feed as a maker of brigantines at least from 1459 to 1462,[109] and another brigantine maker, John Clement, was feed in 1473.[110] Brigantines were jackets in which plates or scales of metal were riveted together beneath a cloth covering and were thus more secure than jacks. Two plates from a brigantine found at Coldingham Priory are all that remain of a garment which must have been quite common in Scotland well into the seventeenth century.[111] John Clerk was appointed principal jackmaker to the king in 1542 and was also entered as a gunner.[112]

We have tried to trace in the above account royal attempts to improve standards of workmanship and increase home production of arms and armour in Scotland in the fifteenth and sixteenth centuries. Three different but interrelated approaches to achieving this can be distinguished: firstly, the importation of foreign craftsmen; secondly, the establishment of royal workshops; and thirdly, the appointment of craftsmen to feed positions as royal arms or armour makers. That this policy had some measure of success seems clear from the documentary evidence and is suggested by the surviving weapons. Craftsmanship in Scotland was at the very least competent. Scotland, however, never came anywhere near to being self-sufficient in the manufacture of munitions, though it must be doubtful if this could have been seriously envisaged. The most notable achievement was the provision of artillery for the royal armies, ships and fortresses; but it may be possible to trace some sort of indebtedness to this royal encouragement in the seventeenth-century achievements of Scottish craftsmen.

NOTES

1. P. Hume-Brown, *Early Travellers in Scotland* (Edinburgh, 1891), 47-48. Compare Andrea Trevisano quoting Ayala, ibid., 52.
2. D. Laing, 'A Contemporary Account of the Battle of Flodden . . .', *Proc. Soc. Antiq. Scot.* vii (1866-8), 150.
3. *Acts Parl. Scot.* [APS], ii, 48 (1456).
4. *APS*, ii, 9 (1425); ii, 346 (1535); ii, 372 (1540).
5. E.g. *Treasurer Accts.* [TA] i, 69 (1474); v, 458 (1531); vi, 413-14 (1538).
6. *Prot. Bk. Grote*, no 287.
7. *Reg. Sec. Sig.* [RSS], no 2428. A previous grant to the master melter, David Rowan, alone, 17 Mar. 1549-50, is to the same effect, giving him power to trade 'as he wer creat and maid fre burges of the said burgh [Edinburgh] be the provest and baillies thereof' and gives him freedom from all customs on goods exported abroad, ibid., iv, no 596.
8. E.g. *TA*, ii, 22 (1501); iv, 105 (1507).
9. The earliest use of guns is claimed by W. D. Simpson, *Dundarg Castle* (Aberdeen, 1954), 131, to have been at the siege of Dundarg Castle in 1334 but his evidence is not very conclusive. 'Uno instrumento dicto gun' was bought for Edinburgh Castle in 1384 (*Exch. Rolls* [ER], iii, 672), but this does not seem to have been made by Theodore/Dietrich as suggested by R. Nicholson, *Scotland, the Later Middle Ages* (Edinburgh, 1974), 195.

10. John Dunbar was allowed payment 'pro fabrica et reparacione certorum instrument-orum bellicorum' in 1456/7, and these were probably guns used at the siege of Threave Castle (*ER* vi, 293).

11. *ER*, vi, 383.

12. According to Fordun (*Joannis de Fordun, Scotichronicum . . .* , ed. W. Goudall (Edinburgh, 1759), 490), James I had a large bombard called the Lion brought over from Flanders in 1430 and the exchequer rolls of that date record the importation thence of a great bombard and other munitions (*ER*, iv, 677, 678, 681). The making of Mons Meg at Mons in 1449 and its gift by the Duke of Burgundy to James II in 1458 has now been discovered by C. Gaier, 'The Origin of Mons Meg', *Journ. Arms & Armour Soc.*, v (1967), 425-52. Its arrival in Scotland is apparently recorded in *ER*, vi, 383. See also the paper in this volume by R. B. K. Stevenson.

13. *APS*, ii, 45.

14. Ibid., ii, 99-100, 105 (1471, 1473).

15. Aberdeen was prepared to field 19 carts (from 43 people and the litsters, cordiners and fleshers) in 1497, but many of these may have been able to carry equipment rather than guns. (*Aberdeen Council Register*, 61, 63-64). Carts, apparently for guns, were to be got ready in 1512 and 1514 as well (ibid., 83, 92-93), but it is to be noted that in all these cases the concern was for the defence of Aberdeen alone. Both Aberdeen and Edinburgh, however, were prepared to lend their artillery out: Aberdeen to the Earl of Bothwell in 1539 (Ibid., 166) and Edinburgh to Kirkcaldy of Grange in 1567 and to Jedburgh in 1570 (*Edinburgh Burgh Recs.*, iii, 240, 275).

16. *APS*, ii, 345-6; ii, 371.

17. According to Don Pedro de Ayala (1498), the Scots had some modern French guns of metal (i.e. bronze) given to the father of the present king (i.e. to James III) by King Louis in payment of what was due to him as co-heir of his sister, the Queen of Scotland (Hume-Brown, *Early Travellers*, 48). The writer sees no reason to doubt the veracity of Ayala's eye-witness account of seeing modern French guns but his explanation for them being in Scotland is nonsensical. Louis XI of France had been married to a daughter of James I and it may be to a settlement in connection with this that Ayala refers.

18. *TA*, i, 74.

19. Ibid., i, 65.

20. Ibid., i, 68. See also pp. 48, 49, 52, 54, 66, 67, 70 for other references to the gun-making.

21. *ER*, ix, 434 (1483-6).

22. Ibid., vii, 234, 275.

23. *TA*, iv, 105. The gunmaking in Edinburgh Castle in the 1480s was probably mostly just of wrought iron guns. See *ER*, ix, 218n., 286, 291, 416.

24. For this gunmaking see in general *TA*, iv, 109-13, 116, 117, 127, 132, 133-6, 139. J. B. Paul believed there was gunmaking in Edinburgh at this time because Alexander Bow, an Edinburgh potter, was involved and mention is made of a gun mould being made 'in the Abbey' (*TA*, iv, lxv). There can be little doubt that by 'the Abbey' is meant Holyrood, but that Bow was of Edinburgh is hardly convincing evidence. 'Potter' in this context means a maker of bronze pots, and not a maker of pigs (earthenware pots).

25. *TA*, iii, 139.

26. Ibid., iv, 276, 277, 372, 378, 438.

27. Borthwick was already 'zettare of the Kingis gunnys' by the end of 1511 (*RSS*, i, no. 2374) and 'master meltare of the Kingis gunnis' by the end of the succeeding year (*TA*, iv, 442). For the story of the 'seven sisters' see Pitscottie, *Historie*, i, 259.

28. *Henry VIII Letters & Papers*, i, no. 3577.
29. Ibid., nos. 216, 922, 923.
30. These guns are described in various places. See especially *TA*, iv, 515-17 and Laing, 'The Battle of Flodden', 146.
31. A new furnace was built in Edinburgh Castle in 1515 and workmen were hired for the casting (*TA*, v, 18, 37, 66-67).
32. These bells are described by H. E. L. Dryden, *Description of the Church dedicated to Saint Magnus and the Bishop's Palace at Kirkwall* (Kirkwall, 1878), 20-21, and in the *Orkney Inventory* (*Roy. Comm. Anc. Hist. Monuments Scot.*, 1946), ii, 146.
33. Appointed 30 Apr. 1532 (*RSS*, ii, no. 1213).
34. Ibid., iii, no. 2719.
35. Peris was given a letter of recommendation to the officers of the ordnance of Francis I by James V dated 20 June 1534, as he was going to France to recover debts (*Henry VIII Letters & Papers*, vii, no. 866), and was given £10 on 21 Mar. 1538/9 to help him on his way to France (*TA*, vii, 150). His two sons (David and Thomas?) were apprenticed in France at the command of James V (Ibid., vi, 402).
36. Illustrated previously in *Renfrew Archaeol. & Hist Coll.*, i (1885), pl. vii; text, ii (1890), 207. Perhaps it was lost at the siege of Castle Semple and the 'house in the lough' in 1560 (*Cal. State Papers Scot.* i, 489).
37. *TA*, x, 101, 115, 151.
38. One of these guns from Castle Menzies, with the I and H inadvertently reversed, has been illustrated by D. P. Menzies in *The 'Red & White' Book of Menzies* (Glasgow, 1894), opp. p. 172; and also in *Proc. Soc. Antiq. Scot.* (1895-6), 314-16. There is a photograph of another three in L. Mann, *Mary Queen of Scots at Langside* (Glasgow, 1918), opp. p. 74. They are described more fully in a forthcoming paper by the author.
39. This measure is now in Huntly House Museum, Edinburgh. It has been illustrated in *Scottish History & Life*, ed. J. Paton (Glasgow, 1902), 199, fig. 235. The payment to David Rowan is to be found in *Edinburgh Burgh Accts.*, i, 204.
40. See D. Wilson, *Memorials of Edinburgh in the Olden Time*, 2nd edn. (Edinburgh & London, 1891), i, 161.
41. *TA*, x, 437-42; *Cal. State Papers Scot.*, ii, 636.
42. The culverins got from Stirling for the field in 1489 were presumably handguns. Culverin was a term also applied to a class of artillery, but such guns normally have qualifying terms like gros culverin, culverin moyan, etc.
43. See, for instance, *TA*, iv, 98, 105, 110, 111.
44. Ibid., iv, 115, 130.
45. Large quantities of half haggis and culverins were imported in 1541. (*TA*, vii, 498; viii, 120), and more were gifted by the French, e.g. in 1543 (*Hamilton Papers*, ii, 103). James V requested guns from Frederick I of Denmark in 1528 (*James V Letters*, 150) — unsuccessfully.
46. *Reg. Privy Council*, iii, 398.
47. *TA*, vii, 422; xi, 63, 71.
48. Ibid., iv, 112. Pettigrew was a priest (ibid., iv, 101), hence the 'sir' used by those priests who were not entitled to the university distinction of 'Master'.
49. Ibid., ii, 159.
50. Ibid., iv, 121.
51. Ibid., iv, 276, 333, 374, 379, 439 (508-12?); V, 32-33, 69.
52. Ibid., v, 375 (1529), etc.
53. John Bikcartoun, smith and culverin maker, entered to work as a gunner in Edinburgh Castle, 28 July 1541 (*TA*, vii, 499).

54. See n. 16.

55. The wearing of them was banned on numerous occasions but a contemporary account remarks of the ban of 1569, 'the town of Edinburgh being alwayis exceptit'! (*Diurnal of Occurrents*, 163).

56. Two Dutchmen were apprehended in Stirling in May 1549 for wounding a Scotsman with a pistol (*Stirling Recs.*, 56).

57. *Cal. State Papers Scot.*, iv, 182.

58. Six late 16th century Scottish gun barrels are illustrated and described by C. Blair, 'Scottish Firearms', *Bull. American Soc. Arms Collectors*, xxxi (1975), 61-101.

59. In 1532, however, the Master of Semple gifted eight two-handed sword blades to James V (*TA*, vi, 88).

60. For Selkirk see *ER*, xi, 234-5; J. Smith, *The Hammermen of Edinburgh and their Altar* (Edinburgh, 1906), xcii; *TA*, i, 22, 33; ii, 476; iv, 105; etc.

61. The elder Rae was probably appointed in 1513 (*RSS*, i, no. 2506). The son's appointment is ibid., v, no. 2279.

62. *RSS*, vii, no. 1538.

63. Evidence mainly from *Edinburgh Burgesses*.

64. There are line drawings of these in C. G. Young, 'Remarks on the Sword, Dagger and Ring of King James the Fourth of Scotland . . .', *Archaeologia*, xxxiii (1851), 335-40.

65. See J. Wallace, *Scottish Swords and Dirks* (London, 1970), 11-12, nos. 9-11.

66. C. Blair & J. Wallace, 'Scots — Or Still English?', *Scottish Art Review*, special no., *Scottish Weapons*, IX, i (1963), 11-15.

67. Illustrated by Blair & Wallace, 'Scots — Or Still English?', 23, pl. 3.

68. *ER*, viii, 189, 191.

69. Ibid., x, 78, 196, etc.

70. In a consignment of bows in 1539 the Scots ones were valued at 9 shillings each, the English 16 (*TA*, vii, 194).

71. John Bowmaker, Englishman, or 'The English Bowyer'. *TA*, v, 407, 408, 431; vi, 30, 36, 209, 358.

72. *TA*, iii, 373, 374.

73. *RSS*, ii, no. 2271.

74. Ibid., ii, no. 3068.

75. *TA*, vii, 356.

76. E.g. an antler crossbow nut from Urquhart Castle. See A. MacGregor, 'Two antler crossbow nuts . . .', *Proc. Soc. Antiq. Scot.*, cvii (1975-6), 317-21.

77. A. V. B. Norman, 'The Armour on the Van der Goes Altarpiece at Edinburgh', *Journ. Arms & Armour Soc.*, ii (1957), 127 (cf *ER* vii, 33).

78. *TA*, ii, 359 (1502-03).

79. Ibid., vii, 13.

80. Ibid., iv, 114 (1508), 417 (1513); viii, 30, 124 (1541).

81. *APS*, ii, 45 (1456) 'Quhite harnes', i.e. plate armour, is included in the armour to be worn at the wapinschawings in 1491 (*APS*, ii, 226).

82. *ER*, ii, 130, 174.

83. Ibid., v, 156, 181 (1443-5); vi, 4 (1454-5).

84. William Moncur: *ER* vii, 424; viii, 40 (1465-6, 1468-71). John Moncur: Ibid., viii, 189, 191 (1472-3).

85. *TA*, i, 268, 306, 373.

86. For Andrew Moncur see *TA*, iii, 361, 381, 384, 385; Smith, *The Hammermen of Edinburgh*, p. xcii, 18; *Edinburgh Burgh Recs*, 91, 149, 174; etc.

87. *ER*, viii, 316; *TA*, i, iii; *Reg. Mag. Sig.*, ii, no. 2477; etc.

88. *ER*, xiii, 96; *TA*, iii, 39, 112; etc. Cochran was working for James IV as early as 1501

(*TA*, ii, 93), but may not have been feed any earlier than 1508.

89. *RSS*, i, no. 3402.
90. Ibid., ii, no. 2873.
91. *TA*, i, 264; ii, 392; etc.
92. Ibid., i, 270.
93. Ibid., ii, 281. A payment was ordered by the king on 16 June 1503 to Sir Thomas Tod's wife for the mail of the houses where the armourers work. (*TA*, ii, 375). Tod was an Edinburgh burgess of some note and by the context armourers here can only refer to Passing and his colleagues. A payment made in Linlithgow in the previous month to the armourers when they took the king's measurements to make him an armour (*TA*, ii, 370) is less convincing as evidence that they worked there, as previously claimed by several writers.
94. *TA*, ii, 365.
95. Ibid., ii, 411.
96. Ibid., ii, 430, 432.
97. Ibid., iii, 129, 279, 406, 408.
98. See *Accts. Masters of Works*, i, 101-02, 242, 290, 309; *TA*, vi, 34.
99. *TA*, v, 439.
100. Ibid., vi, 75, 94.
101. Ibid., vi, 90.
102. *Balcarres Papers*, i, 18.
103. For Leschender see *TA*, vi, 382 (Mar. 1537/8); vii, 105, 140; viii, 54; etc.
104. James Young, armourer, Elgin, 1593 (W. Crammond, *Extracts from Elgin Kirk Session records, 1564-1779* (n.p., n.d.), 17; see also H. Lumsden & P. H. Aitken, *The History of the Hammermen of Glasgow* (Paisley, 1912), 7.
105. Of 16th cent. date there is a burgonet in the National Museum of Antiquities, Edinburgh (Prof. Duns, 'On a Helmet Found at Ancrum Moor', *Proc. Soc. Antiq. Scot.*, xxx (1895-6), 317-18), found at Ancrum Moor, Roxburghshire; a Spanish morion from Appin (W. Reid, 'A Knapscall from Appin', *Scottish Art Review*, X, i (1965), 21-23), and another morion from Blair at Blair Atholl Castle. A third morion in the National Museum comes from Manton Walls, Ancrum. There is a composite suit of armour, largely of 16th cent. date, in Provost Skene's house in Aberdeen, which came from the Aberdeen townhouse.
106. Manuscript Corpus Christi College, Cambridge, no. 171. All four of its illustrations are shown in *Facsimiles of National Manuscripts of Scotland* (Edinburgh, 1870), ii, pls. LXXXIII, LXXXVI.
107. Most of these monuments are described and illustrated by R. Brydall, 'The Monumental Effigies of Scotland . . .', *Proc. Soc. Antiq. Scot.*, xxix (1894-5), 329-409, and there are detailed studies of two of these at Dunkeld and Corstorphine by A. V. B. Norman: 'The Effigy of Alexander Stewart, Earl of Buchan and Lord of Badenoch (?1343-?1405)', *Proc. Soc. Antiq. Scot.*, xcii, (1958-9), 104-13; 'A Scottish Military Effigy of the 15th Century', *Scottish Art Review*, special no., *Scottish Weapons*, ix, 1 (1963), 24-25.
108. W. de G. Birch, *History of Scottish Seals*, i, *The Royal Seals of Scotland* (Stirling & London, 1905), no. 40.
109. *ER*, vi, 496-8, 581; vii, 34, 145.
110. *TA*, i, 65, 68.
111. D. H. Caldwell, 'Fragments of a brigantine from Coldingham Priory, Berwickshire', *Proc. Soc. Antiq. Scot.*, cvi (1974-5), 219-21.
112. *RSS*, ii, no. 4691.

6 Artillery and Major Places of Strength in the Lothians and the East Border, 1513-1542

Iain MacIvor

This essay describes the provisional investigation of a very small plank from the shipwreck of time — much of it badly shattered. It could not have been undertaken without the generous help of David Caldwell, especially on early guns and the siege of Tantallon; Dr Marcus Merriman on all aspects of Berwick-upon-Tweed; and Bent Petersen on visualising the emplacement of guns. I am, however, entirely responsible for all mistakes of interpretation and deduction. The places chiefly considered are Dunbar Castle and Berwick, with the castles of Tantallon and Blackness. There are also brief notices of Norham, Wark, Cessford and Craignethan Castles.

1. Introduction: To 1513

Dunbar Castle in East Lothian, slighted in 1488, was reconstructed for James IV in 1496-1501.[1] The reconstruction, taking in fortifications and internal buildings, was initiated by the conflict with England caused by the support given by James to Perkin Warbeck's claim to the English throne. The place had assumed a new importance in the defence of the East Marches since the loss of Berwick in 1482. The principal new fortification at Dunbar was the rebuilt gatehouse and forework (figs. 41, 42),[2] which partly survives below parapet level, protected by inward-splayed loops opening as 'inverted keyhole' apertures of modest scale, the circular gunhole itself measuring externally about 200 mm. in diameter. The wallhead is nowhere extant. The destructive power of attacking artillery was apparently looked on with some nonchalance, for the forework was commanded at a distance of only 45 m. by a promontory, across a sea-swept chasm. The promontory was itself difficult of access from the mainland, from which it was almost disjoined by a deep and wide cleft: perhaps this degree of isolation led James IV's master mason to ignore its offensive possibilities. Breech-loading forged iron guns for the castle appear in 1497, when a payment was made to Johne Lam, smith, for

> iij serpentinis gunnis to Dunbar; with ilkane tua chameris, their mykkis and thair slottis.[3]

The word serpentine, taken from the French, was used in Scotland and

Figure 41. Dunbar Castle, aerial view showing (left) the blockhouse and (centre) the traverse wall, forework and main ward of the castle

England throughout the period of our narrative, and remained in currency until the seventeenth century. The term does not closely define the weapon. Serpentines might be made of forged iron, cast bronze or (in England) cast iron; there were muzzle-loaders and breech-loaders with detachable chambers to hold the gunpowder charge; they had shot of stone, iron or lead.[4] As one might expect from the name, a serpentine seems to have been usually long-barrelled in proportion to its calibre. In England in 1497 a standard iron shot weight for serpentines was 5 lbs., giving a calibre of about 95 mm. But English guns were often not identical with Scottish ones and over the span of its existence the bore of serpentines varied, down to about 40 mm.

What seems to us an imprecise nomenclature of early guns deserves remark at the outset. We sha'l meet it throughout in relation to forged iron pieces. We have a clear picture of the biggest of them, the *great bombards*, for several great bombards exist including the 460/496 mm. Mons Meg of 1449,[5] described elsewhere in this volume by Robert Stevenson. The generic term *bombard*, however, is much vaguer, being (exceptionally?) used to describe pieces with a bore down to 90 mm.,[6] thus conflating the type with serpentines in terms of calibre. The rest are

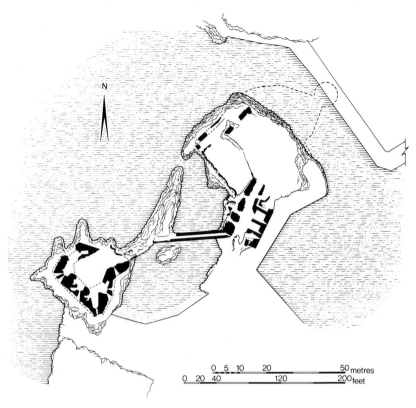

0 5 10   20   50 metres
0 20 40   120   200 feet

Figure 42. Dunbar Castle, general plan to show relationship of the castle and its fore-work/gatehouse to the traverse wall and the blockhouse.

equally indistinct. The name *curtow* was eventually used in England to describe cannon (as defined below) but they were originally larger than cannon.[7] *Slangis*, *slangs*, or *slings* may sometimes be coterminous with serpentines, as well they might be from their derivation (*Schlange*, a serpent), but sometimes they may be distinguished as separate natures of gun which may be heavy pieces of up to 5.5 m. long and 200 mm. bore.[8] *Heidsteikis* were also large. *Berses*, *basses* or *bases*[9] and *cutthrottis*[10] were usually fairly small, down to 1.2 m. long and 45 mm. bore, though again there were large bases in England. Of these names, *curtow* was not used by the Scots; *heidsteik* and *cutthrott* were not used by the English. All the names may embrace specified variants of size within the type, as *quarter-slings*, for example.

In the fifteenth century the chief battering gun in a royal siege train was the great bombard. These giant pieces were cumbersome, very slow to load and therefore had a minimal rate of fire. They had a limited breaking strain and so gave a low impact velocity. Other types, including curtows and slings, were also used as battering pieces; the rest were deployed as field artillery or as fortress guns. Stone shot was originally the norm for all save the smallest pieces; hence the generic term gunstones, a word later used for shot of either stone or iron. In spite of the inherent constructional weakness of forged iron guns, Mons Meg and others in the later fifteenth century were provided also with iron shot which, because of its greater weight, at once had a greater impact and imposed a correspondingly greater strain on the gun.

The forged iron guns were produced by techniques already well established from the middle of the fifteenth century.[11] The barrel of any iron gun wrought by a smith was made up either of staves welded around a cylindrical mandrel, or from a sheet of iron hammered to a cylinder, and in both cases strengthened with hoops of iron shrunk on. The breech-piece had to be made separately, and it took several forms. It could be permanently plugged into the barrel and secured there to make a muzzle-loader, or it could be screwed into the barrel like the breech-piece of Mons Meg, which was probably used in action as a muzzle-loader. Or — and this is the construction which we shall commonly meet, and the construction which survived longest — the breech-piece could be a separate forged iron chamber to hold the charge, shaped like a tall narrow beer-mug with a handle, and tapered to push into the barrel (fig. 32). In guns with chambers the barrel fitted into a groove-like chase cut in a long wooden stock, to which the barrel was lashed or strapped with leather, cord or iron bands. The chamber dropped into the rear part of the chase, and was driven home into the barrel by a wedge, in Scots a *slot*, as in the 1497 serpentines for Dunbar. We meet a crux with the *mykkis* or *mitches* of the guns for Dunbar, for the word seems to have more than one meaning. It may be a stirrup-shaped piece of iron forming part of the mounting, plausibly as a swivel pin; or it may be an iron member of similar shape which, fixed to the barrel, is sometimes used further to secure the chamber in position.[12] Stocked forged iron guns without any further mounting may have been the original armament of some of the casemates in the towers of Threave Castle, Kirkcudbrightshire as early as the 1450s. Fig. 43 shows an 80 mm. piece (see p. 100) emplaced in a Threave casemate. Like the subsequent armament drawings, it must be regarded as a very tentative sketch.

The technique of forging iron guns seems to have changed little through the later fifteenth and the sixteenth centuries. Their traditional manufacture contrasted with improved processes of bronze-founding which produced a new generation of 'brass' guns, beginning to appear in Scotland during the reign of James IV (1488-1513) and in England during the reign of Henry VII (1485-1509). Some of the Scots' pieces were gifted by their French allies, others were manufactured in the royal gun-foundries.

Cast bronze guns of all sizes were by no means new. In 1430 James I had imported a great 'brass' bombard, called the Lion, from Flanders:[13] the technique, after all, was not superficially dissimilar from that used to cast a large medieval bell. Practice, however, seems to have belied theory, and forged iron guns seem to have been preferable in terms of efficiency as well as cost. Once design — particularly the breech re-inforcement — and quality of casting had been bettered, in time, bronze had inherent superiorities over forged iron. It could be cast with a much stronger breech, and with a truer bore, so that iron shot could be fired as a norm, to carry accurately over longer ranges with a substantially greater impact velocity.

From the beginning of the sixteenth century several different types of cast bronze gun become clearly distinguishable, conforming to more or less similar specifications of size and weight throughout Europe. With a re-use and standardisation (sometimes with changed significance) of old names, the largest were the cannon and some of the culverins, which were battering guns; a comment made much later was probably true from the outset:

> Culverins and demy-culverins serve to pierce and slice out in
> Batteryes, what the Canons have loosened and shaken.[14]

A *double cannon, great cannon* or *cannon royal* had a bore of about 215 mm., a *cannon* or *demy-cannon* about 170 mm.[15] The largest culverin, the *gros* or *great culverin*, about 135 mm.; the *demy-culverin* about 110 mm.[16] All the culverins were relatively longer than cannon and so had a greater range.

There were several lesser natures of culverin, from which I may select for mention the *culverin pikmoyen* (Scots) or *saker* (English) of about 95 mm.,[17] and the smaller *culverin moyen*. An English *lizard* may have been a lesser culverin. Then come the various natures of falcon: from the *double falcon* of perhaps 65 mm. to the *quarter falcon* of about 40 mm. All of these were carriage-mounted field guns, which could be used as anti-personnel weapons by a besieging force. We shall encounter them also as fortress pieces. Smallest were *hagbuts of crok* or *hackbuts*, which had hooks on the underside of their barrels for mounting them, instead of trunnions.[18] Bronze and forged iron hagbuts co-existed: they also were field pieces and fortress weapons. Trestles were provided for mounting hagbuts at Dunbar Castle in 1515, and are found in Berwick em-placements in 1539, suggesting that these were defensive guns. In the field hagbuts seem to have been normally mounted on carts. Almost all the bronze guns were muzzle-loaders. Though breech-loaders with separate chambers were made,[19] they were much rarer and ran counter to sound construction in the material. The manufacture of cast iron guns seems to have begun in England quite early in the sixteenth century,[20] though it was a long time before the technology of ironfounding reached the sophistication necessary for the production of reliable weapons in this material. Cast iron guns appear only hazily in our narrative (see p. 134 on the armament of Berwick in 1539).

The word *cannon,* once a generic term for artillery, was first used in its new specific sense in 1506 in Scotland,[21] where James IV was amassing a considerable arsenal. It is likely that most of his bronze guns were utilised in the Flodden campaign of that year (some others were mounted on shipboard; two were sent to Ireland). The artillery train taken with the army was primarily intended for siege work, and it compelled the surrender of the castles of Norham and Wark as well as the lesser holds of Ford and Etal. The bronze guns consisted of five cannon, two gros culverins, four culverins pikmoyen and six culverins moyen.[22] The 'other dyvers small ordenances' listed presumably included forged iron pieces.

The future was by no means entirely to favour the new bronze guns. They replaced bombards in the siege train (Mons Meg, which had gone to Norham for the siege of 1497, was left behind in Edinburgh Castle in 1513); but while they seem to have replaced most forged iron muzzle-loaders we will note examples of the latter still possibly emplaced in 1539 (p. 134). Forged iron breech-loaders were still sufficient, and perhaps better adapted, for a variety of uses which did not involve distant targets or battering power, particularly on shipboard and in fortifications as shorter-range and anti-personnel weapons.[23] Bronze guns, usually the culverins and falcons, were clearly well qualified because of their long range and accuracy for parapet mountings, where they could discomfit the besieger's men and artillery on advantageous terms (occasionally, even cannon were later so emplaced).[24] Such qualities were not needed to counter close investment, or assault: and for these purposes forged iron guns remained in use, and in production. As breech-loaders they were more convenient for use in casemates, since they did not have to be pulled back for reloading, and where the level surface behind a parapet was not wide enough to pull the gun back. They were also much cheaper than cast guns, and so tended to be deployed where cast guns gave no clear benefit. There were occasions where forged iron guns seem to have been used as fortress pieces purely for reasons of thrift: as late as 1584 at Stirling Castle bombards were still being kept in reserve as flanker guns,[25] presumably to fire multiple shot, where something less sluggish might seem to have been more desirable.

This development of artillery was to cause further change in fortress

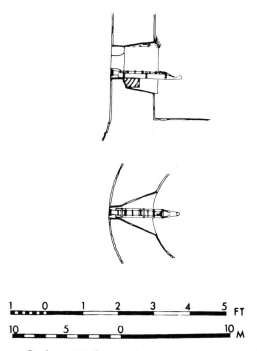

Figure 43. Threave Castle, c.1450. Section of casemate opening to 'dumb-bell' gunloop, with sketch of possible armament: a stocked forged iron breech-loading gun of about 80 mm bore of a type which may have been called a *serpentine*. No attempt has been made to conjecture detail of mounting

design. Up to the end of the reign of James IV, there is no evidence of major innovation at Scottish places of strength to take account of gunpowder weapons in attack and defence. Improvement was rather a conservative adaptation of traditional castle planning, as far as one may judge from the surviving evidence. The only recognisable common theme in the extant physical evidence is the emergence of specially designed gunholes with internal splays: the 'inverted keyhole' pattern which we have seen at Dunbar, and the 'dumb-bell' pattern. Both appear in what may be the earliest extant Scottish fortifications with gunholes, Threave Castle, Kirkcudbrightshire, and Ravenscraig Castle, Fife, of 1460-83.[26] The same designs continue, though with smaller external apertures, at for example the foreworks of Dunbar Castle and Stirling Castle.[27]

If the gunstones found during Christopher Tabraham's excavations at Threave (described by him elsewhere in this volume) relate to the earliest armament there, we have pieces of about 65 mm. and 80 mm. bore, which might well have been called serpentines (fig. 43). Similar guns may have armed some casemates of all these pre-Flodden fortifications. The wallheads of none of these works survive intact as built, so there is no physical evidence for parapet guns. John Slezer's late seventeenth-century drawing, however, shows the wallhead of the Stirling Forework intact,[28] without any apparent provision for special armament apart from small pieces resting on the crenels or fired from trestles. There is no physical or documentary evidence for very heavy ordnance emplaced anywhere, though the case against their use is certainly not proven. When bombards are found in Scottish castles, they seem to have been part of the siege train, not guns of position.

There is no surviving evidence of a striking increase in wall thickness, save at Ravenscraig Castle where the high and massive round-fronted towerhouse has a maximum wall thickness of as much as 4.4 m. This is the only pre-1513 gunlooped work with an extraordinary reinforcement of wall thickness that may be taken as a response to the threat of bombardment. The walls of the Ravenscraig frontal work are not, however, consistently so thick, for they are reduced at the angles of the internal vaults and rooms to 3.3 m., and are weakened by a mural chamber at a higher level. Elsewhere, no work with gunholes has thicker walls than the stoutest traditional works without them, such as the mid-fifteenth-century towerhouse at Cessford, Roxburghshire.[29] Some are surprisingly slight, notably the walls of the gatehouse towers of the Stirling Forework, which are only 1.1 m. thick. Wall thickness, whether of stone or, in the case of later ramparts, of stone reinforced by earthwork or earthwork alone, like every characteristic of a fortification, varies according to the threat which that part of the work is designed to withstand. A work intended to resist a 'siege royal', assault by the full resources of a royal train, will look very different from a work intended to repel enemies of more limited means, or without artillery of any kind. Parts of a fortification designed to withstand battery will be much stouter than those which are not. (On my first visit to Inchkeith in the Firth of Forth several years ago, I found it salutary to note that the little shoreline 'blockhouses', built for small arms defence against a landing immediately before the First World War, had concrete walls only 300 mm. thick. These slight works co-existed with far more massive gun emplacements designed to oppose the principal armament of the Kaiser's fleet). At Stirling Castle, unquestionably a stronghold of the first magnitude, there were outer defences beyond the Forework: nevertheless one might have expected that the latter would have been more substantial.

In England, where the earliest visible account taken of gunpowder weapons was also in loophole design, there were in the south earlier signs than in Scotland of a major break with tradition: notably with the centrally placed round guntower, dodecagonal mantlet wall and stirrup-shaped flanking positions at the first Camber Castle of 1511-14, a geometrical plan not altogether unlike some of the late fifteenth-century designs of Francesco da Giorgio Martini.[30] Concerning armament, there is a requirement in 1512 for Great Yarmouth to provide four iron bombards for its defence.[31] They were not as big as the word at first suggests, being 9 feet long and only 3½ inches in calibre (2.74 m. and 90 mm.); but they were to have a range of a mile — a reminder that one must not under-estimate the capability of iron pieces. On the east Border, there were bombardelles or lesser bombards lying unmounted in the donjon or great gatehouse of Berwick Castle in 1539.[32] While these may again have been part of the siege train, we cannot discount the possibility that they had been emplaced at Berwick at an earlier date.

There was artillery in Berwick from the early fifteenth century, and Henry IV's guns were brought against the place when held by the Earl of Northumberland in rebellion. We do not know, however, when the first improvements were made to adapt the castle and town to defence by and against gunpowder weapons. The castle, to north-west of the town, had defences which may in part have ante-dated the Wars of Independence, but which seem to have been largely reinforced after the capture of Berwick in 1296 by Edward I (whose White Wall down to the Tweed survives) and thereafter improved through the fourteenth century. The extant polygonal Constable's Tower at the south-east angle of the enceinte, with defensive fish-tailed slits, may indicate the appearance of similar works elsewhere now destroyed or buried. The town was surrounded by defences laid out after 1296. The defences (fig. 44) had an approximately rectangular plan, with the castle cutting off the north-west angle, and were strengthened by medium-sized or small half-round or half-octagonal towers. The west and south fronts followed the bank of the Tweed estuary. Of the landward fronts, the north front lay towards Scotland, the east front separated the town from the undeveloped land, known as the Snook, which extended to low cliffs above the sea. Edward's broad ditch remained; the palisade on the bank behind it was replaced piecemeal by masonry defences. Of the numerous towers of the town's landward defences only two polygonal works are visible above ground: the lower part of the Damned Tower (known since the upper part was rebuilt in Elizabeth's reign as the 'Bell Tower'),[33] and a smaller tower on the east front, to which an artillery work called the Murder Tower was added in 1522 (see p. 120).

Nowhere in town or castle is there surviving physical evidence of adaptations for artillery which may certainly be dated before Flodden. From documents I know only one specific reference relating to this

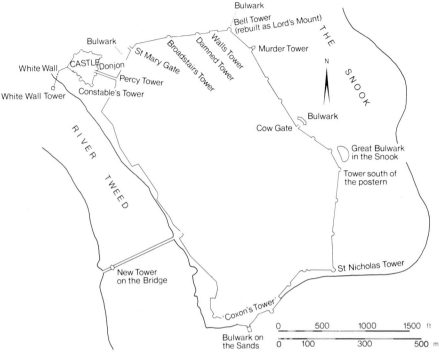

Figure 44. Berwick-upon-Tweed, diagrammatic outline plan of town and castle based on the survey of 1532x5. The location of works mentioned in the text is shown

period: in the time of Sir William Tyler, captain of Berwick 1489-98, and also controller of His Majesty's Works, a masonry seaward defence designed to hold guns (later called the Bulwark on the Sands) was built, projecting into the estuary beyond the medieval tower now known as Coxon's Tower.[34] Some other works mentioned in a survey of 1532 x 35[35] may also conceivably be pre-Flodden improvements including the countermure described below (page 121). Unspecified operations were being carried out right up to 1513, with for example £500 being paid in the previous year for fortifying the town.[36] There was a tower for artillery ('mayd for occupyynge of ordenance') in the river at the southern end of the White Wall; and a rectilinear tower called Walls Tower of slight projection and with a long face towards the field on the north front of the town, between Damned Tower and the tower at the north-west angle of the town enceinte, the original Bell Tower. Cow Gate was also provided with gun positions. Some or all of these improvements[37] may conjecturally have been carried out up to 1513, besides the possible slapping of some gunloops in the towers.

Our picture of the earliest armament of Berwick is even more shadowy than our understanding of its earliest gun positions. Conjecture must be based on documents of 1539 and later,[38] by which time there had been substantial changes to the parapets (page 134). Nevertheless one may cautiously look at the detail then given for the casemated armament of the new and modified works just mentioned. Within the Bulwark on the Sands were two iron serpentines 'stokkyd with mytche and forloke' with two chambers to each, and eight iron hagbuts. The White Wall Tower, damaged by tempest in 1532,[39] was unarmed in 1539 (it was subsequently rebuilt on a different site), and the casemates of Walls Tower were unserviceable, as were those in several of the modified medieval towers. But the armed tower casemates also have hagbuts and breech-loading iron serpentines stocked with mitches. In an inventory of 1545[40] the hagbuts and serpentines were still there, and the latter are itemised as stocked *upon* mitches, suggesting that here the mitch is some kind of mounting, most plausibly a forked swivel. These may be the type of weapon for which the emplacements were designed. Parapet armament is beyond conjecture.

The only surviving physical evidence of improvement on the East Border is at the Bishop of Durham's Castle of Norham in Northumberland. A casemated wall there, north-east of the gatehouse, has been dated to 1509.[41] Each of the three casemates had an internally splayed rectangular gunport about 350 mm. high and between 250-350 mm. wide, with no evidence of swivels. The gunports are at floor level, for pieces mounted on a stock or timber baulk. The pieces intended for the casemates may have been similar to those proposed for Great Yarmouth, the whole arrangement resembling that of the floor-level positions at Threave or Ravenscraig though with differently shaped apertures. The corresponding parapet at Norham is lost; but there may have been substantial pieces here, and at Berwick.

Nothing is so far known of the use of earthwork in artillery fortification during the period and area covered by this preliminary sketch in either Scotland or England.

2. 1513-1523

On 26 November 1513, twelve weeks after Flodden, the Scottish Estates were summoned to reply to ambassadors from Louis XII of France. One of the ambassadors was Antoine d'Arces, Sieur de la Bastie, who was to remain in Scotland until his violent death in 1517. The two proposals of the Frenchmen were accepted: that the 'Auld Alliance' be continued, and that John Stewart Duke of Albany, second in succession to the Scottish throne, be sent to Scotland as Governor, with men and arms. In the country's vulnerable condition after her disastrous defeat, ruled on behalf of the infant James V by a Council of Regency with the widowed Queen Margaret Tudor (Henry VIII's sister) as Regent, French succour was an agreeable prospect to many — though by no means all — Scotsmen. Faced with English raids, the regime soon looked to the country's defences. In January 1514 the Council considered how the strengths of Fast Castle and Dunbar might be provided with men, artillery and victuals.[42] In February de la Bastie and Robert Borthwick, master gunner 'hes devisit bulwerkis and trinchis' to be made before Edinburgh Castle, and were planning to 'stuff' the place with men and artillery.[43] It is doubtful whether the Edinburgh works were carried out, though the reference is interesting as the first use of the word 'bulwark' in the region covered by this essay that has been brought to my attention. Over the next three decades, until it acquires the specific meaning of an Italianate angle bastion, 'bulwark' seems to be used loosely for a strongpoint generally, of earth or masonry.

At this time, traditionally, the Flodden Wall was begun by the Town Council of Edinburgh. The work consisted of a wall about 1.2 m. thick and a maximum surviving height of 7.35 m., with rectilinear towers, pierced by 'dumb-bell' loops.[44] The design of the loops is similar to that of the Stirling Castle Forework, though on the Flodden wall the top and bottom circles are externally flared to trefoils. Such a wall thickness was not designed to resist battery by heavy ordnance: it might be capable of holding off a lightly armed raid. In its design it does not show any evidence of innovation.

Rather more enterprise was being shown south of the Border, where Flodden had induced a sense of alarm rather than complacency. Indeed, in March 1514 there were reports of Scots preparations against Berwick.

The little turrets which survive, greatly ruined, attached to the curtain of the outer ward of Norham, and the larger Clapham's Tower attached to the curtain of the inner ward, have for some time been conjectured as part of the repairs and improvements, largely of 1513-15 following the siege, and continuing to the end of the decade, directed by William Franklyn, the bishop's treasurer[45] (fig. 45). The angular faces of the Norham works have prompted the suggestion that their designer had some acquaintance, however distant, with the plan-form of the much larger angle bastions then being developed in Italy. Not only in plan-form, but also in scale, the lesser turrets are almost identical with Martini's *capannate* or prototype caponiers.[46] The resemblance stops there: the Norham structures were not vaulted and stone-roofed above a loopholed gallery as were those proposed by Martini, but seem to have been raised at least

Figure 45. Norham Castle, 1738 engraving by S. & N. Buck showing small angle-faced turrets on outer curtain, similar and larger Clapham's Tower on inner curtain

to the height of the curtain. They seem moreover to have missed the functional point. Martini's *capannate,* like the flankers of angle bastions, were intended to provide low-level flanking fire along the faces of the walls to counter assault. At Norham, however, the surviving structures and the 1728 Buck engraving[47] show only loops in the faces of the little turrets, none in the flanks to 'scour' the curtains. Clapham's Tower has a flank casemate, but it covers the bridge, not the adjacent curtain. All of these surviving Norham casemates are narrow and cramped, suggesting handguns resting on their sills, rather than anything heavier. Works were also carried out at Berwick after the battle, with an intriguing reference 'to make certain fortresses' there in 1514. The nature of these fortresses is unknown. The master mason was involved in their construction[48] and so they must have incorporated at least some element of mason work. The problem is discussed further below, p. 120.

Henry recognised the serious implications of French intervention, but his diplomacy only succeeded in delaying Albany's arrival. On 20 November 1514 de la Bastie appeared before the Council:

> Comperit schir Anthone Dercy monsieur de la Baty, procurator and in name of my lord duk of Albany governor of Scotland on the tan part and mastir Robert Forman, dene of Glasgow, Kepar of the castell of Dunbar under my lord of Murray on that uthir part

and agreement was reached to deliver the castle to de la Bastie on 6 December 1514.[49] Dunbar Castle thereafter became Albany's principal base in Scotland. It seems to have been little changed since the works completed for James IV at the beginning of the century; and it is possible, though incapable of proof, that de la Bastie now began to devise the 'bulwark' or 'great outer blockhouse' which survives today as the most remarkable feature of the site (figs. 46, 47).

Albany himself arrived in Scotland on 17 May 1515. Robert Lindesay of Pitscottie tells us[50] that the Governor brought six cannon, six great field pieces (culverins?) and other small guns with him from France, but the activity of carting guns from Dumbarton and Glasgow back to Edinburgh detailed in the Treasurer's accounts at this time may only relate to the Scots' own guns off the royal ships, the *Margaret* and *James,* which had returned home in 1515 with Albany. The shifting interests of the Scottish nobility ensured that Albany's welcome was mixed. Soon Alexander Lord Home fortified Fast Castle, that remote place of huge natural strength on the sea cliffs of Berwickshire, against the new Governor. Although Home had joined in the invitation to Albany, his relations with England were ambiguous, and he presumably had had second thoughts about the positive French commitment entailed in the

Figure 46. Dunbar Castle Blockhouse. Blockhouse, its salient with gunhole extreme left; traverse wall in middle leading to castle (right)

new government. Albany reacted vigorously, and occupied Fast and Hume Castles — the latter a place of commanding position in the East Borders — while Home fled to England, returned to give himself up, was placed in Edinburgh Castle, then escaped to England with his gaoler Archibald Douglas Earl of Angus. The latter headed one of the greatest families of Scotland, co-equal with the Hamiltons, and had attained an especial prominence as the second husband of Margaret Tudor, the Queen Dowager.

Although a truce was concluded with England in January 1516 through French good offices, the English soon re-opened their intrigues with Scottish dissidents against Albany, using Thomas Fiennes Lord Dacre as a principal agent. Albany riposted by seizing Home, bringing him to trial and executing him on 8 October 1516. The events of 1516 caused stress in Anglo-Scottish relations, though without any outbreak of hostilities. England responded by looking to her defences. By June 1517 Lord Dacre, warden of the East and Middle Marches, had received £480 for the king's works and had the master-mason at Berwick sent to Wark Castle to devise new fortifications there.[51] The most interesting innovation which resulted at Wark was in the four-storeyed keep. Two years later, again according to Dacre, each storey had 'fyve grete murdour holes . . . So that grete bumbardes may be shot out at icheon of them'. But while re-marking on Wark's ample provision for bombards, Dacre seems to have

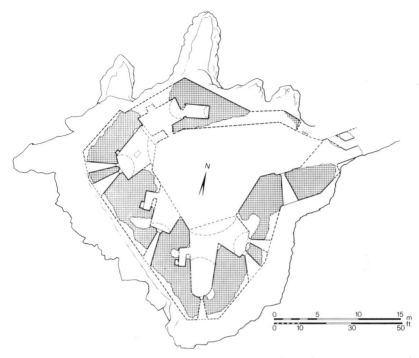

Figure 47. Dunbar Castle Blockhouse. The cross-hatching shows those surviving parts of the work of 1515x23; heavy broken line shows the probable completion of the plan as then built

asked for rather less, requesting 10 serpentines, 2 slings and one greater piece of ordnance (not further detailed) for scouring the fords of Tweed.

The Governor left Scotland for France on 7 June 1517, ostensibly for a six months' absence, leaving de la Bastie in charge of his interest and of Dunbar Castle, and Warden of the East Marches in succession to the late Lord Home. Dunbar Castle appears to have had five French gunners under James IV's gunner Master Wolf by or before 1 October 1517.[52] The complement is perhaps larger than seems necessary for the castle as re-built in 1496-1501, and the 'great outer blockhouse' already mentioned may possibly have been built by this time. Certainly Albany's departure in June, leaving behind him a less than tranquil situation in Scotland, would be easier to understand if he had established a really secure base at Dunbar, which by the addition of the blockhouse was later described as 'impregnable'. While we only know beyond contradiction that the block-house had been built for Albany at some date before 1523, there is no surviving Scottish documentary evidence for major works there in the whole period between Flodden and 1523, and there are hints (discussed below on p. 119) that it may have been in existence for some time before the latter date.

Albany's Scottish arrangements proved distinctly unfortunate: de la Bastie, venturing from Dunbar, was killed in revenge for the execution of Home. The incident, however, had no effect on Dunbar Castle, which was still retained in the French interest with de St Jacques as Captain. In France, the Auld Alliance was renewed as already agreed in principle by the Scots. Francis I wished at this juncture, however, to maintain friendship with England, and Albany, still nominally Governor of Scotland, was prevented from returning thither as his return would have been seen by Henry VIII as a hostile act. The factions in the Scottish Council of Regency were left to their own devices, which included a notorious street fight in Edinburgh (1520) between Hamilton and Douglas supporters of Arran and Angus, in which the former's bastard son James Hamilton of Finnart, who will appear later in other roles, played a conspicuous part.

During 1521 Anglo-French relations deteriorated and so there was no reason why Albany should be kept in France. He landed at Dumbarton for his second visit on 19 November. Dumbarton, Inchgarvie on the Forth and Dunbar Castle were 'stuffed with Frenchmen'. Dunbar was then described as a place of Albany's own, 'only five hours' march from Berwick'[53] (presumably for a force unimpeded by a siege train, as the two are 30 miles apart). Attempts were made to stave off open war by negotiation: for example Albany intended a meeting with Dacre on 28 January 1522, to arrange a continuation of the existing truce — the possible relevance of this meeting to our present theme is noted below (p. 119). Nevertheless hostilities eventually broke out; and a year of tension was reflected in the hasty strengthening of Berwick, described below on pp. 119-122. In September, with an English army in France, Albany moved on the western Border. After this show of strength he remained in Scotland until 25 October 1522 before again sailing to France.

In the winter of 1522-3, during Albany's absence, half-hearted attempts were again made to establish peace. In December 1522 Clarencieux Herald met the Scottish Chancellor at Stirling and reached a short-lived agreement; but in the spring of 1523 Henry VIII decided instead on a series of heavily armed raids to persuade the Scots to agree to a child-marriage between his daughter Mary and James V. Annan was attacked in April. The requisition of the lighter Dunbar artillery on 15 May was a precaution against the next impending raid, though it did not see action. On 18 May the Earl of Surrey, with Dacre and others and a force of over 2,000 men, crossed the Border into Roxburghshire. He took with him three heavy siege guns and eight lesser pieces; a curtow and a culverin (his best guns), a demi-culverin, four lizards and four falcons. After brief and successful sieges of minor towers the force reached Cessford Castle, seat of the Warden of the East Marches, Sir Andrew Ker. Ker was absent but his men defended the place with determination. Surrey, in a letter to Henry VIII,[54] described the place as 'vawmewred with earth of the best sort I have seen'. A *vawmure* was an earthwork raised against the face of a wall: in this case the slight masonry barmkin wall which surrounded the massive mid-fifteenth-century tower already mentioned (a *countermure* was raised behind a wall: see p. 121 below). Cessford held out against battery and assault all day, and the garrison showed no inclination to give in until Sir Andrew returned and surrendered the place on being allowed to depart with bag and baggage. Surrey admitted that, if the defence had been continued, he did not see how it could have been taken — remarking with perhaps understandable exaggeration that, after Dunbar Castle and the inaccessible Fast Castle, he reckoned that Cessford was the strongest place in Scotland.

The resistance offered is not altogether surprising. The curtow broke an axle in the early stages of the action; the weather was appalling; and moreover this was no siege in form: though powerful, Surrey's equipment was certainly not a complete siege train. Meanwhile a greater invasion of Scotland was being contemplated. Seeking preliminary intelligence, Cardinal Wolsey asked Dacre for information about Dunbar Castle. Dacre supplied it at the end of a long letter dated 26 June 1523:[55]

> And ffinally touching the state and strenth of the castell of Dunbar whereof your grace is desirous to be advised, I assure your grace it is a thing in maner unprenable for I have bene in it. It standith upon a crag and there is no waye to go to it but one which is strongly and substantially made with a new bulwerk and sett with ordinance as can be devised by the Duke of Albany for in the said castell is all the said Dukes trust. And if the said Bulwerk could be won I think there is no doubt but the castell might be won semblably be reason that the said castell stands low upon a crag and the erth without it is hygh about it, and so there could nothing stirr within it but the ordinance that were without the castell shulde bete it.

The surviving remains show that Dacre's 'bulwerk' is the same structure as that described by Pitscottie, who has it that Albany came

> into his awin castell of Dunbar, and thair remanit ane quhill; and gart craftismen and maissouns fall to work and build in the samin ane great staine house and insche callit the uttward blokehouse and garnist it witht artailzie pulder and bullatis.[56]

'Insche' (island) describes the isolated site of the work. In this passage Pitscottie, not the most reliable of historians, gets the date wrong, for he has it built during Albany's third and final visit to Scotland, after the unsuccessful siege of Wark — several months after Dacre had written to Wolsey describing the bulwark or blockhouse complete and armed. We

Figure 48. Dunbar Castle Blockhouse. Traverse wall linking castle (left) to blockhouse (right). The breach made by the sea reveals the passage within the thickness of the wall

shall return to consider further the date of construction. The physical remains of the work described are identifiable beyond dispute.

West of the structures rebuilt or repaired by James IV, the great block-house stands on the neighbouring island-like promontory already described; the cleft between the tip of the promontory and the general mass of the mainland may have been artificially improved to its width of 15 m. The blockhouse was joined to the castle by a stout traverse wall (fig. 48) built across the tidal chasm, containing a roofed-in passage. Above the passage there probably existed a rampart walk.

The blockhouse has a masonry rampart, the facing of which is almost entirely dilapidated but which has been up to 6.5 m. thick, graded in thickness according to the degree of threat from battery. It has measured externally about 28.5 m. maximum north to south by 23 m. east to west. The plan is polygonal. Towards the south the straight faces converge, and the salient seems to have been truncated as a short straight length of wall. The general shape is rather like that of a contemporary Italian angle bastion, though the similarity is probably accidental, dictated by the natural bounds of the precipitous rock faces which surround the whole work. Loss of the facework has blurred the original profile of the scarps.

Figure 49. Dunbar Castle Blockhouse. Interior showing casemates part-blocked by accumulated soil and debris

There is a hint that the scarp, at least on its west side, may have been vertical on a battered base, though without a photogrammetric survey the true profile can only be guessed at. The gorge has always been open towards the castle, and the interior of the work has always been unroofed.

Four large ground-level casemates with segmental vaults are deeply recessed into the rampart (fig. 49), reducing its thickness to a minimum of 2.5 m. The casemates are open to the rear. The soffits of two of the casemates are pierced with vents to help disperse the smoke from emplaced artillery (fig. 50). The rampart at the front of two of the casemates has been pierced by a gunhole; one gunhole opening through the salient has been subsequently blocked; the two other casemates have two gunholes each. A seventh gunhole, to the east, has no casemate but opens through the whole thickness (at that point 3.6 m.) of the rampart. Internally, the gunholes have circular throats within shallow cupped recesses. The throats are all large, varying in diameter from 300 mm. up to 380 mm. From the throats the gunholes splay outwards to horizontal slits with rounded ends (fig. 51): the largest external opening measures 1.75 m. by 0.75 m. The gunhole throats are all big enough to receive, with a reasonable margin for sighting, substantial pieces of artillery. The

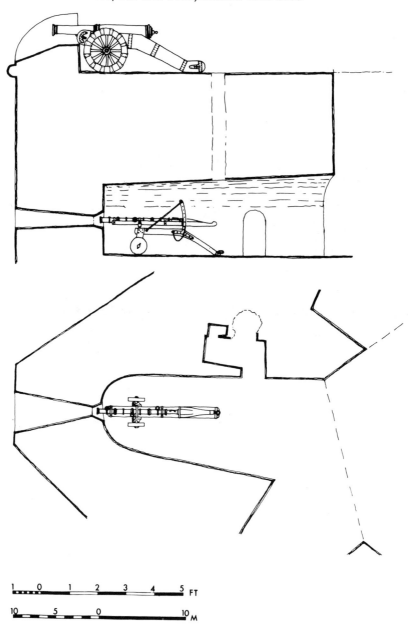

Figure 50. Dunbar Castle Blockhouse. Sketch of restored section showing conjectural parapet and casemate armament, plan showing casemate armament. On the parapet, a cannon on a heavy carriage with shod wheels; in the casemate, a stocked forged-iron breech-loader similar to but shorter than the weapon shown in fig 43, on a trestle mounting. It must be emphasised that these armament sketches are meant only as very tentative visual aids

Figure 51. Dunbar Castle Blockhouse. Characteristic external aperture of gunhole, a horizontal slit with rounded ends.

armament is discussed further below. Because of the accumulation of soil within the casemates the height of the gun mountings from the ground cannot be precisely determined.

We may note in passing that the blockhouse gives the earliest datable appearance of this particular form of gunhole, having horizontal external apertures with rounded ends, which in various sizes establishes itself as the type most characteristic of Scottish works, many of them towerhouses with very much more modest defensive ambitions than the formidable work which we are describing. If the gunholes at Dunbar do represent the earliest appearance of the type in Scotland, it is itself instructive. From the circumstances of its erection one would expect that the master-mason who designed the blockhouse would be a Frenchman in Albany's train (see p. 110). Gunholes of this precise external form with rounded ends certainly existed in France.

Two of the casemates have recesses in their sides which may be interpreted as expense magazines. (In addition, there are several irregular recesses apparently carved out of the rampart core. A possible explanation of these is that they were hacked out in 1567, when the place was demilitarised, in order to place explosive charges and so to effect the complete ruin of the blockhouse, and that the intention was never carried out. Instead, the parapet alone was thrown down.)

Towards the northern, seaward, side of the blockhouse are two rectangular vaulted chambers measuring 4.7 by 2.5 m. and 2.8 by 1.6 m. The larger chamber, the back of which has collapsed into the sea, has had a fireplace. These chambers seem to provide barrack accommodation.

Above the casemates there is still evidence of a massive parapet: masonry loss at this level makes it difficult to estimate the parapet thickness, but it must have been about 2 m. thick. The parapet may have had the curvilinear profile of Italian origin as found at, for example, da San Gallo's bastioned *fortezza* at Pisa, and best known in Britain from its use in Henry VIII's forts of c. 1539-42. A principal emplacement for a gun at the salient is indicated by a broad shallow recess with splayed ingoes: the turf cover makes it impossible to see more than fragments of other parapet emplacements, and their full definition, like the definition of the casemate floors, must await excavation. The parapet was approached by a broad ramp, or a gentle flight of steps, on the northern side, and a flight of narrow steps on the opposite side. Before excavation there are only glimpses of its inner face through the turf cover.

The armament of the blockhouse must be guesswork. 'Most of the artillery of Scotland' is said to have been in Dunbar in June 1523,[57] and while this gives wide scope we do not know what was exclusively the field train and what was emplaced as artillery of position (some of which might of course on occasion be removed for use in the field). On 15 May 1523 the comptroller was 'to send to Dunbar Castle and receive furth of the same culverins moyans, falconis and hagbuttis'[58] for use against English incursions. None of these are heavy pieces — the most considerable, a culverin moyen, had a bore of about 80 mm. Five years later Pitscottie lists a more formidable armament borrowed from Dunbar for the siege of Tantallon: two great cannon, two demi-cannon, two double falcons and four quarter falcons.[59] Although we must remind ourselves again that Pitscottie is unreliable, this weight of metal can hardly be invention. There are also the cannon and (probably) culverins which the Duke is said to have brought in 1515, the most likely destination of which was Dunbar.

The possible natures of weapon, and their mounting, for the exceptionally broad platform behind the parapet at the salient may be more straightforward to conjecture than those elsewhere. Such a position seems usually in the sixteenth century to be designed for long-range pieces mounted on field carriages with two large iron-shod wheels and a long heavy trail, the trunnions of the guns being half-countersunk in the fore part of the carriage. In the sequel (because such carriages were not at this period used exclusively in the field) such mountings will be referred to as 'carriages with shod wheels', following the quotations given in the next paragraph. Within the period immediately following there is evidence elsewhere for a variety of parapet guns on carriages with shod wheels, from falcons up to cannon. The parapet emplacement at the Dunbar blockhouse salient is sufficiently large for a cannon to be run back, and a cannon is illustrated on the Dunbar armament sketch section (fig. 50) to show its feasability. Elsewhere the Dunbar parapet may have mounted two or three more guns — not so large, and perhaps differently mounted, for there the platform is less broad.

This may be an appropriate point to enlarge on the subject of parapet mountings. It is conventionally assumed that in England, through the reign of Henry VIII and after, where the parapet guns of a fortress were muzzle-loaders usually of cast bronze, they were mounted on carriages with shod wheels. The assumption is reasonable because such carriages, and no others, are shown on contemporary drawings of fortress parapets.[59] Field carriages appear in inventories as, for example, at Berwick in 1545:

> a culveryne of brasse mounted upon her cariage with shoddwheles lymbers ladell and spunge.[60]

The same carriages appear in Scotland: at Edinburgh Castle in 1566[61]

> upon the tour heid ane moyane of found mountit as said is with stokkis quheillis and aixtree garnesit with iron.

Sometimes the carriages in Scotland had a third wheel, apparently a smaller one attached to the trail; again at Edinburgh Castle

> on the foirwall foure new cannonis of found mountit upoun thair stokis quhellis and aixtreis garnisit with iron quhilkis were brocht last yeir out of France having als thre aixtreis of iron for third quheillis.

The assumption is beyond doubt generally true, in Scotland as well as England, but it may not be universally so. A muzzle-loading gun behind a parapet requires a considerable breadth of platform, additional to the overall length of the carriage, to take account of recoil and to allow the gun to be run back for loading. In the mid-eighteenth century an 18 or 12 pounder gun (that is, a gun of culverin size), on a compact garrison carriage measuring about 1.6 m. overall with four small wheels or trucks, was provided with a platform commonly between 5.5 and 4.9 m. long: that is at least 3.3 m. of the platform was allowed for recoil and loading.

With a sixteenth-century field carriage measuring about 4.5 m. overall one might expect a platform of nearly 8 m. in length. I may cite one example to show that this was not the case. Part of the west front, and all of the north front of the curtain of the inner ward of Carlisle Castle were remodelled for parapet guns at a date which is unsettled but which appears to fall around the middle years of the sixteenth century, perhaps 1539-42. In the remodelling, a broad platform behind the medieval curtain was provided, at the west front supported on transverse arches, at the north front on an earthen countermure revetted with masonry at the rear. The platform width at the west front is now 5.8 m., and at the north front 5.45 m. These widths can never have been greatly different since the original building, and they are clearly too narrow for field carriages.

An inventory of pieces at Carlisle in 1545[62] makes no mention of carriages with shod wheels. Instead, many guns, including sakers (the largest) and falcons are itemised as being mounted on carts. While these carts may be solely for moving the pieces from one place to another, rather than mounts for action, such an interpretation would be at odds with other inventory evidence. We know that mountings with trucks (or truckles: small wheels) existed before the middle of the sixteenth century, and we shall later notice examples at Berwick.[63] These cart and truck mountings may represent primitive four-wheeled garrison carriages, and such carriages may have been used on the Dunbar parapet, elsewhere than at the salient.

The Dunbar casemates present different problems. In general, casemate guns were not mounted on field carriages because of restricted space, difficulty in running the gun back and difficulty in aligning the muzzle of a gun rotating on conventionally-placed trunnions to the gunhole. At Dunbar the first two considerations need not apply, for the casemates are spacious and open to the rear, where the whole interior of the blockhouse was not improbably level with the casemate floors. The third consideration, however, does apply, and exactingly so: the very slight elevation and depression feasible in the vertical section between gunhole throat and external aperture requires a mounting pivoting as near as possible to the gunhole throat — as near as possible to, but not at the throat, which has itself no provision for fixing the barrel of a gun or a stock attached to it. This implies some form of trestle mounting with the very limited elevation and depression possible contrived by a rack or wedge to the rear. The nature of Dunbar's casemated guns is less easy to surmise than that of its parapet armament. The persistence of breech-loading iron-forged guns in such positions noted below at Berwick (p. 000 etc) makes one think that such guns may well have been used at Dunbar also: breech-loaders were used in situations elsewhere where it was physically possible to run the pieces back.

We may only say with certainty that the great blockhouse which has been described existed by late June 1523. Dacre, however, was then reporting his impressions from a visit made some time before. While Dacre peaceably entered Scotland from time to time in pursuance of his duties as Warden (he had, for example, met Albany at Smailholm on 11 September 1522),[64] he seldom had cause to go very far into the country. The most proximate occasion that a meeting at Dunbar may have been hinted at is on 28 January 1522.[65] If this be indeed the date of Dacre's visit, it would push the latest date of construction back to the building season of 1521, and on balance of likelihood further back still, to the first period of Albany's Governorship. We must of course take into account Dacre's description of the bulwark as 'new' in 1523, and perhaps conclude rather lamely that the work was built somewhere between 1515 and 1523.[66]

The invasion of Scotland mooted in the summer of 1523 did not materialise, but English raids prompted a response from Albany to demonstrate the value of the French alliance. In October 1523 he came to Scotland for the last time, landing at Dumbarton with a great professional army: a letter to Surrey lists it with some awe and maybe some inaccuracy: 100 heavy horses, 500 light horses, 4,000 foot, 500 men at arms, 1,000 hagbuts, 900 serpentines and falcons, and 16 cannon.[67] This display of military might was to join with the Scots, intending, it was believed, the recapture of Berwick. The month produced foreboding English messages, and urgent work; but there was no attack on the frontier town. The Governor's artillery played on Wark Castle from the Scottish side of the Tweed, his French corps made an unsuccessful assault, and he was compelled to withdraw, frustrated by extremely bad weather (the Border climate affected both sides) as well as lack of enthusiasm from his Scots allies. Soon afterwards Albany left Scotland for the last time.

The constant major threat from Albany's enterprises had been the loss of Berwick, which was ill prepared to withstand a siege. Although works were carried out in haste in the seasons of 1522 and 1523, spies reported in October 1523 that Albany was still confident that Berwick could not hold out for six hours against him. Surrey in the previous month had given the castle eight hours against six 'curtowtes' (i.e. cannon, a word not frequently used by the English).[68] It may be useful to review our knowledge of the state of the defences at that date.

The artillery works existing in the late autumn of 1523, and surviving today only as a few scattered, mostly indistinct, fragments, represent accretions over a long period. Some operations have been touched on already: the adaptation of medieval towers for ordnance; the construction of the Bulwark at the Sands, the White Wall Tower and Walls Tower. There was clearly more besides. Early in 1522 it was reported that four bulwarks had fallen down and the fifth was in decay.[69] One of these may have been the stone Bulwark in the Sands. The nature and location of the others is quite uncertain: unfortunately, for it would be valuable to know more of the nature of the various strongpoints which might at this date be called 'bulwarks'.

The certain works of 1522[70] were structures by Richard Candishe, master of the ordnance at Berwick, projecting from the enceinte or detached beyond the enceinte. These were: earthen bulwarks at the Bell Tower and beyond the wall between St Mary Gate and Percy Tower, a Murder Tower with thin masonry walls, attached to a tower on the town's east front, and a major repair of the Bulwark in the Sands.

Of these, the largest enterprise documented was 'the gret bull werk by the belle Tower'. It is not clear whether this bulwark was attached to the walls or disjoined from them. It was reached by a postern in the Bell Tower itself, and measured 21 yards (19 m.) across its base towards the walls, projected for 70 yards (64 m.) outward from the Bell Tower, and measured 9 yards (8.2 m.) across its outer extremity, giving a curiously elongated shape. Some timber seems to have been used in its construction ('rotten and fallen in decay' in the 1533 x 5 survey suggests this) perhaps for the revetment of parts of scarp and parapet, but it also had masonry 'gown holes' and 'loupes of stone'.[71] The form, and indeed the exact location, of the bulwark between St Mary Gate and Percy Tower is unknown.

The Murder Tower was attached to, and gained access from, the medieval tower immediately south of the Bell Tower.[72] Its ground plan seems to have resembled that of the little turrets at Norham already mentioned, though with walls only 2 feet (600 mm.) thick. The interior at the ground floor was 8 feet (2.45 m.) wide and 8 feet high. In 1539 it contained[73] two iron breech-loading serpentines 'with mytches and forloke with two chambers a pece', and seven iron hagbuts. 'Upon the hed of Murther's towre' (that is, on the parapet) there was a muzzle-loading brass serpentine mounted on shod wheels. There is no reason to think that this was not the original armament. The Murder Tower was a purpose-built work to scour the ditch on each side, and to provide a defence towards the field from its parapet.

The Murder Tower may have been built because the ancient tower (the stump of which survives today, with a very small fragment of the Murder Tower north wall) to which it was attached was too small to accommodate artillery, and elsewhere the adaptation of some of the larger old towers as 'murderers' may belong to the 1522-3 programme. The ground-floor vaults of ten of the medieval towers of the enceinte were adapted as gun casemates[74] by slapping loops in their flanks to cover the ditch on either side: although some early gunloops may already have existed, a more comprehensive provision of flank defence seems complementary to the building of the Murder Tower in 1522. The 1539 armament of these improvised 'murderers' was likewise breech-loading iron serpentines and hagbuts and — although in several cases the armament seems to have been withdrawn during the intervening period of neglect — may likewise represent the original provision. Normally, in the 1539 inventory, there are two serpentines in each vault and between four and ten hagbuts. A not dissimilar provision was made in two of the castle towers, though there the casemates were in the middle of the towers, not at ground level.

The only bulwark which survives today is nowhere dated: we only know that the 'great Bulwark in the snooke' had fallen into decay by 1532x5.[75] Advanced beyond the ditch on the town's east front, and originally reached by a postern in the town wall, this is an asymmetrical D-shaped earthwork measuring approximately (for its scarps are reduced by weathering) 64 m. across its base by 38 m. from centre of base to rounded salient. A fourth earthen bulwark, in front of the Cowgate, is also mentioned as being in a state of decay in 1532x5.

One further major reinforcement described in the 1532x5 survey, part of which is extant on the north front of the town, is also undatable: the earthen backing or countermure raised behind the landward enceinte of the town, and behind part of the castle enceinte. An earthen backing to a stone wall is an ancient military device which came into new prominence as a reinforcement against artillery and, with masonry knitted to earthwork by internal buttresses or counterforts, was to become the norm for rampart construction from the mid-sixteenth century. The device was employed at Berwick in its simplest form,[76] with such an earthwork countermure varying between 18 and 28 feet (5.5-8.5 m.) in thickness for the town, about 5 yards (4.6 m.) for the castle. Tunnels with masonry side walls and timber roofs were built to give access through the countermure to the towers and posterns. Most of the towers appear to have been reduced in height (some parts of the walls may have been similarly reduced), and the towers were filled with earth — either completely filled, or excluding the casemates of the casemated towers — to the top. These earth-filled towers seem to have had their own earthen platforms, and parapets possibly also earth-backed, the platform being apparently level with the broad platform formed by the top of the countermure. A parapet armament for the towers, and maybe at intermediate points on the curtain platforms, seems to have been intended from the time of construction of the countermure. The parapet armament in 1539 consisting of muzzle-loading pieces — a culverin, sakers, serpentines and falcons — may again suggest the originally intended armanent.

There is no direct evidence for the date of the countermure, or whether indeed it all belongs to a single campaign. We know that it had existed for some time in 1532x5, for the timber lintels of the tunnels were then badly decayed and the tunnel roofs in many places had partly collapsed. One possible date for it is in 1522-3, though it could also belong to the period around the Flodden campaign or even earlier. It is also an intriguing possibility that the four earthen bulwarks noted were more or less drastically remodelled in 1522-3 from earlier originals, giving (with the stone Bulwark in the Sands) the five decayed bulwarks reported on in early 1522. Could they (incorporating some masonry features) even be the 'fortresses' of 1514?

3. 1524-1542

After Albany's final departure from Scotland his 'impregnable' castle of Dunbar continued, with its French garrison, pending the arrangement of a French match for James V. The Council of Regency seems to have asked for the return of Dunbar in 1527, but Albany did not trust the ability or the will of the Scottish government to hold the place against the English, and was able so to convince the King of France. The French garrison remained after James V had escaped from the tutelage of Angus in 1528 and, at the age of 17, personally assumed the reigns of government. Co-operation seems to have been readily given to James from Dunbar when in the same year he endeavoured to assert his authority against Angus in an attack on the latter's principal stronghold, Tantallon Castle in East Lothian. James, with a powerful train of artillery, could not take the place by bombardment though he shortly afterwards gained it by negotiation.

Then, as now, the most conspicuous defence of Tantallon was the medieval towered curtain wall across the neck of the promontory site.[77] The curtain was high, and stout: about 3.70 m. thick, though pierced by a number of mural chambers and stairs. There are today several earthworks beyond it. One of these is a ditched redan which clearly belongs to a later period of fortification than that which we are considering here. There are, however, several indications that the easternmost earthwork, a massive bank and ditch extending across the promontory, and from superficial evidence[78] a work of several periods, existed in some form in 1528. It is likely that it had originally been raised to bound the medieval outer ward. By 1528 its gateway, and its ditch by the gateway, seem already to have been defended by a traverse wall and a small round tower, furnished with gunholes similar in design to those of the Dunbar blockhouse but much smaller, with throats of some 170 mm. diameter. I make this conjecture because the traverse and tower as they exist today show evidence of repair to damage which is most readily interpreted as damage caused by bombardment; and because the clearly visible repairs are largely executed in the greenish stone found in most repairs carried out in the decade after the siege. I claim only that it is more reasonable to assume that the traverse and tower existed in 1528, than to assume they did not. It may therefore plausibly be guessed that these works were built by Angus earlier in the decade, acknowledging the example of Dunbar in their gunhole design, and belonging to the same family as the 'murderer' and adapted medieval towers at Berwick noted above in their concept of flank defence of a ditch. The tower at Tantallon has walls up to 2.1 m. thick at the most vulnerable side, though the traverse is only 1 m. thick. The greatest Scottish magnates like Angus had resources not unequal to those of the crown, and so it would be hardly surprising to find that their enterprises in fortification were ambitious. The enigmatic flanking turret at the Hamilton stronghold of Cadzow Castle, Lanarkshire, which has been variously interpreted,[79] may represent an analogous addition by Arran of about the same period.

The existence of the advanced earthwork front at Tantallon, in itself much more resistant to gunfire than the high medieval walls which it shields at their most vulnerable lower part, may help in some measure to explain the failure of the siege.

James took advice from his chief gunners, Robert Borthwick and John Drummond, on what was necessary for the siege, and they reckoned on four cannon and one culverin battard.[80] Here Borthwick and Drummond may have been more influenced by what was available than by what was desirable. To the list of things thought necessary by the gunners was appended a memorandum 'to send for the masoune of Dunbar and to consider his engyne'.[81] Our only source for the result of this putative discussion with the Dunbar master-mason is Pitscottie, who says that James got from Dunbar two great cannons, two great battards, two moyens, two double falcons and four quarter falcons.[82] James also had four falcons from the Scottish arsenal besides the pieces recommended by Borthwick and Drummond.[83] Even though we make due allowance for the unreliability of Pitscottie, it seems unreasonable to think that there was not a respectable augmentation from Dunbar. The number of guns present, however, is by no means the only element in the equation. Complementary to the provision of guns was the provision of cannon balls and gunpowder. Gunpowder was certainly made in Scotland at this time, but not enough, and much had to be got from abroad. Before the siege was finished we know that James had either run out of powder or was greatly hampered by lack of it. At this time all the cast iron shot fired by the larger guns had to be imported from abroad since the Scots lacked the technological capability to cast iron, with the consequence that they only had a limited supply of iron shot. Borthwick and Drummond recommended thirty shot for each gun of the king's taken,[84] and again we can only suppose that this figure reflects what was available since a well operated gun could shoot forty shot in one day. James must have got more shot from Dunbar Castle or other sources or else the siege would not have been worth undertaking in the first place.

A final difficulty in mounting the siege (shared by Albany, and by later Scottish leaders) was the fact that the king could not field a force for longer than a few weeks. Traditionally he could not call on the services of the host for any longer than a period of forty days in the year, and normally service was shorter than this. For the siege of Tantallon James asked for only twenty days' service after which his force went home.[85] This was presumably bad organisation on James's part, as Albany demonstrated that this problem could at least partly be solved by calling out the host a quarter at a time. After Tantallon was surrendered to him, James repaired and strengthened the principal masonry front: in Pitscottie's words he

> caussit maissouns come and rainforce the samin wallis that was left waist of befoir, as transses and throw passagis and maid all massie wark.[86]

Whether this was done almost immediately, as the context of the quotation implies, or after an interval, is not certain. What is clear is that the strengthening of the castle, perhaps extending intermittently over the next decade, took in much more than the filling of voids in the medieval walls. To this we shall return below (p. 000).

The next major fortification begun in Scotland, Craignethan Castle in Lanarkshire, lies outside the topographical limits of the present essay but deserves an exceptional notice here because of its place in the development of flank defence.[87] Craignethan was a private stronghold of the Hamiltons, built by Sir James Hamilton of Finnart from around 1530. The neck of its spur site was cut by a deep, straight and narrow ditch with vertical masonry counterscarp and scarp, the latter rising to form a high and thick rampart at the west of the defended perimeter. The ditch defence was a fully developed caponier, a vaulted and loopholed gallery extending right across the ditch (fig. 52).

The rampart, unlike the curtains and towers of Tantallon, was not protected by any outer earthwork; on the contrary, to the west, the ground rises abruptly to overlook the whole site at a distance of 82 m.

Figure 52. Craignethan Castle, Caponier. Inner castle to the left

from the west rampart. The height and brute mass of the latter was clearly still judged sufficient to counter the threat of besieging guns on the high ground, bearing in mind that the base of the rampart, its most vulnerable part, was protected by the ditch. On the other sides of the site, beyond the ravines, the nearest high ground is about 120 m. distant. On these less exposed sides there was a much slighter wall, 1.7 m. in general thickness, with rectilinear towers, in plan not unlike the Flodden Wall. The defensive armament is unknown. The caponier and the enceinte were pierced with gunloops of the Dunbar blockhouse type with circular throats splaying to horizontal external apertures with rounded ends, but much smaller, and suitable only for light firearms resting (not swivelled) on the sills, or mounted on trestles. The surviving west parapet of the residential towerhouse within the enceinte, and the destroyed parapet of the west rampart, may have accommodated wheel-carriage mounted pieces of moderate size; documentary hints, though inconclusive, point to falcons.

Its intended capability of defence is likewise unknown. Craignethan's designer would have been optimistic if he imagined it could have withstood battery by contemporary great artillery. Once again, however, we must remember that there are several gradations of threat which a fortification may be designed to withstand, from formal siege down to attempted intrusion. Craignethan's intended capability may fall some way below the former, and appreciably above the latter. Craignethan seems to have been an internal Scottish affair: a powerful house strengthening its hand against its peers, and if necessary against the authority of the crown. The design, incorporating the concept of 'perpendicular fortification' in its arrangement of west rampart, ditch and caponier, is a development of the theme of flank defence which we have seen at Norham and Berwick.

On 28 February 1532 the Imperial ambassador in London, Eustace Chapuys, wrote to Charles V[88] describing *inter alia* an interview with the Duke of Norfolk. Norfolk had shown him several plans for fortifications on the Border, among them a plan for a citadel at Berwick to resemble that at Tournay, built following Henry VIII's occupation of that place in 1513. The ambassador was uncertain whether the English really had any fear of the Scots, or whether these plans were merely a device for raising money. Over the next decade, we may share the same uncertainty concerning both sides. There is no military crisis like that of the last years of Albany's governorship, and neither intermittent mutual raids nor the political and religious context quite explain the concern with fortifications shown by both James V and Henry — that is, until the general crisis which began in 1538-9.

The Berwick citadel was not built, and at the end of the year the decayed defences of the place suffered further damage in a storm which caused great harm to the White Wall tower.[89] In January 1533 Sir Thomas Clifford wrote to Henry VIII[90] reminding him that he had often informed the king of the ruinous state of Berwick, which was being viewed by Sir Christopher Morice, Master of the Ordnance, and Richard Candishe, who would report in due course. Clifford observed that, with recently increased deterioration, no defence could be made against an enemy except upon 'the high of the walls, for the bulwarks are clearly decayed, and the towers and murderers in such case as, for danger of falling of the same to the ground, there can none ordnance be occupied by the gunners within the most part of them'.

This may be the occasion when the detailed survey, already referred to, of the defences of the town and castle[91] was written. The undated survey was tentatively ascribed in the Calendar of *Letters and Papers*[92] to 1539, but further evidence suggests that it must have been made between 1532 and 1535:[93] I have referred to it as the 1532x5 survey. The survey emphasises the weakness of the castle; which

> standith in such forme and so lowe under the town, as yf the town by any means be against the castell . . . the said castell can no waies hurte or danger the town, and the town greatly hurte and danger the castell.

The castle was also threatened by high ground to the north-west; and it is curious that, with its recognised defects, more effort seems to have gone into strengthening the town than strengthening the castle. It is equally curious that, throughout our period, comparatively little attention seems to have been paid to reinforcing the middle lengths of the north front of the town enceinte; why was there no middle bulwark here, corresponding to the Great Bulwark in the Snook? The general bad condition of the defences may be appreciated by a summary of the findings of the survey for the north and east fronts of the town.

On the north front, there were holes eroded in the walls of Marygate, which seems to have been too slightly built for an armament of anything heavier than hagbuts. Broadstairs Tower and the Bell Tower, filled with earth above the vaults of their lowest level, afforded no provision for parapet guns, and access to the improvised flanking casemates in their vaults was either hindered or prevented by the collapsing rotten timber roofing the access tunnels through the countermure. The other two towers were filled with earth from the ground up and again seem to have had no parapet guns. What parapet armament existed seems to have been emplaced on the countermure behind the walls: the deterioration of the towers seems to have been so advanced that it was dangerous to mount guns on them. Most of the temporary repair of the curtains in stone and black earth was about to fall down, and 19 yards of the old wall between Walls Tower and the Bell Tower had already fallen. Candishe's bulwark beyond the Bell Tower, though only eleven years old, was 'rotten and fallen in decay'.

On the east front, rainwater penetrating the flags of its upper platform rendered the flank emplacements at Cowgate unusable for casemated ordnance; and the casemated towers of the front all suffered from the decay of their countermure tunnels. Two of the towers, the unnamed tower south of the postern and St Nicholas Tower, were structurally so dangerous that ordnance could not be put in their casemates, or on their parapets: none of the towers on this front also could be used for parapet guns save Murder Tower, where the timberwork was decaying but could still accommodate ordnance. There had been a recent rebuild of 80 yards of wall between Bell Tower and Murder Tower. Elsewhere the antique curtains were in indifferent repair but their state appears to have been a little less perilous than on the north front. Limited repairs at Berwick followed, but there is no evidence for new works.

In 1533 commissioners reported on Wark in terms which give some insight into the different levels of defensive capability which a fortified place might have. Wark could not withstand a 'siege royal', as *inter alia* its situation offered such opportunities for mining, but 'consyderynge the Scottes and especyally the borderers to be men of no great experyence or engyne in the assaillinge of fortresses' the castle might at little cost be strengthened sufficiently to hold up an army until relief came.

In 1536 control of Dunbar Castle passed for the first time since 1514 into the hands of the Scottish crown. One of the clauses of James V's marriage treaty with Marie de Vendome, assuring the continuation of the Auld Alliance, stipulated that the French garrison was to relinquish Dunbar. The French my still have had misgivings about the Scots' ability to hold the place, but now that the Auld Alliance was assured by the marriage treaty and James's inclinations, it was no longer necessary to maintain a permanent French base in Scotland. During his visit to France, when he abandoned the intention of wedding Marie de Vendome in favour of the much prettier Madeleine de Valois, James at Orleans appointed Moyse Martin, sometime master-mason at Dunbar Castle, to be his master-mason.[94] It is an intriguing possibility, though no more, that Martin was not only the mason whose 'engyne' had been sought for the siege of Tantallon in 1528, but also the designer of the great block-house for Albany.

Be this as it may, it is at least a remarkable coincidence that in August 1536 provision was made to fund 'the reparacioun and bigging' of the royal castle of Blackness in West Lothian, and that at Blackness there survives a work which in plan (figs. 53-55), though not in elevation, bears a remarkable similarity (discounting later alterations) to the Dunbar blockhouse, of which the Scots in 1536, for the first time, could take full cognisance. I propose to explore the multi-period reinforcement of the defences of Blackness, and the modification of the tower in the middle of the site apparently used throughout the sixteenth century as a state prison, in a separate paper. Here I intend only a summary appropriate to the present purpose.

When the castle, first documented in 1449, was annexed to the crown after its capture by James II and Mary of Gueldres in 1453, it had probably assumed the basic plan which it retains today. The plan was dictated by the site, a narrow elongated spit of rock jutting into the Forth,

Figure 53. Blackness Castle, drawing of 1794

then surrounded on three sides by sea or salt marsh. The spit was isolated by a ditch and enclosed by a 1.5 m. thick barmkin or curtain wall, with a blunt polygonal front on the south, tapering northward to a point at the tip of the rocky spit. The barmkin was of modest height, with a simple crenellated parapet flush with the main wall face.[95]

In 1534 James Hamilton of Kincavil, hereditary captain and keeper of Blackness, fled to England to escape trial on a charge of heresy and was forfeited. The charge was urged by his kinsman Sir James Hamilton of Finnart, whom we have already encountered fighting the Douglases in Edinburgh in 1520 and building Craignethan Castle ten years later. From 1534 until 1540, when he was executed on a charge of treason, Sir James had custody of Blackness under the king. Up to his death he was also in charge of royal works at Blackness and Linlithgow Palace.

On 17 August 1536 Patrik Hepburn of Wauchtoun, Jhone Simpson and Robert Walson were bound by the Lords of Council to

> pay to schir James Hammiltoun of Fynnert, knycht, the soum of i[m] li. restand awand in ane obligation maid by the saidis persouns to the Kingis grace for the said Patrikis eschet gudis and in compleit payment of the hale obligatioun at the Kingis gracis command for the reparatioun and bigging of his castell at Blaknes, . . . at the termes contenit in the said obligation, that is to say v[c] li. at Yule nixt tocum and uthir v[c] li. at Witsonday nixt thareftir in the yer of God i[m] v[c] xxxvii yeris; . . .[96]

One may perhaps deduce that the two-instalment sum of £1,000 was to be expended during the building season of 1537. Subsequent payments to Sir James entered in the Treasurer's Accounts show the programme continuing:

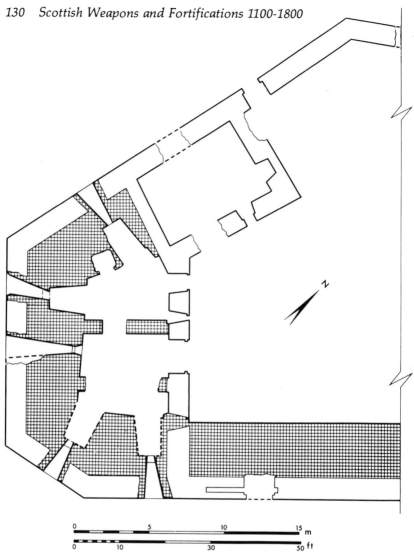

Figure 54. Blackness Castle: the reinforcement of the south front as proposed in 1537, with reinforcement of the east curtain as possibly proposed at the same date. Proposed reinforcement shown cross-hatched; structures of the 15th-cent. castle in outline only

> 1538 delivered to Sir James Hamilton in payment for sums owed to him by the King's grace for expenses on the palace of Linlithgow and the castle of Blackness . . . £180.[97]
>
> 1540 to Sir James Hamilton for the rest of his account for works of Linlithgow and Blackness . . . £300.[98]

and in 1542 the parson of Dysart was paid £133.6.8 'to complete the work of the Blackness'.[99]

Figure 55. Blackness Castle, aerial view with south front in foreground. Parapet rebuilt by Office of Works in the 1930s

When the parson had completed the work, the place is for the first time described as formidable. On 16 July 1543, after the death of James V and the accession of his infant daughter as Queen of Scots, Ralph Sadler advised Henry VIII that Governor Arran

> will go to Linlithgow until his whole force assemble, and if his enemies come forward he will remove the Queen to Blackness, which is impregnable.[100]

—repeating the adjective used by Dacre twenty years earlier to describe Dunbar.

The work which we would identify here as that begun in 1537 is at the polygonal south end of the castle. A variant of the plan-form of the Dunbar blockhouse has been reproduced at the lowest level by slapping large gunholes through the fifteenth-century curtain wall, while internally reinforcing the wall with masonry giving an overall maximum thickness of 5.5 m., interrupted by segmental-vaulted casemates. The gunholes opening from the casemates have throats up to 400 mm. in diameter, slightly larger, that is, than the biggest of the gunhole throats at Dunbar. The size of the external apertures is also closely comparable to those at Dunbar. So far there is a near resemblance between the two works. But whereas at Dunbar the parapet was set immediately above the casemated level, at Blackness the south front was carried up vertically to a high tower, filling in the fifteenth-century crenellations and building above them with a further internal masonry reinforcement. This new tower contained the principal residential accommodation. During the extended repair of Blackness at the end of the seventeenth century it was specified that one of the hall windows was to be suitable for the emplacement of a 'great gun' in time of need. Such a gun would command the high ground which, as at Craignethan, confronts the fortification and seems considerably to weaken the site. A great gun may have been provided for in this location from the beginning, augmented by whatever armament was emplaced on the parapet. The design of the latter with a simple crenellated parapet as shown in a drawing of 1794 may represent the original form: in the nineteenth and twentieth centuries the wallhead has been completely rebuilt. Again reliance was placed on a brute mass of high masonry to resist artillery.

The reinforcement of the east curtain of Blackness to a thickness of 5 m. may have been planned also at this stage, but the work may have remained incomplete until a later date.

Work now appears to have reopened at Tantallon with accounts showing expenditure of £472.17.0 in 1538-9.[101] This may represent a further stage of improvements carried out intermittently since the 1528 siege, and more may have been done after 1539, perhaps even completed after the castle was handed back to Angus by the new Scottish regime in 1543, when Angus returned from exile in England. In this period the defences of the castle were refurbished in a number of significant ways. We have already noted Pitscottie's reference to the strengthening of the medieval walls, apparently relating to works soon after the siege. The mural stairs and chambers in the high medieval curtains were infilled with masonry, and the resulting solid rampart was topped by a crenellated parapet 1.75 m. thick, rising from continuous corbelling, suitable for hand-held guns resting on the crenels. The 1538-9 works may possibly take in the reinforcement of the towers. The landward face of the east tower of the front was strengthened to give it a thickness of some 4.5 m., and pierced at several levels with Dunbar-type gunholes with throats as large or larger than those of Dunbar, up to 400 mm. in diameter. The corresponding tower at the opposite end of the front is so greatly ruined that no evidence survives of a possible parallel reinforcement there, but the later armament of its wallhead suggests that such a reinforcement was carried out. The central tower with its gate and barbican had added to it a massive forework (the Fore Tower) with rounded angles, having large gunholes with 360 mm. throats at the level of the entrance pend and below it to flank the inner ditch, and a smaller gunhole commanding the length of the bridge.

The long-range armament of the castle seems to have been concentrated on the wallheads of these three towers. Suffolk in 1543 did not specify the location of the 'ordinaunce that wolde shote two mylys and ynough of it';[102] but an inventory of 1556[103] may be taken, with circumspection, as an approximate guide to at least some of the pieces which may, from the beginning, have been intended:

On the eist tourheid
Ane culvering myoun with hir furnist stok and quhelis.

On the foir tour heid
Ane culvering myoun with hir stokkis and quhelis
Ane singill falcoun of font.

On Douglass tourheid
Two singill falconis of font
Two slangis of irne without stokkis and with two chalmeris to ather of thame.

On the wallheads of the towers the cast-bronze lesser culverins and falcons contrast with the dismounted slangis of the older fashion. Slangis, as has been noted above (p. 000), were substantial, and sometimes very elongated, long-range pieces. No casemated armament is noted in position for the East Tower or the Douglas Tower. 'In the entries of the zet', plausibly the emplacements in the sides of the Fore Tower flanking the inner ditch, there were two single cutthrottis and a double cutthrott. There was also a single cutthrott 'abone the brig', again plausibly at the small gunhole in the front of the Fore Tower which gives a longitudinal command of the bridge over the inner ditch. The small guntower and traverse at the gate of the outer ditch seem to have had no weapons in position.

I have already noted the patching of guntower and traverse after the siege. The earthwork behind the outer ditch may have been augmented in 1538-9 and, at least in part, given a masonry scarp, rising vertically from the rock-cut outer ditch, 1.3 m. thick and today surviving to a height of some 5 m. The place in the sequence of the stone scarp, like the repairs to the traverse and small gun tower adjacent to it, is suggested by the greenish stone of which it is constructed. This stone scarp formed the major obstacle to the Cromwellian siege in 1651, and was a principal target for Monk's considerable siege train: hence its present state of ruin. The combination of masonry and earthwork reverses the sequence at Berwick, where the masonry came first: like Berwick, the reinforcement of Tantallon foreshadows the future, and the overall remodelling of the castle is ingenious.

While these operations at Blackness and Tantallon were in progress a major European crisis had developed. In the summer of 1538 France and the Empire signed a ten-year truce, and soon an invasion of England to re-establish the authority of the Roman Catholic church there seemed inevitable. Henry had fears also from Scotland; commissioners were sent north to report on the ordnance and munitions at Berwick, which they began to survey on 20 January 1539. The report,[103] which shows that some work had been done in the preceding years to remedy at least some failings (many places which earlier in the decade had been unfit for ordnance were now armed), is of the highest interest.

At both the town and the castle the armament of the wallheads of towers and curtains consisted entirely of muzzle-loaders. These are all brass pieces save for two iron sakers. The latter are the only guns which we shall encounter that might be of cast iron. Excluding a large number of iron hagbuts, the casemated armament consisted entirely of forged iron breech-loaders, mostly serpentines.

About the town, the tower parapets were armed with one culverin, four sakers, three serpentines (brass muzzle-loaders) and three falcons; parapets of curtains with one saker and two falcons. The tower casemates had fourteen serpentines (iron breech-loaders) and no less than 57 hagbuts. There were besides two brass muzzle-loading serpentines mounted on a garret by St Mary Gate, and five hagbuts in the gate itself. The castle's tower parapets had two sakers and two falcons; on the walls between the towers and on the roof of the great chamber one saker and two falcons. The casemates of the castle towers had one fowler and six serpentines (iron breech-loaders). There were also two culverins on the hill before the castle — an outwork probably dating from 1522.

The mountings of the guns are given in some detail. Most of the parapet armament is 'mountyd upon shod wheles with ladell and sponge', with one gun unmounted (with a pair of shod wheels beside it), another mounted upon an old stock with shod wheels with ladle and sponge: there is however one exception, a brass serpentine stocked and mounted upon a capstan (some form of turntable) with ladle and sponge. All but one of the casemate serpentines is specified as being 'with mytch and forloke', i.e. swivelled, if our conjecture above (p. 000) is correct, in some cases stocked with mitch and forelock. One serpentine, and the fowler, are simply inventoried as stocked and bound with iron. In two of the tower casemates there are trestles for the hagbuts ('A Trestell of wood to shot hagbusshes'): the towers in question contained four and five hagbuts respectively, suggesting that hagbuts were discharged successively from the same trestle.

The Duke of Norfolk was sent to the northern counties in March 1539[104] to take general direction of the seaboard and the castles there. At Berwick he was astonished to find the town and the castle so weak — he had last visited it 14 years before, just after its hasty refortification during the crises of Albany's Governorship — and in spite of shortage of money set 300 workmen to improve the defences.[105] Work seems to have gone on over the whole season — in October[106] the master of ordnance at Berwick sent the master mason to Cromwell to report the progress of the king's works there — and proceeded until at least 1542.

Much effort was doubtless expended in the ultimately hopeless task of piecemeal repairs to the walls: Stefan von Haschenperg was involved in the rebuilding of one special length.[107] In addition, a new tower on the White Wall may have been built to replace the earlier tower where the storm damage of 1532 had never been repaired. The tower which exists today, incorporating a postern, lies at the bottom of the sloping length of the White Wall. The sizes given in the 1532 x 5 survey show that the damaged White Wall tower then existing (and not armed in 1539) lay much further into the river — at low water mark — than the extant tower, which corresponds approximately to the position of the postern noted in the survey. 'The whyte wall tower' was armed in April 1545,[108] and I suggest that this is a new tower built in the interval, most likely in the period of activity between 1539 and 1542.

The casemated ground level of the White Wall tower has outward-splayed rectangular gunports, 320 mm. wide and 450 mm. high at the throat. The ports have sills 0.8 m. high, indicating that the guns were fired from an adjustable mounting of some kind, not lying on the floor. Although the casemates are still cramped they could accommodate pieces of 'serpentine' size. Two of the casemates effectively flank the curtain wall: the other commands the low-level approach to Berwick along the bank of the Tweed. The whole of the ground level is taken up by the vaulted casemates and a vaulted central passage forming a postern.

The first floor consists of a room with a fireplace (for the garrison or guard) from which open deep recesses with smaller gunports 190 mm. wide and 500 mm. high. The sills of these upper ports have rectangular chases sunk in them, above which have been set iron bars (subsequently torn out) which appear to have been intended to hold the pins of swivel-guns. All the gun positions at both levels have smoke-vents. Walls at the upper level, allowing for lost facework, have been about 3 m. thick.

The parapet above the timber-roofed first floor has been massive: again allowing for lost facework, about 1.8 m. thick and over 2 m. high — the parapet may have been exceptionally high to protect those within it from the high ground to north-north-west. In April 1545, the tower had at parapet level a (muzzle-loading) brass falcon 'with ladell and spunge', conjecturally mounted on a field carriage: this is presumably the original parapet armament. The casemated armament is not known: the swivel guns intended for these emplacements must have been fairly small.

Figure 56. Lord's Mount before excavation. Exterior robbed of facework, with gunport. Upper part demolished c.1560

More important, however, was a completely new fortification (fig. 56) at the north-east angle of the town enceinte, where the medieval Bell Tower stood with Richard Candishe's bulwark beyond it. The new work seems to have been designed with a high central turret to accommodate the day watch again, and for several years it was still called the Bell Tower. By 1564, however, the work had been renamed Lord's Mount, and the latter name will be used here from the beginning, for greater clarity. The purpose of Lord's Mount was to improve the defence of the north-east angle by a massively built structure in the latest fashion which would require less maintenance, and would require fewer men to guard it,[109] than Candishe's earthwork. The original plan had the rare distinction of having been devised by Henry VIII himself; though the royal engineer's ability is only cloudily illustrated by the surviving remains, for as we shall see Lord's Mount as built differed in unspecified ways from the design.

Much of Lord's Mount seems to have been built in 1541, though it had been begun when Norfolk returned to the north in March 1541.[110] It was either complete, or nearing completion, in the spring of 1542. In April of that year Henry VIII ordered the military engineer John Rogers to go to

Figure 57. Lord's Mount, interior of surviving lower level showing casemates during excavation

Berwick with Lord Lisle and others to view the fortifications in progress, as Rogers knew the plats. The party was disconcerted by what it found there.[111] Comparing the fortifications newly made with the plats devised by the king, they found that the works differed from the plats, and found also a difference of opinion between Thomas Gower, the controller of the works, and George Lawson, the master mason, of whom Rogers had a low opinion. By the date of the visit 20,000 marks had been spent. Lord Lisle, communicating this information to the Council, added that he had caused the master mason to draw a plat of the fortification now made at the Bell Tower which, with the plat devised by the king, would be sent up to London by John Rogers as soon as the latter had completed his business. No documents recall further proceedings in the matter, though Lawson appears to have escaped royal wrath for his initiatives, for he retained his offices until his death in 1543.

The debris-filled interior of Lord's Mount (fig. 57) was excavated by the author for the Department of the Environment in 1970-3. It was wrapped round the north-east angle of the town wall with its foundations below the level of the bottom of the Edward I ditch and thus well below the footings of the medieval works on the bank. In consequence, the medieval angle tower had to be completely demolished, and the ends of the north and east town walls had to be underpinned. The new work included at its core a polygon which may, by coincidence or intent, resemble the demolished angle tower. Conjecturally the polygon rose to some height above the main work so that it might serve as a vantage point for the day watch. The massive curved front of the bulwark, 32.5 m. in external diameter and subtending 245°, was 6 m. thick faced with large ashlar blocks. The lower level of the gun tower was externally indicated by a plinth; above the plinth were two roofed levels surmounted by a parapet. A ditch was dug around the work, its bottom corresponding to that of the Edwardian ditch.

The lower level (fig. 58) had six deep casemates with three-centred vaults opening externally to double-splayed gunports. Each casemate had small aumbries in the side walls, presumably expense magazines. The throats of the ports had detachable shutters. As revealed during the excavation, the sills of the gunports had been damaged, probably during later slighting, when the upper part of the work was demolished.[112] The sills were pierced by circular holes of about 40 mm. diameter, apparently corresponding to holes pierced in iron bars resting longitudinally on the sill and solidly built into the jambs. The bars had been torn out but their form and function were clear: they were rests for swivel guns (fig. 59). The floors of the casemates had also been altered.

The annular space between the central polygon and the frontal wall was sub-divided for use as a kitchen and for other accommodation. The flagged kitchen had a large fireplace, oven and well. There were two other rooms containing fireplaces with four-centred lintels. The ventilation of this level was helped by angled open shafts from the central polygon. The latter was roofed with timber and lead at the lower floor level and was, one must surmise, a shell pierced with apertures above, having a platform for the watch at the wallhead. The roofed ground floor of the central polygon may have been a magazine or may simply have been used for domestic storage. Entrances to the lower floor of the bulwark from the town were designed from its west and south-west extremities, piercing the ingoes of the casemates. From the first-floor level of the polygon a flight of wooden steps descended to the kitchen, and a flight of stone steps descended to the west compartment. From the latter opened a latrine contrived in the frontal wall.

There are only limited physical remains of the upper level of the gun-tower. It was separated from the lower level by a timber floor. A comparison with related Henrician works gives some insight into the probable nature of the upper level. It would contain the principal accommodation with the captain's lodging, with window embrasures that might be used as firing positions in time of need. The lost parapet

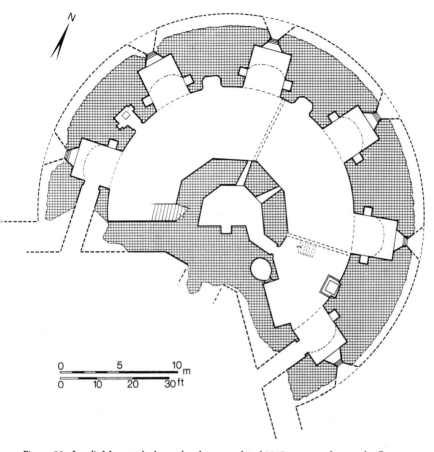

Figure 58. Lord's Mount, the lower level as completed 1542 or soon afterwards. Cross-hatching shows surviving parts of the work; heavy broken line shows the probable completion of the plan

probably had the heavy curvilinear profile deriving from early sixteenth-century Italian forms and the most common Henrician type. It would be embrasured for substantial pieces of artillery.

The armament of the guntower is evidenced by both documents and archaeology. An inventory of ordnance prepared by Thomas Gower and Archani in the spring of 1545 for the fortifications of Berwick in general[113] has the following entry for the Bell Tower:

> Item upon the bell tower a culveryne of brasse mounted upon her cariage with shoddwheles lymbers ladell and spunge.
> Item a saker of brasse mounted upon shoddwheles ladell and spunge.

Figure 59. Lord's Mount, throat of gunport showing position of iron bar for swivel pin, removed during c.1560 demolitions with consequent damage to jambs

Item in the bell tower benethe v porte peces of iron with — chambers apece stocked upon trockelle.
Item hagbusshes of irone viii.

The culverin and saker were therefore mounted at parapet level on field carriages of the kind frequently shown on contemporary illustrations. These medium-heavy long-range guns contrast with the forged-iron breech-loading port pieces beneath; the latter seem to have been stumpy guns of shorter range and larger bore, up to 255 mm. in the case of later examples. They might fire 'murthering shot' to repel close assault. The hagbuts would provide lighter support at shorter range — they might be used at first floor level. The inventory of 1545 was certainly not that intended originally as far as the port-piece mountings was concerned, for the trucks or truckles imply a primitive garrison carriage. Such a carriage would not work with the swivel holes in the sills of the embrasures.

Before considering the archaeological evidence of the shot of stone, iron and lead recovered during the excavation of 1970-3, we must take note of a later inventory of ordnance of 1547-8.[114] By that date an additional bastion-shaped work had been built out beyond Lord's Mount, its site approximating to that of Richard Candishe's demolished bulwark; hence presumably the additional guns. The inventory itemises at the Bell Tower:

    on the parapet: 1 brass cannon
                      1 brass culverin
                      2 iron falcons
    in casemates: 1 brass falconet
                      5 iron port pieces
                      6 double bases
                      8 hagbuts

How these were disposed does not really concern us here, though it is perhaps worth noting that a cannon (of what size is not specified) may possibly have replaced the saker on the wallhead of Lord's Mount.

The shot of stone, iron and lead recovered during the excavation seems to conform for the most part to the 1545 inventory, with one or two puzzles. The partial demolition of the gun tower took place circa 1560; it was then abandoned until the civil wars of the seventeenth century when, its fill of debris levelled and provided with an earthwork parapet, it was adapted as a battery. The shot recovered was stratigraphically sealed by destruction debris of c. 1560. Most straightforward are the culverin and saker, represented by iron shot of 89 mm. and 108 mm. respectively. Lead shot in groups of 48 mm. and 38 mm., and one specimen of 63 mm., are for the lesser armament of the 1547/8 inventory, though the smallest of the lead shot is too big for the eight hagbuts, which seem to be unrepresented in the finds. The 38 mm. shot may be for the falconet and the 63 mm. shot for the falcons, leaving the 48 mm. short for the double bases — a gun type of which we know very little save that it was one of the smaller natures.

The puzzles arise with the largest shot: disregarding a very irregular and presumably unfinished stone, there were an iron ball of 165 mm., several stone and iron shot varying between 216-219 mm., and two stone shot of 270 mm. The 165 mm. shot would be suitable for a demi-cannon; the 216-219 mm. shot, though a little large, may be suitable for a double cannon (the 1547 Inventory does not specify which). On the other hand some of these, and even the 270 mm. shot, may be for the port pieces. We have already noted that in their later development (where alone we have information on calibre) port pieces were very large — but 270 mm.

seems excessive, for this is approaching the size of a large bombard.

While the report of 1542 indicates that the design of Lord's Mount was in some way flawed in execution, the deviations from Henry's scheme cannot now be identified, though the swivelled casemate armament, soon to be replaced by port pieces on truck carriages, may possibly represent a divergence of detail.

The first armament sketch of Lord's Mount (fig. 60) shows a culverin above a gun of serpentine size on a swivelled trestle mount below. The second and third sketches (figs. 61, 62) show two possible truck mountings for the port pieces. Fig. 61 shows the floor level unchanged; fig. 62 interprets the not-quite-conclusive evidence of two steps at the opening of each casemate as evidence for the raising of the floor within: thus raising it to a height more suitable for a four-wheeled carriage.

4. Envoi

The events in the three decades which have been sketched belong to an interim period of development in the history of artillery fortification in Britain. For a period of 60 years before, some provision had already been made for the emplacement of gunpowder weapons in Scotland, and for much longer in England. We are able to set this interim period of development against contemporary events in Italy, where the evolution of systematic fortification using the pointed angle bastion was sufficiently advanced by 1527 to produce da San Gallo's *Fortezza da Basso* at Florence. It must be said at the outset, however, that while there may have been indistinct glimpses of *la nuova fortificazione* available to a well-informed man producing works of military engineering during our selected period, no convincing imitation appears in Britain until 1544/5. None appears in the places which have been noticed above, although those particularly described were fortifications considered with great respect by contemporaries, and works which one would expect to conform to the latest ideas current on defence insofar as means or time allowed.

Our awareness of the background, which was to metamorphose fortification through Europe and the Europeanised world, may blunt our recognition of what is going on in the foreground. The improved defences of Berwick as they existed in late 1523, though we may visualise them only indistinctly, represent not the least remarkable development. Their provisions for defence by and against artillery do not seem to have been part of a single scheme, and most of their features were improvisations. The resultant whole had major defects — the prototype flankers, for example, were nowhere articulated with the bulwarks. Yet Berwick in 1523 provided, as it were, a kit of parts for the fully articulated systems

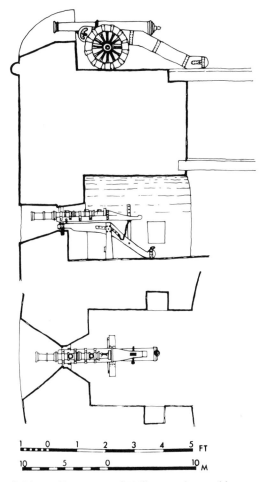

Figure 60. Lord's Mount. Figs 60, 61 and 62 illustrate the possible parapet and casemate armament in three different permutations of the documentary and structural evidence. All three have a restored section of the parapet and a casemate and a plan of a casemate.

Fig 60: as apparently intended by George Forman, master mason of Berwick. On the parapet, a culverin on a heavy carriage with shod wheels. In the casemate, a stocked forged-iron breech-loader (? a *serpentine*) similar to the weapons shown in figs 43 and 50, on a swivel mounting

which later emerged under Italian influence: walls of moderate height reinforced with earthwork, through which ran tunnels to flanking emplacements scouring the ditch on either side, with advanced strongpoints placed at intervals.

The Dunbar blockhouse illustrates different elements in the complex pattern of change. It introduced new and enduring standards of defensive

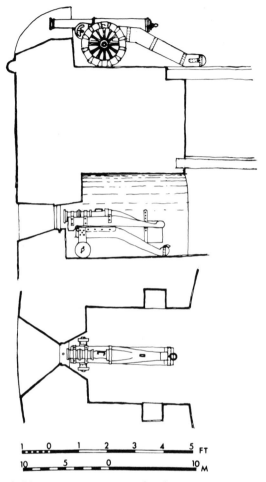

Figure 61. Lord's Mount: an attempt to visualise the armament as inventoried in 1545 assuming no raising of the casemate floor. On the parapet, a culverin as in fig 60. In the casemate, a forged-iron breech-loading port piece on a high mounting with two trucks

strength in the massiveness of its construction, and in its generous provision for emplaced artillery, especially at the level of its stout parapet. Yet the blockhouse was in some ways idiosyncratic because of the site and its function, and its importance is in general terms only. Its site, a tower-like crag, most probably conditioned the precocious low profile and the angle-bastion-shaped plan. Its function as an advanced redoubt meant that there was no need to articulate it into an overall system of defence. Moreover, beyond generalities, its detail of tunnel-like loops piercing greatly thickened walls had an influence extending over little

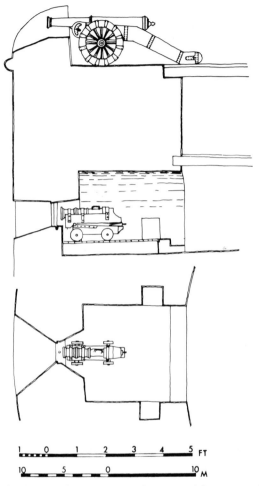

Figure 62. Lord's Mount: as fig 61, assuming the raising of the casemate floor by two steps. On the parapet, a culverin as before. In the casemate, a port piece as in fig 61 on a primitive garrison carriage with four trucks

more than a generation. The combination reappeared at Blackness and Tantallon; then finally, beyond the period of our present study, in the surviving gunhole built at Edinburgh Castle north of David's Tower in 1546,[115] apparently as part of the Forewall (of a scale generous enough to be armed with four cannon and two gros culverins[116]) begun two years before.[117] The gunhole type survived, but suffering a sea-change, widely used in slighter works and buildings of far less defensive capability.[118] Wall thickness was reduced in the scarps of subsequent Italianate bastioned works with their generous earthen backing. The scarp of Sir

Richard Lee's 1558 Berwick system was about 3.35 m. thick at the base above the foundation; by that date the scarp wall was further stabilised, and bound to the earthwork behind, by substantial internal buttresses or counterforts.[119]

In terms of overall strength, though not of detail, Lord's Mount may be compared to the Dunbar blockhouse: of about the same size, with walls of about the same thickness, heavily armed on two levels. The origins of the two are clearly different. Dürer's 1527 treatise on fortification with round *Pasteien*,[120] and von Haschenperg's involvement with Henry VIII's south coast castles and the citadel at Carlisle,[121] suggest Germanic influence for the 'round bastion' used so extensively in Henry's works. At the same time one must remember that circular plans were in the mainstream of European fortification generally, with low round towers continuing in the south of Italy until the 1540's. Lord's Mount is not very closely paralleled elsewhere in the large corpus of Henrician fortification. Its simple line and lack of a scarp gallery relate it more closely perhaps to a tower of the Carlisle citadel; there is certainly no near resemblance to Deal, Walmer or (from our limited knowledge) Sandown, the south coast castles supposedly devised by the king.

The value of earthwork was clearly recognised on both sides of the Border. The outstanding example of Berwick has been examined in detail. Cessford Castle is also a key example, where the vawmure gave a new degree of defensive capability to a medieval stronghold. A vawmure did not necessarily protect the whole masonry scarp: perhaps more usually, it protected only the lower and more vulnerable part of the scarp, acting as a substitute for an integral battered base. Such a low vawmure was raised around the Berwick enceinte, and around Lord's Mount, both probably after 1542. A secure interpretation of the principal earthwork at Tantallon will only be achieved with archaeological investigation, but superficial inspection suggests that it is a very early example of masonry added to earthwork to give stability.

There remain contradictions and uncertainties, besides experiments such as Craignethan. There is no outright rejection of high exposed walls, and there is no evidence of battered scarps save for the possible hint of a battered base at Dunbar. High and apparently vulnerable masonwork continued well beyond the limits of the present essay, one of the most remarkable examples being the post-1573 Half-Moon Battery at Edinburgh Castle. The stepped profile of the scarp of the Half-Moon gives it an appearance of durability, but the wall base is in places no more than 1.75 m. thick.[122] Yet both the Half-Moon and Blackness were being repaired as serious fortifications in the later seventeenth century. Here lack of resources — an important factor in any consideration of the art of defence — may be a contributory encouragement to conservatism.

Figure 63. The Siege of Edinburgh, 1573, showing the Italian-designed flanked 'bulwark' or 'spur' of 1547-50; a variation of the theme shown also at Eyemouth of a central flanked bastion to defend a narrow front (from Holinshed's *Chronicles*)

The artillery that had been developed by the early sixteenth century changed hardly at all during the course of our survey — and, as far as cast-bronze pieces were concerned, was to change only by gradual refinement long after its conclusion. The challenge which it represented was

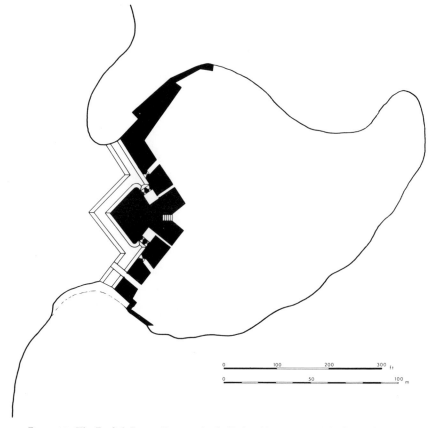

Figure 64. The English Fort at Eyemouth, Sir Richard Lee 1547-48. The faces of the central Italianate bastion are protected by casemates in the rampart. Plan at ground level based on Belvoir MSS, MSS letters etc, ii, folios 58-59

met by the general adoption of the Italianate angle bastion. Within our region, the next chapter of the story sees the appearance of bastioned systems during the Anglo-Scottish war of 1547-50. Among the earliest works were variations of a single flanked bastion at Edinburgh Castle and Eyemouth (figs. 63, 64). The first, the 'fort of the castle hill', was devised by an unknown Italian for the Scots; the second was devised by Thomas Petit for the invading English army under Protector Somerset. A norm thereafter existed for major fortification against which future achievement might be set. The new and expensive mode was often put aside in favour of obsolescent concepts, especially in Scotland where there were problems of intractable sites as well as of cost, but the period of transition in reaching a commonly agreed desirable solution had come to an end.

NOTES

1. *Treasurer Accts.* [*TA*], i, p. lxxxiii, 323 ff; ii, p. lxxxii.
2. Fig. 42 is based on a survey of Dunbar Castle made by the Royal Commision on the Ancient and Historical Monuments of Scotland for the National Monuments Record. I am grateful to NMR for permission to reproduce this, and the similarly based plan of the blockhouse which appears as fig. 47.
3. *TA*, i, 334.
4. H. L. Blackmore, *The Armouries of the Tower of London* (London, 1976), s.v. 'Serpentine' and Inventory items. A normal bore for English serpentines in 1497 may have been about 80 mm. (firing 5 lb. iron shot): H. R. Schubert, *History of the British Iron and Steel Industry* (London, 1957), 162. Cast-iron guns are rare throughout the span of this paper: H. R. Schubert, 'The first cast-iron cannon made in England', *Journal of the Iron and Steel Institute*, cxlvi (1942), 131-40.
5. C. Gaier, 'The origins of Mons Meg', *Journ. Arms & Armour Soc.*, v (1967), 425-52.
6. *Henry VIII Letters & Papers* [*L & P*], i, no. 1494; and see below, p. 102.
7. James IV's cannon taken by the English at Flodden were equated by their captors with 'great curtalles': D. Laing, 'A contemporary account of the battle of Flodden', *Proc. Soc. Antiq. Scot.* [*PSAS*], vii (1866-8), 146. In 1497 34 lb. iron shot was supplied for 'demi-curtows', implying a bore similar to that of a cannon/demi-cannon, i.e. about 170 mm: Schubert, *History of Iron Industry*, 102; Blackmore, *Armouries of the Tower*, s.v. 'Curtow' and Inventory items indicate even larger guns bearing the name.
8. These figures are based on those for one of the guns raised from the wreck of Henry VIII's *Mary Rose*, identified as an English sling, possibly comparable to the slangis in use in Scotland. There were slings in the English royal collection in 1514 over 6.1 m. long. See L. G. C. Laughton, 'Early Tudor Ship Guns', *Mariners' Mirror* (Nov. 1960), 275-8; also Blackmore, *Armouries of the Tower*, s.v. 'sling'.
9. *Papers relating to the Navy during the Spanish War 1585-87*, ed. J. S. Corbett, *Navy Records Soc.*, xi (1898), 318.
10. Cutthrot is a Scottish gun name for which there is no identifiable direct equivalent in other languages, although those captured at Solway Moss were equated by the English with basses: *Hamilton Papers*, i, p. lxiii.
11. F. Deuchler, *Die Burgunderbeute* (Bern, 1963), 302-38.
12. Blackmore, *Armouries of the Tower*, s.v. 'Mitch', and below, p. 134.
13. Fordun, *Scotichronicon*, lib. xvi, c. 17: quoted *TA*, i, p. ccxxi.
14. R. Ward, *Animadversions of Warre* (1639): quoted Blackmore, *Armouries of the Tower*, 224.
15. E.g. Blackmore, *Armouries of the Tower*, cat. nos. 29, 31.
16. Ibid., nos. 30, 34.
17. Ibid., no. 27.
18. D. H. Caldwell, 'A hagbut of crok from Carr, County Armagh', *Ulster Journ. Archaeol.*, xxxix (1976), 53-55.
19. Blackmore, *Armouries of the Tower*, cat. no. 178.
20. Schubert, 'The first cast-iron cannon'.
21. *TA*, iii, 203.
22. *TA*, iv, 515-17; Laing, 'The battle of Flodden', 146.
23. For longevity, Blackmore, *Armouries of the Tower*, s.v. 'Base', 'Fowler', 'Port Piece', 'Sling'.
24. See p. 133 and the list of cannon emplaced at Edinburgh Castle in 1566: *Wardrobe Inventories*, 166 ff.
25. *Hist. MSS. Comm.*, 9th report (1883), appendix, 193.

26. On Threave, C. J. Tabraham's article in this volume; on Ravenscraig, W. D. Simpson, *Ravenscraig Castle* (Aberdeen, 1938).
27. *Inventory of Stirlingshire* (Roy. Comm. Anc. & Hist. Monuments Scot., 1963), i, 193-6.
28. Reproduced ibid., i, pl. 57.
29. *Inventory of Roxburghshire* (Roy. Comm. Anc. & Hist. Monuments Scot., 1956), i, 128-31.
30. F. di G. Martini, *Trattato di architettura*, ed. C. Promis (Torino, 1841).
31. *L & P*, i, no. 1494 (57).
32. Public Record Office: E101/60/3.
33. The use of the name 'Bell Tower' for two different towers at different periods has caused confusion. Hereafter the name is used exclusively for the tower at the north-east angle of the town walls.
34. PRO, E36/254: quoted in the calendar entry *L & P*, iii, part 2, no. 2436.
35. PRO, E36/173 published in *Archaeologia Aeliana*, i (1857), 87-94. On evidence for the date of this paper, ascribed in *L & P* to early 1539, see p. 126-7 and n. 93.
36. PRO, E101/483/12.
37. From E36/173; outline plan of towers in Cecil Papers (at Hatfield House), Maps i, 25.
38. PRO, E101/60/3 and SP1/200 (of 1545).
39. *L & P*, v, no. 1630.
40. PRO, SP1/200.
41. C. H. Hunter Blair & H. L. Honeyman, *Norham Castle* (HMSO, London, 1966), 12.
42. *Acts of Council (Public Affairs) [ADCP]*, 7
43. Ibid., 11.
44. *Inventory of Edinburgh* (Roy. Comm. Anc. & Hist. Monuments Scot., 1951), 120-1.
45. Hunter Blair & Honeyman, *Norham Castle*, 9, 17-19.
46. Martini, *Trattato di architettura*. In plan-form and scale they also resemble a work east of the Byward Tower at the Tower of London: *History of the King's Works*, ed. H. M. Colvin (London, 1963), i/ii Plans, plan no. 2.
47. S. & N Buck, *The south-east view of Norham Castle.*
48. *L & P*, I, ii, no. 2709.
49. *ADCP*, 27.
50. Pitscottie, *Historie*, i, 288.
51. J. R. Kenyon, 'Wark Castle and its artillery defences in the reign of Henry VIII', *Post-Med. Archaeol.*, xi (1977), 50-52, for this and the immediately following references.
52. *TA*, v, 161-2.
53. *L & P*, III, ii, no. 1976.
54. Ibid., no. 3039.
55. British Library, *BM Add.* 24965, fo. 161.
56. Pitscottie, *Historie*, i, 303.
57. *L & P*, III, ii, no. 3114.
58. *ADCP*, 173.
59. Examples may conveniently be seen in B. M. Morley, *Henry VIII and the development of coastal defence* (London, 1976). Also e.g. Belvoir MSS, MSS letters etc., ii, fos. 56-57, being the plan of Thomas Petit's 1548 fort at Lauder, Berwickshire.
60. PRO, SP1/200.
61. *Wardrobe Inventories*, 166 ff.
62. *L & P*, XX, i, no. 280.
63. SP/1200: see p. 140.
64. *L & P*, iii, no. 2532. Mr Fraser, of the School of Scottish Studies, has kindly advised me that the most likely identification of *Solame/Solem* Chapel is Smailholm.

65. *L & P*, iii, no. 1949. It is no more than a vague hint. A meeting was proposed by Albany writing from Dunbar, and Dacre accepted the proposal, but the location of the meeting is not given. It is, however, the best hint we have. Dacre's copious correspondence gives no indication of a possible visit later, when the state of Anglo-Scottish relations was anyway less propitious for an invitation to enter the Governor's stronghold.

66. The identification of the blockhouse with Albany's work has already been made, by merely following Pitscottie, in *Inventory of East Lothian (RCAHMS*, 1924), 27.

67. *L & P*, III, ii, no. 3403.

68. Ibid., nos. 3445, 3365.

69. Ibid., no. 1976.

70. Named in PRO, E36/254; described E36/173.

71. E36/254.

72. This and the following detail from PRO, E36/173.

73. PRO, E101/60/3.

74. PRO, E36/173.

75. Ibid., 'mayd of erth and duffet [turf] . . . and is now sore waisted and decayed, and verray nedfull to be repayred'.

76. The following description from E36/173.

77. *Inventory of East Lothian*, 61-67.

78. Archaeological excavation would be necessary before the sequence of construction of the earthwork could be determined.

79. S. H. Cruden, *The Scottish Castle* (Edinburgh, 1960), 313; J. G. Dunbar, *The Historic Architecture of Scotland* (London, 1966), 57-58.

80. *ADCP*, 285. I am indebted to Mr D. H. Caldwell for the following analysis of the siege.

81. *ADCP*, 285.

82. Pitscottie, *Historie*, i, 331.

83. *ADCP*. 285.

84. Ibid., 285.

85. The host was summoned to muster aι Edinburgh on 20 Oct. (*ADCP*, 284). The siege was apparently over before 14 Nov. when Magnus reported on its failure to Cardinal Wolsey (*L & P*, IV, ii, no. 4924).

86. Pitscottie, *Historie*, i, 330-3.

87. I. MacIvor, 'Craignethan Castle, Lanarkshire: an experiment in artillery fortification', *Ancient Monuments and their Interpretation*, ed. M. R. Apted & R. Gilyard-Beer (London, 1977), 239-62.

88. *L & P*, v, no. 832.

89. *L & P*, v, no. 1630.

90. *L & P*, vi, no. 37. *L & P*, vii, no. 85(2) dates a copy of this letter to 1537. The later date cannot be correct: see n. 93.

91. PRO, E36/173 (n. 35 above).

92. *L & P*, XIV, i, no. 187.

93. The survey refers to the storm damage at the White Wall Tower, giving a *terminus post quem* of 1532. It also refers to the walls east and south of St Mary Gate as badly decayed, with several makeshift patches of stone and black earth, and parts of the two lengths 'lyke to fawll to the grounde within breve tyme'. In 1535 walls are being rebuilt east and south of St Mary Gate (*L & P*, ix, no. 637). Since E36/173 mentions new walls where they exist, it seems inescapable that the survey was made before the 1535 repairs.

94. *Accts. Masters of Works*, p. xxxiv.

95. The following analysis of the first period of the reinforcement of Blackness Castle substantially modifies the account in *Inventory of West Lothian* (RCAHMS, 1929), 192-6.

96. *ADCP*, 453.

97. *TA*, vii, 91.

98. Ibid., 302.

99. Ibid., viii, 73.

100. *L & P*, XVIII, i, no. 897.

101. *Accts. Masters of Works*, 198, etc.

102. *Hamilton Papers*, ii, 169.

103. PRO, E101/60/3. This important source has been cited already.

104. *L & P*, XIV, i, p. xvi.

105. Ibid., no. 625.

106. Ibid., no. 674.

107. Ibid., XXI, ii, 462.

108. PRO, SP1/200.

109. *L & P*, xvi, no. 650.

110. Ibid.

111. Ibid., xvii, no. 318.

112. The date of the slighting is unrecorded, but may be presumed to have taken place in about 1558 in order to reduce a point of vantage from which Sir Richard Lee's newly begun bastioned enceinte, cutting off the castle and northern part of the town, might be vulnerable. In April 1558 (*Cal. State Papers Dom. 1601-1603* [*with Addenda 1547-1565*], 474-5, no. 89) permission was given to take down the inside of the castle to a convenient height to prevent its hurting the defence of the realm: it is reasonable to think that Lord's Mount, which represented a greater threat to the new works than the castle did, would be seen in a similar light.

113. PRO, SP1/200.

114. Society of Antiquaries of London, MS 129, fos. 347-59. Mr J. R. Kenyon was kind enough to draw my attention to this document.

115. *TA*, viii, 463: 'for 1x peces of stanis to the goun holl in the castell'. The entry confirms 'gunhole' as Scottish usage for artillery apertures of this type. The gunhole is shown (though in a survey that requires correction) in *Inventory of Edinburgh*, 16, fig. 69.

116. The armament in 1566: *Wardrobe Inventories*, 166.

117. *TA*, viii, 305.

118. S. H. Cruden, *The Scottish Castle*, 218-24.

119. I. MacIvor, 'The Elizabethan fortifications of Berwick-upon-Tweed', *Antiquaries Journ.*, XLV (1965), 67-70.

120. A. Dürer, *Etliche underricht zu befestigung der Stett . . .* (Nurnberg, 1527).

121. B. H. St J. O'Neil, 'Stefan von Haschenperg, an Engineer to King Henry VIII, and his Work', *Archaeologia*, xci (1945), 140 ff.

122. *Inventory of Edinburgh*, 16, fig. 69.

7 The Early Basket-Hilt in Britain
Claude Blair

1. Introduction

The problem of the origin of the distinctive form of basket-hilted sword
used by the Scottish Highlander — the 'claymore'[1] of Scottish official
military terminology — is one that has exercised students of arms and
armour for nearly a century. During this period two main theories have
been put forward. The earlier one, apparently first promulgated openly
in 1890, both by the authors of *Scottish National Memorials* and by
Maurice Maindron, is that it derived from the schiavona, the basket-
hilted sword carried by the Dalmatian troops in the service of the
Venetian Republic.[2] This does not seem to have been based on any
stronger evidence than a superficial similarity between the two forms
that is, in fact, common to most basket-hilted swords, coupled with a
belief, certainly mistaken, that the schiavona basket-guard developed at
an earlier date than did the Scottish one. The validity of the theory was
questioned as early as 1899 by Lord Archibald Campbell, and subsequently by a number of other writers.[3] Nevertheless, it still appears to
enjoy a fairly wide acceptance on the Continent.

The second theory was put forward by Mr Holgar Jacobsen of
Denmark in an article published in 1940[4] in which he carefully analysed
the construction of a wide variety of different types of basket-hilt. One
result of this was to establish that there are major constructional differences between the Scottish basket-hilt and that of the schiavona which
make it improbable in the extreme that there could be any direct connection between them (see below, pp. 189-90). Mr Jacobsen pointed out,
however, that there do appear to be similarities between the Scottish hilt
and one of the forms found on the late-sixteenth century German curved
sword, now usually known as a Sinclair sabre *(Sinclairsäbel)*, of which
very large numbers survive in Norway. He therefore suggested tentatively that it was here that the prototype of the Scottish hilt was to be
sought. This theory, which Charles E. Whitelaw, the leading authority of
his day on Scottish weapons, had hinted at as early as 1902,[5] is probably
the one to which most informed modern students would subscribe.

Proponents of both the theories outlined above apparently take it for
granted that the Scottish hilt-form must derive from a Continental pro-

totype. Mr Jacobsen did, however, include the comment in his article: 'of course there always remains the possibility that this basket may have developed on English soil from primitive types unknown to the author'.[6] More recently, Dr Heribert Seitz, discussing the schiavona theory in his *Blankwaffen*,[7] has pointed out that there appears to be earlier evidence for the use of basket-hilts in Scotland than for the existence of the fully developed schiavona guard, though he very properly adds that this does not necessarily mean that the Scottish form is the older of the two. In fact, as Dr Seitz makes clear, both here and elsewhere in his book, we know so little at present about the origins, dating and development of the different forms of early basket-hilt that it is manifestly absurd to try to find international links between them. Before this can be done, an adequate number of individual studies of the different hilt-types within the areas where they chiefly occur must be made available, and work on these lines has hardly begun. The main reason for this lack of basic published material is undoubtedly the scarcity of evidence for the firm dating of any of the hilt-constructions. That this should be so is hardly surprising. The basket-hilt was almost exclusively a utilitarian military one, and examples therefore rarely bear any decoration that might provide a clue to date, appear in portraits, or are clearly identifiable in accounts and inventories. This is not to say that no evidence is available for the historical development of the early basket-hilted sword, and where the Scottish form is concerned, enough can be found to provide a very tentative and broad typology, as I hope to demonstrate.

Before going further it would be as well to define what is meant by the Scottish form of basket-guard.[8] This was, of course, subject to many variations of detail, but certain characteristics that appear to be common to all fully-developed examples can be identified. The guard (fig. 65) is frontally symmetrical in construction[9] and shaped approximately like a melon, more-or-less truncated at top and bottom, and scooped out at the back for the hand. Its basic construction is a framework of bars grouped to form a series, of pointed arches or pointed ovals, usually three, the longer axes of which — and this is important — run parallel to that of the blade. The upper points of the framework are set symmetrically round half, or rather more than half, the diameter of the pommel, and some examples are linked by a washer-like ring or half-ring formed in one with them; on others they merely touch the pommel, are fitted into slots or a groove in it, or are attached by screws. Two loop-shaped foreguards are usually, though not invariably, fitted to the front of the main guard over the base of the blade,[10] and there is also usually a short quillon at the rear.[11] The spaces within the basic framework are filled with other bars that are found arranged in a wide variety of shapes, among which saltires, either straight or curved, are very common. All the bars often incorporate small plates of varying sizes and shapes, sometimes decoratively pierced.

2. Documentary and pictorial evidence

The factors that make the study of all forms of the basket-hilt difficult apply as much, or more so, to the Scottish one. The earliest dateable ex-

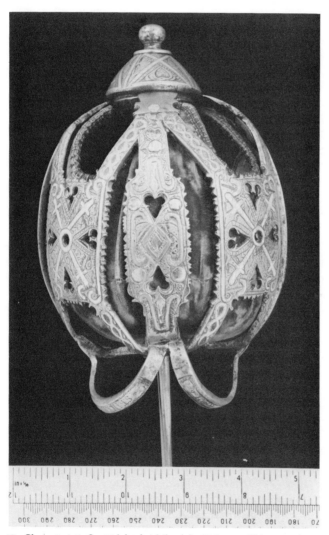

Figure 65. Characteristic Scottish basket hilt of the 18th cent. This example is signed by John Allan, senior of Stirling and dated 1716. *National Museum of Antiquities of Scotland* (MCR 1)

ample in a Scottish context so far identified is in a portrait of c. 1670, Joseph Michael Wright's well-known 'Highland Chieftain' in the Scottish National Portrait Gallery (fig. 66),[12] and is a so-called West Highland guard of the 'ribbon', 'snouted' or 'beak-nosed' type.[13] All known surviving basket-hilted swords of *proven* Scottish origin date from the same period or later. There can be no doubt, however, that the basket-hilt was in use in Scotland at least as early as the beginning of the seventeenth century, for in his account of a visit to Shetland, the Highlands and Orkney in c. 1617 the Reverend Richard James describes the arms of the Highlanders as comprising 'a long basket hilt swoarde, and a longe kinde of dagger broad in the backe and sharpe at ye pointe which they call a durcke; and longe bowe and arrowes with which they are verie expert'.[14] At what is thought to be approximately the same date, the anonymous author of the satirical song *Jocky will prove a Gentillman*, presumably an Englishman disgruntled at the favours lavished by James VI & I on his fellow Scots, included in it the following verse:

Thy sword at thy arse was a great black blade
With a great basket hilt of iron made;
But [now] a long rapier doth hang by his side,
And huffling doth this bonny Scot ride.
Bonny Scot, we all witness can
That England hath made thee a gentleman.[15]

Again, Arthur Wilson (ob. 1652) in his *Reign of James I*, published in 1653,[16] says in his account of the wooing in 1623 of Frances, Countess of Hertford, by Ludowick Stewart, Earl of Richmond and Duke of Lennox, albeit the lady's husband was alive at the time, that the Duke paid his addresses to her 'in such odd disguises' — odd, that is, to an Englishman unacquainted with the Highland dress — of which one was 'a blew Coat with a Basket-hilt sword'.

The evidence for the use of the basket-guard in Scotland before the beginning of the seventeenth century is more tenuous. What is usually regarded as the earliest reference to it is an entry of 1576 in the Inverness Burgh Records which mentions 'ane pair of Heland hiltis wyth the plwmet thairof . . . to be put on ane sourd bled'.[17] Contrary to the modern practice of using *hilt* as a collective term for the guard, grip and pommel of a sword or a dagger together, it is normally used in early texts to refer to the guard.[18] A 'pair of hiltes' originally meant what modern writers would call a 'pair of quillons', and it is possible therefore that the Inverness guard was no more than a simple cross intended for that very characteristic Highland weapon, the large, cruciform, two-hand claymore. Some support for this interpretation seems, at first sight, to be provided by the essay produced by James Robertson, Lorimer of Perth, for his admission into the local Hammermen's Guild on 28 May 1589:

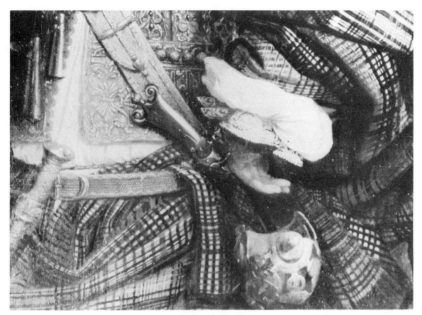

Figure 66. Detail of the hilt of the sword shown in J. M. Wright's 'Highland Chieftain' of c.1670. *Scottish National Portrait Gallery*

ane heland hilt with the plummet wrocht
be him with two pair ane handit soword gairdis
the ane of thame varnesit blak and the uther tynnit.[19]

Hammermen's essays, however, so often consisted of objects of widely disparate kind[20] that one cannot assume the consistency that would be implicit in the conclusion that because two of the guards were described as being for one-handed swords, the other, the 'heland hilt', must have been for a two-hand, or hand-and-a-half sword.

By the mid-sixteenth century, as already noted, the term *hilt* had come to be applied to any kind of guard, and the fact that it is given in the plural in the Inverness document, if of any special significance at all, may only mean that the one in question was equipped with a pair of quillons. As will be shown later, many early basket-hilts have quillons, so the problem of the precise meaning of 'ane pair of heland hiltis' in this particular document will probably never be resolved beyond doubt. Nevertheless, it is likely enough that it refers to a basket-guard, for there is evidence for the existence of a form of this that was regarded as specifically Highland at only a slightly later date. Richard James's description of the arms of the Highlanders indicates that the basket-guard was in general use among them in the early seventeenth century, and it is reasonable to assume that it was not then a recent innovation. It is likely, therefore, that the following entry, dated 30 September 1591, in the accounts of Alexander, Laird of Cawdor, refers to a basket-hilted sword:

> Item giffin for ane new skabart to your
> heland sowrd cutting and dressing and ane
> newe fische [i.e. fish-skin] hande, all . . . xxs.[21]

Some support for the suggested interpretation of the Inverness and Cawdor references is provided by the fact that more or less continuous usage of the terms *Highland sword* and *Highland hilt* (or *guard*) can be traced until long after the date when the two-hand claymore had been generally supplanted in the Highlands by the basket-hilted broadsword.[22] For example, the Edinburgh armourers' essay in 1649 was 'an mounted sword, with a new scabbard and an Highland gaurd', while the minute-books of the Glasgow Hammermen record the following essays:

> 4 September 1694: by John Rankine, 'Ane best sort of a hiland hilt and ane horsmans hilt two bard'.
> 17 August 1695: by Archibald Sympsone, 'ane mounted shable wt ane hieland hilt shorne'.
> 22 March 1711: by John Simpson the Younger, 'Ane broad Hieland sword with hilt and mounting yrof [thereof].[23]

Among these, the entry of 1695 is of special interest, for a shable was a type of sword with a curved blade[24] that could not possibly be connected with the two-hand claymore. But far more significant than this is the fact that in early seventeenth-century England, as will be shown later, the Scottish form of basket-hilt was apparently regarded as Gaelic in origin.

As will also be shown later (p. 162), the terms *close-hilt* and *basket-hilt* were synonymous in England in the early seventeenth century. It is probbable, therefore, that the 'ten ryding swordis wt. clois gairdis', in the inventory of the effects of Thomas Hislope, armourer of Edinburgh, drawn up after his death on 2 November 1600, were basket-hilted.[25]

The remaining piece of evidence for the use of the basket-hilt in Scotland in the last quarter of the sixteenth century is provided by a Flemish manuscript (No. 15662) in the Bibliothèque Royale in Brussels. This is described in the catalogue as 'Ouevre poétique de Willem de Gortter, surnommé Sombeke, membre de la Chambre de Rhétorique de Malines (DePeone). Illustré de nombreuses aquarelles réprésentant les costumes de l'armée des Pays-Bas de 1577 à 1583'.[26] Among the figures illustrated are four ensigns of the Scottish Brigade, shown in pairs on two plates, of which one pair are identified as Captains Blair and Gordon (fig. 67), and the others merely described as 'Scottish ensigns then in camp at Rijmenam' (fig. 68). All are dressed in normal Western European civilian costume of the time — in one case accompanied by a plate gorget — and three of them wear basket-hilted swords with straight blades, globular pommels and long quillons. The guards of the swords carried by the two anonymous ensigns are apparently formed of a trellis of vertical and horizontal bars, similar to those on some Sinclair-sabres, and the ends of the quillons are recurved. The constructional details of the guard of the other sword — worn by Captain Blair — are less clear, but it appears to consist of fairly wide vertical bars and straight quillons. None of the hilts show the foreguards that are characteristic of the developed form of Scottish guard.

The author of the manuscript, Willem De Gortter, was not born until 1585 and it is not known when he compiled it, though it was almost certainly completed before 1620. The accuracy of the details of costume and heraldry in the illustrations suggests, however, that they may be copies of lost originals made at the time of the events to which they relate.[27] Nevertheless, they clearly are not primary sources of evidence for the precise forms of the swords carried by the Scottish ensigns. They can, however, be regarded as providing a reasonably firm indication that some of their swords were equipped with basket-hilts of some kind.

One other sixteenth-century Scottish reference to what has been thought to be a basket-guard remains to be considered briefly before we examine the evidence for the early use of the hilt in England. In 1792 William Charles Little published an article on the Hammermen of Edinburgh in which he mentioned that 'in the year 1583, Robert Lyal being admitted a gairdmaker, wrought for his essay, a pair of clain skellit gairds, and ane pair ribbit gairds.'[28] There was once a not very clearly defined feeling among students of Scottish arms that a 'clain skellit' guard was likely to be a basket one, perhaps because 'skellit' sounds as though it might be a corruption of 'skeleton'! In fact, this is not so, for the original entry actually reads 'ane pair of clam schellit gairdis'[29] and must refer to the latest form of true claymore guard on which the cross is supplemented in the centre by a pair of iron shells, bent towards the hand, that together resemble a half-open clam.[30] If this interpretation is correct, the entry provides the earliest evidence for the existence of this type of guard yet discovered.[31]

The available English material for the study of the early basket-hilt is more extensive than the Scottish, though for the period before 1600 it is scanty enough. The term *basket-hilt* is first recorded in Shakespeare's *Henry IV, Part II*, of 1597, where in Doll Tearsheet's tirade against Pistol she calls him 'a basket-hilt stale juggeler' (II, iv, 141). In 1600 Samuel Rowlands mentions it in his *Letting of Humours Blood in the Head Veine* (V. 72),[32] while on 28 April, 1601 horse posted for service in Ireland were ordered by the Privy Council[33] to be armed with 'curattes, murryons, horsemen's staves and long pistoles, Turky swordes[34] with baskett-hiltes, and horsemen's coates'. Infantry on the same service were to be armed —

Figures 67-68. Scottish ensigns in the Low Countries, 1577-83. Fig 67 identified as Captains Blair and Gordon. Early 17th-cent. watercolours in MS 15662 in the *Bibliothèque royale, Brussels* (fols. 5r & 10r)

Schotsche vendrichs die te rijmelant van Laghen
oock vromelyck hún Lyf teghen Don ian waghen

presumably in addition to their muskets, calivers or pikes — 'onley with good swordes with baskett hiltes and Turky blades'.[35] Similar swords are mentioned in several subsequent orders of the Council concerning the same troops until their final departure for Ireland in 1602.[36] The Council's initial instructions of 26 June, 1600[37] for raising the troops says, however, that their swords are to be 'of Turkie blades and close hiltes, of which there hath bin verie ill choise made heeretofore . . .'. It would seem to follow from this that *close-hilt* and *basket-hilt* are synonymous,[38] and that the type of hilt to which they refer had already been in use in the English army for some time before 1600. Henceforth, both terms occur fairly frequently in written sources of all kinds, but, as none of those known to me establishes anything beyond the continued and widespread use of the hilt-form in England, no discussion of them is called for here.

Basket-hilt and *close-hilt* were almost certainly generic terms that could be applied to any form of basket-guard. A third term found in seventeenth-century texts, 'Irish hilt', appears, however, to have referred to a specific type that is of considerable importance in relation to the present study. The term is first recorded in the declared accounts of Sir Henry Lee as Master of the Armouries covering the period January 1601/2 — December 1610,[39] as follows:

> Also allowed . . . for money yssued paide and defrayed . . . for provicon of one thowsande swordes furnished sent into the Realme of Irelande for his Ma^{tes} service in that kingdome . . . allowed by force of his highnes warravnte vnder the privy seale dated the xth of November 1607 in the fifth yeare of his Ma^{tes} raigne . . .
>
> Armynge Swordes wth Irish hiltes ⎫
> furnish wth girdles and hangers m^{l} ⎬ Vc li
> at x^{s} the pece ⎭

After this date Irish hilts are mentioned not infrequently in accounts and military text-books until the middle of the century,[40] the latest reference known to me being in a contract of 1 April 1653 between the English Committee for the Ordnance and William Walker, in which the latter agrees to supply 1,000 new swords 'with stronge Irish Hilts and large for ye hand well ioyned over ye shoulder of ye Blade'.[41] Three references are of particular interest in that they show that the use of the Irish hilt was by no means confined to the plain munition swords carried by the ordinary troops. All come from the records of payments for weapons supplied by the royal sword-cutler Robert South of London, contained in the Wardrobe Accounts of King Charles I when Prince of

Wales,[42] and are as follows, the dates being those of the warrants authorising payment:

9 June 1618:
'More for a sword wth an Irish hilt, damaskt wth.
gold and wrought wth. silver   iij li xs'

20 June 1622:
'j Irishe hilte richlie damasked wth gold with a
broad blade and wyre handle   iiij li xs'

24 June 1622:
'one Irishe hilt richly damasked wth gold wth a
broad blade and wire handle   pr. iiij li xs'

Some indication of the form of the Irish hilt is provided by references in two military text-books. Edward Davis in his *The Art of War*, published in 1619, says that a pikeman should 'have a good back sword with an Irish basket hilt and hanged in a strong belt,[43] while Francis Markham's *Five Decades of Epistles of Warre*, published in 1622, contains the following passage about the arming of a musketeer:

He shall also have by his left side a good and sufficient Sword with a basket hilt of a nimble and round proportion after the manner of the Irish; strong Scabards of liquord or well rosend leather, Chapes of yron, and Girdles and Hangers suitable to the same; as for the Blade, it should be broad, strong, and somewhat massie of which the Turkie, or Bilboe are the best.[44]

It would seem to be clear from the evidence given above that the Irish hilt was a basket one of rounded form and that — in the period round about 1620 at least — it was fitted to swords used by the aristocracy as well as to plain munition swords. It was also sometimes elaborately decorated with gold damascening and might, in addition, be 'wrought with silver'. Among surviving English swords of the first half of the seventeenth century it is not difficult to find a series of hilts that fit these specifications exactly.

The best known of these swords is the one, now in the Metropolitan Museum of Art, New York (No. 49.163.6), that is believed to have belonged to Sir William Twysden, Bart. (1566-1629) of Roydon Hall, Kent.[45] This magnificent weapon (fig. 69) has a hemispherical basket-guard of almost classic 'Scottish' form. It is composed of curved flat-section bars arranged in three groups of three set in the same line as the blade and forged together to form a homogeneous whole. Each section is drawn together at the top into a short tongue attached to the pommel by a screw, and where the centre section touches the others on either side the two adjacent bars form a saltire-like feature with a disc-shaped centre; each of the remaining bars widens in the centre. At the front are two loop-shaped foreguards. The pommel is large and globular and equipped

Figure 69. Silver-encrusted hilt of the sword believed to have belonged to Sir William Twysden. English, c.1610-20. *Metropolitan Museum of Art, New York* (No. 49.163.6)

with a prominent button. The external surface of the guard and the pommel are heavily encrusted with chased silver designs in very high relief consisting of foliage involving winged terms, grotesque birds and animals, and masks, all against a granulated ground that bears trace of having been entirely gilt originally. The broad two-edged blade is grooved and pierced and is stamped with the letters NMMSSS.

A number of similar swords exist in collections in Britain, for example: the Tower of London Armouries;[46] the Victoria and Albert Museum;[47] Warwick Castle;[48] the Leicester Museum; Temple Newsam House, Leeds (traditionally that of the Parliamentary Commander Colonel John Lambert); the York Museum, York;[49] and Middle Claydon House, Buckinghamshire (fig. 70) (from the old Verney family armoury).[50] An example is also illustrated in a portrait of an unknown man of c. 1620-5, once called William Shakespeare (fig. 71), in the collection of Her Majesty the Queen,[51] and another, with long slender quillons, recurved at the tips, in a portrait of c. 1645, called Colonel John Booth, at Dunham Massey Hall, Cheshire (fig. 72).[52] None of the surviving swords is so elaborately decorated as the Twysden sword and only the Claydon one is in such good condition, but all have hilts that are basically of the same form and construction though there are minor variations in detail; and all known examples, except one that is entirely damascened with fine gold scrollwork,[53] are encrusted with designs in silver. Decoration of identical type is found on a whole series of swords with other forms of hilt which, in view of the number of examples surviving in Britain, the frequency with which they appear in early seventeenth-century English portraits, and their rarity on the Continent, must be regarded as English. They are too well known to require any discussion here, but attention must be drawn to one feature that is found on them very frequently, namely a large spherical pommel of the kind fitted to swords of the Twysden type.[54]

In addition to these decorated basket-hilted swords a number of plain military weapons with hilts of closely similar form can be found in the context of early seventeenth-century England — and also incidentally early seventeenth-century America[55] — though, as is commonly the case with the cheaper objects used in the past, they have survived in smaller numbers. Among places in England where examples are to be seen are: the Ashmolean Museum, Oxford;[56] the Wakefield Museum, Yorkshire (from the site of Sandal Castle) (fig. 73); the Preston Museum, Lancashire (found at Walton Flats in 1875); the Lewes Museum;[57] the Sheffield Museum; the Chepstow Museum; Audley End, Essex; and Bardwell Church, Suffolk (fig. 74).[58] Another was once in the museum at Basing House, Hampshire but was stolen a few years ago (fig. 75).[59] All have guards of similar construction to that of the Twysden sword but

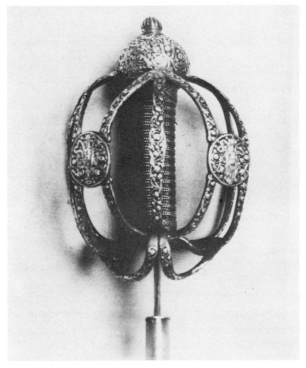

Figure 70.   Silver-encrusted sword hilt, English, c.1620-25. *Middle Claydon House*

made of thinner bars and in some instances either without attachment screws on the pommel or with merely a single one holding the top of the centre section. The pommels are globular, with the exception of that on the Bardwell sword which is bun-shaped,[60] but rather smaller than those on swords of the Twysden group.

The Basing House and Sandal Castle swords are of particular interest in that they can be dated to before 1645 and 1646 respectively, the years in which the buildings on whose sites they were excavated were deliberately destroyed after being çaptured by Parliamentary forces.[61] A sword of the same type is also depicted in Sir Peter Lely's portrait of General Sir Edward Massey (c. 1619-74), now in the National Gallery of Canada, Ottawa, which is believed to have been painted in about 1651 (fig. 76).[62] Despite their similarity to the Twysden sword which, as we have seen, probably dates from about 1620, there is no reason to think that these swords were old-fashioned in the mid-seventeenth century. They well illustrate one of the major difficulties encountered in the study of the

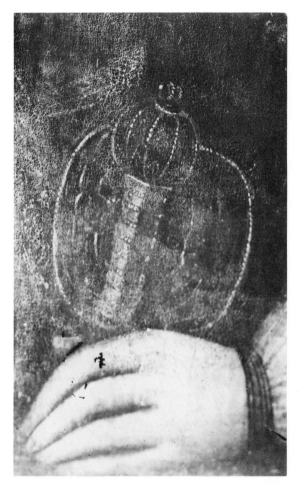

Figure 71. Detail of a portrait of an unknown man, English, c.1620-25. *Collection of Her Majesty the Queen*

basket-hilt, namely, the long periods during which particular forms remained in use with comparatively little change.

As will be shown later, a number of variations on the hilt-form described above are to be found, but no basket-hilt construction that differs from it fundamentally is recorded from a British context prior to the Civil Wars. In view of this, and in light of the evidence given above, it can hardly be doubted that it was this form that was known as an Irish hilt in the first half of the seventeenth century. We can therefore equate the Twysden group of swords with the entries in Prince Charles's Ward-

Figure 72.   Portrait called Col. John Booth, c. 1645. *Dunham Massey Hall, Cheshire.*

Figure 73. Sword excavated on the site of Sandal Castle (destroyed 1646). *Wakefield Museum*

robe Accounts and the Basing-Sandal group with those mentioned in the Privy Council orders and the Ordnance contract.

The reason why this particular type of hilt was called 'Irish' was not, as might at first seem likely, because it was the one used by English troops on service in Ireland. Francis Markham's instructions quoted above, that a musketeer should be armed with a basket-hilted sword 'after the manner of the Irish', make it clear that the hilt was regarded as being Irish

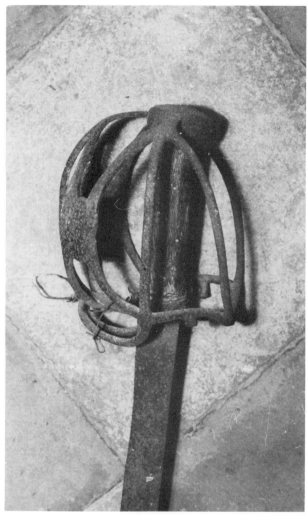

Figure 74. Sword, English, second quarter of 17th cent. *Bardwell Church*

in origin, but this does not necessarily mean that it was thought to originate in Ireland. From the Middle Ages until the eighteenth century the term 'Irish' was widely used in England and the Scottish Lowlands to refer to the Gaelic-speaking inhabitants of both Ireland and Scotland. One of its definitions in the *Oxford English Dictionary*, supported by a series of quotations from early texts, is 'Belonging to the Scottish Highlands or the Gaelic inhabitants of them. Obs.[olete]'. A similar definition, with supporting evidence from early Scottish texts, is given

Figure 75. Sword excavated on the site of Basing House (destroyed 1645). Present where-abouts unknown

under *Irische* in the *Dictionary of the Older Scottish Tongue*. An extract from one of these texts, *The History of the Church of Scotland* (London, 1665, 9) by John Spottiswood (ob. 1639), is worth quoting here:

We oft finde the Scots called Irishes,
like as we yet term commonly our Highlandmen,
in regard they speak the Irish language.

This dual significance of the term 'Irish' at the period with which we are concerned here of course presents a problem. Was the Irish hilt regarded in early seventeenth-century England as originating in Ireland or in the Scottish Highlands? The weight of the evidence is over-whelmingly in favour of the latter place. The studies of the late Professor

Figure 76.   Detail of a portrait of Sir Edward Massey by Lely, c.1651. *National Gallery of Canada, Ottawa*

G. H. Hayes-McCoy and others have shown that the characteristic sword of the inhabitants of Ireland in the sixteenth and early seventeenth centuries was a cross-hilted weapon of very distinctive outline.[63] No evidence has ever been adduced to suggest that any form of basket-hilt was native to the country, and I know of only three early examples found there,[64] and they could well have been brought into Ireland from outside. On the other hand, as I have already demonstrated, the basket-hilt was certainly in general use in the Scottish Highlands at the beginning of the seventeenth century and probably as early as the 1570s. There can be little doubt, therefore, that *Irish hilt* was the English term for what in Scotland was called a *Highland hilt*. That the form of guard to which the term was applied in England was regarded as originating in the Scottish Highlands as early as 1607 provides, as has already been noted, additional evidence in support of the view that the swords mentioned in 1576 in the Inverness Burgh records and 1591 in the Laird of Cawdor's accounts had basket hilts.

The first known reference to an Irish hilt is in the Privy Council order of 1607 mentioned above. But three earlier references to Irish swords have been noted in English documents. Two of these are in the Revels Accounts of King Edward VI in 1550/1 and 1553/4 and relate to theatrical performances, of which one was 'an Irisshe playe of the state of Ireland', that involved the making of 'an Irysshe sword' of wood.[65] The nature of the play makes it clear that the sword had nothing to do with the Scots-Irish, and it is very probable, therefore, that it and the other mentioned in the account were simple cross-hilted weapons.

On 15 March 1602/3 the London Cutlers' Company 'redelivered to Willm Griffyn his two Arminge swords and the Irrishe sworde', weapons that had apparently been impounded as not being up to standard.[66] This reference is more ambiguous and it is, of course, quite impossible to say whether it refers to a true Irish sword or to a Highland one. The fact that it dates from only four years before the period when we know that 'Irish hilt' was commonly used to denote a basket-guard seems, however, to make the second meaning the more probable one.

The fact that the term 'Irish hilt' is not recorded until after the accession of James VI to the English throne in 1603 suggests that the Scots who came with him were responsible for introducing the type of guard concerned to the English. Unfortunately, the matter does not seem to be quite so simple as that. The influx of Scots may well have led to its increased use, and to the spread of the term 'Irish hilt', but there can be no doubt that a basket-hilt of a form closely similar to that now usually called Scottish was known in England long before James succeeded Elizabeth I.

A sword equipped with what is perhaps an early form of basket-hilt is carried by one of the Yeomen of the Guard depicted in the left foreground of the well-known painting of the Field of Cloth of Gold of 1520 at Hampton Court Palace, discussed on pp. 202-3 below, but the rendering is too small and sketchy to permit absolutely certain identification. The earliest known certain evidence for the use of the basket-hilt in England is provided by a three-quarter length panel portrait in oil (fig. 77), by an unknown artist, showing a member of the royal bodyguard known as the Gentleman Pensioners[67] dressed in the costume of round

Figure 77. Portrait of a member of the Palmer family of Lemmington (probably William Palmer), c.1540. Formerly in the E. G. Spencer Churchill Collection

about 1540, and bearing the arms and crest of Palmer of Gloucestershire and Warwickshire.[68] The sitter has been identified as William Palmer of Lemington, near Todenham, Gloucestershire, since before 1784, when the picture was in the possession of the Delabere family at Southam-

Delabre in the same county.[69] William, who died in 1573, appears on the earliest recorded list of Gentlemen Pensioners, that of 1539, as 'Palmer of Glouc. sonne',[70] a description which suggests that his father had also been a Pensioner not very long before. There is a possibility, therefore, that the portrait may represent the father, John Palmer, also of Lemington, who died in 1553:[71] the absence of a label (indicating an eldest son) from the coat-of-arms might be regarded as evidence in favour of such an identification if we could be certain that the arms are precisely contemporary with the painting of the picture, which we cannot.[72] It has recently been suggested that the artist responsible for painting the portrait was the German Gerlach Flicke, who came to England c. 1545 and died there in 1558.[73] If this attribution could be substantiated it would, of course, make the identification of the sitter as William Palmer virtually certain and would also point to a date very early in Flicke's career in England, since the costume shown is of a kind that was already fashionable in the late 1530s, and was becoming obsolete by the time he arrived there.[74] Unfortunately, the attribution cannot be regarded as anything more than an educated guess, so, for our present purpose, we must be content with a dating of c. 1540 for the portrait.

Palmer is shown holding the polaxe of a Gentleman Pensioner in his right hand, while with his left he grasps the handle of a sword suspended on a girdle and hanger. The surface of the painting has unfortunately suffered damage, and the angle at which the artist has viewed the sword, almost directly from above, is not the best one for precise identification of the details of its hilt. Nevertheless, its general form and construction are clear enough. The pommel is a large oblate spheroid divided by ribs into segments and has a prominent spherical button. The visible portions of the guard comprise six slender bars, apparently circular in section, arranged in two groups, each of which consists of three bars that curve round the hand from the direction of the blade and converge into a triangular tongue that touches the pommel (fig. 78). One group forms the outside of the hilt and the other the front. No other details can be made out, but the arrangement of the bars on the guard — which perhaps included a third group on the inside — leaves no doubt that it is a basket one. The whole hilt — using the term in its modern sense — seems in fact to have been similar to those of the swords illustrated in figs. 104-11 which are discussed in more detail below.

Five other sixteenth-century illustrations of basket-hilted swords in an English context are recorded. In c. 1570 the Flemish artist Joris Hofnaegel painted a festive scene on the opposite bank of the Thames to the Tower of London. This picture, which is now usually called *A Fête at Bermondsey*, is preserved at Hatfield House[75] and shows, among a group of very small figures in the right foreground, a lady and gentleman followed by a

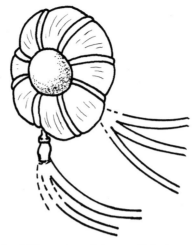

Figure 78. Drawing of the visible portions of the sword hilt shown in fig 77

Figure 79. Detail of J. Hofnaegel's 'Fête at Bermondsey', c.1570. *Hatfield House*

Figure 80. Drawing of the sword hilt in fig 79

servant who holds a sword by its blade with the hilt projecting backwards over his right shoulder (figs. 79, 80). A circular buckler hangs over
his back, apparently from the hilt of the sword. The guard is clearly a
basket one composed of diagonal bars and equipped with long quillons
and looped foreguard, but it is painted to such small scale that it is impossible to form any accurate idea of the details of its construction. A
very similar group of figures is the subject of a water-colour illustration
in a manuscript, *Théâtre de tous les peuples et Nations de la terre,* by
Lucas de Heere, another Flemish artist, who worked in England from
1567 to 1577, now preserved in the University Library at Ghent.[76]
Labelled *Gentilshommes Anglois,* it shows a lady and gentleman walking
along followed by a servant who carries a sword and circular shield in
the same manner as the figure in the Hatfield painting, but over his left
shoulder (fig. 81). The hilt of the sword is partly obscured by his hat, and
is drawn somewhat sketchily so that, apart from its large ovoidal fluted
pommel, the precise details of its form defy reconstruction. There seems
to be little doubt, however, that the guard is a basket one formed partly
of curved bars running on the outside of the hilt from the knuckle-bar
and across the line of the grip; other bars on the inside are visible through
the spaces between them. A long straight quillon (presumably one of a
pair) is shown at the junction of the guard and blade. It looks very much
like the hilt of a German sword at Abbotsford (fig. 82).[77]
     Another basket-hilted sword is depicted in a second watercolour illus-
tration by De Heere in his manuscript *Beschrijving der Britische Eilanden,* executed between 1567 and 1574, now in the British Library.[78] This
shows a group of two English peers, dressed respectively in Parliament

Figure 81. Detail of Lucas de Heere's *Gentilshommes Anglois*, 1567-77. *University Library, Ghent* (MS 2466)

and Garter robes, and a Yeoman of the Guard (fig. 83).[79] The last-named carries a halberd over his left shoulder and wears a basket-hilted sword hung from a diagonal girdle. The hilt is again partly obscured, this time by the Yeoman's trunk-hose, but the guard appears to be formed of two curved bars, running vertically to join the globular pommel, with the space between them filled by a curved saltire.

The fourth illustration is a woodcut in George Silver's *Paradoxes of Defence*[80] of 1599 showing a swordsman armed with a sword and dagger (fig. 84). The dagger has a simple cross-hilt, but the sword has a guard of longitudinal curved bars (of which three are visible), perhaps similar to those discussed on pp. 221-33 below, above a simple cross; the pommel, which is set above the guard, is globular, divided into longitudinal segments and fitted with a prominent button.

The remaining illustration, which is by far the most important of the five under discussion, occurs on a portrait of Edward Lyttleton of Longford, Shropshire (ob. 1592) in the possession of Lord Cobham at Hagley Hall, Worcestershire (fig. 85).[81] Lyttleton is shown three-quarter length wearing trunk-hose, a slashed and pinked doublet of buff leather with a high collar below a small ruff, matched by ruffs at the cuffs of the

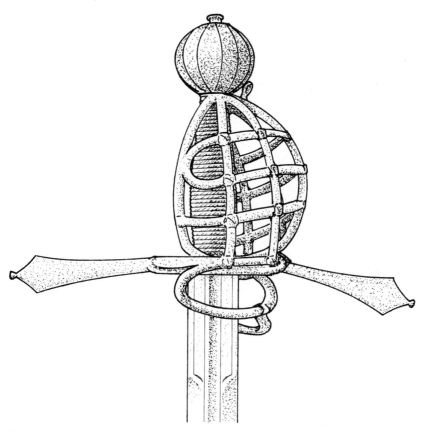

Figure 82. Sword, German, c.1570. *Sir Walter Scott Collection, Abbotsford*

close-fitting sleeves. Round his neck is wound a heavy gold chain incorporating two rectangular plaques, each enamelled or painted with what appears to be a human skeleton. Round his waist is a narrow girdle, with metal mounts, supporting a dagger on the right, of which only the large ovoidal pommel is visible projecting from behind his hip. It is divided into segments by broad longitudinal gilt bands and a narrow horizontal one, the visible segments being decorated, apparently in gold and silver damascening, with a hound and plants like Christmas trees. Suspended over his left thigh is a basket-hilted sword, its hilt tipped towards the front of his body at an angle of forty-five degrees and, unfortunately, cut across by the lower edge of the picture (figs. 86-87). The pommel is decorated *en suite* with that of the dagger, while the exterior of the guard is damascened with running foliage; the interior appears to be gilded. To the right of Lyttleton's head (left of the spectator) is a shield bearing the

Figure 83. A Yeoman of the Guard by Lucas de Heere, 1567-74. *British Library* (Add MS 28300)

elaborately quartered arms of Lyttleton, surmounted by a crested and mantled helm, above which is the date *AN.DNI.1568.* The third figure of the date has been tampered with, but the dress of the sitter is entirely characteristic of the period round about 1570, so the reading given can be accepted.

  The hilt of the sword is depicted clearly but, because of the artist's lack of understanding of perspective, is distorted, and, as already noted, is cut across by the lower edge of the picture. This means, in effect, that, when viewed as if held vertically with the point of the blade downwards, everything below a line drawn at approximately forty-five degrees through a point just above the centre of the quillon-block is obscured. Nevertheless, enough is visible to reveal quite clearly that, under the terms of the definition given on pp. 154-5 above, the hilt can be classi-fied as a fully-developed 'Scottish' one. The basket guard (fig. 87) is of

Figure 84. Woodcut from George Silver's *Paradoxes of Defence*, 1599

'scooped-out-melon' shape, and made of flat bars drawn together at the tops into a series of pointed arches with tongue-like apexes set round the centre of the large pommel, which is ovoidal in shape and equipped with a prominent button. The rim of the oval opening for the hand slopes down and away from the pommel and is formed of a single bar that also forms the rear edge of the rear arch on either side. Projecting from the bottom of the opening is a flat rear quillon, straight for about half its length and then bending at an angle towards the blade before widening into a small disc-shaped terminal ending in a small finial. The rear arch on the outside of the guard is bisected by a vertical bar, from the lower visible part of which two other short bars curve up to merge with the

Figure 85. Portrait of Edward Lyttleton of Longford, 1568. *Hagley Hall, Worcestershire*

sides of the arch: the result is that the upper part of the arch has the appearance of being filled with a pointed oval divided by a longitudinal bar. The lower rear part of this oval is linked to the hand-opening, under

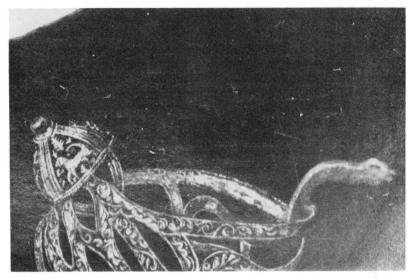

Figure 86. Detail of the sword hilt shown in fig 85

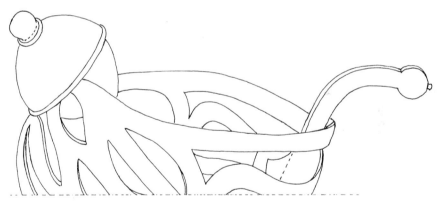

Figure 87. Drawing of fig 86

the rear quillon, by an S-shaped bar, while part of a corresponding bar can be seen on the inside of the hilt. There does not seem to be a corresponding oval feature, which suggests that the hilt may have been slightly asymmetrical, though the fact that this section of the guard is partly obscured by the bars on the outside makes its precise form uncertain. No further details of the construction of the guard are visible on the portrait, though it can be observed that the arrangement of the upper ends of the bars at the front of the outside of the hilt is consistent with their forming the top of a saltire-like feature. It should be mentioned also that most of the spaces between the bars in the guard are formed as narrow pointed ovals, sometimes flattened on one side.

The visible portions of the guard of the sword on the Lyttleton portrait are closely similar in construction — allowing for the distortion already noted — to the corresponding portions of the guard of a sword formerly in the collections of the Duke of Abercorn and Mr H. C. Haldane of Clark Hall, Wakefield, Yorkshire, and now in the National Museum of Antiquities of Scotland, Edinburgh (figs. 88, 89).[82] This is made of rather broader bars, has a pommel of different shape, is undecorated and has wider piercings, but its general outline is the same, as are also the shape of its rear quillon and the arrangement of the tops of the bars and the spaces between them at the front. In addition, the top of the rear arch contains a similar oval feature with a central bar, linked to the bottom of the hand-opening by an S-shaped bar. It seems very probable, therefore, that the concealed portions of the Lyttleton hilt were also of similar form to the corresponding parts of the Edinburgh hilt, and that a description of this last will more or less cover both.

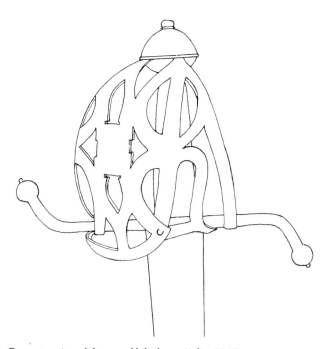

Figure 88. Reconstruction of the sword hilt shown in figs 85-87

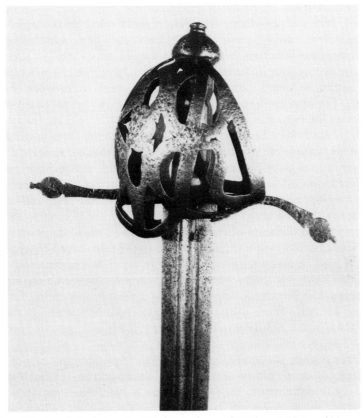

Figure 89. Sword, English or Scottish, late 16th or early 17th cent. *National Museum of Antiquities of Scotland* (LA [1966])

The guard of the Edinburgh sword is frontally symmetrical and is equipped with a forward quillon of the same outline as the rear one, but curved slightly upwards. The quillons together form a one-piece cross, threaded over the tang of the blade in the usual manner and originally made separately from the basket and then welded to it at two points. The construction represents two symmetrical halves linked at the front by what is, in effect, a knuckle guard, formed as a figure eight bisected by a vertical bar and curving up from the quillon to the pommel. On each side of this is a feature resembling a saltire, centring on a small rectangular plate with rounded corners and with inward curving arms, each pair of which, above and below, merge at the tips into a tongue-like prolongation. The upper tongue joins the pommel, and the lower one the centre of one of a pair of loop-shaped foreguards that flank, and curve below the rear half of the front quillon. The space between the saltire and the bar that forms the rim of the hand-opening is filled by a feature that can be likened to a slightly elongated figure eight divided by a longitudinal central bar, and with the rear half of its lower loop broken at the top and bent down to run horizontally and join the bottom of the hand-opening near the rear quillon, so forming the bottom edge of the guard behind the foreguards; the longitudinal central bar is prolonged to form one of these guards. The upper loop of the figure eight is, of course the 'oval feature' shown on the Lyttleton portrait, and the S-shaped bar that also appears on the portrait links the bottom of this to the tip of the hand-opening just above the bottom bar of the guard. The fact that this last is not visible in the portrait suggests that on the Lyttleton sword it may have merged with the S-shaped bar before joining the rim. Each of the two bars that form the bottom of the guard has a small tongue-shaped extension projecting towards the under side of the rear quillon, so protecting the gap between it and the sides of the basket. The pommel is equipped with a prominent button, and is shaped like two flattened rounded cones placed base to base. It is encircled by a groove in which the upper ends of the guard are held. The grip is of wood, spirally grooved for a wire binding (missing). The broad two-edge blade has a wide central gutter on each face of the forte flanked by narrower gutters, and containing the signature *ANDREA FERARA* in punched letters. Also stamped on each face of the blade is a half-moon mark.

As has already been noted, one of the major problems encountered in studying the development of the basket hilt arises from the fact that the same forms remained in use, virtually unchanged, for long periods. It would be unwise, therefore, to assume that the similarities between the Lyttleton and Edinburgh swords indicates that the latter must also date from the 1560s. The quillons, with their disc-shaped terminals, are, however, of a form found on swords down to about 1630 only,[83] and the guard is not likely to be much later than this. It can therefore be dated with reasonable confidence to within the period c. 1570-1630. The blade appears to be one of the many bearing the spurious signature of the sixteenth-century Italian smith Andrea dei Ferara produced in Solingen for export to Scotland, and is of a type that is usually dated to the seventeenth century.[84] In fact, it is not known when these spurious Andrea Ferara broadsword-blades were first made and we cannot say, therefore, that this example could not date from within the sixteenth century. On the other hand, it is possible that it is a later replacement for the blade originally fitted to the hilt.

The precise date of the guard of the Edinburgh sword is less significant to our present study than the light it throws on the construction of the hilt of the sword shown in the Lyttleton portrait. This would seem to establish beyond doubt that the fully-developed 'Scottish' basket guard was already in use in England by the 1560s and, in view of its complexity, it follows that it is likely to have started to evolve long before. The fact that Lyttleton was English does not, of course, mean that his sword must have been made in England, and he may well have acquired it in Scotland. The Edinburgh sword came originally from the collection — or more probably the armoury — of the Dukes of Abercorn, who belonged to the old Scottish family of Hamilton, which suggests that, it at least, may be Scottish. The Lyttleton sword and its accompanying dagger are, however, much more sophisticated products and the style of decoration is certainly not Scottish in inspiration. In fact, the damascening on the pommels of the two weapons, with its illustrations of hounds and Christmas-tree-like plants, is reminiscent of the work of the Spanish damascener Diego de Çaias and his presumed pupil Damianus de Nerve or Nerven.[85] The former is recorded as working for the French and English Courts respectively during the periods 1535-42 and 1542-c.1550. Nothing certain is known of his subsequent career, or of the career of de Nerve, who worked in a closely similar style, but a little evidence exists to suggest that one or both of them may have continued to work in Antwerp until the 1560s. It would be going too far to suggest that either artist had anything to do with the decoration of the hilts of the Lyttleton sword and dagger, and the affinity between it and their work cannot, on the evidence available, be regarded as anything more than an indication that the damascener responsible was strongly influenced by Continental styles. He may well have been a foreigner working in either England or Scotland, but so little is known about damascening in either country at this period that no useful comment can be made on this point.[86]

It would be interesting to know if Edward Lyttleton ever visited Scotland, and so had an opportunity to acquire the sword there, but, unfortunately, I have been unable to discover any detailed information about his career. He was nicknamed 'Long Edward', was the second son of John Lyttleton of Frankley, Worcestershire (ob. 1532) and was probably born in about 1522. He married Elizabeth Talbot (née Wrottesly) who had been the second wife of Sir John Talbot of Albrighton, Shropshire, and was buried at Albrighton on 28 September 1592.[87]

On 20 October 1591 Lyttleton made his will[88] and on 10 March 1591/2 he drew up an inventory of all his possessions at Longford (his home near Albrighton), including his armoury.[89] His swords and dagger are listed in this in a single entry:

Itm a sworde and a dagger a Rapier
and a dager and Armeinge sworde
a tohand sworde and ij bucklers
and ij sworde girdles of velvet and Lether

The sword and dagger shown in the portrait are perhaps the first two items in the entry, and also the ones — 'my sword and buckler and dagger' — he bequeathed to his servant Richard Howle. It is tantalising that both the inventory and the will should be so uninformative about these arms, and particularly so in view of the fact that both documents give short descriptions of some of his other possessions, including the distinctive neck-chain shown in the portrait.[90]

The Lyttleton portrait brings us to the end of this discussion of the recorded documentary and pictorial evidence relating to the early use of the basket-hilted sword in Britain. The conclusions to be drawn from this can be summarised as follows:

1. Basket-hilts were already in use in England as early as c. 1540, and had probably become fairly common there by the 1560s. By at least as early as c. 1600 they were in widespread use.
2. The 'Scottish' form of basket had already developed fully by the 1560s. The single piece of evidence for this — the Lyttleton portrait — provides only a firm *terminus ante quo* and, where the problem of the origin of the hilt is concerned, can only be regarded as showing that the form was known in England at this period.
3. In the early seventeenth century, if not before, the 'Scottish' form of basket was regarded in England as being of Highland Scots origin. The term used for it, 'Irish hilt', was almost certainly the English equivalent of the Scottish 'Highland hilt', first noted in 1576. There is thus good reason for thinking that the basket-guard was in use in Scotland by c. 1570 at the latest, though no absolutely certain evidence has been noted earlier than c. 1617.

3. Surviving basket-hilts

So far in this paper we have considered surviving basket-hilts only as sources for the interpretation of the documentary and pictorial evidence. We can now turn to a more general discussion of them and their possible typological development. It must be said at once that they add virtually no firmly-dateable evidence to that discussed in the earlier parts of this paper, and that theories about their typological development must be based almost exclusively on supposedly progressive variations in their construction and form. I say supposedly because we cannot at present be certain when variations *are* progressive and when they are merely manifestations of differences in individual taste or workshop methods, while it is only necessary to compare the hilts of the Civil War swords from Basing House and Sandal Castle with that on the Lyttleton portrait (figs. 73, 75, 88) to realise that greater complexity does not necessarily indicate later date. These remarks must be borne in mind when reading the remainder of this paper.

Before proceeding further, it would perhaps be as well to dispose of the theories that the Highland hilt — as I shall call it from now on for convenience — is derived from either the schiavona or the Sinclair sabre.

As was pointed out at the beginning of this paper, the theory about the schiavona goes back to the late nineteenth century. At this time it was thought that the fully-developed forms of schiavona hilt date from within the sixteenth century.[91] We now know that not only is there no evidence for so dating them, but that they were current in the eighteenth century, and almost certainly did not develop fully until well after 1600.[92] The original basis for the theory under discussion is therefore fallacious. Since it was first propounded, however, attention has been drawn to a few schiavone that may well date from within the sixteenth century. The most recent account of these, by L. G. Boccia and E. T. Coelho, ascribes them to the late sixteenth century, and states that the schiavona basket-guard was first developed at this period in the Veneto, probably in Belluno, though does not adduce any supporting evidence.[93] This is hardly surprising, for there does not, in fact, appear to be any firm evidence available at present for the dating of these swords: all that can really be said about them is that their guards are typologically much earlier than those, referred to at the beginning of this paragraph, from which our nineteenth-century predecessors suggested that the Highland guard developed, and later than the one 'schiavona' so far recorded which can be dated with some confidence to a period well within the sixteenth century. This is an excavated sword in the collection of the late Dr Giorgio Bini of Rome, which is known to me only from a drawing published by Dr Heribert Seitz in 1965.[94] It has long quillons, recurved horizontally, and a series of guards round the base of the blade that together form a simplified version of the corresponding guard on the developed schiavona hilt. A simple, flat, knuckle-bar extends from the pommel to the base of the forward quillon: the tip of this, where it meets, but is not fixed to, the pommel is linked by a diagonal bar on the outside of the hand to the middle of the rear quillon. The pommel, which is more or less shield-shaped, with a prominent boss on each face, resembles the pommels on a number of swords, dating apparently from the late fifteenth and early sixteenth centuries, in the Palazzo Ducale, Venice.[95] On the rather uncertain evidence of this resemblance the sword has been dated by Dr Seitz to the early sixteenth century, but there can be little doubt that this is much too early. The pommel is also very similar to those on some of the schiavone dated by Boccia and Coelho to the late sixteenth century, while the arrangement of the guards round the base of the blade is reminiscent of the corresponding guards on a group of Italian rapiers dating from the period c. 1540-80.[96] It seems likely, therefore, that the Bini sword should really be dated to the third quarter of the sixteenth century, and this view is confirmed by the representation of a sword with a closely-similar hilt, though a different pommel, in an Italian portrait of a knight of the Order of Santiago, dating from the third quarter of the sixteenth century, in the Gemäldegalerie, Berlin-Dahlem.[97] The evidence of the William Palmer portrait shows, however, that a fairly well-developed basket-hilt, different in design from the Bini one, and almost certainly of 'Highland' form, was already in use in Britain by c. 1540: the prototype schiavona hilt on the Bini sword, therefore, cannot possibly be regarded as being also the prototype of the Highland hilt.

Finally, before leaving the subject of the schiavona, Mr Holger Jacobsen's very pertinent comments on the constructional differences between its guard and that of the Highland hilt must be quoted: 'Typical of the finished Schiavona is, that the prevalent parts of the basket . . . all spring from the end of the crossbar like the crown of a palmtree, further, that nearly all the principal lines of the construction are *askew* on the axis of the blade, while they are *parallel* to it on the Scottish basket. One look on the diagrams [fig. 90 here] ought, really, to be enough to show the difference in construction and consequently the improbability of the theory, that one should have developed from the other.'[98]

The term *Sinclair sabre* (Norwegian *Sinclairsabler*) is often applied to a form of curved basket-hilted sword of which many examples occur in Scandinavia, and especially in Norway. According to a romantic tradition there, they were originally the weapons of a unit of Scots mercenaries, commanded by Colonel George Sinclair, which was virtually annihilated by Norwegian peasants at Kringelen in Gudbrandsdalen on 26 August 1612. The story of this unit is an authentic one[99] — though George Sinclair was only a Captain, and the unit was commanded by Lieutenant Colonel Alexander Ramsey — but nobody appears ever to have produced the slightest evidence to connect any 'Sinclair sabres' with it. In fact, as several writers, commencing with Mr Holger Jacobsen in 1934, have shown, these swords are found in Norway because they were part of the equipment of the local militia of that country, and most, if not all, of them were almost certainly imported from Germany and Austria as a result of the military reforms of Christian IV of Denmark and Norway (1588-1648). The name by which they were originally known was the German one *Tessak, Dussack* or *Dussäge,* and the earliest Norwegian document in which they have been noted is Christian IV's law of 1604 concerning the arming of the militia, which supplanted a law of 1276, though some may have been included among the unspecified arms purchased in Germany for Norwegian peasants in 1589.[100] The swords

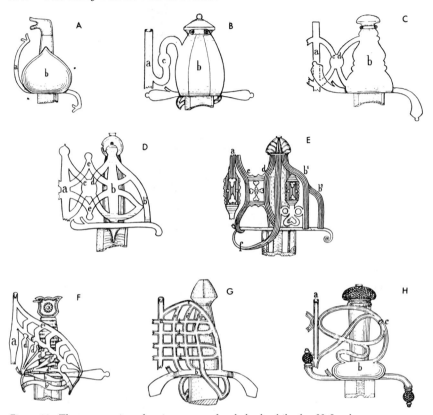

Figure 90. The construction of various types of early basket hilt after H. Jacobsen

were thus already in use in Norway some eight years at least, and perhaps much longer, before the date of the Scottish expedition. The term 'Sinclair sabre' is therefore a misnomer, and the most recent writer on swords of the kind to which it is normally applied, Major E. Eyvang, has discarded it in favour of *Tessak*.[101]

Tessaks with both curved and straight blades and a variety of guards of basket type are found in Norway. Major Eyvang divides them, according to their form and construction, into eight groups, each designated by a letter. The last group, H, is a miscellaneous one which includes a number of swords with 'Highland' hilts of generally similar design to the sword in the National Museum, Edinburgh, described on pp. 184-6 above,[102] but, in most instances, without foreguards (fig. 91), and with langets and much shorter quillons. There is no reason to think that these are earlier, or even as early, as the sword on the Lyttleton

Figure 91. Sword, English or Scottish, late 16th cent. *Norsk Folkmuseum, Oslo* (No. 998-24)

portrait of 1568, or that they are anything other than imports from Britain: they could, in fact, be the real relics of the Scottish expedition of 1612.

The remaining groups, though they are related primarily by Major Eyvang to swords from Norway, also cover every known form of early basket hilt, other than those already mentioned in this article, and the hilts of the *Schweizersäbel* and *Katzbalger* briefly discussed below. None can be shown to date from an earlier period than the fully developed hilt shown on the Lyttleton portrait, and only one of them, Type F — which incorporates a solid triangular plate on the outside — shares with the Highland hilt the characteristic of having its main lines of construction parallel to the axis of the blade. It was this form only, which is first recorded in the 1560s in Austria, that Mr Jacobsen, on the basis of a theoretical constructional evolution, suggested might be the prototype of the Highland hilt.[103] His suggestion was, however, based on the assumption that the Highland hilt was a comparatively late development: now, in light of our knowledge that it was already fairly well developed by c. 1540, and fully evolved by the 1560s, we could legitimately reverse the order of the drawings illustrating his theoretical constructional evolution to demonstrate convincingly that it was Eyvang's Type F hilt that developed from the Highland one!

Of the two other types of sixteenth-century basket-hilted sword that have not yet been mentioned here, one is the very distinctive large sabre which appears to have been used exclusively by the Swiss, whence it is now usually called a *Schweizersäbel*, though it appears originally to have been known as a *Schnepf*.[104] In its developed form, which is not recorded until the end of the sixteenth century, this often has a half-basket guard, mainly protecting the outside of the hand, where it sometimes incorporates a solid triangular plate, rather like the guard of Eyvang's type F *Tessak*. This developed form is very different in design and construction from the Highland hilt, but it can be traced back to a prototype which, on the evidence of its construction only, might be regarded as an ancestor of the Highland guard also. It is found on a group of sabres with spirally-twisted pommels and quillon-terminals that can be dated on stylistic grounds to the second quarter of the sixteenth century, and which also appear to be exclusively Swiss in origin.[105] The guard comprises: a pair of straight quillons, horizontally recurved at the ends, set between a pair of side-rings, and sometimes accompanied by one or two finger loops ('arms of the hilt'); a rudimentary half-basket formed of two slender bars which curve respectively from the base of the forward quillon and the centre of the edge of the outside side-ring to merge at the pommel, and a diagonal S-shaped bar which fills the space between them. The appearance of this half-basket is not unlike a section taken out of a Highland guard, and one might reasonably postulate, therefore, that the latter is a development from the former. The dangers of typologies based only on apparent constructional similarities has, however, already been demonstrated, and, in the absence both of hilt-types representing possible intermediate stages of development, and of the slightest evidence to suggest that there were mutual influences between Switzerland and Scotland in any field in the sixteenth century, the possibility that the hilt of the early *Schweizersäbel* could really be the ancestor of the Highland hilt seems to be a remote one.

The second type of early basket-guard that has not yet been mentioned developed around the characteristic early sixteenth-century Landsknecht short-sword, known as a *Katzbalger*, on which the quillons are looped round to form a figure eight. The origins and subsequent evolution of this sword have still to be studied but it is not unlikely that it first appeared in Switzerland at the end of the fifteenth century.[106] The form remained in use unchanged until at least the middle of the sixteenth century,[107] but a very small number of examples with more developed hilts are recorded. One such is sword No. IX. 898 in the Tower of London[108] Armouries (fig. 92). The quillons are here supplemented by a

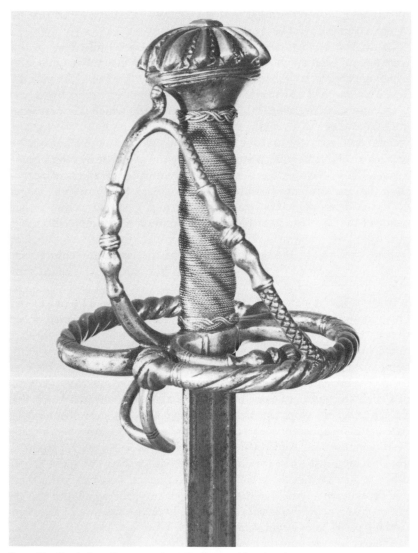

Figure 92. *Katzbalger,* German, c.1540-50. *Tower of London Armouries* (No. IX.898)

slender, central knuckle-bar linked by a similar diagonal bar to the centre of the looped quillon on the outside; the upper end of this diagonal is bent over like a hook, so that it runs into the knuckle-guard well below where it joins the pommel. A ring-guard is set within the outside quillon, while below the inside one, at the front, is a loop-shaped foreguard of the kind already mentioned several times in this study. The pommel is

Figure 93. *Katzbalger*, German, c.1550-60. *Tower of London Armouries* (No. IX.169)

shaped somewhat like an oval mushroom, decorated on top with prominent radiating flutes. A number of swords with very similar hilts are depicted in the manuscript *Kriegsordnung* of the Master H. D. (identified as Hans Döring) in the Staatsbibliothek, Munich, which is dated 1545.[109] The Tower sword, therefore, may reasonably be ascribed to the period c. 1540-50.

Another sword (fig. 93) in the Tower Armouries (No. IX 169)[110] has a form of guard that seems clearly to be a development from the last. There is no foreguard, but a ring-guard is set within each quillon, and the diagonal bar on the outside is balanced by a corresponding bar on the inside. As on the diagonal guard on the other sword at the Tower, the upper ends of these bars are bent over like hooks before they merge with the knuckle-guard: unlike it they are prolonged, and curve back and away from the knuckle-guard again, until they rejoin themselves just above the quillons. The result is a symmetrical basket guard with an arch-shaped outline which is linked to the pommel only by the tip of the knuckle-bar. The pommel is similar to that on the other Tower sword, but circular. Since this type of hilt, as already noted, is clearly a development from the form represented by the other Tower sword, and since it is not depicted in Döring's *Kriegsordnung*, it is likely to date from after c. 1545. It can perhaps be dated tentatively to c. 1550-60.

There is thus no evidence to suggest that the *Katzbalger* type of basket guard had developed earlier, or even as early, as the type of basket shown in the Palmer portrait of c. 1540. Also, the two types of guards differ so much in construction — notably in the way in which their upper parts are set in relationship to the pommels — as to rule out any real possibility of a link between them. On the other hand, it is very probable that the guard of the more developed of the two Tower swords represents the prototype from which Eyvang's Types A to E[111] developed, for all have in common an arch-shaped or circular basket built round a knuckle-bar which is the only part of the guard to touch the pommel. The earliest dateable example of one of these known to me is the illustration of what appears to be a Type C guard in the Hofnaegel painting referred to on pp. 175-7 above.[112]

In light of the foregoing, it seems probable that the origins of the Highland hilt are to be sought in Britain. It is, in fact, possible to suggest a line of evolution based entirely on swords from this country (fig. 94), though, as none of these can be firmly dated, it must necessarily be very tentative. Before discussing it some preliminary remarks are necessary:

1. It must be emphasised again that the basic framework of the Highland guard consists of bars set in the same line as the blade. It is also unusual, if not unique, among hilts of all kinds in being fitted commonly with *two* loop-shaped foreguards over the base of the blade.

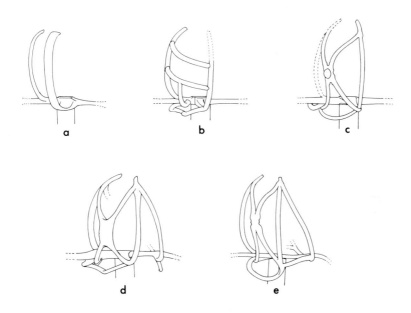

OUTSIDE

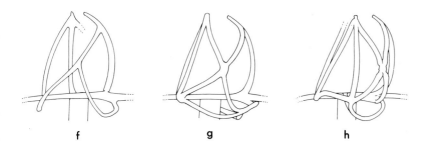

INSIDE

Figure 94. Suggested evolution of the Highland guard. The drawings are based on the following: *a*, sword formerly in Redfern Coll; *b*, sword at Boughton House; *c*, sword in Bolling House Museum; *d* & *f*, Sword from Pembridge Castle; *e* & *h*, sword in author's coll; *g*, sword in Castle Museum, York

2. It is clear from the construction of the hilts themselves that the basket-guard is built up round a simple cross-guard which, in the seventeenth century, lost its fore-quillon.

3. The Highland guard seems to have developed in the sixteenth century from a simple cross hilt to a construction of considerable complexity which was almost certainly the precursor of the so-called West Highland 'snouted' or 'beak-nosed' guard:[113] it was, however, one of the intermediate forms that survived to become, with slight modification, the standard Irish hilt of the seventeenth century. No evidence has been found to suggest that any of these later hilts was anything other than symmetrical in construction, so, for the purposes of typology, I have assumed that all guards of asymmetrical construction belong to the initial period of development towards the complex form. Some support for this assumption, as will be shown, is provided by the way in which the fore-guards evolved.

4. The typology is only intended to show a suggested general line of development of the hilt during the period before the Civil Wars. I have not attempted to classify all the variations in its form that I have noted.

As a starting point for our typology — a simple cross-hilted sword of British origin — we can take the mourning sword of the City of Exeter (fig. 95), the gilt latten hilt of which was almost certainly made in 1530-1.[114] I have selected this merely as a type, because it has a large, globular, hollow pommel, a feature found on many early British basket hilts, and a cross of about the right proportions for our purpose. I must emphasise, however, that I do not regard it in any way as being itself a prototype of any form of basket-hilted sword.

The typology proper begins with a sword that was formerly in the W. B. Redfern collection (fig. 96), and which, as its present whereabouts are unrecorded, can be studied only in an illustration in an article by him published in *The Connoisseur* for March 1923.[115] Unfortunately, he does not give any indication of the source from which he obtained it, merely calling it Venetian, an attribution for which there is no obvious reason. It has every appearance of being an excavated piece and this, in the context of the Redfern collection, which included a number of pieces with old connections with this country, makes a British find-site a possibility. The possibility is strengthened by the existence, in the Museum of London, of the detached guard of what must have been an almost exactly similar sword (No. A5455) from White Cross Street, London (figs. 97, 98).[116]

The hilt of the Redfern sword appears to be entirely of iron, and comprises: a large, globular, hollow pommel; a pair of straight, circular-section quillons of medium length, with trumpet-shaped tips cut off flat at the ends; a flat knuckle-bar joining the pommel to the base of the front quillon, and a corresponding bar on the outside, springing out at right-

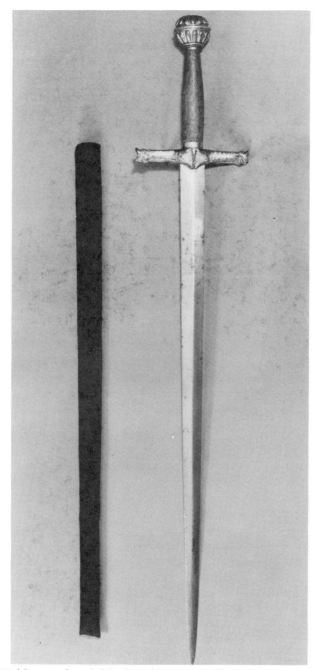

Figure 95. Mourning Sword of the City of Exeter, probably made 1530-1. *Guildhall, Exeter*

Figure 96. Sword, English (?), early 16th cent. Formerly in the W. B. Redfern Collection

angles from the centre of the cross before curving up to join the pommel. Each quillon is encircled immediately behind its tip by three engraved lines, while the bars of the guard are decorated with a hatched pattern and bordered by longitudinal engraved lines. The blade is single-edged with a rudimentary ricasso and a narrow gutter bordering the back.

So far as I am aware, the Redfern sword and Museum of London guard are the only ones of their kind recorded, and it would be foolish, therefore, to attempt to attach any firm date to them. There does not, however, appear to be any evidence for the existence of anything other than single knuckle-guards before the sixteenth century,[117] so these examples, with two such guards, probably date from after c. 1500. On the other hand, their simple form, without counter-guards over the base of the blade, suggests that they are not likely to have been produced very long after. We can therefore ascribe them tentatively to the very early years of the sixteenth century.

The significance of the Redfern sword at once becomes obvious when we compare it with the next sword, which forms part of the old Montagu family armoury at Boughton House, Northamptonshire (figs. 99-101).[118] This again has an iron hilt, now painted black, with a large, globular, hollow pommel and a guard which, apart from being made entirely of circular-section bars, closely resembles the White Cross Street guard and that on the Redfern sword in its basic construction, even to the design and decoration of the quillons. The basic construction, however, is supplemented by a number of additional bars, as follows: two parallel diagonal bars filling the gap between the knuckle-guard and the corresponding guard on the outside, of which the one nearest the cross is joined in the centre by a short L-shaped bar linking it to the base of the forward quillon; also springing from the base of the forward quillon is a loop-shaped foreguard which curves under the quillon towards the inside, almost at right-angles, and then curves back under itself to join the longitudinal guard on the outside at the point, level with the cross, where it begins to bend towards the pommel. The blade is double-edged with a central gutter at the forte and a long ricasso bordered on each face by a single engraved line. Two-thirds of the longitudinal side guard have been broken off.

The constructional similarities between the hilts of the Montagu sword and the Redfern one are so close as to leave little doubt that the former developed from the latter. It is hardly necessary to point out that the Montagu sword also has some of the basic characteristics of the developed Highland guard, notably a basket — or rather half-basket — based on longitudinal bars, and a loop-shaped foreguard. Its date is, of course, as uncertain as that of the Redfern sword, but, as the guard is clearly very much less developed than that shown on the Palmer portrait of c.

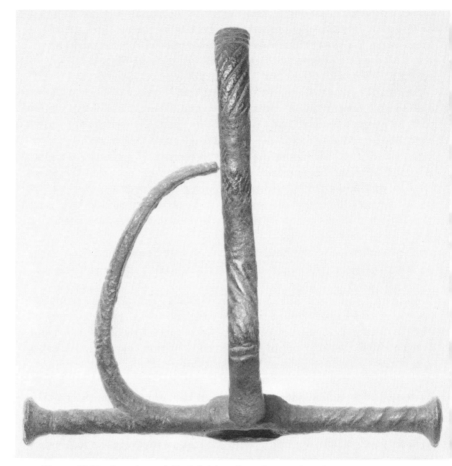

Figures 97-98. Sword guard, English (?), early 16th cent., found in White Cross Street, London. *Museum of London* (No. A5455)

1540, it can reasonably be dated rather earlier, say to c. 1520-30. Such a date is perhaps supported by an illustration of a sword-hilt on the well-known painting *The Field of Cloth of Gold* in the collection of Her Majesty The Queen at Hampton Court Palace. This depicts some of the events centring round the famous meeting of King Henry VIII and Francis I of France near Guisnes in June 1520, among which is the English royal procession. One of the Yeomen of the Guard, shown in the left foreground, taking part in this procession carries a sword with a guard which might have been of similar form to that of the Montagu sword (figs. 102, 103), though it is represented on such a small scale that it is im-

possible to be absolutely certain of this. The picture has been attributed tentatively to Johannes Corvus and ascribed to a date very shortly after the events it depicts.[119]

In order to convert the guard of the Montagu sword into a clearly-recognisable version of the Highland hilt, it would only be necessary to substitute a saltire-shaped arrangement of bars for the transverse bars in its half-basket. What appears at first sight to be a hilt of exactly the form that would thus be produced occurs on a backsword excavated in the area of Bradford, Yorkshire, and now in the Bolling Hall Museum there

Figures 99-101. Three views of sword, c.1520. *Boughton House*

(fig. 104).[120] This must, however, be treated with great caution for the hilt is damaged — the knuckle-guard and rear quillon, for example, are certainly missing — and it bears what appears to be traces of other bars, suggesting that in its original form it belonged to the same group as the

Pembridge Castle Guard described below. As it exists now it has what we may deduce to be the appearance of the missing link between this group of swords and the Montagu sword. All the bars are of circular section, and the space between the two main longitudinal ones (that is, including the missing knuckle-guard) is filled with a saltire-shaped arrangement of bars with a small central plate decorated with a rivet with a prominent head. The surviving quillon is recurved horizontally and terminates in a small knob, but has adjacent to it a loop-shaped foreguard almost exactly like that on the Montagu sword. The large, hollow pommel is shaped like an oblate spheroid, made in two halves joined horizontally, and segmented by inlaid strips of silver so that it looks like a peeled orange. This pommel, of course, resembles that on the Palmer portrait of c. 1540 very closely, which, for reasons given below, is perhaps further evidence for thinking that the whole hilt was originally similar to the Pembridge Castle one, and therefore rather later in date than our theoretical missing link.

With the next guard to be discussed we are on firmer ground, and it can be regarded as the earliest with recognisably 'Scottish' features to be identified with certainty up to now. It is a detached sword-guard found in the moat of Pembridge Castle, Herefordshire, now in the Tower of London Armouries (No. IX. 1404), but formerly in the collection of the late Dr Richard Williams (figs. 105, 106).[121] It has a pair of quillons of the same form as the one surviving on the Bolling Hall sword, is made of bars of similar type, and, though in excavated condition and broken in places, has every appearance of being complete. Its basic framework, including the shape of the single foreguard, is strikingly similar to the guard of the Montagu sword, but added to this are a number of other bars. Firstly, as on the Bolling Hall sword, the space between the knuckle-bar and a longitudinal bar in line with the blade on the outside is filled with a saltire, which centres on a small rectangular plate; sloping back and downwards from the apex of the side bar is another similar bar which joins it to the centre of the quillon. On the inside is a guard shaped like a curved, inverted Y, of which the tail merges with the upper end of the knuckle-guard near the pommel, and the two arms connect respectively with the centre of the rear quillon (opposite the rear longitudinal bar outside), and with the point on the foreguard, on the inside, where it begins to curve back on itself.

With the Pembridge Castle guard we reach a form that can be related to the guard shown on the Palmer portrait, for, viewed from the same angle, it shows exactly the same arrangement of two groups of three slender bars converging on the pommel. We may reasonably date it, therefore, to the period round about 1540, though with a certain amount of caution, because it is just possible that the Palmer sword was of a still

Figure 102. Detail of 'The Field of Cloth of Gold', c.1520-5. *Hampton Court Palace*

more developed type with more bars, now obliterated, on the inside of the hilt (cf. figs. 78, 115).

What must be the next stage of development is illustrated by the guard of a sword found near Ripon, Yorkshire, and now in the Museum there (figs. 107, 108).[122] Apart from the loss of its quillons — which may have been removed deliberately — this is complete and in good condition. Its construction is exactly the same as that of the Pembridge Castle guard, except that two additional lateral bars, set one on each side of the cross, link the foreguard to each side of the bottom of the back of the basket. The lateral bar on the inside is shaped like an elongated horizontal S. A four-petalled flower is roughly chiselled on the centre of the saltire-shaped feature on the outside. The guard is mounted on a single-edged blade, without grooves, bearing a demi-orb and cross and S marks, and is accompanied by a bun-shaped pommel with a very prominent rounded button. The pommel, though it has clearly been with the sword for a very long time, is not original to the guard since it is pierced with three horizontal slots to take the upper ends of a symmetrical ribbon guard.[123]

The next identifiable stage of development is illustrated by a number of swords. It affected the bars on the inside only, and was achieved, firstly, by converting the inverted Y into a large saltire (if a rather distorted one) by prolonging its forward arm upwards and backwards in a

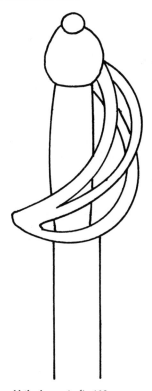

Figure 103. Sketch of the sword hilt shown in fig 102

flattened curve until it rested against the middle of the pommel in line with the centre of the grip. Secondly, the two rear arms of the saltire were linked by a longitudinal bar, outside the hilt. On all the examples known to me the bottom lateral bar inside is more or less straight and not S-shaped as on the Ripon hilt.

I know of the following swords fitted with guards of this form:

1. A sword from the Timperley Collection, now in the Castle Museum, York (No. T 454) (figs. 109, 110). The guard is formed of bars of similar section and thickness to those on the Ripon sword, and the quillons are horizontally recurved and terminate in writhen conical buttons. The saltire outside the hilt centres on a small rectangular plate incised with a cross within a rectangle. The pommel is a large hollow sphere, made in two halves brazed together round the centre, where it is also encircled by two shallow grooves. The small button, which forms part of a circular washer, is made separately. The wooden grip is of flattened oval section, ribbed longitudinally, and covered with what appears

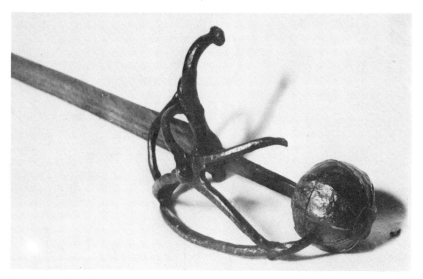

Figure 104. Sword found near Bradford, mid-16th cent. (?) *Bolling Hall Museum*

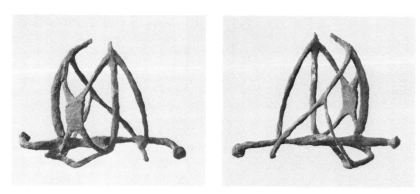

Figures 105-106. Sword guard from the moat of Pembridge Castle, c.1540 (?) *Tower of London Armouries* (No. IX.1404)

to be thin canvas (now dark brown in colour); it would probably have been bound originally with wire. The straight two-edged blade has a ricasso, both faces of which are bordered by a single groove on each edge and roughly engraved with rather indeterminate scrollwork. The blade proper has a shallow central groove on each face, and a running wolf mark on one. Nothing is known of the history of the sword before it was presented to the Castle Museum by the late E. Timperley.[124]

Figures 107-108. Sword found at Clotherholme, c.1550 (?). *Ripon Museum* (No. B.5)

2. A sword in the National Museum of Antiquities, Edinburgh (No. LB 8), said to have been found in Ireland in 1851, in the River Shannon at the head of Keelsay Falls.[125] It is in poor condition but the form of the pommel and of the surviving parts of the guard are so similar to the corresponding features on the York sword as to leave no doubt that the two originally looked very much alike, and probably came from the same workshop. The wooden grip, which is not fluted, retains part of its binding of copper wire. The blade has a long ricasso, and a double central groove. This, it should be mentioned, is the only sword of its kind with Irish connections so far noted.

3. A guard, mounted with a pommel that clearly was not made for it, and a rapier blade that is almost certainly also associated, now in the Museum of the U.S. Military Academy, West Point (No. 2132) (fig. 111).

Figures 109-110. Sword, c. 1560 (?). *Castle Museum, York (Timperley Collection)*

It is almost identical in design to the guards of the York and Keelsay Falls swords, except that the saltire outside the hilt centres on a disc, and the quillons are slightly longer and terminate in plain conical buttons. Its particular interest to the present study lies in the fact that the whole sword is said to have been found in a tomb in the churchyard at Nether-bury, Dorset.[126] Unfortunately, enquiries at Netherbury have failed to produce any confirmation of this story,[127] and the good condition of the surface of the weapon does not lead one to give it much credence.

4. A sword in the Rijksmuseum, Amsterdam (No. N.M. 10858), found in the Haarlemermeer in 1854 (fig. 112), and possible a relic of the battle fought there in 1573.[128] It has a guard of similar form to the three just described, but of rather better quality, decorated with mouldings and spiral ribbing, and with straight quillons. The pommel resembles those on the Palmer portrait and the Bolling Hall sword.

It is not difficult to see how the form of basket just described could be evolved into a symmetrical basket with a double foreguard, and a saltire set between the knuckle-bar and a central longitudinal bar both inside and outside the hilt. The earliest examples of this development I have noted so far are on two backswords, respectively in an English private collection and in my own collection (figs. 113-115).[129] Both have large

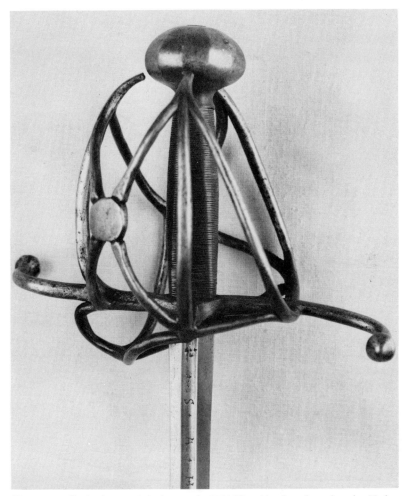

Figure 111. Rapier (composite), the guard c.1560 (?), said to have been found at Nether-bury, Dorset. *Museum of the U.S. Military Academy, West Point* (No. 2132)

globular hollow pommels made in the same way as the pommel on the York sword, but that on my own sword is decorated with close-set longitudinal gadrooning on either side of a horizontal central moulding set between two narrow grooves. The pommel on the other privately-owned sword is correspondingly decorated in the upper half with a design of incised leaves. Both swords have quillons of the same design as those on the York sword (on my own sword one is a restoration and the other lacks a quillon) and the two foreguards are made as if they were extensions of the lower ends of the longitudinal side-bars, curved for-

Figure 112. Sword found in the Haarlemermeer, c.1560 (?). *Rijksmuseum, Amsterdam* (No. N.M.10858)

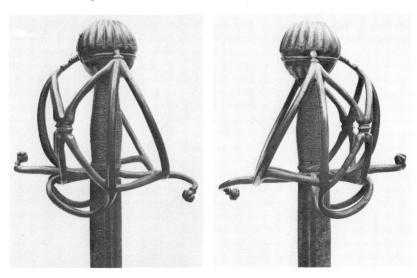

Figures 113-115. Sword, c.1560-70 (?). *Author's Collection*

wards and upwards until they merge with the front quillons under the knuckle-bar.

With these two swords we reach the first fully-developed form of the Highland guard which, apart from the quillons, is identical in construction to the Irish hilt of the seventeenth century. Their close relationship to the swords with asymmetrical baskets and single foreguards, and their large, spherical, hollow pommels made in two halves joined round the

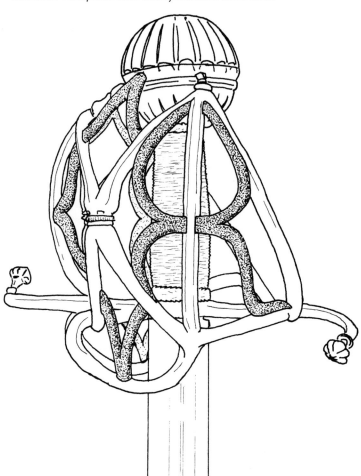

Figure 116.   Drawing demonstrating how the form of guard shown in fig 113 developed into the form shown in fig 117

middle, suggest, however, that they are very early examples of the form, and probably much earlier than the more complex guard illustrated on the Lyttleton portrait of 1568. They can therefore probably be dated tentatively to round about 1560.

The way in which a guard of the type just described developed into one of similar construction to that on the Lyttleton portrait is demonstrated in fig. 116, where the additional bars are shown shaded.[130] The form

Figure 117. Sword, c.1570 (?). *National Museum of Antiquities of Scotland* (SW 11)

so produced — with slender bars instead of the ribbon-like ones of the Lyttleton picture — is almost exactly like that of the guard (lacking its quillons) of a sword in the National Museum of Antiquities, Edinburgh (No. SW 11) (fig. 117).[131] The pommel of this sword differs in form from those on the two swords referred to in the last paragraph, being solid, rather elongated and faceted, and has the upper elements of the guard screwed to it instead of merely abutting. Another sword with a rather more elaborate version of the same basic form of basket, in the Preston Hall Museum, Stockton-on-Tees (Spence Collection), is equipped with a pommel of closely similar type to that on the sword in my own collection, and is almost certainly from the same workshop (fig. 118).[132] The blade bears an S and sickle mark and the grip retains its original plaited leather binding.

The constructional similarities between the guards of the swords referred to in the last paragraph and the guard of the sword on the Lyttleton portrait suggests a possible date for them of about 1570. This view is supported by the evidence of a sword in the Nederlands Leger en Wapenmuseum 'Generaal Hoefer', Leiden (No. OP 156) (fig. 119),[133] of which the guard, now much damaged, was originally similar in construction to that of the Edinburgh sword just described, though made of thinner bars. The pommel is shaped like a double gourd, with the smaller half uppermost,

Figure 118. Sword, c. 1570 (?). *Preston Hall Museum, Stockton-on-Tees (Spence Collection)*

Figure 119. Sword found in the River Maas, near Mook, c.1570(?). *Nederlands Leger en Wapenmuseum 'General Hoefer'* (No. OP.156)

and is very close indeed to the pommel of the rapier depicted on a portrait dated 1568 of Sir Thomas Tresham at Boughton House, Northamptonshire.[134] The Leyden sword was found in the River Maas, near Mook, and has been associated with a battle fought there in the early-seventeenth century, but the evidence of the pommel again suggests a possible date of about 1570. Two swords with comparable guards and

Figure 120.　Sword guard, c.1570 (?), found on the site of Colonial Jamestown, Virginia. *Site Museum, Jamestown*

pommels are in respectively the Haermuseet (No. HAO 5160) and the Norsk Folkemuseum (No. 998-24), Oslo.[135]

I have used the words 'possible date' in connection with these swords advisedly, for basket guards of the same form have been found in early seventeenth-century contexts at Colonial Jamestown, and other sites in Virginia, U.S.A. (fig. 120). These, however, could have been old already when they were abandoned.[136] The remains of another sword with one of these guards is in the museum at Rochester, Kent. Unfortunately, nothing certain is known of its history, except that it was presented to the Museum by 'R. A. Arnold of the Precincts, Rochester' and is likely, therefore, to have been found locally.

As has already been mentioned, it was the simpler form of thin-barred guard that survived in England as the Irish hilt. That it survived much longer than is generally supposed is shown by an example in the National Museum of Ireland, Dublin, which is chiselled with profile busts of William and Mary (1689-94) (figs. 121, 122).[137] Where the form of guard made of flat bars, as on the Lyttleton portrait and the Abercorn sword, is

Figures 121-122. Sword chiselled with portraits of William and Mary, 1689-94. *National Museum of Ireland, Dublin*

concerned, there is no evidence to suggest that it remained in use in England much beyond the sixteenth century.[138] It seems certain, however, that it was the direct precursor of the form of guard made of very wide bars, and with only rudimentary quillons, and no foreguards which is probably Scottish (fig. 123). This form usually has small langets over the base of the blade, like those found on the so-called Lowland type of two-hand sword and also on the so-called 'mortuary' swords of the English Civil Wars, of which the latter can date from as late as the 1650s.[139] Whatever its origins, there can be little doubt that it was, in turn the direct precursor of the so-called West Highland 'snouted' or 'beak nosed' guard of the kind found on the Michael Wright portrait of a Highland chieftain of about 1670, which, as was mentioned at the beginning of this paper, is the earliest dateable example of such a hilt in a Scottish context.

Another early type of basket-guard found in Britain must be discussed (figs. 124, 125). This is similar in general form to the developed Highland guard, but is constructed mainly of slender, close-set, longitudinal bars, some of which are often arranged in pairs that are slightly bowed towards each other and linked centrally by a small flat plate. These pairs

Figure 123. Sword, Scottish (?), early 17th cent. *Tower of London Armouries* (No. IX. 1015)

of bars resemble very narrow, elongated versions of the saltires found on the developed Highland guard. In the front part of the basket, the bars are spaced to form at least two open panels which are filled with solid plates decorated with a few piercings. There are no foreguards, but at the front is a single quillon bent back towards the hand. This kind of basket guard seems always to be accompanied by a flat disc-shaped pommel, set across the line of the tang, and with a very prominent rectangular

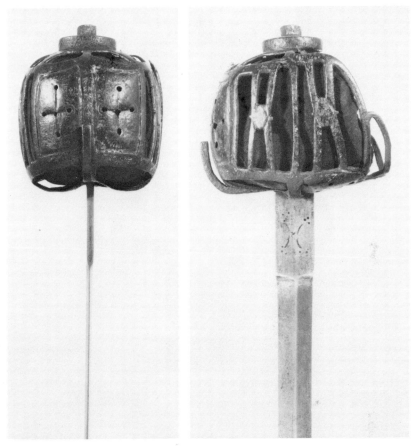

Figures 124-125. Sword, Lowland Scots (?), late 16th or early 17th cent. *National Museum of Antiquities of Scotland* (LA 84)

button.[140] It is also usually fitted with a long, tapering blade of flattened-diamond section, like the blade of a heavy rapier, with a long rectangular ricasso below the guard.

Examples of swords of this kind are not very common, and the few known to me that have any kind of pedigree — that is, are from old family armouries or of known archaeological provenance — are distributed impartially between England, Scotland and the United States. Swords in old family armouries are at Inveraray Castle (Duke of Argyll), Ardvorlich (Stewart of Ardvorlich),[141] and Littlecote House, Wiltshire (Popham family armoury); swords of known archaeological provenance are in the Salisbury Museum (found in a house at Seend, Wiltshire), in

Figure 126. Sword found in the Thames, Lowland Scots (?), late 16th or early 17th cent. *Reading Museum*

the Reading Museum (found in the Thames) (fig. 126) and the Irish National Museum, Dublin (No. 116-1943; found at Lough Oughter Castle, County Cavan),[142] while — of special interest — a detached guard was excavated a few years ago on the site of a fort dating from about 1619-25 at Flowerdew Hundred, a plantation established in 1618 near Jamestown, Virginia by Governor Sir George Yeardley (1580?-1627).[143] Other swords, without associations, are in the Dick Institute, Kilmarnock, the Glasgow Art Gallery and Museum (No. 11-29-GW; with later pommel and blade) and the National Museum, Edinburgh (No. LA 84; with a japanned hilt),[144] while another was in the L. F. McCardle Collection at Sheffield Park, Sussex.[145] Mention must also be made of what appears to be a developed form of this type of basket hilt found on a broadsword, now in the Wakefield Museum (No. 23.03) (fig. 127). According to an unconfirmed tradition, it belonged originally to the Parliamentary commander Colonel Sir John Bright (1619-88)[146] and, like the sword in the National Museum, it is japanned. The guard resembles

Figure 127. Sword, early 17th cent., said to have belonged to Col. Sir John Bright (1619-88). *Wakefield Museum (No. 66/432/4)*

those on the hilts under discussion in being made of close-set longitudinal bars, but is of heavier construction, does not involve rectangular plate or saltires, and the pommel is large and globular with a prominent button. It also has a pair of vertically recurved quillons.

I have mentioned above that these hilts are usually found fitted with blades like those of some late sixteenth- and early seventeenth-century

Figure 128. Left-hand dagger, Lowland Scots (?), late 16th or early 17th cent., found in the River Fleet, London. *Museum of London* (No. 7773)

rapiers. There is evidence to suggest that, in such a combination, this is, in fact, what they were. Preserved in the Museum of London is a dagger (No. 7773) (fig. 128), found in the River Fleet in 1863,[147] with a horizontal disc pommel and a basket guard that is merely a reduced version of the type under discussion, supplemented by a pair of strongly arched quillons like those found on the conventional left-hand dagger or poniard of the late sixteenth and early seventeenth centuries. It was clearly made to match, and to be used in conjunction with, a basket-hilted sword in sword and dagger play. Such a garniture of sword and dagger is perhaps referred to in a passage in the early seventeenth-century poem *Robin Hood's Birth, Breeding, Valour and Marriage:*

> And then Robin got on his basket-hilted sword
> And his dagger on his tother side.[148]

That the dagger here need not necessarily have been a basket-hilted one is shown by the evidence of the Lyttleton portrait and the George Silver woodcut: Nathaniel Field in his *Amends for Ladies* of 1618, however, describes something as being '. . . as flat as a basket-hilt dagger',[149] while Ben Jonson in his *Tale of a Tub* of 1633 speaks of 'Your dun, rusty pannier-hilt poniard',[150] which can hardly have been anything other than a basket-hilted left-hand dagger. George Silver also, writing in 1599 about fencing, mentions 'a close hylted dagger',[151] as also does Joseph Swetnam writing in 1617.[152]

Three other pannier-hilt poniards are recorded, all with guards of similar construction. One (fig. 129), formerly in the Morgan Williams, W. B. Redfern and E. Timperley collections, is now in the Castle Museum, York.[153] Its basic form is that of a standard left-hand dagger of the late sixteenth or early seventeenth century, with slender arched quillons and a single side-ring filled with a solid plate, but made in one with these last is a basket guard made of slender bars of circular section. In shape it resembles a narrow lancet-like arch within a large rounded arch, the two being joined together at the top. The feet of the larger arch spring from the bases of the quillons, and those of the smaller one from the rim of the side-ring, and the whole guard curves out and then back to join the pommel, to which it is attached by a screw passing through a small lug. The smaller arch is filled by bars shaped to form a narrow saltire with a central open crosspiece; above and below the crosspiece are small, rectangular, ribbed 'collars'. The pommel is bun shaped.

A second dagger is in the collection of Mr D. G. Harris (fig. 130).[154] The basic construction of the guard here is the same as on the York dagger, but it is made of wider, flat-section bars, the quillons are straight and spatulate at the ends, the outer arch of the basket is horseshoe shaped, the inner arch is replaced by bars formed as a Staffordshire knot, and the pommel is ovoidal. The side-ring has lost its pierced plate.

The third dagger (fig. 131) is in the Haermuseet, Oslo (No. HAO 20230B) and is one of a group of arms transferred from the Historisk Museum, Bergen in 1964-5.[155] I know it only from a photograph, but it appears to resemble the McCardle dagger closely, except that the outer

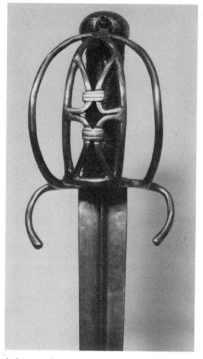

Figure 129. Left-hand dagger, Lowland Scots (?), late 16th or early 17th cent. *Castle Museum, York* (No. T.38)

arch of the basket is formed as a large oval ring, and the Staffordshire knot is replaced by a flat knuckle-bar that widens in the centre into a large disc.[156]

A detached, and slightly imperfect, dagger-guard in a private collection[157] is perhaps related to the guard of the York dagger (fig. 132). Also made of slender bars of circular section, it is similarly constructed round a conventional left-hand dagger guard, with quillons, swelling at the tips, and a side-ring. The quillons are, however, straight and are supplemented by a pair of unusual antenna-like 'sword-breakers' which would frame the base of the blade; the inner edges are cut to form saw-like teeth and each terminated in a long barb, of which only one survives. The basket is slightly asymmetrical, with a bias towards the outside, and consists basically of three longitudinal bars which curve out and back to join the pommel (missing), of which one bar springs from the base of the front quillon, and the other two from either side of the rim of the side-ring. Each of the two spaces between the bars is filled with pairs of addorsed S-shaped scrolls, one above the other, which join in the

Figure 130. Left-hand dagger, Lowland Scots (?), late 16th or early 17th cent. *Collection of Mr D. G. Harris*

middle to form a small, lozenge-shaped frame with its side points prolonged laterally to join the centres of the main bars on either side. The centre of the rear main bar is also linked to the centre of the rear quillon by another longitudinal bar, while the side-ring is balanced on the inside by a horizontal loop-guard. At most of the points where bars merge are small 'collars', rectangular, or formed like mouldings.

The four complete daggers are fitted with blades of a distinctive type, which provide a clue to the origin and provenance of the whole group, including, of course, the swords with the same form of guard and

Figure 131. Left-hand dagger, *Haermuseet, Oslo* (No. HAO 20230B)

pommel as the Museum of London dagger. The type is fairly broad (about 32 mm. across the base), double edged, leaf shaped, and of very flat section with a strong, narrow medial rib running the full length of each face, except, normally, for a short section at the base of the face against which the thumb was placed when the dagger was being used for parrying. Similar blades are found on a number of left-hand daggers of

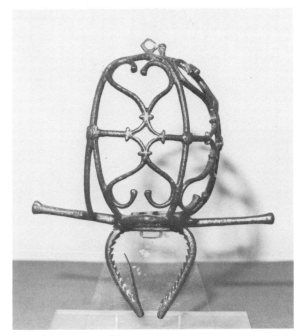

Figure 132. Guard for a left-hand dagger, late 16th or early 17th cent. *Private Collection, England*

conventional late sixteenth- or early seventeenth-century form, found in Britain, of which several have horizontal disc-shaped pommels. An example found in the Harrogate area was in the collection of the late W. J. Kent of Tatefield Hall, Beckwithshaw,[158] two, excavated locally, are in the Taunton Museum, another in excavated condition is in the Lewes Museum, and one found in the River Thames is in the Reading Museum.[159] A dagger with a blade of the same type but a completely different form of hilt was found in the London Thames in 1978 and is now in the Tower Armouries (No. X. 588).[160] The blade is inlaid on each side with a copper mark in the form of an orb and bears traces of etched and gilt figures and foliage. The guard is a small circular plate, cut off sharply at the back and with escalloped edge, and the pommel is a flattened hollow sphere divided into segments by ribs, and made in two halves, brazed round the middle, rather like the pommels on the Palmer portrait and Bolling Hall swords. It retains its sheath-locket of iron and two by-knives.

The key piece among these daggers, however, is one belonging to the Department of Medieval and Later Antiquities at the British Museum (No. 56/7-1/2256) (fig. 133)[161] which came originally from the Charles Roach Smith collection, and was therefore almost certainly found in

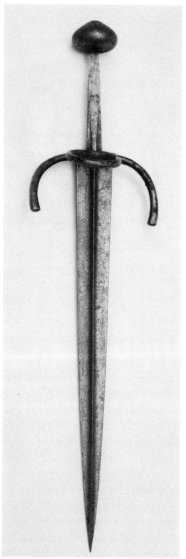

Figure 133. Left-hand dagger, Lowland Scots (?), dated 1593. *British Museum* (No. 56/7-1/2256)

London. It has arched quillons — one quillon being twisted forward, the better to catch an opponent's blade — a side-ring originally filled with a solid plate, and a disc-shaped pommel drawn up to a very flattened cone on top. The blade is of the form described at the beginning of the previous paragraph, and is etched all over with arabesques, filled with hatching and arranged in panels. Near the point on one face is the inscription, in script, 'In my defence God me defend', while in a corresponding position on the other face is an illegible inscription ending in the date 1593'.[162]

The style of the decoration on the blade of the dagger is very similar to that on the well-known group of early seventeenth-century ballock-knives of Lowland Scots origin of which an account was published in 1963 by Mr John Wallace and myself.[163] The inscription 'In my defence God me defend' is recorded, with minor variations, on at least three of these, and the words form the first line of a prayer which was much used in Scotland in the sixteenth and seventeenth centuries.[164] It seems likely, therefore, that these blades are also of Lowland Scots origin, from which it follows that basket-hilts of the type found on the Museum of London dagger are probably also from the same area, while the date on the British Museum dagger and the evidence of the guard from Flowerdew Hundred indicate that they were in use in the late sixteenth and early seventeenth centuries. The apparently rather odd combination of guards of sub-Highland type with rapiers and poniards would perhaps seem less odd in a Lowland Scots context, for Lowland fashions, on the whole, followed those of England and Continental Europe, but were subjected to influences from the Highlands.

So far as I am aware, only one early form of basket-guard with British association has not been mentioned here. It is a very rare form, for I have noted only four examples: in the National Museum of Ireland, Dublin (No. 494-1902, found in County Cavan), the Scottish United Services Museum, Edinburgh Castle (No. 1930-28) (fig. 134) (information from Mr A. V. B. Norman), the Museum at Whitby, Yorkshire (probably excavated locally), and the J. D. Forman Collection (formerly in the McCardle Collection) (fig. 135).[165] On all of these the basket, which is equipped with two loop-shaped foreguards, is symmetrical and has a basic framework of three pointed arches, the tips of which touch the pommel. Each arch is bisected by a central bar which forms a spine for a series of curved bars, set at intervals like ribs, linking it to the sides of the arch. The Grimsby and Dublin Swords have horizontally-recurved quillons (the front one missing from the latter) ending in buttons, and globular pommels of moderate size with buttons, and are fitted with long, rather narrow blades of flattened diamond section of the type mentioned on p. 223 above. The Whitby sword has the unusual feature of having a pair of bars springing from the base of each quillon and bending back under the guard where they terminate in buttons.

The baskets of the Whitby, Scottish United Services Museum and Dublin swords are made of thin bars of circular section. That of the Forman sword is made of flat bars of which those forming the main

Figure 134. Sword, late 16th cent., *Scottish United Services Museum* (No. 1930-20)

framework are wider than the others, and it has lost its quillons. It is accompanied by a large hollow, globular pommel of the form described on pp. 209, 212-13 above, made in two halves brazed round the middle where it is encircled by a narrow double groove, and is fitted with a prominent rectangular button of the kind found on the disc-shaped pommels described on pp. 222-3 above. The blade is a broad triply-

Figure 135. Sword, late 16th cent., *J. D. Forman Collection*

grooved one with an Andrea Ferrara signature, and may well be later than the hilt.

The evidence of the blades of the Whitby and Dublin swords and of the pommel of the McCardle sword suggests that the whole group is related to the hilts with both globular and disc-shape pommels discussed. It can therefore be dated to the late sixteenth and early seventeenth centuries.[166]

A left-hand dagger with an arch-shaped guard for the back of the hand formed like a single section of one of the sword hilts is illustrated in an album of drawings of pieces from the W. B. Redfern collection in the Library of the Tower of London Armouries (ex Richard Williams collection). It has a single foreguard and originally had quillons of which only the stumps remain. The pommel is globular and the blade flat with a groove on each face inscribed *IOHAN*. On one face are the running wolf and orb and cross marks. According to an accompanying note the dagger had a wooden grip with traces of gold wire, there were 'Signs of silvering on hilt', and the whole was 'much corroded'.

Finally, we must propound the question, did the form of basket hilt we have been discussing originate in England or in Scotland? The answer is that we still do not know for certain. All that can be said is that, apart from the indications that in early seventeenth-century England the basket guard was thought to have originated in the Scottish Highlands, there appears to be only one rather indeterminate piece of evidence in favour of a Scottish origin. During much of this paper a good deal of attention has been drawn to the large, spherical, segmented or fluted pommels found on early examples of the Highland hilt. Very similar pommels occur on a number of examples of the two-hand claymore, a type of sword that seems to have been confined to the Gaelic-speaking parts of Scotland and Ireland,[167] though some of them may actually have been made elsewhere. If it could be shown that these dated from an earlier period than, or were precisely contemporary with, the earliest British basket hilts — which is not yet possible — it would, in my opinion, provide strong evidence for regarding hilts of this type as Scottish in origin.

Acknowledgements

First and foremost, I owe a great debt to the late Dr C. R. Beard. After his death in 1958 his extensive notes for a study of the history of the basket-hilted sword in Britain were deposited in the Department of Metalwork at the Victoria and Albert Museum. They contained most of the information that I had already discovered for myself by that date, and a good deal more besides — especially literary references — which I have made use of here, acknowledging the source in the appropriate Notes. Dr Beard's views about the development of the early basket-hilt were broadly similar to my own, but, since his death, I have been able to discover more information on the subject, and my final conclusions therefore differ in detail from his. He must, however, be given full credit for his important pioneer work, and it is very much to be regretted that he never published it himself.

Secondly, a special word of thanks is due to Mr William Reid, Director of the National Army Museum. He and I originally intended to produce this article jointly, but when the part that I had agreed to write grew disproportionately large he very generously suggested that I should publish the whole, including his material, by myself. I am very grateful to him for allowing me to do this, and I have acknowledged in the appropriate Notes where I have made use of his material.

I am also especially grateful to Mr A. V. B. Norman, Master of the Tower of London Armouries who has always been prepared to share his great knowledge of the history of the sword with me. He has discussed many of the problems raised in this paper with me and made many helpful suggestions, and has also been kind enough to produce sketches of the illustrations of basket-hilts in paintings for me. My grateful thanks are also due to Mrs A. V. B. Norman who has very kindly made the drawings reproduced as figs. 87 and 88. Colin Hendry of the National Museum, Edinburgh has drawn or re-drawn several of the illustrations and I am very grateful to him also.

Guldsmedemester Holgar Jacobsen of Copenhagen, whose pioneer publications on the problems of the origins of the basket-hilt are mentioned more than once in this article, very generously offered to let me make any use I wished of any part of them. I have accepted with gratitude and reproduced some of his drawings of hilt-constructions as figures.

Other people to whom I should like to express my gratitude for help of one kind or another in the preparation of this article, in addition to those who have been acknowledged in the text and Notes, are: Mr A. J. Aitken, Editor of the *Dictionary of the Older Scottish Tongue*; Mr N. J. Arch, Keeper of Military History at the Castle Museum, York; His Grace the Duke of Argyll; The Curator of the Bolling Hall Museum; Mr P. J. Boylan, Director of the Exeter Museum; Mr Roy Butler of Messrs Wallis & Wallis, Lewes; Dr Nolfo di Carpegna, Director of the Odescalchi Collection, Rome; Miss Priscilla Copeman of the Courtauld Institute of Art; Mr Ian Eaves and Mrs B. M. A. Ellis of the Tower of London Armouries; Mr J. K. Ellwood; Major Eivind Eyvang, Director of the Haermuseet, Oslo; Mr J. D. Forman; the late Mr Leslie I. Gibson; Mr George A. Gordon; Mr D. G. Harris; Mr Ivor Noël Hume of the Colonial Williamsburg Foundation; the late Mr B. W. J. Kent; Mr J. B. Kist of the Rijks-museum, Amsterdam; Mr Richard E. Kuehne, Director of the West Point Museum; the late Mr Clement Milward; Mr A. R. E. North of the Victoria & Albert Museum; the late Mr Harold L. Peterson; the Curator of the Preston Hall Museum, Stockton-upon-Tees; Mr Stuart Pyrrh of the Metropolitan Museum, New York; the Rev. Canon M. H. Ridgway; the Curator of the Ripon Museum; the Curator of the Rochester Museum; Mr J. G. Scott, late of the Glasgow Museum; Major John Stewart of Ardvorlich; Mr John Wallace; Miss Rosemary Weinstein of the Museum of London.

Finally, I must mention Mr Stuart Maxwell, Deputy Director of the National Museum of Antiquities of Scotland, and Mr David Caldwell of the same institution. Both have helped in many ways with the preparation of this article, while Mr Caldwell has also edited it for the press with great care. I am very grateful to both of them.

NOTES

1. The word *claymore* has been applied to the basket-hilted Scottish sword since at least as early as 1679, and the view that it should be restricted to the Highland two-hand sword is an arbitrary one for which 19th-century antiquaries are entirely responsible. See pp. 378-84 below.

2. *Scottish National Memorials. A Record of the Historical and Archaeological Collection in the Bishop's Castle, Glasgow, 1888*, ed. J. Paton (London & Glasgow, 1890), 259; M. Maindron, *Les Armes* (Paris, 1890), 258-60.

    Joseph Anderson, who was responsible for the text and captions in J. Drummond's *Ancient Scottish Weapons* (Edinburgh & London, 1881), implied (p. 18) — as did also Drummond's selection of illustrations — that there was a direct connection between the schiavona and the Scottish basket-hilted sword, but he did not say so outright. W. Boeheim, in his *Waffenkunde* (Leipzig, 1890), 264, was similarly non-committal, despite the fact that he used the phrase 'Die schiavona der Schotten'. The responsibility for the widespread acceptance of the theory over a long period almost certainly belongs to Sir Guy Laking. In his catalogue, *The Armoury of Windsor Castle* (London, 1904), he wrote (p. 217): 'The basket-hilted sword was not of Scotch origin, but was first used in Venice by the *Schiavoni*, or hired soldiery, their particular form of sword being called the *schiavona*. After its introduction into England in the first years of the 17th century it became a favourite cavalry weapon . . . From England it was introduced into Scotland, where it found ready favour among the stalwart Highlanders, and where it received its now universally known, though as before stated, inaccurate name of the claymore'. He also wrote on similar lines in his immensely-influential *Record of European Armour and Arms* (London, 1920-22), ii, 302; iv, 325-6.

    The source of the theory is probably a passage in A. Demmin's *Guide des Amateurs d'Armes* (Paris, 1869), 390-1, which is translated as follows in the English edition of the book, *An Illustrated History of Arms and Armour* (London, 1877), 371:

The real Scotch claymore had a plain cross-guard, without the basket hilt which protected the whole of the hand: swords and sabres with these hilts are often wrongly called claymores, but they were used only by the Venetians, and were called *schiavone*, being the weapon used by the Doge's guards in the sixteenth and seventeenth centuries, as may be seen in pictures of that time; in Scotland they were not known till the eighteenth century.

3. Lord A. Campbell, *Highland Dress, Arms and Ornament* (Westminster, 1899), 44-5; C. E. Whitelaw, 'Scottish Weapons', in *Scottish History and Life*, ed. J. Paton (Glasgow, 1902), 236; J. G. Mann, 'The evolution of the basket-hilted sword', *XIIIe. Congrès International d'Histoire de l'Art, Stockholm 1933, Résumés des Communications Présentées au Congrès* (Stockholm, 1933), 241-43; I. Finlay, 'Highland Weapons at the Royal Academy', *Connoisseur*, Feb. 1939, 76-77; J. G. Mann, *Scott Collection of Arms & Armour: Introductory Guide* (Corporation of Glasgow Art Galleries and Museums, 1940), 14-15.

4. H. Jacobsen, 'Kurvfaester', *Vaabenhistoriske Aarbøger*, iii (Copenhagen, 1940), 90-105.

5. Whitelaw, 'Scottish Weapons'.

6. Jacobsen, 'Kurvfaester', 105.

7. H. Seitz, *Blankwaffen*, 2 vols. (Brunswick, 1965 & 1968), ii, 113-14.

8. The problem of what the conventional position of a sword should be for description is particularly acute in an article of this kind in which swords have to be described in relation to the contemporary illustrations in which they are depicted. The one I have adopted, because it seems to me to be the most convenient for this particular study, is to describe each sword as if it were worn vertically, point downwards, in the normal sheathed position on the left side. In this position, the main part of the guard is, of course, towards the front. I have called the part against the body the inside of the hilt, and the side away from the body the outside. I have used *interior* and *exterior* of the hilt to refer to its inner and outer surfaces.

9. I must emphasise the words *in construction*. Many basket-hilts are, of course, asymmetrical in form, though rarely greatly so.

10. On the earliest basket-hilts (e.g. figs. 105-16) the sword can be gripped with the fore-finger hooked round the front quillon, in which position it is protected by the fore-guards. On later swords this is not possible and the foreguards appear to serve no practical purpose.

11. This is the last vestige of the cross-guard round which the earliest basket hilts developed. See below, p. 198.

12. For a discussion of the date and possible identity of this portrait see C. R. Beard, 'Two Disputed Portraits at the Royal Academy', *Connoisseur*, Feb. 1939, 94-96; J. T. Dunbar, *History of Highland Dress* (Edinburgh & London, 1962), 55-56. What might be a basket-hilted sword is shown in a portrait, dated 1574, of the young James VI at Hardwick Hall. Unfortunately, it is a 17th-century copy of an earlier picture made in England and this, coupled with the fact that it is by no means certain that the sword really has a basket hilt, destroys its value as evidence. See R. Strong, *The English Ikon* (London, 1969), 258. I am grateful to Mr R. E. Hutchison of the Scottish National Portrait Gallery for his opinion on this portrait.

13. J. Wallace, *Scottish Swords and Dirks* (London, 1970), 23, 26 and figs. 15 & 20. The story that these hilts were produced in the Western Highlands has never, so far as I know, appeared in print, although it is current among collectors. It is likely enough, but it does not seem to be based on any definite evidence.

14. Richard James, 1592-1638, 'Description of Shetland, Orkney and the Highlands of Scotland', ed. E. MacGillivray, *Orkney Misc.*, i (1953), 51.

15. *The North-Country Chorister; an Unparalleled Variety of Excellent Songs. Collected and published together, for general Amusement, by A. Bishoprick Ballad-Singer* (Durham, 1802), 16. Reprinted as part of J. Ritson's *Northern Garlands*, London, 1810. A different version of the poem, without any reference to arms, was published by F. W. Fairholt in *Satirical Songs and Poems on Costume* (Percy Society, London, 1849), 127-30. References from C. R. Beard's notes.

16. A. Wilson, *The History of Great Britain being the Life and Reign of King James the First* (London, 1653), 258. References from C. R. Beard's notes.

17. *Inverness Recs.*, i, 252. See also C. E. Whitelaw, *Scottish Arms Makers* (London, 1977), 252, where the date is given incorrectly as 1572.

18. F. Deters in *Die Englischen Angriffswaffen zur Zeit der Einführung der Feuerwaffen* (Heidelberg, 1913), 7-9, denies that this was so while, paradoxically, drawing attention to a passage in the fourteenth-century *Story of England* by Robert Mannying of Brunn in which *hilte* clearly can only mean a sword-guard:

    ffro the hilte vnto the pomel
    Was twenti vnche large, meten ful wel

    A. Schultz, in *Das Höfische Leben zur Zeit der Minnesinger*, vol. 2 (Leipzig, 1880), 12-13, says, quoting supporting texts, that the equivalent medieval German words *helze* and *gehelze* referred to the grip and quillons together, and there is some evidence of a similar use of *hilt* and *hilts* in English medieval texts. For example: the whalebone and parchment swords made for the tournament at Windsor in 1278 had gilded 'pomell hilt' (*Archaeologia*, xvii [1814], 302); the inventory of the goods and chattels of Thomas, Duke of Gloucester at Pleshy in 1397 includes several swords and daggers described as having 'pomel & hilte' with other fittings but without any references to grips (*Archaeol. Journ.*, liv [1897], 306); in a roll of arms of the third quarter of the 15th century in the British Museum (*Harleian Ms.* 2169) a simple cruciform sword, with a grip, in the arms of Our Lord is blazoned merely as 'wt gold pomell and hyltte' (*Ancestor*, ix [London, 1904], 178). By the end of Henry VIII's reign the word was undoubtedly being used in the sense of guard. This is shown by the many entries in the well-known inventory of the king's possessions, made after his death in 1547, describing swords as being equipped with hilts (both in the plural and singular), pommels and hands (or handles), for example '. . . an armynge swourde wch was William Conquerors . . . the pomell and hiltes couerid wt silver plate . . . the hande wounde aboute with wier of Silver' (British Museum, *Harl.* 1419B, f. 410; *cf.* also *Archaeologia*, li [1888], 272). The normal word for guard in the inventory is *hilt*, though *cross* also occurs occasionally. In two instances the words are used together — for example, '. . . A bearinge Swourde . . . the Crosse pomell and hiltes of Silver and guilte' — a combination which presumably indicated a sword with long quillons with supplementary guards in the centre (*Harl.* 1419B, f. 410). Similarly, in an order of 8 June 1580 made by the Perth Hammermen a distinction (undefined) is apparently made between 'hilts' and 'gairdis' (Whitelaw, *Arms Makers*, 271). The noted Elizabethan fencer George Silver uses *hilt* several times in his *Paradoxes of Defence* of 1599 in a manner which indicates clearly that he is referring to sword-guards (Shakespeare Association Facsimile, London, 1933, Dedication, and pp. 17, 32, etc.), while as late as 1688 R. Holme in his *Academie of Armory* (Roxburghe Club, London, 1905, 125) refers to a sword as having 'Hilt, handle, and pommell'. By 1692, however, the modern usage of *hilt* had been introduced, for Sir William Hope, in the second edition of *The compleat fencing-master* (London, 1692), 2, says, 'The Hilt is divided into three parts, the Pomell, the Handle, and the shell.'

19. Whitelaw, *Arms Makers*, 270.

20. Ibid., passim.

21. *The book of the Thanes of Cawdor,* ed. C. Innes (Spalding Club, 1859), 204.

22. Apart from a suggestion of doubtful reliability published by Thomas Pennant in 1774 (*A Tour of Scotland . . . MDCCLXXII,* 289), that they were used extensively at Culloden in 1746, all the available evidence points to the two-hand claymore having gone out of general use long before the end of the seventeenth century. The consensus of opinion among modern writers on the subject is that it was no longer made after the seventeenth century. See pp. 385-6, notes 3 & 18.

23. H. Lumsden & P. H. Aitken, *The History of the Hammermen of Glasgow* (Paisley, 1912), 290, 291. I am grateful to the Glasgow City Archivist and Mr J. G. Scott for providing corrected transcripts of the two earlier entries from *Minute Book No. 1* (pp. 229 & 232) of the Incorporation of Hammermen of Glasgow.

24. See: *Oxford English Dictionary* under *shable;* W. Grant & D. D. Murison, *Scottish National Dictionary* (Edinburgh, 1931-76), under *shabble;* Whitelaw, *Arms Makers,* 22.

25. Ibid., 296.

26. See W. H. Finlayson, 'Two Early Paintings of the Scots Brigade', *Scot. Hist. Rev.,* cvi (1949), 119-20. I am very grateful to Dr Nolfo di Carpegna for examining the original manuscript for me and providing sketches of the sword-hilts.

27. Finlayson, 'Two Early Paintings', 120.

28. W. C. Little, 'Observations on the Hammermen of Edinburgh', *Archaeologia Scotica,* i (1792), 170.

29. I am grateful to Mr A. J. Aitken, Editor of the *Dictionary of the Older Scottish Tongue,* for first suggesting that this might be the correct reading and to Dr W. H. Makey, Edinburgh City Archivist, for very kindly establishing that it is by looking at the original entry (*Records of the Hammermen,* vol. iii, 9 Jan., 1583/4). Dr Makey has also corrected another misleading transcription published by Little. The 'great hit sword' which he states was the Armourers' essay in 1590 was actually 'ane graithit sword', that is a sword ready for sale, the adjective being derived from the verb 'to graith', (ibid., 11 Feb., 1590/1).

    Since the present study was written the correct version of one of the entries has appeared in Whitelaw's *Arms Makers,* 170.

30. See Wallace, *Scottish Swords and Dirks,* 11, 20.

31. The entry also contains what appears to be the earliest recorded use of the term 'ane pair of ribbit gairdis', the precise meaning of which is unknown. It presumably referred to a guard made of ribs or bars, and this description applies equally to the earliest form of basket-guard (e.g. figs. 99-120) and to the normal European swept rapier hilt of the period. Little's reference (p. 171) to 'ane pair of small ribbit sword gairds . . . of the French fashion', which seems to provide support for the swept hilt identification, is misleading. The source (which Little does not indicate) is clearly the record of the admission of Robert Borthwick, Lorimer on 10 July, 1589, when he presented as his essay 'ane pair small ribbit gairds, ane mollet bit of the french fassioun, ane peir steirrup irnes and ane pair of spurris of the frenche fassioun' (Whitelaw, *Arms Makers,* 164).

32. Both quoted in the *Oxford English Dictionary* under *Basket hilt* and *Basket hilted.*

33. *Acts of the Privy Council of England,* n.s. vol. xxxi (London, 1906), 312.

34. The inventory of a lottery of arms and armour held in London in 1586 includes several references to 'semitaries or Turky swordes' (F. H. Cripps-Day, *Fragmenta Armamentaria,* II, ii [Frome, 1938], Lots 23-25, 32, 38). It seems likely, therefore, that a Turkey blade was a curved one. The Cutlers' Company and others were supplying swords with Turkey blades for the City trained bands in 1614 (R. R. Sharpe, *London and the Kingdom,* ii [London, 1894]), 65, while in 1622 Francis Markham wrote that

the blade of a musketeer's basket-hilted sword 'should be broad, strong and somewhat massie of which the Turkie, or Bilboe are the best' (see p. 163). The 'Bilboe', which derives its name from Bilbao in Spain, appears to have been a straight, broad blade, or a sword equipped with such a blade, though this is not absolutely certain (see *Oxford English Dictionary*, s.v.). A number of swords with early basket-hilts of British type are preserved in Scandinavian museums (see E. Eyvang, 'Tessaken', *Haermuseets Arbok 1973-1975* [Oslo, 1975], 112). Another sword with such a hilt and a curved blade bearing an inscription with English connections is in the Tower of London Armouries (No. IX.1015). See n. 138 below.

35. *Acts of the Privy Council of England*, xxxi, 316, 324.

36. Ibid., xxxii, 224, 236, 443, 473.

37. Ibid., xxx, 414.

38. This conclusion is confirmed by a passage in Sir William Hope's *New Method of Fencing*, 2nd edn. (Edinburgh, 1714), 157:

> . . . when a Man has a Back-sword with a closs Hilt or Guard, and that now a days ther are but few such Swords made use of, except amongst the *Highlanders* in *Scotland*, and Backsword-Masters or *Gladiators* in *England* . . . If I mistake it not, the Royal Regiment of *Scots* Dragoons are furnished with such closs *Hilted Swords* . . . or as they are more commonly termed by the Vulgar, *Shell* or *Sheephead* Hilts.

See also p. 158 above.

39. Public Record Office [PRO], London, E351/2963.

40. See below, p. 163; also *Calendar of the State Papers relating to Ireland . . . 1615-1625* (London, 1880), 543.

41. PRO, W.O. 47/2, Minute of 2nd June 1653. I am grateful to Mr. H. L. Blackmore for this reference.

42. PRO: E101/434/9, p. 36; E101/435/16, p. 12; E101/436/3, mem. 4.

43. E. Davis, *The Art of War* (London, 1619), 135. I am grateful to Mr A. V. B. Norman for this reference.

44. F. Markham, *Five Decades of Epistles of Warre* (London, 1622), 34. I am grateful to Mr W. Reid for this reference.

45. This has been illustrated and described many times, for example, Laking, *European Armour & Arms*, iv, 325, and C. Blair, *European & American Arms* (London, 1962), pl. 167. It was originally in the collection of the Baron C. A. de Cosson, but it is not known where he obtained it. In his own catalogue of his second sale held by Christie's 2-4 May 1893 (Lot 205) he says, 'There is reason for believing that this sword belonged to Sir William Twysden of Roydon Hall in Kent, Knighted by James I in 1603, and Baronet in 1611', but does not say what the reason was. The Sir William Twysden in question was born in 1566 and died in 1629 and could very well have owned the sword. Unfortunately, his will (PRO Prob. 11/155) contains no mention of his personal possessions, while I am informed by Dr Felix Hull, Kent County Archivist, that there is no material among the Twysden manuscripts under his care at Maidstone which might contain information about the sword. It is not mentioned either in the very well documented history of the family by Sir J. R. Twisden and C. H. Dudley Ward, *The Family of Twysden and Twisden* (London, 1939), or in A. R. Cook's history of Roydon, *A Manor through Four Centuries* (Oxford, 1938).

46. Nos. IX 1021 & 1114. *Swords & Daggers in the Tower of London*, pl. 51a.

47. No. 472-1936.

48. [Sir] J. G. Mann, 'Die Waffensammlung auf Warwick Castle', Pt. II, *Zeitschrift für Historische Waffen- und Kostümkunde*, xv (1937-9), 53.

49. At present on loan to the Tower of London Armouries.

50. This has been fitted to a Light Cavalry sabre of the British 1796 pattern, presumably for use by a Yeomanry officer.

51. O. Millar, *The Tudor, Stuart and Early Georgian Pictures in the Collection of Her Majesty the Queen*, 2 vols. (London, 1963), No. 77.

52. Reproduced in R. N. Dore, *The Civil Wars in Cheshire* (Chester, 1966), pl. 9, where it is captioned 'A Cheshire Officer for the Parliament: probably Colonel John Booth', an identification which does not appear to be based on any firm evidence. It shows the full-length figure of a young man wearing a harquebus armour (without the helmet) over a buff coat with quilted sleeves. The sword, which has a globular pommel of medium size, is hung at his left side and viewed from the inside, while a combined priming flask and wheel-lock spanner *(charging spanner)* hangs from a long cord round his neck. His right hand holds the muzzle of a carbine with its butt resting on the ground: despite the spanner this is fitted with a snaplock with a cock resembling that of a Spanish 'miquelet' lock.

    I am indebted to Mr J. L. Nevinson for the information that the style of costume shown in the portrait suggests a date of c. 1645. It therefore provides the latest evidence known to me for the survival of long quillons on a basket-hilt of this type. It is, of course, possible that the sword was already an old one when the portrait was painted.

    I am grateful to Mr P. A. Hayes of the National Army Museum, London, for drawing my attention to the reproduction of the portrait in Dore's book, and to Canon Maurice H. Ridgway, Vicar of Bowdon, Cheshire, for information about it.

53. Sotheby's, 20 Dec. 1963, Lot 13B (not in the catalogue). It is now in an English private collection.

54. See C. Blair, *The James A. de Rothschild Collection at Waddesdon Manor: Arms, Armour and Base Metalwork* (National Trust, London, 1974), 83-86.

55. See H. L. Peterson, *Army and Armor in Colonial America* (Harrisburg, Pennsylvania, 1956), 84, pls. 90-93; J. L. Cotter & J. P. Hudson, *New Discoveries at Jamestown* (Washington, 1957), 56, 70; J. L. Cotter, *Archaeological Excavations at Jamestown* (Washington, 1958), 112, 178. See also p. 220 below.

56. C. ffoulkes, *European Arms and Armour in the University of Oxford* (Oxford, 1912), No. 20.

57. No. 70.17. According to a label attached to it the sword was given by Mrs Bowthorpe's Estate and belonged originally to 'Sir John Hobbs'. The identity of Sir John Hobbs is not recorded at the Lewes Museum.

58. This was almost certainly originally part of the parish armour.

59. Stephen Moorhouse, 'Finds from Basing, Hampshire (c. 1540-1645): Part Two', *Post-Med. Archaeol.*, v (1971), 54, pl. IIIA.

60. This is not to say that bun-shaped pommels are rare on swords of this type. They are, in fact, quite common. See, for example, two swords in the L. I. Gibson collection sold at Sotheby's 17 May 1977 (Lots 259, 266). The guard of one of these (Lot 259) is decorated with roughly-incised profile heads in morions.

61. The Sandal Castle finds have not, at the time of writing, been published. For an account of Basing House see S. Moorhouse, 'Finds. Part One', *Post-Med. Archaeol.*, iv (1970), 31-40.

    What appears to be another sword of this type was excavated at Helmsley Castle, Yorkshire in 1928, and is illustrated with other objects from the same site, in *The Times* for 16 Nov. 1928. These finds are said to have been deposited with the Ancient Monuments Branch of the old Ministry of Works (now Department of the Environment), but are no longer traceable. The sword was probably a relic of the Civil War siege which ended with the surrender of the Castle to Parliamentary forces on 22 Nov. 1644. [Since this went to press the sword has been traced in the Ancient Monuments store at Fortress House, Savile Row, London (No. 670819). It has an Irish ribbon hilt and a pommel like that of the Ripon sword described on p. 208 above.]

62. See: F. Hyett, 'Notes on Portraits of Sir Edward Massey', *Trans. Bristol & Gloucestershire Archaeol. Soc.*, xliii (1921), 239-251; *The National Gallery of Canada: Catalogue of Painting and Sculpture*, i, ed. R. H. Hubbard (Ottawa & Toronto, 1957), 119.

63. G. A. Hayes-McCoy, *Sixteenth Century Irish Swords in the National Museum of Ireland* (Dublin, 1959), passim.

64. See above, pp. 211, 224, 233 and n. 137.

65. A. Feuillerat, *Documents Relating to the Revels at Court in the time of King Edward VI and Queen Mary*, (Louvain, 1914), 49, 134, 142.

66. *Cutlers' Company Court Minute Book 1602-70*, Guildhall Library Ms. 7151/1, f. 6v. I am grateful to Mr Gerald Mungeam for this reference.

67. See W. L. Nevinson, 'Portraits of Gentlemen Pensioners before 1625', *The Thirty-Fourth Volume of the Walpole Society, 1952-1954* (Glasgow University Press, 1958), 6, 12, and pl. IIA.

68. The evidence for the precise identification of these arms in the records of the seventeenth-century heraldic Visitations is a little confusing. As pointed out by Mr Nevinson (ibid., 12), exactly the same arms and crest (but differenced by a crescent) are given to Palmer of Compton Scorfen (now Compton Scorpion), Warwickshire, in the return for Camden's Warwickshire Visitation of 1619 (*Harleian Soc., xii* [1877], p. 220). This family was a recent branch of the family of Palmer of Lemington, near Todenham, Gloucestershire, see also n. 69, the members of which, well back into the Middle Ages, are also shown in the Visitation pedigree. The same Visitation return includes an entry for Palmer of Lemington (ibid., 170-71), of which the pedigree more or less duplicates a small section of the much more elaborate pedigree of Palmer of Compton Scorfen, but is accompanied by a completely different coat-of-arms. These same arms and approximately the same pedigree are also given for Palmer of Lemington in the return for the Gloucestershire Visitation of 1623 (*Harleian Soc., xxi* [London, 1885], 119). There can be little doubt, for reasons given below, that the portrait is of a Palmer of Lemington, so the arms must either have been added later and inaccurately (which is not impossible), or else the arms given for this family in the two Visitations are incorrect. The quarterings included in the arms on the portrait are appropriate to Palmer of Lemington, while the pedigree with the return for Palmer of Compton Scorfen is undoubtedly a much more thorough piece of work than the other two. In my view, therefore, we must accept that it is the one that is the most likely to be accurate and that the arms on the portrait could have been used by both branches of the family.

69. R. Bigland, *Historical, Monumental and Genealogical Collections, Relative to the County of Gloucester*, i (London, 1791), 377 n., in which the picture is described in detail. Bigland died in 1784, so the information he gives here about it must be earlier than that. He attributed it to Andrew Wright, Serjeant Painter to King Henry VIII, apparently merely on the evidence, obtained from reading Horace Walpole's *Anecdotes of Painting*, that Wright was active in England when the portrait was painted. The available documentary evidence about Wright indicates, however, that he was an archtitectural and heraldic painter only (E. Auerbach, *Tudor Artists* [London, 1954], 144-45).

   The Palmers do not appear to have had any direct connections with Southam-Delabere, and, according to Bigland, the portrait under discussion, and portraits of

Giles Palmer, William's younger brother and heir, and of his grandson, the ill-fated Sir Thomas Overbury, 'belonged to Sir John Hales, and, with his own Portrait, were brought to *Southam*, in Consequence of the Marriage of Kinard De La Bere and Joan his daughter, in 1650'. This refers to Sir John Hales, Bart. (ob. 1677) of Coventry, but I have been unable to trace any connection between him and the Palmer and Overbury families. It seems reasonable to assume, however, that he somehow acquired a collection of pictures that had belonged to Giles Palmer's daughter Mary, wife of Nicholas Overbury.

The portrait remained at Southam until 1947 when it was sold by Lord Ellenborough's executors (Sotheby's, 11 June 1947, Lot 77). The photograph reproduced as fig. 77 shows it at the time of the sale. It subsequently appeared, restored, as Lot 10 in the Captain E. G. Spencer Churchill sale at Christie's on 25 June 1965. In 1977-8, much repainted, it was in the possession of Sabin Galleries of Cork St., London.

70. *Henry VIII Letters & Papers*, XIV, i, 345. His name is substituted for 'Barmeston' in the list, which suggests that he had just joined the Gentlemen Pensioners when it was drawn up. He appears under his full name in later lists (ibid., XIX, i, 161-3; XX, ii, 558), so there can be no doubt that he is the same person as 'Palmer of Glouc. sonne'. A list of pensioners, alleged to date from 1526 in which his name appears (ibid., IV, i, 871) actually dates from about 1540.

Palmer is described in the 1619 Warwickshire Visitation (*Harleian Soc.*, xii [1877], 222) as 'unus ex generosis pencionarijs Hen. octavij'. He is last recorded as a Gentleman Pensioner at the funeral of King Edward VI on 8 Aug. 1553 (*Archaeologia*, xii [1796], 387). He probably left the royal service because the new régime of Mary was not congenial to him, or perhaps because the death of his father in the same year (see n. 71) made it necessary for him to return to the family estates in Gloucestershire. He died between 22 July 1573, when his will was signed, and 19 Dec. of the same year when it was proved (P.C.C. 38 *Peter*. PRO Prob. 11/55/ff. 288-89).

71. His will was signed on 10 July 1553 and proved on 8 August of the same year (P.C.C. F16 *Tashe*. PRO Prob. 11/36/f.117). In the pedigree of Palmer given in the much enlarged second edition of Sir William Dugdale's *Antiquities of Warwickshire* (London, 1730), ii, 633, he is described as 'unus ex Generosis Pensoniarius regis Henrici 8'. It does not describe William Palmer in this way so it is conceivable that the reference to John being a Gentleman Pensioner is the result of a mistranscription of William's similar entry in the 1619 Warwickshire Visitation pedigree (see n. 70).

72. Their style is consistent with any date between c. 1540 and the early seventeenth century.

73. The suggestion is made in a duplicated account of the portrait and its history produced by Sabin Galleries in 1978. For an account of Flicke see Auerbach, *Tudor Artists*, 163.

74. The costume, especially the hat, shown in the portrait is very similar to that shown on Holbein's drawing of William Parr, later Earl of Essex and Marquess of Northampton, at Windsor Castle (Nevinson, 'Portraits of Gentlemen Pensioners', 6, pl. IIB), which must date from before 1543, the year of the artist's death. I am grateful to Mr J. L. Nevinson for kindly giving me his opinion that the costume suggests a period in the late 1530s for the Palmer portrait, but that a date as late as 1546 is not impossible.

75. E. Auerbach & C. K. Adams, *Paintings & Sculpture at Hatfield House* (London, 1971), No. 49. This contains a discussion of the possible connection between figures in the picture and the drawings by Lucas de Heere at Ghent discussed below.

76. Ms. 2466, fol. 70. I am grateful to Dr Albert Derolez, Keeper of Manuscripts of the Universiteit-Gent Centrale Bibliotheek for supplying me with a photograph of the illustration. See also n. 78.

77. There is no reason to think that this sword has any early Scottish connections. See also p. 196.

78. Add. Ms. 28, 330, fol. 31. For a full description of the manuscript and a discussion of its connection with the manuscript referred to in n. 76, see Th. M. Chotzen & A. M. E. Draak, *Beschrivning der Britische Eilanden door Lucas de Heere* (Antwerp, 1937).

79. He is labelled 'Eenen halbardier der Magesteit'.

80. Silver, *Paradoxes of Defence 1599,* 28.

81. I am very grateful to Dr J. F. Hayward for drawing my attention to this important portrait and for generously allowing me to publish it here. In fairness to the late Dr C. R. Beard, it must be recorded, however, that he appears to have been the first person to realise the significance of the portrait as a document for the history of the basket-hilt. He saw it at the *Heraldic Exhibition* held at the Birmingham City Art Gallery and Museum in 1936 (Catalogue No. 882), and a discussion and sketch of the sword-guard are included in his unpublished notes on basket-hilted swords. I am also grateful to the late Viscount Cobham for allowing me both to examine the picture and to publish the photograph reproduced as fig. 85 here.

82. No. LA (1966). Sold Christie's, 14 Apr. 1966, Lot 174. I am grateful to the late Mr H. C. Haldane for the information that the sword came from the Duke of Abercorn.

83. See Seitz, *Blankwaffen,* ii, figs. 66, 75 for late examples. Fig. 75 shows a sword at Veste Coburg dated 1637 on the blade.

84. See G. V. Irving, 'On Andrea Ferrara swords', *Journ. British Archaeol. Assoc.,* (1865), 316-34; Baron de Cosson, 'Arsenals and Armouries in Southern Germany', *Archaeol. Journ.,* xlviii (1891), 122-3; Wallace, *Scottish Swords and Dirks,* 25.

85. C. Blair, 'A Royal Swordsmith and Damascener: Diego de Çaias', *Metropolitan Museum Journal,* 3/1970 (1971) 149-98.

86. For English damascened work of this period see: J. F. Hayward, *The Art of the Gunmaker,* ii, 2nd edn. (London, 1965), 120-7; I. Eaves, 'Further Notes on the Pistol in Early 17th Century England', *Journ. Arms & Armour Soc.,* viii, (1974-7), 284. Whitelaw, *Arms Makers,* 126, records three 'Damaskers' working in Edinburgh, in the late sixteenth and early seventeenth centuries.

87. Prattinton's manuscript collections relating to the history of Worcestershire in the Library of the Society of Antiquaries of London include (Vol. XIV, f. 35) a pedigree of the Lyttleton family which contains the following information about the children of John Lyttleton and his wife:

    By her he had seven sons & two Daughters.

    1. *John* 2. *Edward* nicknamed Long Edward, who married the Lady Elizabeth [Talbot], daughter of Wrottesley of Wrottesley in Staffordshire, & widow of *Sr John Talbot* of *Grafton* from whom descend the *Talbots* of Salwarp, Worvil & the late Lord Chancellor Talbot . . .

    For the date of his burial see J. B. Blakeway, 'History of Albrighton', *Trans. Shropshire Archaeol. & Nat. Hist. Soc.,* xxii, (1899), 74.

    See also T. R. Nash, *Collections for the History of Worcestershire,* i (London, 1781-2), pedigree opposite p. 494; *Hist. Mss. Comm., Various Collections,* ii (1903), 309-10.

88. P.C.C. 76. PRO *Prob.* 11/80. Proved 26 Oct. 1592.

89. Salop County Record Office, Shrewsbury. I am grateful to Miss M. C. Hill, County Archivist, for providing me with a xerox of the relevant parts of the inventory. A slightly inaccurate transcript is in the Prattinton Ms. at the Society of Antiquaries (Vol. XV, 1-9).

90. It was bequeathed to his son-in-law John Talbot: 'my chaine of golde wch I vse to weare with the picture deathes head vppon yt'. This is presumably the 'Chain of gold

of 40 oz with twooe pictures in the same' listed in the inventory.

91. See most of the sources quoted in n. 2.

92. See C. Blair, 'A Schiavona Rapier', *Journ. Arms & Armour Soc.*, v, (1965-7), 453-4; G. Seifert, 'Blankwaffen: Schiavona', *Deutsches Waffenjournal*, ii, no. 12 (Dec. 1966), 42-7; Seitz, *Blankwaffen*, ii, 122-26; *Swords & Daggers in the Tower of London*, pl. 45; L. G. Boccia & E. T. Coelho, *Armi Bianche Italiane* (Milan, 1975), pls. 488-98, 765-73. In the Museum at Kotor, Dalmatia (Yugoslavia) a portrait of Captain Peter Zelic de Bijela, Knight of Malta, dating from c. 1760, shows a schiavona.

93. Boccia & Coelho, *Armi Bianche*, 23, pls. 488-95.

94. Seitz, *Blankwaffen*, i, 171, fig. 107.

95. Boccia & Coelho, *Armi Bianche*, pls. 150-2, 165-7.

96. Ibid., pls. 333, 380.

97. No. 259A. I am grateful to Mr A. V. B. Norman for drawing my attention to the similarity between the sword shown in this portrait and the Bini Sword. The portrait was formerly attributed to Sebastiano del Piombo (ob. 1547) and is illustrated by Pietro d'Achiardo in his book on this master (*Sebastiano del Piombo* [Rome, 1908], 223, fig. 48). The attribution was rejected by L. Dussler, *Sebastiano del Piombo* (Basel, 1942), 150, No. 82, and the painting is listed as 'Piombo?' in the *Verzeichnis der Ausgestellten Gemälde des 13. bis 18. Jahrunderts in Museum Dahlem* (Berlin, 1964), 89. I am indebted to Mr J. L. Nevinson for the information that the type of hat shown in the portrait is not likely to be earlier than about 1540, and for his opinion that the general style of the costume suggests a date in the 1550s or 1560s. Similar costume is shown, for example, in Titian's portrait of Phillip II of Spain, dated 1551, at Naples. See C. Bernis, *Indumentaria Española en Tiempos de Carlos V* (Madrid, 1962), fig. 162.

98. Jacobsen, 'Kurvfaester', 103-4.

99. See T. Michell, *History of the Scottish Expedition to Norway in 1612* (London, 1886).

100. H. Jacobsen, 'De norske "Sinclairsabler"', *Vaabenhistoriske Aarbøger*, i (1934-6), 25-37; Idem., 'Die norwegischen "Sinclair-Säbel"', *Zeitschrift für Historische Waffen- und Kostümkunde*, xv (1937-9), 169-73; Seitz, *Blankwaffen*, i, 360-1; Eyvang, 'Tessaken', 74-115.

101. Ibid.

102. Ibid., 112, fig. 20. Swords of this kind are to be found in Scandinavia in the following collections: Haermuseet and Folkemuseet, Oslo; the Sandvig Collection, Lillehammer; Tøjhusmuseet, Copenhagen.

103. Jacobsen, 'Kurvefaester', 102 and 93, figs. 1-5. Eyvang's Type F is exactly the same as very many of the Tessaks in the Landeszeughaus at Graz, Austria (Styria), of which some, if not all, were produced locally in the last quarter of the sixteenth century. See F. Pichler, *Das Landes-Zeughaus in Graz* (Leipzig, 1880), 106-7, 76-7, pl. xxiv, 6, P. Krenn, *Das Steiermärkische Landeszeughaus in Graz. Eine Übersicht über seine Geschichte und seine Waffen* (Graz, 1974), 39-40.

104. E. A. Gessler, 'Die Entwicklung des "Schweizersäbels" im 16. bis 17. Jahrhundert' and 'Ein Nachtrag zum "Schweizersäbel"', *Zeitschrift für Historische Waffenkunde*, vi (1912-14), 264-77, 303-13; xiii (1932-4), 271-5.

105. Gessler, 'Die Entwicklung', 270-1, nos. III & IV.

106. See Seitz, *Blankwaffen*, i, 173-5, 273-6; E. A. Gessler, 'Eine Sinnbildliche Jahrzahl mit Wiedergabe von Altschweizerischen Waffen', *Zeitschrift für Historische Waffen- und Kostümkunde*, xiv (1935-6), 86-89; H. Schneider, *Beiträge zur Geschichte der Zür-cherischen Bewaffnung im 16 Jahrhundert* (Zürich, 1942), 23.

107. See Seitz, *Blankwaffen*, i, 276; also n. 109.

108. *Swords & Daggers in the Tower of London*, pl. 17a.

109. E. Ehlers, *Hans Döring. Ein hessischer Maler des 16. Jahrhunderts* (Darmstadt, 1919), pls. XXII-XXV, XXVIII, XXX, XXXIV. In contrast to these, a soldier in pl. XXVI appears to be wearing a simple Katzbalger without extra guards. See also D. Miller & G. A. Embleton, *The Landsknechts* (London, 1976), 9-10.

110. *Swords & Daggers in the Tower of London*, pl. 17b.

111. Eyvang, 'Tessaken', 84-85.

112. A sword of this type in the Fitzwilliam Museum, Cambridge is fitted with a blade dated 1591. It is of the right type for the hilt but may, of course, have been made as a replacement for an earlier blade in 1591.

113. See above, p. 156. This form of guard, it should be noted, represents only one line of development, for it does not have the foreguards which are, of course, usually found on eighteenth century hilts.

114. The mourning sword, carried before the Mayor on occasions of mourning and great public solemnity instead of the normal civic sword. The pommel and cross are of gilt latten and only one reference to such occurs in the documents about the Exeter civic swords published by H. L. Parry in 'The Exeter Swords and Hat of Maintenance', *Report & Trans. Devonshire Assoc.*, lxiv (1932), 420-54. This is as follows (p. 432):
    It paid John Walle for vi li of laten of ii sortys for the hayfte of the sword xxiid.
    The blade is probably that of the sword acquired in 1497-8 (ibid., 430). See also L. Willoughby, 'Corporation Treasures Belonging to the City of Exeter', *Connoisseur* Jan. 1909, 17-18.

115. W. B. Redfern, 'On Some Choice Sword-Hilts with Notes on their Evolution', *Connoisseur* Mar. 1923, 141, No. 2. It was included in Lot 119 in the sale of the Redfern Collection at Sotheby's on 20 June 1934, bought by a Major Smith for 18 shillings.

116. I am grateful to Mr A. V. B. Norman for drawing my attention to this guard.

117. For the earlier forms see C. Blair, *European and American Arms* (London, 1964), 4 and pls. 57-61. The earlier dateable double knuckle-guard known to me is on a sword depicted in Holbein's well-known design for a cutler's sign executed in about 1530 (Seitz, *Blankwaffen*, i, 248, fig. 161).

118. The house was built by the Montagu family in the sixteenth century and remained in their possession until it passed by marriage to the Dukes of Buccleuch in the late eighteenth century. The second Duke of Montagu, who was Master General of the Ordnance from 1740 to 1749, seems to have brought some of the pieces now in the Boughton armoury from the Tower of London. If the sword under discussion came from the same source, which is uncertain, it would be tempting to link it with the Yeomen of the Guard on the evidence of the Hampton Court painting discussed on pp. 202-3 above. I am grateful to the late Duke of Buccleuch and Queensberry, for permission to study, photograph, and publish the Sword.

119. There is, inevitably, disagreement about the attribution and precise date, but there seems to be no obvious reason why it should be substantially later than the events it depicts. See Miller, *Tudor, Stuart & Georgian Pictures*, No. 25; S. Anglo, 'The Hampton Court Painting of the Field of Cloth of Gold Considered as an Historical Document', *Antiquaries Journ.*, xlvi (1966), 287-307; J. B. Trapp & H. S. Herbrüggen, *'The King's Good Servant'. Sir Thomas More 1477/8-1535* (National Portrait Gallery, London, 1977-8), No. 67.

120. I am grateful to Dr J. F. Hayward for drawing my attention to this sword.

121. I am grateful to the late Dr Williams both for allowing me to study and photograph the guard, and for the information that he bought it in about 1954 at a sale held in Pembridge Castle. The castle is near Welch Newton in S. Herefordshire.

122. No. B.5. It was found at Clotherholme, two miles north of Ripon.

123. Compare, for example, Wallace, *Scottish Swords & Dirks*, pl. 15.

124. It is not mentioned in the catalogue of Timperley's initial gift to the Museum, published in 1941.
125. *Catalogue of the National Museum of Antiquities of Scotland* (Edinburgh, 1892), 303. The late Professor G. A. Hayes-McCoy very kindly tried to identify the find-site for me, but without success.

     A drawing of what, at first sight, appears to be an exactly similar hilt made for left-handed use, reproduced by Drummond & Anderson, *Ancient Scottish Weapons*, pl. XVI, 9, is probably actually the hilt of the sword under discussion shown in reverse. I am indebted to Mr David Caldwell of the National Museum, Edinburgh, for the information that Drummond's original drawing, preserved in the Library there, is exactly like the published version.
126. Presented to the West Point Museum by Mrs W. R. Whitehead, it was formerly in the collection of W. Wareing Faulder of Manchester. He, in an article 'On Eight Swords', published in *Cambridge Antiquarian Communications,* iv (1876-80), 378-9, gave the following account of its history:

     Upon the death of a former rector of Netherbury, Beaminster, Dorsetshire, a grave was made for him just outside the east end of the chancel of his church, and in doing this an old tomb was opened in which was a coffin, and upon the lid being removed this sword was discovered. The weapon remained in the possession of the sexton for a long time, and from him passed into the hands of the head master of the Grammar School, from whom I obtained it.

     The tomb from which the sword came has always been considered by local antiquaries to be that of a Knight Templar of the 13th or 14th century . . . but supposing it to be true, interments must have been made in the tomb at a later time, as the sword is undoubtedly of a date between 1550 and 1580 . . . The hilt is of a shape extremely rare, and very interesting on account of its being the original form from which was developed the basket-hilt of the broadsword (commonly but erroneously called a Highland claymore) used generally by horsemen during the 17th century.

     The sword was exhibited in the *Exhibition of Industrial Art etc.* held at Ancoats Hall, Manchester in June and July 1881 (Cat. No. 239), and illustrated in Egerton Castles's *Schools and Masters of Fence* (London, 1892), pl. II, 10.
127. I am grateful to the Rev. Peter D. May, Vicar of Netherbury, for making enquiries about the story that the sword was found while digging the grave 'of a former rector . . . just outside the east end of the chancel'. He was unable to discover any information, but informs me that William Brookland, Vicar of Netherbury for 38 years, was buried just outside the east end of the church on 11 March 1842.
128. I am grateful to Mr William Reid both for drawing my attention to this and for obtaining a photograph for me.
129. Both swords were acquired in the sale-room and nothing certain is known of their previous history. My own sword was bought at a sale held by Wallis & Wallis of Lewes from 5 to 7 Sept. 1962 (Lot 1346). It had been put into the sale by a well-known London arms-dealer who informed me that he had bought it privately in the Midlands.
130. I am grateful to Mr William Reid for very kindly providing this drawing.
131. Wallace, *Scottish Swords and Dirks*, pls. 13, 17.
132. Nothing is known of its history before it was acquired by Spence.
133. I am grateful to Dr R. B. F. van der Sloot for photographs of this sword.
134. Cf. also the pommel of the sword depicted in a portrait of c. 1555, attributed to John Bettes I, of Henry Fitz Alan, Lord Maltraver, at Arundel Castle (*Connoisseur* Mar. 1978, 197).

135. A similar pommel occurs on a left-hand dagger in the Nederlands Leger- en Wapen-museum, Leiden, which has vertically recurved quillons with terminals of the same shape. See J. B. Kist, *Jacob de Gheyn, The Exercise of Armes* (Lochem, 1971), pl. 79.

136. A number of guards are in the museum on the Jamestown site; others, from planta-tions in the area, are in the possession of the Archaeology Department of Colonial Williamsburg, the Virginia Historic Landmarks Commission and the Department of Anthropology, College of William and Mary, Williamsburg. They have not yet been fully published, but see: Peterson, *Arms & Armor*, pl. 93; J. L. Cotter & J. P. Hudson, *Jamestown*, 56. A guard, as yet unpublished, was found in a rubbish deposit of c. 1690 on the Joseph Petitt site, Governor's Land, James City Co., Virginia, an in-dication of the long working life that weapons of this kind were likely to have.

      I am grateful to the late Harold L. Peterson for drawing my attention to many of these guards from sites in the U.S.A.. I should also like to express my gratitude to Ms. Merry W. Abbitt of the Virginia Historic Landmarks Commission and Dr Leverette B. Gregory of Southride Historical Sites Inc., Dept. of Anthropology, College of William and Mary, for providing further information and photographs through Mr Peterson.

137. I am grateful to Mr Oliver Snoddy of the National Museum for providing me with photographs of this sword. Another late illustration of the use of this form of hilt is provided by the sword worn by Sir Neill O'Neill on his well-known portrait of c. 1679 by J. M. Wright in the Tate Gallery, London (No. T. 132).

138. The guards discussed on pp. 203-16 above, for example, are all made of thin bars. Sword No. IX. 1015 at the (*Swords & Daggers in the Tower of London*, pl. 52 b-c), however, has a guard made of flat bars of a kind normally called Scottish, but the blade bears the inscription *EDWARDVꝛ PRINꝛ ANGLIE.*

139. See, for example: Wallace, *Scottish Swords and Dirks*, pls. 9-11, 15; *Swords & Daggers in the Tower of London*, pls. 46-2, 52b-c.

140. Pommels of this form also occur on a rare group of heavy rapiers of which the best-known example (with a globular pommel) is probably the one found when making the Thames Embankment and now in the Museum of London. The characteristic feature of the group is a guard comprising vertically-recurved quillons between two large side-rings containing pierced plates, large arms of the hilt, and a knuckle-bar which touches, but is not attached to, the pommel. The Museum of London sword and an exactly similar sword in the collection of the late Leslie I. Gibson of Mirfield, Yorkshire (Sotheby's, 17 May 1977, Lot 270), have globular pommels pierced for a sword-knot. What appears to be an identical form of sword is illustrated on the brass of Sir Edward Gage (engraved 1595) at West Firle, Sussex, so we may reasonably date the whole group to the late sixteenth or early seventeenth century. The remains of another sword of the same type, but with a horizontal disc pommel, from the Salis-bury Canals, is in the Salisbury Museum, while a complete example of unknown provenance was sold by Messrs. Wallis & Wallis of Lewes on 26 Aug. 1976 (Lot 897). A photograph of the blade and pommel (all that survives) of another sword of the same group 'excavated in London during the Blitz' was sent to the Victoria & Albert Museum in 1978 by Mr C. Parkerson of New Orleans. Cf. also the sword with a horizontal disc pommel found on the site of the fort of Älvsborg, near Göteborg, Sweden.

      The sources for the above are: M. R. Holmes, *Arms and Armour in Tudor and Stuart London* (London Museum, HMSO, 1957), 19 and 25 (No. A. 10437); J. Page-Phillips, *Macklin's Monumental Brasses* (London, 1969), 70; H. Wideen, 'Älvsborgs Slott-Grävningsfynd och Byggnadsdata', *Göteborgs Historiska Museum Årstryck 1963* (Göteborg, 1963), 85-86 and fig. 24.

141. See Sir I. Moncreiffe, *The Highland Clans* (London, 1967), 54.

142. I am grateful to Mr Oliver Snoddy of the National Museum for information about this sword.

143. I am grateful to the late Harold L. Peterson for drawing my attention to this guard and to Dr Leverette B. Gregory, Director of Field Operations, Southside Historical Sites, Inc., College of William and Mary, Williamsburg, for providing me with detailed information about it together with a specially-taken x-ray photograph.

144. Wallace, *Scottish Swords and Dirks*, pls. 21-22.

145. Lot 397 in the sale of the contents of Sheffield Park held by Wallis & Wallis of Lewes on 27 Apr. and 25 May 1971. It is now in a private collection in the Channel Islands.

146. No. 66/432/4. The sword, together with an harquebus armour, was bequeathed to the Wakefield Museum by the late Mr C. H. Haldane of Clarke Hall, Wakefield. In 1957 Mr Haldane informed me that he had purchased all the pieces at the sale of the contents of Badsworth Hall, near Pontefract, and that they had belonged to Col. Sir John Bright, whose home it had been. There is no reason to doubt that the pieces came from Badsworth, though they cannot be identified among the rather cursory descriptions in the catalogue of the sale of the contents held by Herbert J. Watson and Lister-Kaye & Co. on 14-17 July 1926. The association with Col. Bright, though likely enough, cannot be regarded as certain. I am grateful to Mr J. E. Cockcroft, Keeper of Social History at the Wakefield Museum and Mr Richard Knowles of Sandal for information about the pieces and the Badsworth sale. Mr Cockcroft also very kindly supplied me with photographs.

147. See: *Catalogue of the Collection of London Antiquities in the Guildhall Museum* (London, 1903), 277, No. 212 and pl. LXXXVII, 6. I am grateful to Mr Max Hebditch, Director of the Museum of London for information about this dagger and also for very kindly supplying me with a photograph of it.

148. J. Ritson, *Robin Hood* (London, 1885), 152.

149. Quoted by Albert Forbes Sieveking in his edition of *Worke for Cutlers or A Merry Dialogue between Sword, Rapier and Dagger . . . 1615* (London, 1904), 66.

150. Act II, Scene 1. Quoted by the *Oxford Dictionary* under *pannier*.

151. Silver, *Paradoxes of Defence*, 107.

152. J. Swetnam, *The School of the Noble and Worthy Science of Defence* (London, 1617), 1, 36, 91, 169.

153. No. T. 38. It was described and illustrated by W. B. Redfern in an article, 'The Dagger and the Main Gauche', *Connoisseur* Apr. 1922, 212, No. 7. It was Lot 121 in the Morgan Williams Sale (Christie's, 26-8 Apr. 1921) and Lot 23 in the W. B. Redfern Sale (Sotheby's, 20 June 1934). I am grateful to Mr N. J. Arch, Keeper of Military History at the Castle Museum, York for kindly giving me permission to examine and photograph the dagger.

154. It was Lot 726 in the sale of the L. F. McCardle Collection, Sheffield Park, (See n. 145). I am grateful to Mr Harris for very kindly bringing the dagger to me at the Victoria & Albert Museum for examination.

155. E. Eyvang, 'Sidevapen fra Historisk museum i Bergen', *Haermuseets Arbok, 1971-1972* (1972), 72-73.

156. A basket-hilted dagger with a guard that may relate to the Timperley/Harris/Oslo group appeared as Lot 409 in the F. R. von Berthold sale, Cologne, 25-26 May 1898.

157. It was acquired in the London sale-room and nothing is known of its previous history. I am grateful to the owner for permission to publish it.

158. Sotheby's, 24 Mar. 1969, Lots 85 and 86 (the latter with a modern pommel). Mr Kent told me that these daggers were both found in Yorkshire.

159. I am grateful to Mr A. R. E. North for this information.

160. Sold at Sotheby's, 14 Mar. 1978, Lot 78. The owner had previously informed me that he had himself found it in the Thames mud, though this information is not given in the sale-catalogue.
161. At present on loan to the Victoria & Albert Museum.
162. Since this article went to press my attention has been drawn to a closely similar dagger, in private possession, which was found in the mud of the London Thames at Bull Wharf on 12 Feb. 1978. It bears an illegible inscription and the date 1592 (?1593) on the blade.
163. C. Blair & J. Wallace, 'Scots — or Still English?', *Scottish Art Review*, IX, i (1963), 11-15, 34-37.
164. Ibid., 35-36.
165. Lot 396 in the Sale of 27 Apr. 1971 (See n. 145).
166. The guard has a certain resemblance to Eyvang's Type B which is undoubtedly Continental in origin. The basic framework of this, however, is a ring which touches the pommel only at the front. The resemblance is therefore probably fortuitous.
167. Drummond & Anderson, *Ancient Scottish Weapons*, pls. XI-XV; Wallace, *Scottish Swords and Dirks*, pls. 8-11.

Addendum

Since this article went to press an unusual hybrid basket-hilted sword has appeared in Christie's (7 May, 1981, Lot 75, illustrated in the catalogue). It has a ribbon Irish hilt, of similar construction to fig. 75, but without a foreguard, and with the lower half of the basket made solid in a manner reminiscent of guards of the form discussed on pp. 221 ff. It has a long tapering blade of flattened diamond section.

8 Some Notes on Scottish Axes and Long Shafted Weapons

David H. Caldwell

Scottish weapons have been little researched and none more so than the various axes and long shafted weapons known to have been in use from the twelfth century onwards. The basic problem, with its two complementary facets, has been firstly to identify those weapons which survive and secondly deduce the nature of those mentioned in documentary sources. There ought to be a fair measure of linkage between the two processes but in the cases where weapons are described in the documentary sources the information is incomplete or open to varying interpretations and many of the weapons considered to be Scottish do not have unimpeachable pedigrees or convincing associations with persons or events which can aid in their dating. Many are, of course, said to have been found on the sites of battles but this in itself can never be taken as evidence of date as battle fields are normally only vaguely known and experience has shown that items of considerably earlier or later date may turn up in such places. Also one might expect that many weapons found on battle fields or elsewhere in Scotland are those of the Scots' main enemy in medieval times, the English.

The fact must also be faced that where a name for a weapon, like 'Lochaber axe', was in use for several centuries, the weapon to which it referred may have changed considerably with the passing of time. Thus, although we know with some confidence what a Lochaber axe was like in the eighteenth century, we cannot automatically suppose that sixteenth-century ones were similar. The following notes on surviving weapons and documentary sources are not offered as a definitive study but merely as a step in that direction. Only weapons are considered which can reasonably be supposed to have been intended for use. Although some of those described were undoubtedly used primarily as badges of office or for ceremonial functions, they could nevertheless be used effectively in warfare.

In 1881 a volume on *Ancient Scottish Weapons* was published in Edinburgh under the name of James Drummond, a notable Scottish artist and antiquary. It consists of a series of coloured lithographs of weapons and other Scottish items with an introduction and notes. Unfortunately, Drummond had died even before all his drawings were completed and the work of compiling the information on the items illustrated and of writing an excellent introduction was undertaken by Joseph Anderson, the Keeper of the National Museum. Thus the notes on the individual weapons, more particularly their whereabouts, are not always as detailed as one would desire. The volume, however, includes several lithographs of axes and staff weapons and is the only major statement on the subject which has been published to date.

Spears

Spears are amongst the simplest of long shafted weapons and have a very long history indeed.[1] Functionally, they can be divided into three major types: spears for fighting on foot, spears for fighting on horseback, and spears for throwing. It is probable that the spear was the main weapon of the Scottish footman from the twelfth century until the seventeenth. It is known that the Scottish host (army) was drawn up in battles (divisions or wings) of spears and, under leaders such as William Wallace and Robert Bruce, was successfully drilled to withstand cavalry charges. There is no contemporary information as to what these spears were like, and most important, how long they were. There are, however, accounts of how they were used by the Scots at the battle of Falkirk in 1298. Wallace's army was weak in horsemen and archers, both of which were the strength of the opposing English. The Scottish footmen were drawn up by Wallace into four battles of circular shape with spears pointing out obliquely in all directions to ward off cavalry charges:

> Statuerunt enim Scotti omnem plebem suam per turmas iiij[or], in modum circulorum in campo duro juxta Fauchircke . . . Scottos lanciarios, qui in circulis sedebant cum lanceis obliquatis in modum silvae condensae,[2]

and indeed this policy was at first successful until the English archers took their toll and created gaps for their cavalry to penetrate.

An act was passed in parliament on 6 May 1471 forbidding merchants from importing spears of less than six ells (5.639 m.) in length and also forbidding bowyers in the realm from making them. Ten years later this was amended by an act for no spears other than those of at least five and a half ells (5.169 m.) or five ells before the burr.[3] Whether of six or five and a half ells in length, these spears were of enormous length and probably considerably larger than any hitherto in use. These were spears, or pikes as they were often called, of the type used so successfully by the Swiss and German mercenaries on the continent and in which the Scots placed so much trust at Flodden in 1513. They were of greatest use when in the hands of well trained and drilled men who could act together in large units. The great length of the pikes meant that several ranks of them could be presented to an enemy in serried rows, making a formidable obstacle to foot and horse alike. It was only if pike units became disarranged or dispersed that they could be defeated and then the length of the pikes could become a severe encumbrance to their owners, as was the case at Flodden.

Nevertheless Flodden was by no means the last occasion on which the Scots were to be drawn up in battles predominantly composed of pikemen. They were so arrayed at Pinkie in 1547, the last major pitched battle between the Scots and English in the sixteenth century. By the time of the civil wars of the middle of the seventeenth century muskets outnumbered pikes in the ranks sometimes by as much as three to two, although in English and continental armies the figures were more often two to one.[4] Pikes by and large do not seem to have been carried by any of those involved in the Jacobite uprisings of the eighteenth century. Their role in warfare had been taken over by the bayonet.

Half pikes which, as the name implies, were pikes with staffs of about half the length of pikes, may have been used more commonly than the one or two references in documents traced by the writer would have us believe. In 1543, in the troublesome times after the defeat of Solway Moss and the death of James V when the country was rent by factions, it was noted by a French observer that not only was the nobility in arms, 'but churchmen, friars and country people only travel through the countryside in large companies all armed with pikes, swords and bucklers and a half pike in their hands, which in this country is called a lance'.[5] A half pike was a more suitable weapon for an individual or for a small group of people since it was handier than the lengthy pike which could only be used successfully by large well disciplined forces. Half pikes were also suitable for use by officers in the army and law enforcement officers in the burghs. The captains of the trained bands of Edinburgh may have been rather tardy in adopting them, as suggested by a minute of 22 May 1678:

> The which day, the citie captaines being mett they taking to their consideration the indecencie of our marching with our staffs in extraordinarie days, and the laudable custom of all other places of the world in marching with the halfe picks, doth unanimouslie appoynt that everie captaine shall march with his halfe pick upon the 29 May 1678, under the paine of sex pounds Scotts money.[6]

In the twelfth and thirteenth centuries great importance was attached by the Scottish kings to the provision of an elite force of heavy mounted troops, clad in mail and armed with spears and swords.[7] The knights, as they were called, used their spears (lances) to deliver devastating charges which no foot soldiers of the time could withstand. The use of stirrups for support allowed the spear to be firmly gripped between arm and body and the charge to be pressed home vigorously. But the training and equipping of such troops was an expensive and time consuming business and Scotland may always have had problems in acquiring suitable sturdy horses. Even King Robert the Bruce is said to have ridden on a palfrey immediately before the main encounter of Bannockburn in order to keep his one good horse fresh for battle,[8] and two hundred years later his descendant James V is said to have sent to Denmark for great horses and mares to breed in his parks to provide offspring for use in the wars.[9] In the fourteenth and succeeding centuries heavily mounted horsemen never seem to have figured on the field as a significant military force.

On the other hand, the Scots made good use at various times of lightly armed horsemen, especially in the sixteenth century, and the border regions in particular. Estienne Perlin, a French visitor to Scotland writing in 1551-2, gives us a description of these horsemen:

> . . . bold and gallant enough, but are not so well armed as the French, for they have very little well made, clean and polished armour, but use jackets of mail in exercising daily with the French, and have the custom of using little ambling nags and small horses; their lances are small and narrow, and they have scarce any large horses, and few are brought to them, except from France.[10]

Javelins are mentioned in some documents of the mid-sixteenth century[11] and these were presumably spears of the type used by horsemen. Javelins were not necessarily for throwing as in the modern sense of the word. In fact there is little evidence for the throwing of spears either from foot or horseback, although the 'galloglaigh' — mercenaries of West Highland extraction — in Ireland are known to have used darts in the sixteenth century. A contemporary account describes how most of them had boys each carrying them three darts which they threw at their enemy before closing in with their axes.[12] In Major's *History of Great Britain*, first published in 1521, there is a description of the battle of Bannockburn in which the weapons described are manifestly those of Major's own time. The throwing of darts is alluded to prior to the main clash.[13] Leslie's *Historie* describes how in 1540 two great ships were sent from France to James V as a gift, loaded with 'speir and Javeling, darte and arrow, Gun and geinzie with all kynd of armour'.[14] These mentions of darts at the very least suggest some familiarity with them as a weapon at that time.

Very few spears have survived in Scotland, and of these most are either so badly corroded that their original form is in some doubt or are stray finds undateable by any archaeological context. A rare exception to this is a spearhead found recently in the excavations at Perth in a context which dates it to the late thirteenth or fourteenth century (fig 136).[15] It has a flattish elongated leaf-shaped blade with a long socket for attaching it to its shaft, but it is not clear whether it was for use on foot or horseback — possibly either. Other spearheads with leaf-shaped blades and

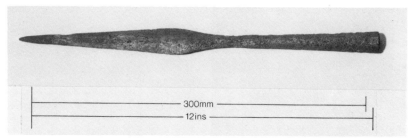

Figure 136. Spearhead from Perth, late 13th-14th cent.

without mid-ribs but generally with shorter and more rounded shoulders and relatively shorter sockets have been found in Scotland, like one in the National Museum from Mouswald in Dumfriesshire (LE 75). The type is also shown on the grave-slab of John Drummond at Inchmahome Priory in the Lake of Menteith, dating to c. 1360 (fig. 137),[16] and seems from the evidence of manuscript illuminations to have been long current in Europe.

Spears are depicted on some West Highland monuments and a particularly good example is on the grave slab of Bricius MacKinnon at Iona which dates to the fourteenth century. The armoured effigy of the deceased man, carved in relief, is shown clasping a spear with a lozenge-shaped blade with prominent mid-rib, and other apparently similar spearheads can be seen on two slabs with effigies from Poltalloch, now in Kilmartin churchyard, dating to the late fourteenth or fifteenth century.[17] Spearheads like this may be derived from a Viking type classified by Petersen as type M. They have a distribution eastwards into Finland and Russia and can be dated by their contexts to the eleventh century.[18] One was found in England in the Thames at Datchet, and is in the London Museum.[19] Manuscript illuminations again suggest the continuation of the type in Europe throughout the Medieval Period.

West Highland and other grave slabs may be used with reasonable confidence as evidence for the types of spearhead in use, but the length of the spear shafts is more open to question. These are shown to be only marginally longer at most than the height of the figures which themselves stretch the length of the stones.

In the Anthropological Museum of Marischal College, Aberdeen University, there are three iron lozenge-shaped spearheads (No. 468) with lozenge cross-sections and sockets (fig. 138). They vary in length from 0.408 m. to 0.441 m. and were purchased together in 1908, being said to have an Aberdeenshire provenance. They are remarkably similar in shape and presumably size to the spearhead on the slab of Bricius Mac-Kinnon but are probably much more recent. Six similar heads are mounted on shafts as half pikes with overall lengths of about 2.1 m. in

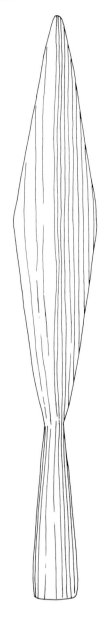

Figure 137. Grave slab of John Drummond at Inchmahome Priory, c.1360

Figure 138. Spearhead from Aberdeenshire, *Marischal College Museum, Aberdeen*

the collection of the Smith Institute in Stirling (Nos. B 4664, B 9871-3, B 9878-9). Unfortunately no provenance is known for them but it is likely that they are half pikes of the seventeenth or eighteenth centuries, possibly carried by a town guard or burgh officials.

Many of the pikes of the late fifteenth century and onwards would probably have had short stubby heads but no recognisable examples have come to the attention of the writer. A good proportion of the spears and pikes in use in Scotland were got from the continent and in the sixteenth century especially large quantities of pikes were imported, like the 3,000 pikes of white ash and 500 pikes of Spanish ash got along with 500 halberds for the king in 1541.[20] In Scotland spears were normally supplied by bowyers, although it is not clear if they made the metal heads as well as the staffs. The heads were certainly made by cutlers like Robert Selkirk of Edinburgh at the beginning of the sixteenth century, and Alexander Wicht, cutler, supplied James V with two gilt spearheads in 1541.[21] Smiths could also be involved, like the Smith of Cambuskenneth who supplied James V.[22]

There are but few representations of lances or spears used on horseback, and such as there are are of little value in providing information on the form of these weapons. The seals of Alexander I and William I have equestrian figures of their owners equipped with spears, and a seal of Walter Fitz Alan, High Steward of Scotland (fig. 139), appended to a charter granting the lands of Mauchline in Ayrshire to Melrose Abbey c. 1170, similarly shows Walter on horseback with shield and lance, a pennon hanging from it.[23] One of a set of six Scottish woodcarvings of the early sixteenth century originally from Fetteresso Church but now set in a door in Muchalls Castle, Kincardineshire, depicts St George slaying the dragon. The saint is on horseback in armour of the period with a lance held firmly between his side and his right arm. A light horseman clad in a jack or a quilted jacket with a spear carried over his shoulder is included in a bookcase in the collection of the National Museum (KL 131). This carving dates to about 1600 and was the work of a carver in the south-west of Scotland.[24] The fine heraldic panel from Cromarty Castle (KG 96), now in the National Museum, displaying the arms of Sir Thomas Urquhart of Cromarty, 1651, has as part of its design two flanking horsemen in cuirassier armour, each armed with light lances held right at the butt.[25]

Axes

Second only in importance to the spear as a fighting weapon was the axe in its various shapes and sizes. Axes were much used by the Scandinavian peoples in the Viking era and many of those in use in Scotland

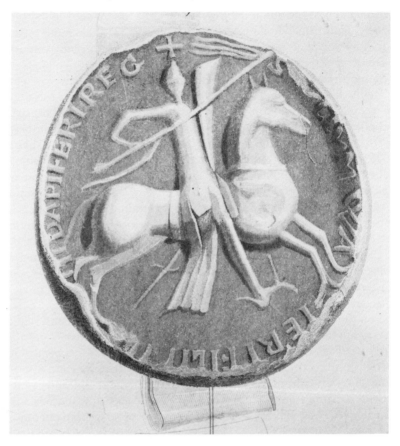

Figure 139. Seal of Walter Fitz Alan, c.1170

from the twelfth century onwards are derived from Viking types. Throughout the medieval period a fair amount of similarity can be traced in the weapons used in both regions. Axes can be divided into several types not only on the basis of their size and shape, but also by how they were used. The ability of the axeman to wield his weapon with one or two hands was undoubtedly an important criterion of type. Axes for use on horseback would mostly have been for use single-handed and would have had fairly short shafts. Axes for fighting on foot if short-shafted could be used single-handed, especially in combination with a shield, but were often wielded in both hands as long-shafted ones certainly were. The difference between long and short-shafted weapons is difficult to define by measurement alone, shafts ranging from about half a metre to over two in length; but many heads were mounted on short shafts which were not put on long ones, and *vice versa.* Generally speaking, short-

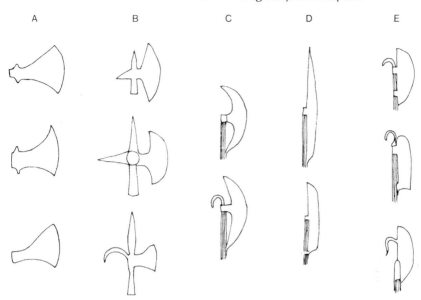

Figure 140. Representative examples of the four main traditions of Scottish battle axes (A-D) and the later Lochaber axes (E)

shafted axes often had shorter blades with relatively heavier heads. It goes without saying that they were also extensively used in wood-working and other such peaceful pursuits. Some of the types to be described were perhaps tools first and foremost and weapons only in necessity. Even the so-called Danish broadaxes of Petersen's type M, described below, are often shown in manuscript illustrations in the hands of carpenters and joiners.[26]

The account of Scottish axes which follows is not only very incomplete but also complex. The interpretation of their types and development favoured by the author is that there were four main forms or traditions (A-D) in which the main types developed (fig. 140). These were as follows:

A: Axes of Petersen's type M, that is 'Danish' or 'broad' axes. They were probably widely in use in Scotland in the period from the eleventh to the fourteenth century, and as late as the sixteenth century in the West Highland region. They were mostly short-shafted.

B: Axes with hammer heads or flukes, either short or long-shafted. Many of the latter are often called halberds.

C: Long-shafted axes with long curved cutting edges. Some later Scottish versions were mounted with a hook behind the blade, projecting from the top of the shaft. The blades themselves derived from axes of Petersen's type M.

D: Glaives, long-shafted weapons with elongated blades for both cutting and stabbing. Their heads were mounted as axes, that is with shaft-holes on the back of their blades, and not on sockets.

Scottish terminology for these weapons was variable and confusing. Thus one of the most characteristic names for Scottish axes from the beginning of the sixteenth century onwards — Lochaber axe — can be associated with weapons of forms A, C and D and probably B. Leith axes may normally have been of form C and Jedburgh staves of form D. By the eighteenth century 'Lochaber axe' and 'halberd' were the only terms to survive in common use. The former was applied to a group of long-shafted weapons, most with two dominant elements — a cutting edge and a hook at the back of it. These are most conveniently regarded as another group — form E — although they vary considerably in structural details. They are the result of the coalescing of axes of form C with those of form D. The term 'halberd' is now used to denote any long-shafted weapon with a head consisting of an axe, a spearhead and a fluke, and was probably so used in the eighteenth century.

Form A Axes

Although axes are often mentioned in medieval documents, they are not normally described in any detail. An early account of their use, which is of some interest, is the description in Barbour's *Bruce* of the fight between John of Lorne's men and Robert the Bruce's in 1306 in which John's men are said to have fought with them:

> Bot the folk off the tothir party
> Faucht with axys sa [felounly]
> For thai on fute war euir-ilkane.
> That thai feile off thar horss has slayne;
> And till sum gaiff thai woundis wid.[27]

There are few other mentions of fighting axes in the fourteenth century and they are not included in the equipment which was ordered by parliament in 1318 to be provided by the lieges for arming themselves in time of war.[28] We thus have in *The Bruce* an association of axes for fighting on foot with the Highlanders — if not in Bruce's day, at least in the lifetime of Barbour in the later part of the fourteenth century. Unfortunately the poem does not describe the shape or size of the axes but we can be reasonably confident that they were fairly long-shafted types for use with two or possibly one hand, of the type represented on the late fourteenth-century cross of Reginaldus of Islay, from Texa, Islay (fig. 141), which is now in the National Museum, Edinburgh (IB 198). Reginaldus is shown wearing a quilted aketon, conical basinet and

Figure 141. Carving of man with axe on the late 14th cent. cross of Reginaldus of Islay.
National Museum of Antiquities of Scotland

camail, presumably of mail. At his waist he has a large single-handed sword and in his right hand he grasps the shaft of his axe, the head of which is level with his face. The head has a broad slightly curved cutting edge and is skewed upwards away from the shaft so that the whole is slightly asymmetrical.

An even earlier representation, purportedly of a Scottish axe, is contained in the initial letter of a charter of Edward II of England to the burgh of Carlisle, 12 May, 1316.[29] This was only a few months after the siege of the town by the Scots under King Robert the Bruce and the charter has on very good grounds been considered to show incidents from the siege, as described in the *Chronicle of Lannercost*.[30] The axe in question is shown wielded in one hand by one of the Scots who carries a heater-shaped shield on his other arm. The axe is of related type to Reginaldus' but with a considerably wider cutting edge and shorter shaft. The owner in this case by his simple dress and lack of armour is a husbandman or retainer rather than a noble.

While the Scot on the Carlisle charter may be intended to be a Highlander, two mentions of the Scottish army in Froissart's *Chronicles* suggest that axes were one of the main weapons of the bulk of those who fought on foot, at least at the battle of Neville's Cross in 1346 and at Otterburn in 1388, where the Scots are said to have carried them over their shoulder (when not in use).[31] It is therefore possible that while axes were not deemed desirable or common for those who fought on foot in 1318, by the mid-fourteenth century they had come greatly into prominence.

Further representations of axes of cognate type to the two previous ones can be seen on another piece of West Highland sculpture, a grave-slab from Kilmory, Knapdale (fig. 142), which dates to the fifteenth century,[32] and on an early fifteenth-century tomb chest at Coupar Abbey in Angus (fig. 148). The former is short-shafted, the latter long-shafted.

Other documentary references back up the use of such axes at this time. An Act of Parliament of 6 March 1429/30 ordered that all yeomen who were not archers and who could not deal with a bow should have a good sure hat and a doublet of fence with sword and buckler (shield), and a good axe, or else a 'brogit staff' (see below).[33] In October 1456 yeomen who could not shoot (that is with a bow) were commanded to have an axe and a targe either of leather or of fine board with two bands on the back.[34] Again, in 1481 it was enacted that every axeman who had neither spear nor bow should have a targe of wood or leather, after the fashion of the example that was to be sent to each sheriff.[35] These references suggest at least two things about axes and their use in the fifteenth century. Firstly, they seem to have been the weapon of a large propor-

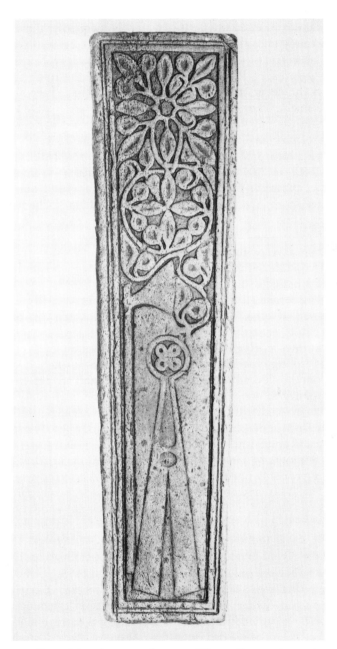

Figure 142. Grave slab with carving of an axe at Kilmory Knap, 15th cent. (cast in the *National Museum of Antiquities of Scotland*)

tion of the yeomen and poorer elements in the host who fought on foot, and despite the royal injunctions for the use and practice of the bow may have been much more in favour by the people. Secondly, the axes were almost certainly short-shafted weapons, capable of being wielded with one hand as it was expected that targes could be used with them.[36] The axes on the cross of Reginaldus of Islay and on the tomb frontal at Coupar are, however, not short-shafted and would have been difficult to use with a shield. They may represent an earlier or alternative tradition. Certainly, in the Highland area, at least, long-shafted varieties of this type of axe may have remained in vogue into the sixteenth century. Whether with long or short shafts, these axes are probably those referred to in the 1500s as Danish. 'Ane Dense ax' is included in an inventory of the tower of Dunbeath in Caithness in 1500, and there were four 'Denishe aixkis' listed in an Aberdeen inventory as late as 1548.[37] The term 'dens ax' even crops up as late as 1688 in Inverness burgh records. In that year tradesmen who could not afford a gun and sword were enjoined to provide themselves with them (see below, p. 000). Whether or not these were anything like the sixteenth-century axes is a point we cannot answer with any confidence.

Danish, or broad, axes, like the one on the cross of Reginaldus of Islay, are called type M, after an important classification of Viking weapons published early in the present century by Jan Petersen.[38] They are also known as Rygh's type 560, while in Britain they have been labelled as Viking type VI.[39] They were current in northern and eastern Europe from the eleventh to the twelfth century[40] and are depicted on the Bayeux tapestry as one of the main weapons of the English at the battle of Hastings in 1066.[41] It is clear that axes of the same general type remained in use in some parts at a later date than this, not only in Scotland but in England and Scandinavia.

Of the few type M axes which have been found in Scotland, the two earliest are probably one from Rescobie Loch in Angus, now in Dundee Museum (fig. 143), and another, now in Dumfries Museum, published a few years ago by Mr. Scott.[42] Its provenance was not known by Scott, but according to a note in the Whitelaw Papers in the National Museum, Edinburgh, it was found on the farm of Kilblain, Caerlavrock, Dumfries-shire, c. 1894. It is 218 mm. long by 200 mm. in breadth across its cutting edge, and its body is only about 2 mm. thick, and twice as thick as that near the cutting edge. This extra thickness at the cutting edge, as Mr. Scott points out, would have given strength where it was needed and would also have provided an edge for grinding. It is more than likely that the edge has been fire-welded on to the rest of the blade. The shaft-hole has been formed by bending the back of the blade over and welding the ends together.[43] Spurs are provided top and bottom for holding the shaft

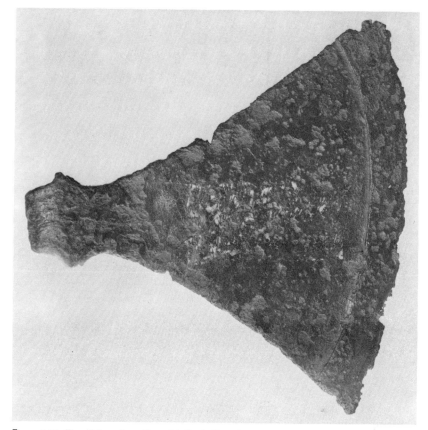

Figure 143. Type M axe from Rescobie Loch. *Dundee Museum*

more securely. Mr. Scott has dated this axe to the eleventh century on the basis of a comparison, firstly with an axe from London which has a sleeve decorated with an incised pattern in the eleventh century *Ringerike* style, and secondly with the axes depicted on the Bayeux tapestry.

The two most important features of this axe which lead us to assign an early date to it are the relative thinness of its neck and the way its upper edge from the tip of the blade to the neck describes an almost straight line. These are traits discernible in a group of type M axes found near Old London Bridge, one of which, with the Ringerike ornamentation, has been referred to by Mr. Scott. All have, in fact, been dated inferentially to the early eleventh century, not just on the basis of the engraved collar on one but also on the supposition that they are the relics of one of the documented Viking attacks at London Bridge at this time.[44] For what

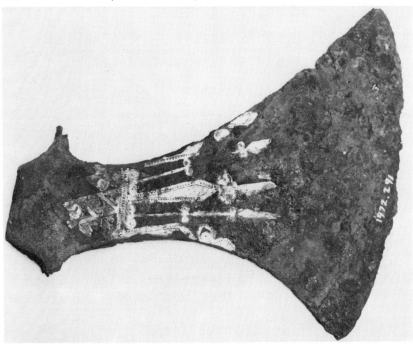

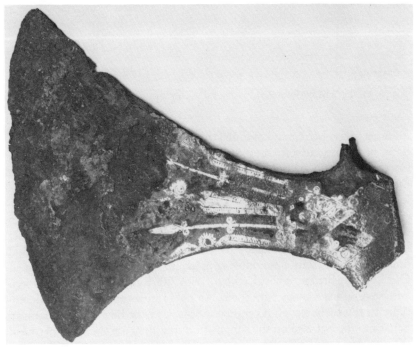

Figures 144a-b. Type M axe decorated with silver, from Loch Leven. *Kinross Museum*

it is worth, many of the axes on the Bayeaux tapestry also show a tendency for their upper edges to be considerably straighter than their lower, but unfortunately, we can adduce little more worthwhile supporting evidence for ascribing such axes to an eleventh-century date alone. Perhaps we should envisage their use in the twelfth century as well. The similar axe from Rescobie Loch may be dated to the same period.

Possibly not much later in date than the axes in Dumfries and Dundee Museums is one said to have been found in Loch Leven (fig 144 a-b). It is now in Kinross Museum (1972.291). It is 189 mm. long but has a shorter cutting edge of only 161 mm., and is unique amongst surviving Scottish axes in being inlaid with silver. At the neck and round the shaft hole the whole of the head is covered with a lattice of silver wire containing spirals, and long strings of decoration radiate from these towards the cutting edge. Other medieval axes inlaid with silver are known on the continent, for example a battle axe from Helmstedt in Brunswick dated to the eleventh century with a similar lattice pattern, each lozenge-shaped void containing a ring; and a type M axe from Masku, Humikkala, Finland, with decoration made of spirals.[45]

Another type M axe has been recovered from the recent archaeological excavations at the High Street, Perth, from a context which dates it to the late thirteenth or early fourteenth century.[46] It has a narrow neck, and like the Dumfries Museum axe, a fairly straight upper edge from blade tip to neck. Other type M axes from Scotland tend to have broader necks, like an axe found in a dug-out canoe near Loch Doon Castle, Ayrshire (fig. 145), now in Kirkcudbright Museum; and another (fig. 146) in Kinross Museum (1972.292). The broadening of the neck has also been noted by Paulsen as a later feature on continental type M axes.[47] The axe at Kinross has a very pronounced upper tip and a wide cutting edge — 250 mm., as against a blade length of 211 mm. The development of the fore-tip of the blade into an acute point can be traced as early as the Dumfries Museum axe and the Loch Leven axe, both of which have their upper tips skewed upwards. Other axes with thicker necks, like two from the moat of Caerlavrock Castle, Dumfriesshire, and one at Cluny Castle, Aberdeenshire, drawn by Drummond,[48] may be regarded as transitional between these early axes and the fully developed form as exemplified by the axe in Kinross Museum. An axe similar to it from the River Thames near Barnes Railway Bridge is illustrated in the London Museum Viking Catalogue,[49] but both most probably date to the thirteenth century at earliest, and possibly a good deal later. An axe with a similarly pronounced fore-tip is represented on a reliquary from Heddals church in Valches, Norway, which is dated to 1200-50,[50] and the same type is represented on the mid-fifteenth century cross of Alexander MacMillan at Kilmory in Argyll.[51] This is the latest representation of one in Scotland,

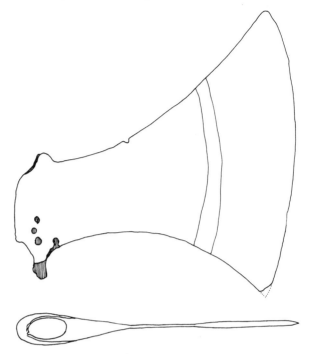

Figure 145.　Type M axe from Loch Doon. *Kirkcudbright Museum*

known to the writer, but the gallóglaigh were apparently still using them in Ireland well into the sixteenth century. In a letter of 1542/3 to Henry VIII of England Sir Anthony Sentleger describes the gallóglaigh as 'having each of them his weapon, called a sparre, made like the axe of the Towre'.[52] The axe of the Tower is presumably the weapon still carried by the Yeoman Gaoler at the Tower of London, a descendant of the Danish axe with a particularly prominent upper horn.[53]

An axe in the National Museum in Edinburgh (IL 727) with thick neck and no spurs on its upper edge is likely also to be a late type (fig. 147). It was found on the farm of Tillychin, Lumphanan, Aberdeenshire, 'near Macbeth's cairn where a battle was fought in 1056'.[54] This provenance, of course, is not in itself evidence of the date of the axe.

The axes on the fourteenth-century cross slab of Reginaldus of Islay and on the fifteenth-century grave slab at Kilmory mentioned above both have heads with narrow necks like the earliest axes in the type M series, but their upper edges instead of being almost straight or concave in outline are markedly convex, a feature not known on any surviving Scottish axes.[55] A similarly shaped axe blade, this time mounted on a long shaft,

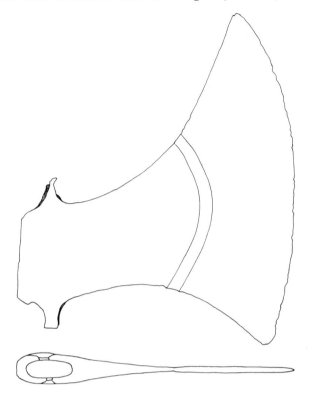

Figure 146. Type M axe. *Kinross Museum*

is shown being carried over the shoulder of a man on the front of a tomb chest at Coupar Abbey in Angus (fig. 148). The carving seems to date to the fifteenth century — to the first half of that century rather than the second, judging by the armour and costume of the figures on it. This is the only representation of such an axe blade in the Lowlands and in being long-shafted could hardly be of the type envisaged by the government when it urged the use of targets by axemen. It, and the axe on the cross of Reginaldus of Islay, are presumably precursors of a long-shafted axe depicted at Rodel.

This carving (fig. 149) is on the tomb of Alexander MacLeod, made in 1528, at Rodel Church in Harris.[56] A man of war carries an axe with the bottom of the shaft resting on the ground and the top of the blade about level with the top of his head. The blade has a long straight cutting edge, convex upper edge and concave lower edge. An axe blade found in Baker Street, Stirling, now in the National Museum (RY 31/MP 277), may have been like it though it is not clear how much of the edges of its blade have

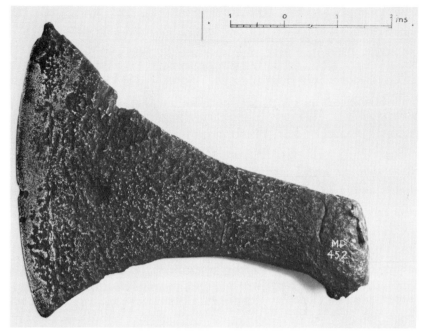

Figure 147. Type M axe from Tillychin. *National Museum of Antiquities of Scotland*

been lost through corrosion and breakage. A similar axe with long shaft is shown on the sixteenth-century tomb chest of Honorina Grace in St Canice's, Kilkenny City, Ireland.[57] Also in this category belongs the axe in Albrecht Dürer's drawing of 1521 of Irish soldiers and poor people. It is drawn held at a slope over one of the men's shoulders.[58] Also to be noted are the long shafted axes shown in the hands of the Irish in a woodcut of a raid on a village, published in Derricke's *Image of Ireland* in 1581.[59]

The Rodel axe is of great interest as it is possible that it is what was referred to at the beginning of the sixteenth century as a Lochaber axe. The district of Lochaber lies in the West Highland region and was well wooded in the medieval period. Royal workmen were even sent there in the sixteenth century to cut wood for making carriages for the artillery[60] and it is certain that there would have been enough timber available to make the long shafts which we suppose Lochaber axes had. In fact, it should be said at the outset that the adjective 'Lochaber' may from the beginning only have been used vaguely for any axes with longish shafts. The first mention of Lochaber axes is in 1501 when 'ane batale ax maid of Lochabir fasoun' was bought for James IV.[61] They are also mentioned in

Figure 148. Carving of man with axe on a tomb front, 15th cent. *Coupar Angus Church*

John Major's *History of Great Britain*, first published in 1521. There they are said to be best for cutting with, single-edged, and used by the Wild Scots (Highlanders) of the north.[62] Major further writes in his *History* that the 'Wild Scots' of his day were armed with small halberds[63] and we should probably interpret this to mean axes of no great length.

This is all very little to go on but at least the axe on the Rodel tomb could fit Major's description of a Lochaber axe, and as we shall show

Figure 149. Man of war with axe on the tomb of Alexander MacLeod at Rodel, 1528

below, Major was careful to distinguish between Lochaber axes which were single-edged and other axes in use in Scotland which were double. Although, as we have pointed out above, axes similar to the Rodel carving were in use in Ireland by mercenaries of Scottish extraction, there is no record of them or any other axes in Ireland being called Lochaber axes.

Lochaber axes do not figure in sixteenth-century documents outwith Major's *History* and the Treasurer's accounts which record James IV's acquisition of one. They are therefore noticeably lacking from the weapons listed by the government at various times as suitable for wapinschawings and hostings and ordained by burgh councils for the maintenance of order in the towns. The axes mentioned in such sources can only be identified as of forms B, C and D. We can only suppose that Lochaber axes at this time were used by Highlanders alone.

This brings us to another problem that may usefully be touched on at this point, the difference in arming between the Highlands and Lowlands. In an Act of Parliament of 1574 ordering the holding of wapinschawings, difference in the arms and armour in the two regions was officially recognised,[64] but this was undoubtedly rather belated appreciation of a situation which had been in existence for a very long time. The question is, can we recognise this difference in any earlier documents, and a possibility that comes to mind is that the 'either/or' instructions for arming in the fifteenth century by which those without bows and spears should be armed with axes and targes might be designed to allow for a Highland preference for the latter weapons. The basis for imagining that axes — and here axes of form A are understood — were favoured more by the Highlanders than Lowlanders rests on their association with the Highlanders in Barbour's *Bruce* and Major's *History* and the representations of them in West Highland sculpture. Admittedly swords and spears are more common on the slabs and crosses but these are the memorials of the nobility who one might expect to be differently armed in any case. Buchanan pointed out in his *History* that the Highlanders in his day were for the most part armed with bows but that a few carried swords or Lochaber axes.[65]

A lot more evidence is needed unfortunately to sustain this hypothesis, but it is a proposition that seems to the writer to be worthy of serious consideration. The use of form A axes — that is type M and derivatives — can be demonstrated in the Highland region as late as the second quarter of the sixteenth century, whereas the evidence for the use of axes in the Lowlands from the beginning of the fifteenth century, with the notable exception of the carving at Coupar Angus, as we shall show below, is largely concerned with other forms of axes. The gallóglaigh in Ireland and other West Highland mercenaries there are known to have fought principally with axes on foot in the sixteenth century, and such little evidence as there is favours the interpretation that this was the case as early as the thirteenth century.[66] A figure, presumably of a galló-glaigh, armed with a type M axe, is carved on the late fifteenth-century tomb of Felim O'Connor at Roscommon Abbey in the County of that name.[67]

On the other hand, two sixteenth-century accounts of the Highlanders and their weapons fail to mention any axes at all. At the muster at Fala Moor in 1542 Pitscottie says there were 20,000 'haberjouns and twa handit swordis, quhilk was the airmor of the hielandis men',[68] and the Irish (Highland) contingent under the Earl of Argyll at the battle of Pinkie in 1547 are described as archers.[69] We would be loath to argue from this evidence alone that axes had fallen completely out of favour by the mid-sixteenth century, especially as they were obviously much used by the Highlanders in the following century. Possibly they were being used only by a small proportion of Highlanders at this time.

In summary we can suggest that axes of form A were in use in Scotland as weapons from the eleventh to the sixteenth century. Type M axes were used throughout the whole country as late as the fourteenth century. Thereafter they may have been used much more commonly in the Highlands. A long-shafted variety was developed which by the early sixteenth century may have been known as a Lochaber axe.

Form B Axes

There is very little evidence for the early use of axes with hammer heads or flukes, and no examples have survived of earlier date than the sixteenth century. It is possible, however, that short-shafted axes with blades rather like type M axes of form A, but extended at the back of the shaft into a spike, were widely known. In the site museum at the abbey of Jedburgh in Roxburghshire there is a sculpture of a man in armour of the fifteenth century, of which only the torso survives (fig. 150). In one hand he grasps an axe which has the upper tip of the blade attenuated into a point as on the axe in Kinross Museum but considerably more spike-like. There are also spikes on top of the shaft and behind it. From the position in which it is held it must be a short-shafted weapon. A carved stone slab, possibly an altar frontal, from Inishail, Argyllshire, shows a warrior with a short-shafted axe by his side with broad curved cutting edge and spike behind the shaft.[70] The Corpus Christi *Scoti-chronicon*, however, in its illustrations of Scotia arriving in Scotland and the Battle of Bannockburn, shows soldiers armed with long-shafted axes with blades not dissimilar to that on the Jedburgh carving.

The *Scotichronicon* illustrations are the earliest representations of long-shafted axes in Scotland, but the earliest reference to them appears

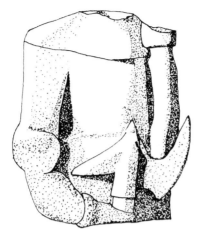

Figure 150.   Carving of man with battle axe, 15th cent. *Jedburgh Abbey Museum*

to come in a parliamentary paper relating to the Borders which may date to the end of the fourteenth century. There is a clause in it headed *De venientibus ad guerram* concerning the arms and armour required by each individual, and it enjoins the use of the 'gysarms quod in Scocia dicitur handhax' amongst those who have less than forty shillings worth of land — that is by the yeoman class.[71] Gisarmes have been variously identified in the past as non-axe-like weapons, but two scholars[72] have recently claimed them as axes with long shafts — an interpretation which fits the Scottish evidence very well. Gisarmes are said to be hand-axes in *De venientibus ad guerram*, and later Scottish documents quite specifically describe hand-axes as long-shafted weapons. For instance, in 1552/3 the burgesses of Edinburgh who had booths or rooms in the High Street were ordered to have 'lang walpynnis therein, sic as hand ex, jedburgh staif, halbert, jawalying and sick lang walpynnis'.[73] Borg more particularly suggests that gisarmes may have had crescentic blades,[74] but conclusive evidence for such a close definition eludes us. We can only assume that 'gisarme' was a term for long-shafted axes. The term is not found in use in Scotland in any other document, and in England is known to have dropped out of use in the last quarter of the fifteenth century, though it survived longer on the continent. Presumably the terms 'battle-axe' and 'hand-axe' replaced it in Scotland while the actual weapons remained in use.

A French document of 1421 describing the Scottish troops of the Earl of Buchan and Sir John Stewart in France, says they were armed with bows, swords and gisarmes, double-edged weapons,[75] and the double-

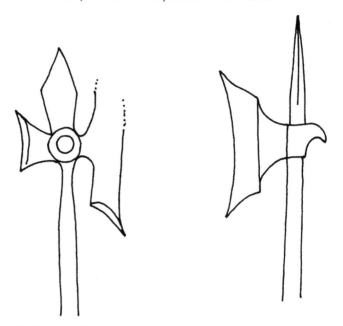

Figure 151.   Battle axe from the late 15th century Crucifixion painting at Fowlis Easter and (right) a halberd from the carvings of the Passion in the chapel of Traquair House, c.1530

edged in this case might refer to the fact that these axes had flukes at the back of their blades.

Long-shafted axes with flukes and spearheads are carried by some of the soldiers in the two illustrations in the Corpus Christi *Scotichronicon*, already alluded to, and such a weapon is also depicted in a fifteenth-century painting of the crucifixion in the church of Fowlis Easter, Angus (figure 151). It has a long straight-edged axe balanced by a smaller blade or fluke. An angular spearhead projects out of the top. A centrally placed roundel is a skeuomorph of the prominent nuts and bolts found on other battle-axes securing axe and spike together.[76] Two surviving Scottish weapons also have this feature. Both have crescent-shaped axe-blades and short straight spearheads and flukes. One (fig. 152) is in the West Highland Museum at Fort William and the other (fig. 153), which is said to have been found at Inverlochy near Fort William, is in the Marischal College Museum at Aberdeen (no. 469/2B). Both may date to the seventeenth century and may be claimed to derive from axes of the type in the Fowlis Easter painting.

Halberds are also long-shafted weapons which by the sixteenth century had assumed a characteristic type of head composed of the three

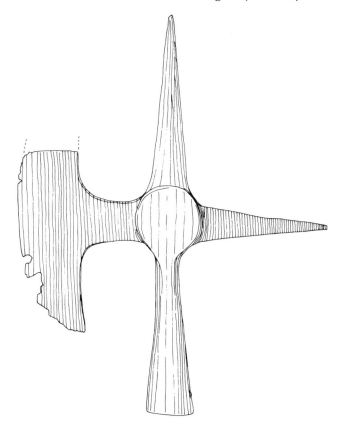

Figure 152. Battle axe, 17th cent. (?). *West Highland Museum, Fort William*

elements, an axe, a spearhead, and a fluke. They are generally thought to
be derived from the so-called 'Swiss vouges', weapons with elongated
blades fixed to shafts with two shaft-holes. They are first mentioned in
Scotland at the beginning of the sixteenth century and regularly thereafter in instructions for wapinschawings and hostings in the first half of
the sixteenth century. They may in particular have been used in combination with hand firearms. The army which the Regent Moray raised
to overawe the defeated supporters of Queen Mary in 1568 is said to
have consisted of 4,000 horsemen and 1,000 harquebuziers and halbert-
men.[77] An Act of Parliament of August 1643 lists the weapons and equipment which were to be carried by the soldiers in the Scottish army. Those
unprovided with pike, musket or sword were to present themselves with
halberds, Lochaber axes or Jedburgh staves.[78] Halberds and the other
axes, however, were probably only borne by a small proportion of the

Figure 153. Battle axe from Inverlochy. *Marischal College Museum, Aberdeen*

army at this time. They continued in use into the eighteenth century, though increasingly they came to be parade-ground weapons. They were also carried by council officials or town guards in many of the burghs.

Halberds were also kept for the defence of the home. Eight were bought for Falkland Palace in 1516 and others for Dingwall Castle and Redcastle in the same year.[79] They were amongst the weapons Edinburgh burgesses were at various times enjoined to keep in their shops for keeping order in the town.[80] In 1517 the young James V was given a guard of twelve footmen with halberds under the command of a captain and they were to guard his bedroom every night.[81] Queen Mary also had a guard of twelve halberdiers when she first returned to Scotland.[82]

Halberds are shown in Scottish woodcarvings and paintings of the sixteenth and seventeenth centuries, some with ornamentally pierced blades and concave cutting edges. In particular we might note the series of carved oak panels portraying scenes from the Passion in the chapel at Traquair House in Peeblesshire. They date to c. 1530 and are said in an eighteenth-century document to have come originally from a chapel in Leith.[83] Halberds such as these and many others in use in Scotland may have been imported from the continent.

There were craftsmen in Edinburgh and Leith who actually described themselves as halbertmakers, and other halberds were produced by blacksmiths.[84] Three halberds are specifically listed as 'skottysh' in an inventory of ordnance and munition belonging to the Earl of Leicester, drawn up in 1583.[85] The earliest surviving weapons, recognisably of Scottish manufacture, date at the earliest to the seventeenth century. They have squat blades and downward curved flukes (fig. 154) as if copying the hooks or bridle-cutters on contemporary Lochaber axes (see below), and may owe as much, if not more, to a battle-axe ancestry as to earlier continental halberds. A typical Scottish halberd from Aberdeen is now in the National Museum, Edinburgh (LE 7), and other eighteenth-century halberds, normally with small narrow axe blades are stamped with 'HYLAND'. There are examples among other places in Perth Museum (fig. 155), and the Hunterian Museum, Glasgow, and Newcastle Museum, but it is not known who was responsible for marking them. Other so-called halberds have oval-shaped blades, like those used by the burgh officers of Irvine in Ayrshire and another illustrated by Drummond which has its axe blade pierced with four hearts in a manner reminiscent of eighteenth-century basket sword hilts (fig. 156). One of the Irvine halberds was displayed in the 'Bishop's Palace' at the Glasgow International Exhibition of 1888 and is said to have been the very weapon used by John Reid, one of the Burgh's officers, to kill a certain Alexander Kennedy during a riot in 1670.[86] There is, in fact, a fair amount of variety amongst seventeenth- and eighteenth-century halberds which may be presumed to be of Scottish manufacture, but we do not intend to itemise all the minor points of difference here. Most characteristically have small axe blades, prominent leaf-shaped spearheads and downward curved flukes. The axes normally have crescent-shaped blades and rarely decorative cusping, piercing or globes at the base of their spearheads (fig. 157). Many of the more decorative varieties with the last mentioned features may not be of Scottish manufacture or may date to the late eighteenth or nineteenth century.

Under the heading of form B axes it will be most appropriate to consider the evidence, slight as it is, for the use of axes from horseback, as many would have been of this tradition. Many a knight undoubtedly favoured axes to the use of swords and maces, including King Robert I

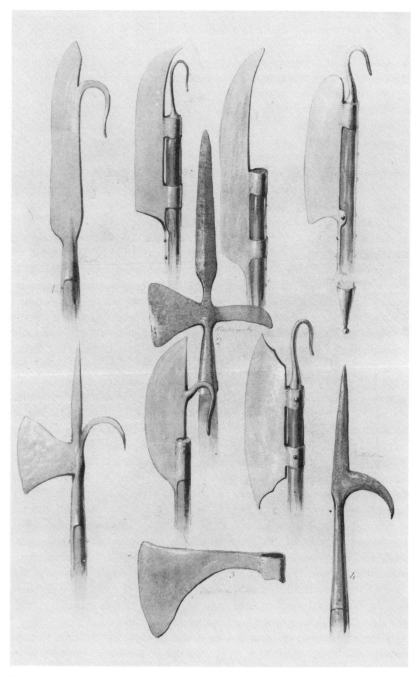

Figure 154. Scottish axes drawn by James Drummond

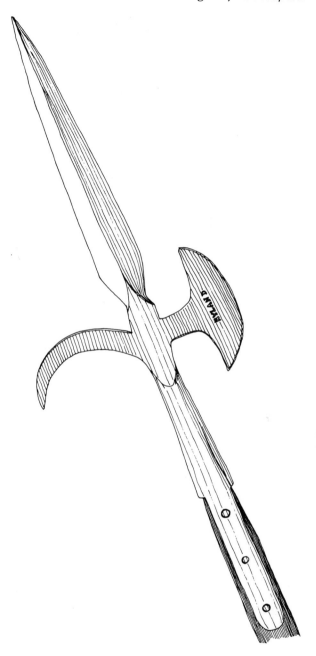

Figure 155. Halberd, 18th cent., stamped HYLAND. *Perth Museum*

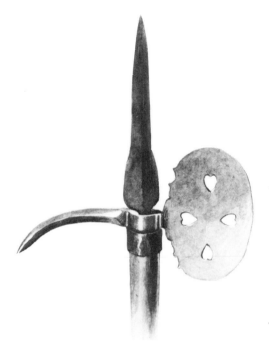

Figure 156. Scottish 'halberd' with pierced blade, drawn by Drummond

himself. In a famous account in Barbour's *Bruce* the king is described riding on a palfrey in front of his troops prior to the main encounter at Bannockburn in 1314. An English knight, Henry de Bohun, eager to gain renown, broke from the English army and charged at him, but:

> Schir Henry myssit the nobill kyng;
> And he that in his sterapis stude,
> With ax that wes bath hard and gude
> With so gret mayn roucht hym ane dynt,
> That nouther hat no helme mycht stynt
> The hevy dusche that he him gaf,
> That he the hed till harnyss claf
> The hand-ax-schaft ruschit in twa,
> And he doune till the erd can ga
> All flatlyngis, for him falzeit mycht.[87]

This episode is depicted in the Corpus Christi *Scotichronicon*, and here Bruce is shown turned in his saddle, both hands grasping a large unwieldy axe with a hammer head (?) behind the shaft. While the use of a large two-handed axe on horseback might appear to be unlikely in

Figure 157. Two decorative halberds, drawn by Drummond

reality, there are other illustrations of them so used, for instance in the mid-thirteenth century English manuscript of the Life of St Edward.[88] This is neither evidence for their use in Scotland at this time or later, but the rest of the arms and armour in the *Scotichronicon* painting seem to be those in use at the time of its execution. One would expect that axes would normally only be used from horseback single-handed and there may be a deliberate element of swagger in the *Scotichronicon* painting and others like it in order to magnify the prowess of the king.

An axe blade in the National Museum, Edinburgh (RY8/MP 16), from Learagan, Rannoch, Perthshire (fig. 158), may be a horseman's axe of the sixteenth century. It has a crescent-shaped blade and narrow spike at the back, possibly at one time more hammer-like as seems to be indicated in Drummond's drawing of it.[89] It would probably have had a spike projecting out of the top of its shaft and would have been rather like an axe (no. VIII.39) in the Tower of London.[90]

On the whole, the evidence for the use of axes of form B is very patchy and there is some doubt as to their confusion with halberds. Long-shafted axes were known by the beginning of the fifteenth century, and Scottish types of 'halberd' of the seventeenth and eighteenth centuries possibly owe more to a native tradition of battle-axes than to continental halberds. Short-shafted axes of form B may have been used on horseback as late as the sixteenth century.

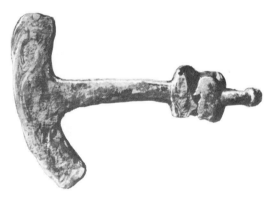

Figure 158. Horseman's axe of the 16th cent. (?) from Learagan, drawn by Drummond. *National Museum of Antiquities of Scotland*

Form C Axes

The Corpus Christi *Scotichronicon* illustration of Bannockburn shows a foot soldier armed with a long-shafted axe with broad crescentic cutting edge, not much broader in this case than many axes of form A, but we have a suggestion of a new type of axe which we shall call form C. Axes of form C are derived from form A and were one of the most characteristic groups in use in Scotland. The two basic features which distinguish them are their long crescentic blades, normally tied to the shaft at the bottom, and their long shafts. In fact, the earliest representation of this form in Scotland known to the writer is carried by St

Matthias on one of the roof bosses in the choir of Melrose Abbey in Rox-burghshire, work executed about the turn of the fourteenth century.[91] A fine example is also carved on the lintel in the south aisle of Roslin Chapel, Midlothian, which depicts the seven deadly sins. It dates to c. 1450 and shows clearly the broad sweep of the blade fixed on the top of its shaft by a narrow shaft-hole. The bottom of the blade is also attached to the shaft while the upper horn projects well above it. The whole may be judged to represent a weapon of about 1.80 m. in length.

Such weapons may have been included amongst those called gisarmes in the late fourteenth-century parliamentary paper relating to the Borders discussed above, but no separate or distinguishing name is known for them throughout the fifteenth century. At the beginning of the sixteenth century, however, we come across the term 'Leith axe', which may be considered to refer to a weapon of this type.

Leith axes are first mentioned in 1512[92] and are described in John Major's *History* of 1521. In translation Major's description reads: 'The double-edged axe of Leith is very much the same as the French halberd; it is, however, a little longer and a more convenient weapon for fighting with. The smiths make a piece of iron in the form of a hook at the end of the stout staff of bills or axes; the English yeomen fight with these useful weapons.'[93] This is a most confusing account but we can try to pick out the following points from it. Although Major does not specifically say so, there can be no doubt that the stout staffs were long ones, as halberds are invariably long-shafted weapons. In his description Major uses the word *bipennis*, strictly 'double-edged axe'. While the blade, or that part of it projecting beyond the shaft, may have been sharpened on both sides, we should not perhaps translate this word too literally as it was possibly intended simply as a synonym for 'axe'. The most interesting part of Major's description concerns the hook which he says was put on the end of the shaft, as these hooks are known on many surviving Scottish axes of a later date and may be considered as a particularly Scottish development.

To sum up, we are suggesting that a Leith axe may be identified as a long-shafted weapon with an axe blade, possibly two-edged, and a hook projecting out of the end of its shaft. Major says the hook was mounted with either a bill or an axe and perhaps by the former he means an elon-gated blade as on the glaives or form D axes we shall decribe below. By axe we would suggest he means a large crescent-shaped blade, and there are at least two weapons of such a form provided with a hook in the top of their shafts, both probably of sixteenth-century date. The first is pre-served in the Musée de l'Armée, Paris (K.74) and has been identified in the past as a Lochaber axe.[94] As we will show below, there is no evidence for weapons with hooks being regarded as Lochaber axes prior to the eighteenth century. The second is illustrated by Boeheim as being in the Imperial Russian Weapon Museum at Zarskoë-Selo.[95] In both, the bottom horn of the blade is fixed to the shaft by a tang for greater security, and but for their distinctive hooks they are very similar to contemporary bardiches, the long-shafted axes in use in Scandinavia, Poland and Russia at this time. Neither is necessarily Scottish but may be the sort of thing Major had in mind as Leith axes. The present whereabouts of the axe illustrated by Meyrick as a Leith axe of the time of Henry VIII, found in a river in Scotland,[96] is unknown. It has a broad crescentic axe blade and a short horizontal spike, but the writer knows of no reason why it should have been thought to be a Leith axe.

Leith axes appear regularly throughout the first half of the sixteenth century in orders for wapinschawings and hostings, but the term then seems to become extinct, if not the weapon itself. The name might suggest that the weapon originated or was manufactured in the town of Leith.

Turning to the seventeenth century, there is much clearer evidence of the existence of axes of form C, now being called Lochaber axes. Two revealing descriptions of these weapons are contained in Irvine's *Nomenclatura*, first published in 1682. Only one of these concerns us at this point and that is that the Rhinns of Galloway — the peninsula at the far south-west of Scotland — is said to be like the edge of a Lochaber axe.[97] There can be no doubt that this Lochaber axe was one with a long crescentic blade and narrow neck. Such a weapon is shown in a picture of 'An incident in the Scottish Rebellion, 1745', by David Morier, painted for the Duke of Cumberland and now in the Royal Collection at Windsor Castle (fig. 159). It has, in fact, been supposed to represent the Battle of Culloden and in it a group of Highlanders are shown opposed to grenadiers, presumably of Barrell's Regiment who were on the extreme left of the Duke of Cumberland's army and suffered heavy casualties.[98] The painting was done very close in time to the event it depicts and impresses one with the accuracy of the costume and weapons in it. The shaft weapon which is of interest to us is wielded by one of the Highlanders and has a long, thin, curving blade, broadening out slightly towards the top and then formed into a point. At the back it is formed into a narrow neck with a shaft-hole for attaching it to the top of its shaft, and the bottom end of the blade curls in to be secured to the shaft at a lower point. The weapon is obviously of the same sort as the ones depicted at Melrose Abbey and on the seven deadly sins lintel at Roslin Chapel, but its closest parallels are with the contemporary bardiches of Northern Europe.[99]

Bardiches have often been confused with Lochaber axes, perhaps largely as the result of an engraving by John Hamilton published in 1795,

Figure 159.   'An Incident in the Scottish Rebellion, 1745' by D. Morier. *Windsor Castle*

purporting to be of the Lochaber axe with which Colonel Gardner, one of the commanders of Dragoons, was killed at the the Battle of Preston-pans in 1745.[100] Hamilton's engraving is of a bardiche in the Tower of London armouries (no. VII.866) which is similar in shape to the axe in Morier's painting, but it is more than likely, as others have pointed out, that Hamilton — or those who advised him — was mistaken in his identi-fication. There is at any rate another axe in the Tower of London much more certainly of Scottish manufacture and a typical example at that of surviving eighteenth century 'Lochaber axes' with hooks, which is claimed by ffoulkes in the catalogue of the Armouries as the weapon which killed Gardner.[101]

None of this is to deny the Scots the use of bardiche-like axes in the seventeenth and eighteenth centuries, and indeed if Hamilton was mis-taken it was most probably because Lochaber axes could be very similar to bardiches. Another explanation is that bardiches were actually used by the Scots. There were two 'Muscoviter poll axes' and a 'Pollonian poll axe' in the House of the Binns in West Lothian on the death of General Thomas Dalyell in 1685.[102] Admittedly, Dalyell had seen service on the continent but so had many others of his contemporaries. In 1675 Lord Cochrane was instructed by the Privy Council to examine James Booll, an Irvine merchant, about some weapons including ten poleaxes he had imported at Bo'ness.[103] These, like the poleaxes at the Binns, may have been bardiches.

From the beginning of the seventeenth century several documents, es-pecially the records of the Privy Council, make mention of pow- or pole-axes being used by Highlanders and other lawless men for nefarious purposes. The MacGregors and their allies are said to have been armed with them at the conflict of Glenfruin in 1603.[104] The 'pole' element derives from the old term for head, 'poll', and does not refer to the pole or shaft on which they were mounted.[105] A study, however, of the contexts in which the word 'poleaxe' occurs in the seventeenth-century Privy Council Records suggests that the term was interchangeable with Lochaber axe.

To sum up, long-shafted axes with long crescentic blades were known by the beginning of the fifteenth century and probably remained in use until the seventeenth century, if not later. Leith axes may have been a six-teenth-century variant with hooks fixed in the top of their shafts. In the seventeenth century they may have been referred to as Lochaber or pole-axes.

Form D Axes

Major gives a description of a long-shafted weapon in his *History* of 1521 which was then known as a Jedwart (Jedburgh) staff, after the town

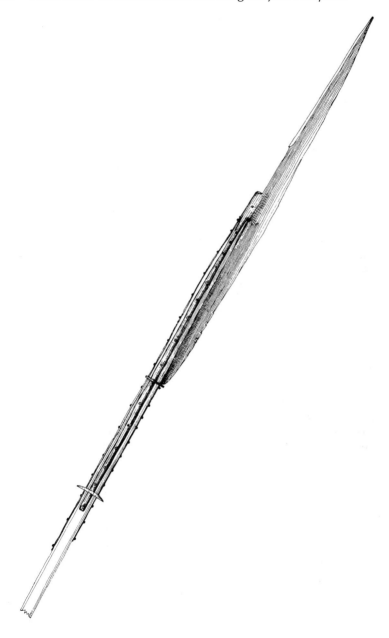

Figure 160. Jedburgh staff (?) from Murthly Castle. *Royal Scottish Museum*

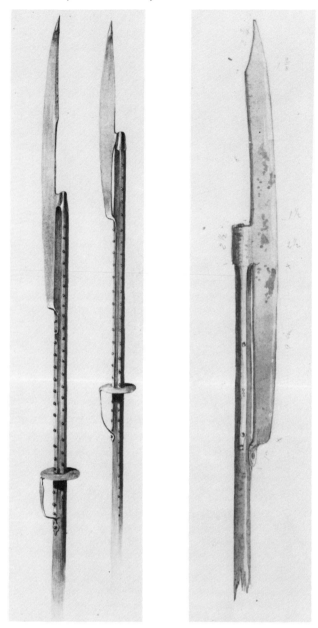

Figure 161. Jedburgh staves (?) drawn by Drummond at Cawdor Castle and in the collection of the *Earl of Seafield*

Figure 162. Axe found in Badenoch, drawn by Drummond. *Inverness Museum*

of that name in Roxburghshire. The weapons were iron-shod shafts, and the smiths of Jedburgh are said to have been able to make steel blades four feet (1.22 m.) long on the end of oak staffs.[106] There survives a small group of weapons in Scotland with long narrow blades of the sort of length indicated by Major which may be considered to be Jedburgh staffs. Three from Murthly Castle in Perthshire (fig. 160), formerly in the Noel Paton Collection but now in the Royal Scottish Museum in Edinburgh (nos. 1905.1081-3) may be considered typical examples. Others are at Cawdor Castle in Nairn and one illustrated by Drummond as belonging to the Earl of Seafield (fig. 161).[107]

The blades in all of them are only a few centimetres wide and stretched into a sharp point beyond the top of the shaft. The upper portions of the blades are double-edged and all are provided with metal roundels — small discs fitted over the shafts a bit below the blades as a protection for the hand and to prevent it slipping. Such devices are often associated with shafted weapons for use on horseback, and if this group of weapons can be identified as Jedwart staves there is good reason to think that they may so have been used at least some of the time. They may date to the sixteenth or seventeenth century.

The blade of another such weapon, supposedly from the site of the Battle of Bannockburn but probably of similar date to the Murthly Castle weapons, is in the Smith Institute, Stirling. It is in three pieces and was originally identified as two separate axes but it is probably one elongated blade which has been wrenched from its shaft and consequently weakened where the shaft-hole(s) was (were) welded on. The three pieces are illustrated in a volume of the Stirling Archaeological Society along with a fourth bit,[108] now missing, which may have been part of the shaft-hole. The upper end of the blade is formed into a narrow spike for thrusting. Another axe drawn by Drummond and said to have been found in Badenoch has a similar elongated blade cut transversely at the top to form a sharp point (fig. 162). Some bardiches are quite similar to these two axes, with solid rectangular bodies drawn into a spike at the top: for instance, one of the seventeenth or eighteenth century in the Tower of London, thought to be of Swedish origin.[109] It is possible that the Scottish weapons were influenced by the Scandinavian ones, or *vice versa.*

The Scottish ancestry of these weapons is not known with any certainty. A representation of St Matthias with a battle-axe in a series of apostles and martyrs carved on one of the arches in the south aisle of Roslin Chapel might be considered an earlier example of this form. The axe blade is cut transversely at its bottom and curves into a point beyond the top of the shaft, and is not of nearly so long and narrow a type as the Murthly Castle weapons. It might, however, be more legitimately considered to be a variant of form C axes.

Long-shafted weapons with blades not unlike the Murthly Castle ones, but shorter, broader and more angular, are depicted in a mid-thirteenth-century manuscript illustrating the landing of William the Conqueror in England. They are stacked upright in the prow of one of the ships along with some spears.[110] Another can be seen on the seal of the French nobleman Roger Bernard, Comte de Foix (1276). The mounted and armoured count is shown with a large heater-shaped shield on his left arm and the weapon held in a couched position under his right arm like a lance.[111] Ellehauge illustrates yet another, this time with a hook, from a fourteenth-century Italian manuscript, and suggests it is a type transitional between a battle-axe and later glaives.[112] Glaives, although many have blades similar in shape to the Murthly Castle weapons, generally have them attached to the top of the shaft by a socket unlike the arrangement in the Scottish weapons in which the shaft extends approximately halfway up the back of the blade and is fitted into shaft-holes. Most surviving glaives are ceremonial weapons of the sixteenth century and later, but the developed type with socket attachment was well known in the previous century. The Scottish method of mounting would seem to be typologically the earlier and gives more emphasis to the weapon's axe-like function and origin.

What may be later examples of the Murthly Castle type often tend to have broader and relatively shorter blades with curved edges. None of them are fitted with roundels. Such is the so-called Lochaber axe lent by HM Office of Works to the Scottish Exhibition of National History, Art and Industry in Glasgow in 1911[113] and another from the Noel Paton Collection, now in the Royal Scottish Museum. It is illustrated by Laking as a Lochaber axe and dated by him to the early seventeenth century. It is said to have been found in a crofter's cottage near Aberdeen.[114] Others have a more rectangular shape of blade, rather like some eighteenth-century axes fitted with a hook. Such is a so-called Lochaber axe (fig. 163) presented by the Burgh of Dunbar in East Lothian to the National Museum (LE 5) and another found at Lochleven Castle, Kinross-shire, and drawn by Drummond (fig. 164). All of these are considered by the writer to be of seventeenth or eighteenth-century date, though it should be noted that the last two are not significantly different from the mid-fifteenth-century axe of St Matthias at Roslin Chapel mentioned above.

Weapons obviously related to these Scottish types are known to have been used in Northern England. In the Blackgate Museum, Newcastle, and the Museum of Artillery at Woolwich are some long-shafted weapons with socketed heads which have semi-circular bodies and spear-like extensions at the top. In appearance and functional capabilities they are not very different from some of the Scottish weapons.

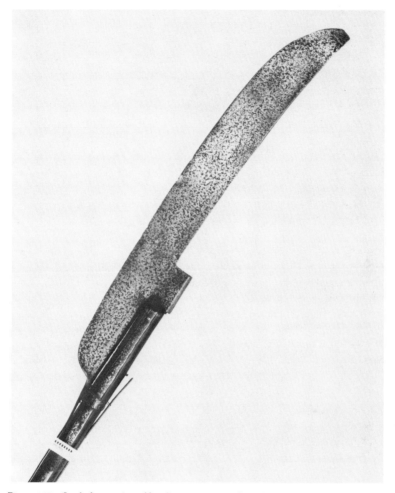

Figure 163. 'Lochaber axe' used by the magistrates of Dunbar. *National Museum of Antiquities of Scotland*

Assuming for the moment that the Murthly Castle weapons were Jedwart staves as described by Major, let us trace the history of this term. It first appears in Scottish documents of the beginning of the sixteenth century. In 1504/5 James IV had 'ane Jedwort hede gilt with bandis' made by the royal cutler, Robert Selkirk, and also a leather case made for the same.[115] The bands most likely refer to the straps extending from the head down the shaft as a strengthening device. The smith of Cambus-kenneth at Stirling supplied more for the royal use in 1507,[116] but rather

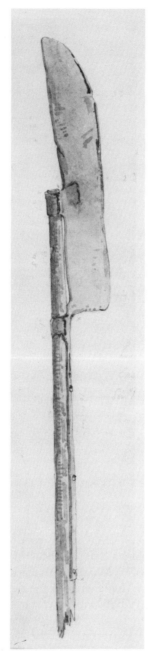

Figure 164. 'Lochaber axe' found at Loch Leven Castle, drawn by Drummond

curiously a few years later in 1515 royal letters were issued banning their use:

> . . . the xxv day of October, to Duncan Riche and certane uthir bearis, for falt of officiaris, xxvj lettrez for samony schereffis, and stewartis of the haill realme for putting doun of jedwart stavis, and for using of speris, axis, halbertis, bowis, and culveringis, deliverit to thair wagis, xlijs.[117]

The reason for this ban is unfortunately not known, though we are tempted to guess at it. Was it because they had been found to be deficient in the Battle of Flodden two years previously? All the Scots fought on foot on that occasion, and while weapons like the Murthly Castle examples would have been ideally suited for a lightly armed horseman, they may have been less successful when used on foot against an enemy army. For one thing, they lacked the length of the pikes which were decreed for the use of the Scots, and secondly they lacked the hacking quality of the halberd or other axes since there was insufficient weight of metal behind any section of the long cutting edge for delivering a really swingeing blow against an armour-clad opponent. All this is mere speculation, but it is noteworthy that in an Act of Parliament of 10 December 1540, laying down the sorts of arms and armour to be used by the lieges, Jedwart staves are still excluded:

> And that na maner of wapnis be admittit in wapinschawingis bot speris pikis stark and lang of vj ellis of lenth axis halbortis handbowis and arrowis corsbowis culveringis tua haudit swordis.[118]

But the Jedwart staff had its uses and was not to be given up readily by the Scots. James V himself did not lack them in this period[119] and they are again mentioned in an order for wapinschawings in March 1546 where they are included with spears, pikes, Leith axes, halberds, bows and arrows, crossbows, culverins and two-handed swords.[120] They are often mentioned in sixteenth-century complaints against people accused of assault and breaking and entering, and their axe-like quality is left in no doubt by accounts such as the following, a complaint by Robert Lindsay, the minister of Birse, against Robert Burnett and others whom he accused of assaulting him on 20 July 1586:

> [they] struke him upoun the heid with an Jedburgh stalff and clave his harne-pan thairwith; like as the said Thomas [Burnett] brak ane Jedburgh stalff upoun him, and left him lying for deid.[121]

Another sixteenth-century document, however, emphasises the spear-like nature of the Jedwart staff. In 1548 there was a fight in the house of Robert Melville, an Edinburgh burgess, between two French merchants in the train of the French army then in the country. One of the Frenchmen grabbed a weapon 'vocato sermone scotica ane Jedwart staff, gallice ane jefflyng'.[122] As we have discussed above, a javelin at this time meant a light horseman's spear rather than a throwing weapon, normally referred to as a dart.

The Murthly Castle type of weapon may also have been used by the gallóglaigh in Ireland. Dymock, in his *Treatice of Ireland*, describes the gallóglach axe as follows: 'the weapon they most use is a battle-axe or halbert, six feet long, the blade whereof is somewhat like a shoemaker's knife, and without a pike'.[123] Unfortunately, Dymock does not elaborate on what he means by a shoemaker's knife — which could either have had a blade like the Murthly Castle weapons or a broad crescent blade.[124] One of the axes in Dürer's drawing of Irishmen of 1521 may be related to the Murthly Castle weapons rather than the Danish axe of form A.

We are suggesting that the Murthly Castle type of long-shafted weapon was known as a Jedwart staff in the sixteenth century. 'Jedwart staff' as a term survived into the next century. An Act of 18 August 1643 enjoined their use by those in the army unprovided with pike, musket or sword,[125] but by the time the arms of the burgh of Jedburgh were recorded in the register of arms in Lyon Office c. 1680 as 'Gules, on a horse salient argent, furnished azure, a chevalier armed at all points, grasping in his right hand a kind of lance called the Jedburgh staff',[126] the weapon described by Major may have ceased to have been a local speciality. In fact, a second description of a Lochaber axe in Irvine's *Nomenclatura* of 1682 seems to describe a Murthly Castle weapon or, as we would have it, a Jedwart staff:

> to feight with Lochaber-axes; which is like a halbert; only the upper part thereof was armed with an axe, above an eln long, narrow below but broader in the middle, which ran to a sharp point, edged on both sides, the two parts of this axe had a socket on the back wherein the wood hand was contained, and all the rest was tyed with iron and armed at the lower end with a strong steal point.[127]

Thus the term 'Jedwart staff' may have been supplanted by 'Lochaber axe' by the later part of the seventeenth century. A further description of a Lochaber axe confirms the continuation of the Murthly Castle type into the eighteenth century. It is contained in a volume on the Highlanders published in the early nineteenth century but based on eye-witness accounts from the time of the 1745 Jacobite uprising. In the context of warfare it says that the Highlanders, in the absence of a musket, or when lacking ammunition, used a Lochaber axe, a type of long lance or pike with a formidable weapon at the end of it adapted either for cutting or stabbing.[128]

By the beginning of the nineteenth century true memory of what Jedwart staves were like seems to have vanished. Sir Walter Scott could write in 1805 in a note to *The Last Minstrel* that 'The Jedwood-axe was a sort of partisan, used by a horseman, as appears from the arms of Jedburgh which bear a Cavalier mounted and armed with this weapon. It is also called a Jedwood or Jeddart staff.'[129] To the present writer's knowledge there is no evidence of the use of the term 'Jedwood-axe' prior to Scott's writing. According to Jamieson's *Dictionary*,[130] Jeddart staves were understood to denote the weapons still carried before the Magistrates of the town or in other processions. 'Some of them resemble the halbert on one side, having a short kind of bill or sharp hook on the other. There are others which exhibit the hatchet on both sides. They are in length from seven to eight feet.' The first of these were weapons of the type normally called Lochaber axes nowadays (see below) and the second probably partisans.[131]

Three other supposed identifications of 'Jedburgh axes' ought to be mentioned here. Drummond illustrates a typical eighteenth-century halberd head and it is described as such.[132] Laking gives an early sixteenth-century German axe and says it is of the same type as the Jedburgh axe, apparently basing this comparison on the opinion of Samuel Meyrick, the noted nineteenth-century English collector of arms and armour, that the Jedburgh axe was a weapon similar to the axe carried by the farriers of the Household Cavalry.[133] The axe in question has the top of its cutting edge drawn into a well defined point and has a horizontal spike or fluke behind. The writer is unaware of any evidence to support either of these ascriptions. Thirdly, a type of long-shafted weapon with a broad flat socketed head formed into a long central point flanked by two flukes has been identified as a Jedburgh axe by ffoulkes, Joubert and others.[134] The weapon seems to be a Northern English type and several of the surviving examples are associated with the burgh of Newcastle-upon-Tyne.[135] There is nothing to suggest that such weapons might have been used in Scotland, nor do they seem to have the characteristics which might be expected for Jedburgh staves from the documentary sources cited above.

In conclusion, we might deduce that form D axes were in use in Scotland by the beginning of the sixteenth century and probably considerably beforehand. A particular variety typified by examples from Murthly Castle may have been known as Jedburgh staves in the first half of the sixteenth century, and were used on horse and on foot. Later form D axes passed as Lochaber axes.

Form E Axes

Thomas Pennant, the late eighteenth-century English traveller, gives two drawings of Lochaber axes and this, as far as we are aware, is the earliest identification of the weapon that is now most commonly recognised as a Lochaber axe.[136] Only a few years later, in 1786, the English antiquary Francis Grose published a drawing of a similar weapon, also described by him as a Lochaber axe.[137] Basically, Pennant's and Grose's drawings are of a type of long-shafted weapon with an axe blade longer than it is broad and with a hook projecting backwards from the top of the shaft. Grose writes that his weapon is five feet (1.524 m.) long.

Sir Walter Scott describes the Lochaber axes carried by the Edinburgh Town Guard in his day or slightly earlier in chapter two of *The Heart of Midlothian* (written in 1818): 'a long pole, namely, with an axe at the extremity, and a hook at the back of the hatchet'. In the National Museum in Edinburgh there are now four long-shafted weapons called Lochaber axes which answer to this description and which are said to have been used by the Edinburgh Town Guard. Of these at least two were gifted by the Town Council in 1849. The Town Guard was first instituted in 1679 for policing the town and to replace the old and unsatisfactory system of watching and warding imposed on the burgesses. On its reconstitution in 1689 the town's Treasurer was appointed to acquire halberds for the guard, and these were evidently supplied by John Munro, an Edinburgh bowyer.[138] In a commission of 1682 by the king for levying a foot company for guarding the town it was proposed that it should have power 'to carie muskets or halberds and other arms necessary'. The first specific mention of Lochaber axes in connection with burgh officials of any sort that the writer has discovered is in 1736 at the time of the Porteous Riots — actually the context in which Scott describes the Lochaber axe in *The Heart of Midlothian*. A contemporary newspaper account describes how the Edinburgh mob 'threws stones in so violent a manner and wounded several of those that attended the magistrates with Lochaber axes and butts of muskets'.[139] They are also mentioned in the indictment of William MacLauchlane who was accused of 'invading the guard room, disarming the guards, and taking the Guns, Halberts, Lochaber Axes and other Weapons kept in the said Room for the Defence of the City' on the night that Porteous was lynched.[140]

It is thus possible that the weapons now in the National Museum date to some time in the eighteenth century prior to 1736. Two of them are marked with the initials 'TS' but it is unknown who these stand for. The only Edinburgh craftsman the writer knows to have made such weapons about this time was Robert Williamson (working in Edinburgh Castle), possibly the Robert Williamson who was apprenticed to William Thomson, armourer, in 1640.[141] On the other hand, in Logan's *The Scottish Gael*, published in 1831, there is an illustration purporting to be one of the Lochaber axes carried by the Edinburgh Town Guard and it is very clearly an axe of form B, or what we would now call a halberd,[142] and such a halberd is shown, in a late eighteenth-century print, being carried by a captain of the guard,[143] and several in the hands of guards in a print of the laying of the foundation stone of the Old College, Edinburgh University. Was there some confusion as to what a Lochaber axe was, or could a Lochaber axe at this time also be a halberd? The National Museum also has two 'halberds' of eighteenth-century date (LE 9-10), said to have been used by the Edinburgh Town Guard.

Edinburgh was by no means the only burgh in the eighteenth century whose guard or other officials are said to have been armed with Lochaber axes. Among the others we may particularly note Stirling and Aberdeen. The former, no doubt alarmed at the approach of the Earl of Mar's Jacobite army, ordered twenty to be made for the use of the burgh in September 1715. The craftsman was John Stivenson, hammerman,[144] but unfortunately none of these are identifiable today. The town of Aberdeen was ordered by Mar to supply 300 Lochaber axes to his army at its camp at Perth in October of the same year, and workmen in Old Aberdeen were duly employed to execute this task.[145] Prior to the uprising of 1745 all the burgh's small arms were removed to Edinburgh Castle so that they would not fall into the hands of the Jacobites, and they were never returned, the burgh receiving compensation for them in 1747.[146] Thus the Lochaber axes presently associated with the town are unlikely to be those manufactured in 1715 and most probably date to the second half of the eighteenth century. The axes in question are preserved in Marischal College Museum, Aberdeen University, and Provost Skene's House in the Guestrow. Each has a crescentic blade with solid body, most of which projects beyond the top of the shaft, and a hook is formed on the back of the blade itself. Logan illustrates one of them with the information that it was formerly used by Aberdeen Town Guard.[147]

A weapon (no. 13) in Perth Museum is probably one of those carried by the Perth Town Guard, since it was gifted to the museum c. 1840 by the Town Council. Like the Aberdeen axes it has its hook formed on the back of the blade, which in this case is elongated and fixed to its shaft by a socket. It thus does not have a very axe-like appearance and, strictly speaking, ought to be considered a member of the 'socketed' glaive family. It is not impossible that it is derived from earlier socketed glaives. The type can be paralleled by weapons depicted in the altar piece of 1482 in the cathedral of Aarhus in Denmark.[148] Perth fell into the hands of the Jacobite insurgents in both 1715 and 1745 and it is therefore likely that this weapon dates to after the uprisings. Axes with their hooks formed on the back of the blade are probably a later development anyway. Perhaps it was discovered that the hooks which were driven into the tops of the shafts could be worked loose quite easily.

Lochaber axes — form E axes — may also have been used by the military in the eighteenth century. Some at Inveraray Castle in Argyll are likely to have belonged to the West Fencible Regiment.

Several of the form E Lochaber axes as illustrated by Pennant and Grose, or of closely related type, survive, probably none dating to any earlier than the second half of the seventeenth century. They can be divided up into several sub-groups on the basis of such features as the following, found either singly or in combination on different examples:

1. the drawing of the top of the blade into a point, normally bent slightly away from the cutting edge and projecting beyond the top of the hook — as on two of the Lochaber axes in the National Museum (LE 3, 4), said to have belonged to the Edinburgh Town Guard, and two in the West Highland Museum, Fort William, from the Breadalbane Collection at Taymouth Castle.

2. axe-heads with crescentic blades and solid bodies — as one in the Tower of London (VII. 1351) signed W HOOD (fig. 165), the Aberdeen Town Guard Lochaber axes and several at Inveraray Castle, both with separate hooks and hooks on the backs of the blades.

3. blades normally of more rectangular outline, the tops of which project but little beyond the top of the shaft — as two of the Edinburgh Town Guard Lochaber axes in the National Museum (LE 1, 2) and the example illustrated by Grose.

4. blades attached to the top of a shaft by a socket rather than by means of one or two shaft-holes on their backs — as the one in Perth Museum described above and another at Inveraray Castle with a near horizontal fluke, rather than a hook, on the back of its blade (fig. 166).

5. hooks set in the top of the shaft — as on the Edinburgh Town Guard ones and the two in the West Highland Museum from the Breadalbane Collection.

6. hooks formed with a sharp inner edge. These are often called bridle-cutters, since this was supposedly one of their main functions. The axe by W. Hood in the Tower of London and others at Inveraray Castle are good examples.

7. hooks formed as one with the back of the axe-head where it projects above the top of the shaft — as the Aberdeen Town Guard axes, another in the West Highland Museum and others at Inveraray Castle (fig. 166).

This list is by no means exhaustive but is solely intended to give some sort of idea of the range in Lochaber axes of form E. All of these weapons are derivative in various ways from those of forms C and D and indeed there may have been little difference at all between some form C axes with hooks — Leith axes as we suggested — and some form E examples. Some weapons which may be regarded as transitional between the two forms in typological terms are some of the axes at Inveraray Castle in Argyllshire which have crescentic edged blades which do not hug the shaft too closely.

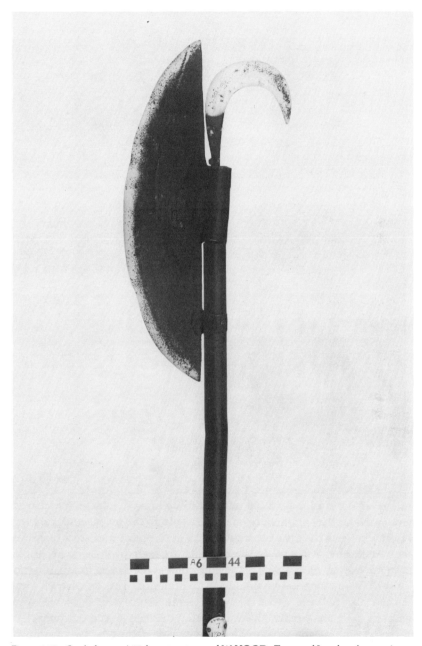

Figure 165. 'Lochaber axe', 18th cent., stamped W HOOD. *Tower of London Armouries*

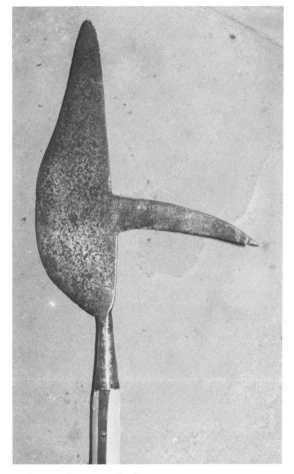

Figure 166. 'Lochaber axe', *Inveraray Castle*

The form of these form E Lochaber axes is not uniquely Scottish, as rather similar weapons, often referred to by arms scholars as *fauchards*, were used on the continent from the fifteenth to the seventeenth century. Normally these have the blade and hook in one piece and are attached to their shafts by a socket, but some, like an axe with a separate bridle-cutter in the top of its shaft, in the collection at the Tower of London (no. VII.875), are remarkably similar. It is stamped with the mark of the Vienna Arsenal and dates to the sixteenth century. It does not seem necessary to the writer, however, to postulate a direct connection between such fauchards and the Scottish axes; rather the two should be seen as parallel developments.

There are some form E axes, identical to the Lochaber axes of Scotland and indeed so-called by modern authorities at least, which are associated with the north of England. In Newcastle Museum there are two types: firstly, those with solid crescent blades and bridle-cutters, and secondly, those with long rectangular blades with rounded tops and hooks in the top of their shafts. Other examples of these are to be found in the Tower of London and in the Artillery Museum at Woolwich — apparently all from the same source, Newcastle. The Town Council of Newcastle gifted two Lochaber axes, one stamped WN, the other IL, to the Museum of Artillery, Woolwich in 1864 (nos. XII, 47-48). It is likely that these axes were copied from the Scottish Lochaber axes in the eighteenth century.

Other Axes

Several other forms of axes are known from Scotland in the Medieval Period, mostly short-shafted ones, but these are normally considered to be woodworking tools rather than weapons. It is worth considering, however, that some of them saw use in battle as this has often been claimed by recent authorities for continental examples.[149] Firstly, there are those with a long socket whose blades are prolonged downwards into an acute point, that is axes of type II in the London Museum Medieval Catalogue.[150] A typical example is one in the National Museum (RY 26/MP 164), from Aberdeenshire, which has a slightly curved cutting edge. Others have straight cutting edges and some, like one from Hunthill in Angus (National Museum: RY 16/MP 24), have a prominent snout.

Secondly, there are those 'bearded' types in which the bottom of the blade is broadened out before returning to the shaft which is normally fairly long. The National Museum has a few examples, including one from Boat-of-Garten, Inverness-shire (RY 25/MP 161), and another from Lochmaben Castle in Dumfriesshire (RY 12/MP 20). A fifteenth-century or later date can be suggested for both of these.[151] A representation of a bearded axe of similar form is carved on a grave-slab at Taynuilt in Argyllshire.[152] Even axes with long thin bodies and short cutting edges, normally only considered as wood-cutting tools, have been considered as weapons.[153] Such an implement from Derryhollagh, County Antrim, Ireland, is illustrated by Hayes-McCoy as probably a gallóglach axe of the thirteenth century or later.[154] Such axes are not unknown in Scotland either, for example one from Knapdale now in the National Museum (RY 39/MP 602).

Finally there is a battle-axe from Birse Castle in Caithness which is distinctly different from the type M axes with which it was probably contemporary. Its long cutting edge is prolonged downwards into a pointed 'beard' and it has a short shaft-hole with no spurs. It may be a development from Petersen's type C axes, possibly of eleventh- or twelfth-century date.[155] It is now in the National Museum, Edinburgh (RY 7/MP 15).

Clubs and Maces

Clubs and maces as a category of weapons include at one end of the scale the simplest, roughly shaped piece of wood and at the other skilfully formed and decorated metal implements. Wooden clubs have always been used by man but because of their simple and often temporary nature and because they were not normally weapons of any prestige, very few of any age have survived anywhere. There is, however, what may be an early example in Kirkcudbright Museum of such an implement. It is about 0.87 in. long with a head slightly at an angle to the shaft, formed at a large knot in the wood. The shaft tapers from the head to the foot in two stages, in the upper of which there is a small hole with iron corrosion, probably the remains of a nail or spike. It was found with one of the type M axes described above either in or next to a dug out canoe beside Loch Doon Castle.[156]

Maces were a development from the more rudimentary clubs and were used especially by mounted troops throughout Europe from the twelfth century onwards. They are thus shown in use on the Bayeux tapestry and in the thirteenth-century English manuscript of *La Estoire De Seint Aedward Le Rei.*[157] Several bronze heads for these maces, to which dates in the twelfth, thirteenth and fourteenth centuries are normally assigned, have survived in Europe, many showing a fair amount of similarity in form — typically with three rows of staggered conical or pyramidal knobs.[158] The heads themselves are normally fairly small, at most about 10 by 7 mm., and judging by manuscript illustrations were mounted on hafts about 0.75 m. long.

Only one macehead with a secure Scottish provenance is known, and that is one ploughed up on Millsteads Farm, Canonbie, Dumfriesshire (fig. 167), now in the Dumfries Museum (no. 1969. 18). It consists of a bronze cylinder, 90 mm. high, on the upper part of which are modelled three staggered rows of four knobs, the top and bottom ones curving down and up respectively. The shaft below the knobs is cast with two pendant fleur-de-lis and has a raised rim. One of the topmost knobs is missing.

Other maceheads from collections in the British Isles are formed with similar bronze shafts and curved knobs, like one in the Tower of London on loan from the British Museum (no. AL 116/562) and two in the National Museum, Dublin (nos. W 297, W 299). Unfortunately the

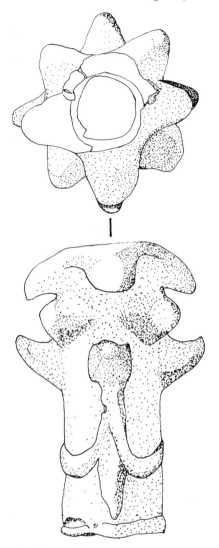

Figure 167. Bronze macehead from Millsteads Farm, Canonbie. *Dumfries Museum*

provenances of all three are unknown.[159] None of them are decorated, but decorated maces occur elsewhere.[160]

Maces remained in use in Scotland into the sixteenth century. Robert Selkirk, the royal cutler, provided James IV with a gilt steel mace containing a dagger in 1507,[161] and maces were used in tournaments at this time,[162] if not very commonly in battle. Forty-two 'irne muschis' were, however, supplied for the ships going on the expedition round Scotland in 1540, each weighing about 4 lbs. 13 ozs. without their shafts.[163] It is possible that these were what otherwise have been referred to as 'brogit staves'.

The parliament in Perth in March 1429/30 enacted that all yeomen who were not archers were to be armed with sword and buckler and a good axe or else a brogit staff.[164] By 'brogit staff' must have been meant a staff weapon armed with spikes like the so-called *Morgensterne* (morning stars) used on the continent in medieval times. Essentially these consist of a shaft with a cylindrical or spherical head round the circumference of which project various iron spikes. They are themselves a form of mace, clearly derived from types in use in the thirteenth century. Seitz illustrates some 'primitive' examples, apparently of the sixteenth century but which were carried in a peasant uprising in Dalarna in Sweden in 1743.[165] They have spearheads projecting out of the top of their shafts and are presumably similar to the 'brogit staff with a spere' which was stolen from Dunbeath Castle in 1500.[166] There are a few other references to brogit staffs about this time, for instance one mentioned amongst the goods of an Aberdeen burgess in 1477,[167] but they do not appear in royal proclamations about arming or royal accounts after 1430. On the other hand, there is an interesting English letter written in September 1513 by Brian Tuke, Clerk of the Signet, to Richard Pace, Cardinal Wolsey's secretary, in which it is said a document was found on one of the dead Scottish nobles at Flodden listing money and munitions sent to the Scots by the French, including 6,000 spears and 6,000 maces.[168] While some of the details about this document may be considered a bit suspect, the attribution of maces to the Scots would not have been unlikely. The English themselves used similar weapons at this time. A Venetian merchant reported in 1513 that the English forces included 12,000 men with a weapon never seen before, six feet long, surmounted by a ball with six steel spikes.[169] The term 'morning star' — to the author's knowledge — appears only once in an early Scottish document. In 1688 the Magistrates of Inverness ordered those tradesmen of the town who could not afford a gun and sword to provide themselves with 'ane dens ax or ane morneing starr with ane sufficient sword'.[170]

Acknowledgments

The writer is greatly indebted to several of his colleagues for the help they have given him in the preparation and writing of this paper. In the first place his thanks go to the curators of the museums who have allowed him access to their collections and also supplied information and photographs of their weapons. Nicolas Bogdan made available the spear and axe from the Perth excavations, and Mrs. K. Antonio of the Scottish Development Department kindly showed the writer the axes from Caerlavrock Castle. Mr. A. V. M. Norman, Dr. Richard Fawcett and Mrs. Helen Bennett all supplied help and information on the carving at Coupar Angus, and lastly a special debt of gratitude is owed to Claude Blair, who read an earlier version of this paper and made several helpful comments. The writer alone, however, is responsible for its remaining imperfections.

NOTES

1. Spears have not attracted so much literature as many other more glamorous or complicated arms, and their simple functional forms and long use have not made their study very easy or rewarding. Recent studies of the spear in Medieval Europe have been made among others by M. Ellehauge, *The Spear* (Tøjhusmuseets Skrifter v, Copenhagen, 1948); J.-E. Cirlot, 'La Evoluccion de la Lanza en occidente' *Gladius* vi (1967), 5-18. See also H. Seitze, *Blankwaffen*, 2 vols. (Brunswick, 1965).
2. *Wallace Docs.*, 37 [Harleian MS 3860, fol. 186].
3. *Acts Parl. Scot.* [*APS*], ii, 100. 132.
4. For a discussion of this see C. S. Terry, *Papers Relating to the Army of the Solemn League and Covenant* (Scot. Hist. Soc., 1917), i, pp. xcv-xcvi.
5. *Brosse Missions*, 23 (translated from the French); but 'lance' normally meant a spear for use on horseback.
6. W. Skinner, *The Society of Trained Bands of Edinburgh* (Edinburgh, 1889), 25.
7. See G. W. S. Barrow's chapter on 'The beginnings of military feudalism' in *The Kingdom of the Scots* (London, 1973), 179-314, for a recent outline of the documentary evidence for knight-service.
8. Barbour, *Bruce*, bk. XIII, lines 18-61.
9. Pitscottie, *Historie*, i, 353.
10. P. Hume-Brown, *Early Travellers in Scotland* (Edinburgh, 1891), 74.
11. *Treasurer Accts.* [*TA*], vi, 337; vii, 124.
12. *State Papers (Ireland) Henry VIII,* III, iii, 444.
13. Major, *History*, 240.
14. Dalrymple, *Historie*, ii, 133.
15. I am grateful to Nicholas Bogdan for furnishing me with information on this spearhead.
16. K. A. Steer and J. W. M. Bannerman, *Late Medieval Monumental Sculpture in the West Highlands* (Edinburgh, 1977), 160-1, pl. 17 B.
17. Ibid., pl. 22 A-B.
18. J. Petersen, *De Norske Vikingesverd* (Kristiania, 1919), 35 and fig. 25.
19. R. E. M. Wheeler, *London and the Vikings, London Museum Catalogues: No. 1* (London, 1927), fig. 12,6.
20. *TA*, viii, 120.
21. Ibid., iv, 121; viii, 54.
22. Ibid., iii, 392.
23. H. Laing, *Descriptive Catalogue of Impressions from Ancient Scottish Seals* (Edinburgh, 1850), pl. 3, 1.

24. S. Maxwell, 'Carved Oak Panels formerly at Greenlaw, Kirkcudbrightshire', *Proc. Soc. Antiq. Scot.*, lxxxii (1947-8), 290-2.

25. W. M. Mackenzie, 'Some Stray Inscriptions', *Proc. Soc. Antiq. Scot.*, lxi (1926-27), 182, fig. 9.

26. See W. L. Goodman, *The History of Woodworking Tools* (London, 1966), 27-33. Type M axes are considered primarily as woodworking tools in the context of medieval Kiev by B. A. Rybakow, 'Das Handwerk', in *Geschichte Der Kultur Der Alten Rus Die Vormongolische Periode*, ed. B. D. Grekow & M. L. Artamonow (Berlin, 1959), i, 139.

27. Barbour, *Bruce*, bk. III, lines 19-23.

28. *APS*, ii, 113.

29. *Royal Charters of Carlisle*, ed. R. S. Ferguson (Carlisle, 1894), 290-4, and reproduction facing p. 13.

30. *Chron. Lanercost*, 230-2.

31. *Les Chroniques de Sire Jean Froissart*, ed. J. A. C. Buchan (Paris, n.d.), i, 254; ii, 720.

32. Steer & Bannerman, *West Highland Sculpture*, 171.

33. *APS*, ii, 18.

34. Ibid., ii, 45.

35. Ibid., ii, 132.

36. On the Bayeux tapestry there is a representation of one of the English at the Battle of Hastings, two hands on a large axe and a shield strapped on his back. The shield in this position is not obviously serving any useful defensive purpose and it seems reasonable to regard this illustration as exceptional. See C. H. Gibbs-Smith, *The Bayeux Tapestry* (London, 1973), fig. 42; P. Paulsen, *Axt und Kreuz in Nord-und Osteuropa* (Bonn, 1956), 15, 21, Abb. 3.

37. *Acts of Council*, ii, 477-8; *Aberdeen Council Register*, 259.

38. Petersen, *De Norske Vikingesverd*, 46-47, figs. 44-45.

39. O. Rygh, *Norske Oldsager* (Christiania, 1885, no. 560. Wheeler, *London and the Vikings*, 25.

40. Paulsen, *Axt und Kreuz*, 19.

41. Gibbs-Smith, *The Bayeux Tapestry*.

42. J. G. Scott, 'An 11th Century War-Axe in Dumfries Museum', *Trans. Dumfries & Galloway Nat. Hist. & Antiq. Soc.*, 3rd series, xliii (1966), 117-20.

43. The constructional details of the axe in Dumfries Museum are similar in all the other type M axes from Scotland and can clearly be seen in many type M axes from elsewhere; e.g. see a fine illustration of one from Finland by T. Leppaaho, 'Späteisenzeitliche Waffen Aus Finland', *Suomen Muinaismuistoyhdistyksen Aikakauskirja*, lxi (1964), Taf. 63.

44. Wheeler, *London and the Vikings*, 14-16, 25.

45. Paulsen, *Axt und Kreuz*, 153, Abb. 82; Leppäaho, 'Späteisenzeitliche Waffen', Taf. 61.

46. N. Q. Bogdan & T. W. Wordsworth, *The Medieval Excavations at the High Street, Perth, 1975-76* (Perth, 1978), 21.

47. Paulsen, *Axt und Kreuz*, 19.

48. The two Caerlavrock axes are to be published shortly but I am grateful to the staff of the Inspectorate of Ancient Monuments of Scotland for allowing me to mention them here. The Cluny Castle axe is Drummond, *Ancient Scottish Weapons*, pl. XXXIV, 6.

49. Wheeler, *London and the Vikings*, fig. 10, no. 5.

50. S. Grieg, 'Hugg-Og Stötvåpen Fra Middelalderen', *Nordisk Kultur. XII B, Vaaben* (1943), 121, fig. 88.

51. Steer & Bannerman, *West Highland Sculpture*, 57, 151-2.

52. *State Papers (Ireland) Henry VIII*, III, iii, 444.
53. Illustrated by A. Borg, 'Gisarmes and Great Axes', *Journ. Arms & Armour Soc.*, viii (1976), pl. CXXI, B.
54. This provenance is given it by Drummond in a note by his drawing of it in the Soc. Antiq. Scot. MSS. This is the axe illustrated by Scot, 'An 11th Century War-Axe', fig. 2, which was formerly in Haughton House, Alford, Aberdeenshire.
55. Paulsen, *Axt und Kreuz*, 19, Abb. 7, h, describes and illustrates a Finnish axe which he dates to the 11-12th cent., which has a convex upper edge.
56. Steer & Bannerman, *West Highland Sculpture*, 78, 97.
57. J. Hunt, *Irish Medieval Figure Sculpture* (Dublin & London, 1974), 292, cat. no. 1486.
58. Illustrated by Steer & Bannerman, *West Highland Sculpture*, pl. 40D.
59. Reproduced in H. F. McClintock, *Old Irish Dress* (Dundalk, 1950), pl. 26.
60. *TA*, vi, 157.
61. Ibid., ii, 111.
62. Major, *History*, 238.
63. Ibid., 49.
64. *APS*, iii, 91.
65. Buchanan, *History*, i, 41.
66. G. A. Hayes-McCoy, 'The Gallóglach Axe', *Journ. Galway Archaeol. & Hist. Soc.*, xvii (1937), 107.
67. Hunt, *Irish Medieval Figure Sculpture*, 251, cat. no. 213.
68. Pitscottie, *Historie*, i, 400. The 20,000 is undoubtedly an exaggeration.
69. Dalyell, *Fragments*, 60 (Patten's Expedicion).
70. Steer & Bannerman, *West Highland Sculpture*, fig. 18.
71. *APS*, i, 388.
72. C. Blair, *European and American Arms c. 1100-1850* (New York, 1962), 24; Borg, 'Gisarmes and Great Axes', 337-42.
73. *Edinburgh Burgh Recs.*, ii, 177.
74. Borg, 'Gisarmes and Great Axes', 339.
75. W. Forbes-Leith, *The Scots Men-at-Arms and Life-Guards in France* (Edinburgh, 1882), i, 16, quoting D. Lottin, *Recharges historiques sur la ville d'Orleans* (Orleans, 1836), i, 194.
76. E.g. a 15th cent. French (?) one in the Wallace Collection, London and another English (?) one of the same date in the Tower of London (no. VII 1509). For the former see J. Mann, *European Arms and Armour* (Wallace Collection Catalogues, London, 1962), ii, no. A926.
77. *Bannatyne Misc.*, i, 28.
78. *APS*, VI, i, 13.
79. *Exch. Rolls*, xiv, 140-1, 163-4.
80. *Edinburgh Burgh Recs.*, ii, 177; iii, 12 etc.
81. *Acts of Council (Public Affairs)*, 392.
82. *Cal. State Papers Scot.*, i, 585.
83. *Inventory of Peeblesshire* (Roy. Comm. Anc. Hist. Monuments Scot., 1967), ii, 323, pls. 111-12.
84. C. E. Whitelaw, *Scottish Arms Makers* (London, 1977), 162-3.
85. *Hist. MSS Comm.* (1925), 196. (Lord de Lisle & Dudley MSS, *Penshurst Place*, i). I am grateful to Mr. I. Eaves for this reference.
86. *Scottish National Memorials*, ed. J. Paton (Glasgow, 1890), 240, fig. 170.
87. Barbour, *Bruce*, bk. xii, lines 50-59.
88. *La Estoire De Seint Aedward Le Rei*, ed. M. R. James (Oxford, 1920), 56, p. 57. The axe in this illustration is wielded by the Norwegian king.

89. Drummond, *Ancient Scottish Weapons*, XXXIII, 6.
90. C. J. ffoulkes, *Inventory and Survey of the Tower of London Armouries* (London, 1915), ii, 257.
91. This boss is illustrated in the *Inventory of Roxburghshire* (Roy. Comm. Anc. Hist. Monuments Scot., 1956), ii, pl. 81, no. 5.
92. *TA*, iv, 458.
93. J. Major, *Historia Majoris Britanniae* (Edinburgh, 1740), 197, ff. Major, *History*, 240.
94. G. F. Laking, *A Record of European Armour and Arms through seven centuries*, 5 vols. (London, 1920-22), iii, 118, fig. 922, followed by Seitz, *Blankwaffen*, i, Abb. 154; H. Laking suggests it dates to the early 17th century while Seitz gives it a 15th century date.
95. W. Boeheim, *Handbuch der Waffenkunde* (Leipzig, 1890), 371, fig. 438.
96. J. Skelton, *Engraved Illustrations of Antient Arms and Armour* (London, 1854), ii, pl. LXXIII, 6.
97. C. Irvine, *Nomenclatura* (Edinburgh, 1682), 201.
98. J. T. Dunbar, *History of Highland Dress* (Edinburgh & London, 1962), 73.
99. See Seitz, *Blankwaffen*, i, 242, Abb. 242.
100. See Borg, 'Gisarmes and Great Axes', 340.
101. ffoulkes, *Tower of London Armouries*, no. VII, 873. It is stamped with a 'B' like another very similar one in the Great Hall of Edinburgh Castle.
102. J. Dalyell & J. Beveridge, 'Inventory of the Plenishing of the House of the Binns . . ., *Proc. Soc. Antiq. Scot.*, lviii (1923-4), 356.
103. *Reg. Privy Council*, 3rd series, iv, 227. There are a few axes of other types with Scottish provenances which are probably of Scandinavian origin. Drummond, *Ancient Scottish Weapons*, pl. XXXIV, 7, illustrates a broad axe of Petersen's type M with pronounced spurs and characteristic backwards bent shaft of the type current in Norway in the 17th century and later (cf. Seitz, *Blankwaffen*, ii, Abb. 243-4). It is from the Loch of Leys, Kincardineshire. Another battle-axe with crescent blade and lozenge-shaped point behind the socket, presently in the Marischal College Museum, Aberdeen (no. 469/4) but dug up by the side of the Loch of Laurieston, may be from the same part of the world (cf. a water colour by Hertzberg dated 1817 of a bride-groom from Kinsarvik, holding such an axe, mounted on a shaft of chest height. R. Kloster, 'Et Bryllop i Kinservigs Praestegield', *Bergens Museums Arbok 1934* (1935), pl. II, fig. 5. A third axe with double blade in Provost Skene's house, Aberdeen (n. 52 21.1) is of a type used till recently by Danish carpenters (cf. Goodman, *Wood-working Tools*, fig. 33). It was found at West Hall, Oyne, Aberdeenshire.
104. Pitcairn, *Trials*, ii, 432.
105. See Blair, *European Arms*, 29.
106. Major, *History*, 240.
107. Drummond, *Ancient Scottish Weapons*, p. XXXI, 1, 2.
108. T. Miller, 'The Site of the Battle of Bannockburn', *Trans. Stirling Nat. Hist. & Archaeol. Soc.*, lv (1933), 89.
109. Borg, 'Gisarms and Great Axes', pl. CXX, B.
110. *La Estoire De Seint Aedward*, 62, p. 63. These weapons are what at a later date would have been called glaives, but although the term was in use in the 13th century it is not clear that it was applied to such weapons — at least not exclusively. See Blair, *European Arms*, 24.
111. J.-F. Finó, 'L'Art Militaire en France au X111e siècle', *Gladius*, vii (1969), 25, fig. 2.
112. M. Ellehauge, *The Glaive* (Tøjhusmuseets Skrifter, ii, Copenhagen, 1945), 8, fig. 7.
113. *Palace of History, Catalogue of Exhibits* (Glasgow, Edinburgh & London, 1911), i, 328, no. 86. Illustrated opposite p. 324.

114. Laking, *European Armour and Arms*, iii, fig. 921.
115. *TA*, iii, 90.
116. Ibid., iii, 392.
117. Ibid., v, 46.
118. *APS*, ii, 362.
119. *TA*, vi, 337; viii, 54; viii, 124.
120. *Reg. Privy Council*, i, 62.
121. Ibid., iv, 118.
122. *Edinburgh Burgh Recs.*, ii, 139.
123. Quoted by Hayes-McCoy in 'The Gallóglach Axe', 105.
124. For an early example of a cobbler's knife see B. A. Rybakow, 'Das Handwerk' in *Geschichte Der Kultur Der Alten Rus*, i (Berlin, 1959), ed. B. D. Grekow & M. L. Artamonow, Abb. 81. Knives with crescent blades are often carved on 18th-19th cent. tombstones, e.g. D. Christison, 'The Carvings and Inscriptions on the Kirkyard Monuments of the Scottish Lowlands . . .', *Proc. Soc. Antiq. Scot.*, xxxvi (1901-02), fig. 40e.
125. *APS*, VI, i, 43.
126. A. Porteous, *The Town Seals of Scotland* (Edinburgh & London, 1906), 160.
127. Irvine, *Nomenclatura*, 215.
128. D. Stewart, *Sketches of the Character, Manners and Present State of the Highlanders of Scotland*, 2nd edn. (Edinburgh, 1822), i, 69. Scythe blades mounted on shafts were also used in the 18th cent., e.g. by the Burgh of Dumfries.
129. Sir. W. Scott, *The Lay of the Last Minstrel*, n. 3.
130. J. Jamieson, *Supplement to the Etymological Dictionary of the Scottish Language* (Edinburgh, 1825), i, 616.
131. Partisans are spears with large triangular blades with projections at each side. They were often very ornate and were used in Scotland, as elsewhere, as ceremonial weapons, e.g. at the Riding of Parliament, and by certain burghs, such as Kinghorn in Fife.
132. Drummond, *Ancient Scottish Weapons*, pl. XXXIV, 1.
133. Laking, *European Armour & Arms*, iii, 120, fig. 924.
134. ffoulkes, *Tower of London Armouries*, ii, 238, nos. 871-2; F. Joubert, *Catalogue of the collection of European Arms and Armour formed at Greenock by R. L. Scott* (Glasgow, 1924), ii (unpaginated). I am indebted to Mr. J. G. Scott for sending me a drawing of the weapon listed by Joubert (39-65qt).
135. There are examples in the Tower of London, Newcastle Museum and the Scott collection in Glasgow Art Gallery and Museum.
136. T. Pennant, *A Tour in Scotland, 1769*, 4th edn. (London, 1776), i, pl. XXXIV.
137. F. Grose, *A Treatise on Ancient Armour and Weapons* (London, 1786), pl. 28,4.
138. *Edinurgh Burgh Recs.*, 36, 277. For Munro see Whitelaw, *Scottish Arms Makers*, 96.
139. *Caledonian Mercury* (9 Sept. 1736). An extract of this is given by W. Roughead, *Trial of Captain Porteous* (Glasgow & Edinburgh, 1909), 238.
140. The indictment is dated 10 March 1737, and there is a copy of it bound in a series of papers and notes on the riot in the library of the National Museum of Antiquities of Scotland.
141. Account for 20 Lochaber axes made for Captain James Coult in 1702. Scottish Record Office, GD 26/6/123/15. I am indebted to Dr. Rosalind Marshall for this reference. See Whitelaw, *Scottish Arms Makers*, 86, for Williamson's apprenticeship.
142. J. Logan, *The Scottish Gael*, 2 vols. (London, 1831), i, 305.
143. Roughead, *Trial of Porteous*, opposite p. 11.
144. *Stirling Recs.*, ii, 140.

145. *Aberdeen Council Register*, ii, 353, 359.
146. Ibid., ii, 376, 387-8.
147. Logan, *The Scottish Gael*, i, 305.
148. Ellehauge, *The Glaive*, fig. 20.
149. See, for instance, Grieg, 'Hugg-Og Stötvåpen', 122-4, fig. 91-96; and Seitz, *Blankwaffen*, i, 238-9; Abb. 154, B, C, D; Abb. 157.
150. *Medieval Catalogue* (London Museum, 1967 edn.), fig. 11.
151. Cf. Grieg, 'Hugg-Og Stötvåpen', figs. 93, 95; Seitz, *Blankwaffen*, i, 239; Abb. 154, D; Abb. 157.
152. Steer & Bannerman, *West Highland Sculpture*, fig. 20, 4.
153. E.g. by Grieg, 'Hugg-Og Stötvåpen, 124, fig. 97.
154. G. A. Hayes-McCoy, *Irish Battles* (London & Harlow, 1969), pl. 6.
155. Paulsen, *Axt und Kreuz*, 24-25; Abb. 8, i; Abb. 9.
156. F. M. Cathcart, 'Account of the Discovery of a number of Ancient Canoes . . . in Loch Doon . . .', *Archaeologia Scotica*, iv (1857), 301; *New Statistical Account of Scotland*, v (1845), 337.
157. Gibson-Smith, *The Bayeux Tapestry*, fig. 35; *La Estoire De Seint Aedward*, 59, p. 60.
158. See, for instance, L. Lindenschmitt, *Die Alterthumer Unserer Heidnischen Vorzeit* (Mainz, 1958), i, Heft VIII, Taf. 2, nos. 1-3, 5; Grieg, 'Hugg-Og Stötvåpen', fig. 98-103; A. Ruttkay, 'Waffen und Reiterausrustung des 9. bis zur ersten Halfte des 14. Jahrhunderts in der Slowakei', *Slovenska Archaeologia*, xxiii (1975), 208, Abb. 29, 32.
159. I am grateful to Mr. Guy Wilson of the Armouries at the Tower of London for supplying me with a photograph and information on the British Museum mace, and to Messrs. R. O'Floinn & E. P. Kelly for photographs and information on the maces in Dublin.
160. See references cited in n. 162.
161. *TA*, iii, 396.
162. Pitscottie, *Historie*, i, 243.
163. *TA*, vii, 355.
164. *APS*, ii, 18.
165. Seitz, *Blankwaffen*, i, Abb. 308.
166. *Acts of Council*, ii, 477-8.
167. *Aberdeen Council Register*, i, 408.
168. *Cal. State Papers Venetian*, ii, 135.
169. Ibid., ii, 99.
170. Council Records of Inverness, vol. 1680-88, fol. 81. (The author has used a typescript of extracts from this in the Whitelaw Papers in the National Museum of Antiquities of Scotland.)

9 The Birth of the Scottish Pistol
Geoffrey Boothroyd

Any study of that unique series of weapons which we today call Scottish pistols must start with the pistols themselves, those examples which a kindly fate has permitted to survive.

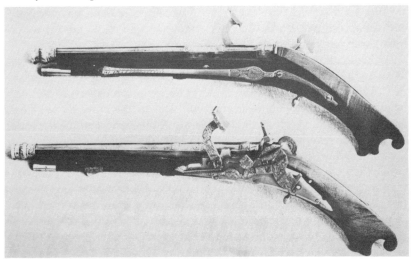

Figure 168. Pair of fish tail pistols dated 1598 (F 316). *Staatliche Kunstsammlungen, Dresden*

The earliest known dated examples are in Dresden (fig. 168), the date 1598. Pistols which can be described as Scottish continued to be made until the opening years of the nineteenth century but I wish to restrict my remarks to those pistols which, admittedly somewhat arbitrarily, I call phase I pistols. With the sole exception of the Dresden pair, all phase I pistols date from the first half of the seventeenth century. From the dated examples the period can be further contracted, 1598-1634.

For convenience I have divided the phase I pistols into two groups. The first group are the 'Fish tail' pistols. The earliest attempt at classification appears to be due to Joseph Anderson, Curator of the National Museum of Antiquities, but in 1923 the late C. E. Whitelaw published an expanded system of typological development and dating which remains in use to the present day. I believe that the term 'fish tail' originated with Whitelaw. I would prefer to use the term 'bird's head' for reasons which will become apparent later, but 'fish tail' has become hallowed with use and I see no real reason for change.

The first fish tail pistols have wooden stocks and these are amongst the earliest of all the phase I pistols. The examples from Dresden have stocks entirely of wood; a pair from Copenhagen dated four years later, 1602, have metal mounts.

Other examples are dated 1611 and 1619. The spread of dated examples is therefore 1598-1619.

These pistols as a group are quite distinctive. Furthermore there is no indication that here is the first fumbling attempt to make a pistol. These are, indeed, the fully developed form; they are confident, nay arrogant, and this presupposes that earlier examples would show how this confident craft had developed.

Unfortunately, no earlier examples have ever come to light and we are left with the supposition that either all the earlier examples have been lost or destroyed or perhaps exist in some museum or collection wrongly labelled. The second supposition could well be the correct one. There are, for example, very few English pistols of this period, and even today the origin of several is in dispute. If, indeed, the craft was imported into Scotland, whence did it come? The answer is very likely to have been either the Low Countries or Germany. There is a body of opinion that favours an English origin for the Scottish pistol. I cannot favour this and feel that both English and Scottish pistols came from a common European heritage and then subsequently developed along divergent lines, the Scottish pistols being in my opinion finer examples of craftsmanship and artistry, although perhaps slightly inferior as weapons. We now have some evidence as to origin in the decoration of the earlier fish tail pistol.

On one example, there is a quite distinct bird's head on the butt terminal (figs. 169, 170). The prototype can be seen in Dresden where a South German wheelock of c. 1590 displays an unmistakable bird's head (fig. 171).

With the evidence available to us this point cannot be stretched any further, so now let us turn our attention to the full metal-stocked fish tail pistols. As the quantity of metallic decoration increased — plaques, straps, butt terminals — it must have seemed quite reasonable for someone to have thought, rather than add metal to wood, why not make the whole stock of metal? When we come to discuss the people who made these pistols, such a line of reasoning appears logical. By whatever means, the fish tail pistols were eventually fully stocked in metal (with one exception all are stocked in brass). It now seems likely that most if not all the brass pistols were in fact originally gilt to prevent tarnishing. The shape, form and style of the wooden butts was faithfully copied in metal. The locks (of which more later), and belt hooks, and the fact that these pistols were made in right and left hand pairs, survive the transition from wood to metal and we have evidence that both types were made

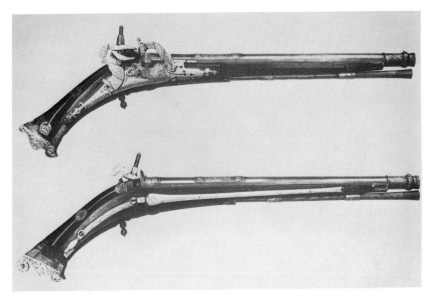

Figure 169. Pair of fish tail pistols signed IL 1602 with walnut stocks and blued barrels with three engraved and gilt panels. The locks are of brass with running foliage decoration, and the stocks are inlaid with silver and brass engraved mounts. The butt terminals have 'bird's head' decoration (B 345a-b). *Tojhusmuseet, Copenhagen*

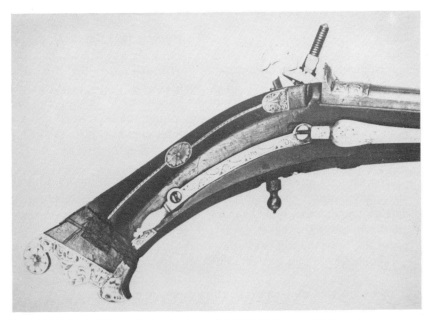

Figure 170. Detail of the stock of a pistol signed IL 1602. *Tojhusmuseet, Copenhagen*

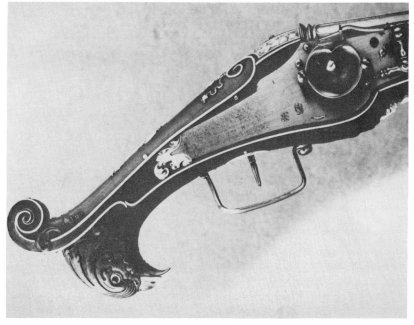

Figure 171.   Detail of butt of a wheel lock pistol dated 1590 in the form of a bird's head (F 188). *Staatliche Kunstsammlungen, Dresden*

concurrently. The earliest brass dated example is 1611 (fig. 172), the last 1626.

It is, however, in the decoration of the fish tail pistols that the maker excelled himself. The pattern and designs employed owe little to Celtic traditions; rosettes are very common, occasionally thistles and leaf scrolls, and scale and cable ornament, running border work and our rather rare bird's head are distinctive features of phase I pistols. The belt hook side of the pistol is often left with minimal decoration and the flattened sides of the barrel are also bare.

Of great significance in our researches, the barrels of these pistols are often dated, also the fence. By far the majority of these pistols bear the date of manufacture, none bear the locus. What we do have, however, are the initials of the maker, invariably impressed on the lock plate. One pistol also bears the maker's initials on the barrel.

I should like to look at a brass fish tail pistol once again in the light of what has been said. These pistols are unique in many respects, in relation to their surviving contemporaries they are quite outstanding.

Sooner or later we must ask the question, what were these pistols like as weapons? From the standpoint of their effectiveness we must look to

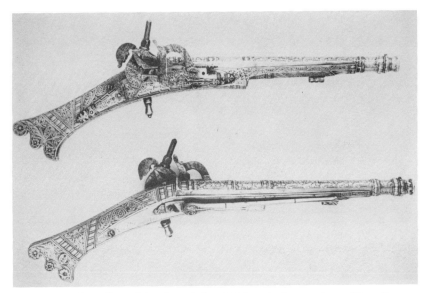

Figure 172. Pair of brass fish tail pistols dated 1611 on the fence and signed IL on the barrel and the lock plate (LH 325-6). *National Museum of Antiquities of Scotland*

Figure 173. Detail of decoration on the top of the barrel and date on a lemon butt pistol signed IA 1613, one of a pair (nos. 1726-7). *Livrustkammar, Stockholm*

22

Figure 174. Arms and initials of Count Axel Oxenstierna (1583-1654) on pistol by IA 1613. *Livrustkammar, Stockholm*

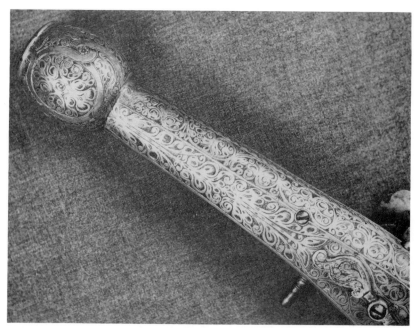

Figure 175. Detail of butt terminal and decoration on pistol by IA 1613. *Livrustkammar, Stockholm*

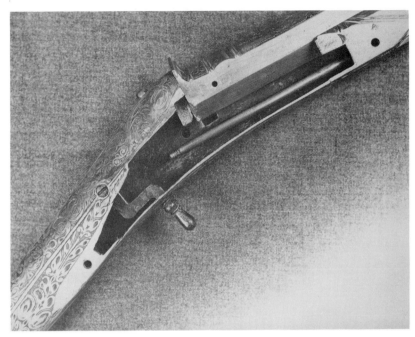

Figure 176. Pistol by IA 1613 with lock removed, showing trigger detail, ramrod, barrel and vent, and general method of construction. *Livrustkammar, Stockholm*

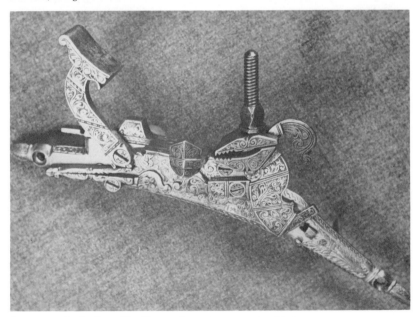

Figure 177. Lock of pistol by IA 1613. *Livrustkammar, Stockholm*

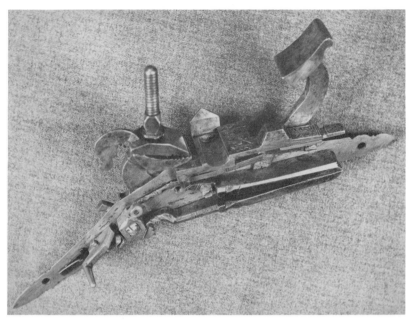

Figure 178. Interior of lock on pistol by IA 1613. *Livrustkammar, Stockholm*

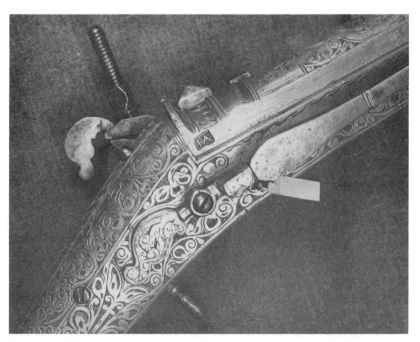

Figure 179. Maker's mark IA on pistol dated 1613. *Livrustkammar, Stockholm*

the calibre, the size of bore which dictates the size of the ball which the pistol could fire. With the type of powder available the velocity of the projectile was limited, so for effectiveness the bore size of pistols was generally quite large. The fish tail pistols have bore sizes of less than 18 mm., and they are quite small, pea shooters in fact, and this has led more than one person to ask if indeed these pistols fired round ball or did they shoot something else, say arrows for example? This is an interesting line of thought but it does provoke several rather serious questions. Do we have any contemporary information about these pistols as weapons? The answer appears to be no. To the best of my knowledge no one has fired a fish tail pistol and recorded his impressions. Very few people who are knowledgeable about pistols as practical weapons have handled fish tail pistols and given their impressions of how they would perform against targets, let alone targets which shoot back. One has therefore to look at this weapon and ask what degree of confidence could be placed in it if one's life depended upon it? Before we go further into this question and the possible answers which might be offered, I think we should examine the other pistols in the phase I period, the 'Lemon Butts'.

Looked at in the broadest possible manner, the term 'lemon butt' has the merit of describing at least a proportion of the phase I pistols which are not fish tails.

Furthermore, it is a term which immediately provides the enquirer with some indication of what he is looking for, pistols with lemon-shaped butts. From the outset it becomes apparent that the close similarity between the fish tails, even from different makers, is lacking in the lemon butt pistols. Here is a far wider divergence of style, shape, ornament and size. One of the points of similarity is that the earliest dated lemon butt pistols were also made with wooden stocks. The pistols are dated 1625, and from the illustration of one in the National Museum of Antiquities (LH 283) we can get a good idea of what the typical lemon butt pistol looks like (fig. 180). The first thing to note is that the lockplate and cock are similar to that on the fish tail pistols and that the stock itself, except for the butt terminal, is again not dissimilar. We can also see why the lemon butt got its name. In this example the butt is roughly lemon-shaped except for the fact that I have yet to see a flat-sided faceted lemon. Again, to change the terminology would be pedantic, and as long as it is realised that few lemon butt pistols have lemon shaped butts there is little reason to change a term which is now firmly established. One alternative would be to call these pistols 'non-fish tail', since the term embraces all those pistols of the phase I period which do not have fish tail butts. Certainly, many of the 'lemons' are rather oddly shaped, but the term is of use since matters would be needlessly complicated if each and every variant were to have its own specific descriptive term, many of

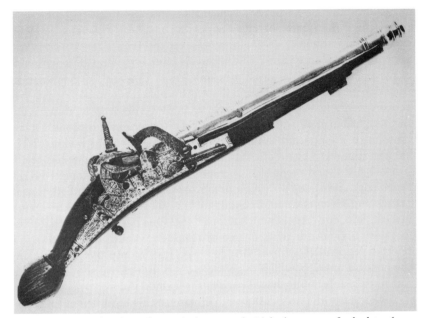

Figure 180. Pistol with snaphaunce lock engraved with leaf ornament. Lock plate of brass with initials RM. Brass barrel with upper surface engraved with interlaced bands enclosing leaf ornaments and bearing the date 1625. Walnut stock lacking mounts and ending in a lemon-shaped, faceted butt (LH 283). *National Museum of Antiquities of Scotland*

which, incidentally, would probably be meaningless to everyone except the originator.

An interesting feature of this particular pistol is the decoration on the facets of the butt. One might be excused for thinking that this was decoration until we have a look at a similar pistol in the National Museum of Antiquities (LH 282) (fig. 181). Here we can see the reason for the 'decorative' holes in the previous example. There were nails in the stock to secure decorative and possibly protective brass plates to the butt terminal. The interesting aspect of this is that both pistols are dated 1625 and both bear the maker's mark 'RM' on the lockplate. It is not unreasonable to suppose that the earlier pistol had similar decorated brass strips, but of significance is the difference in the barrel styling. The barrel of LH 283 is of what we can regard as standard phase I pattern: rounded top and bottom with flat sides. The barrel of LH 282 is composed of a series of flat surfaces almost as if the maker wished to repeat the style of the butt terminal.

As with the fish tail pistols, the lemon butt pistols were made in right and left hand pairs, and the examples from the National Museum in

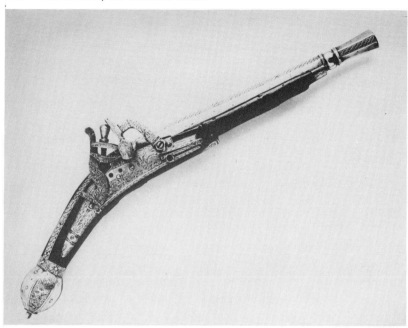

Figure 181. Pistol with snaphaunce lock (top jaw and capstan screw later replacements), brass barrel and lock plate, the latter marked RM. The barrel is dated 1625 and the wooden stock inlaid with brass plates attached to the lemon butt by pins (LH 282). *National Museum of Antiquities of Scotland*

Copenhagen illustrate all the features of these pistols to advantage: the belt hook, the lack of a trigger guard (if trigger guards are fitted they can be regarded as a later addition), and the maker's mark on the lock plate, in this case 'PH'. These pistols are regrettably undated although at some time the fences may have borne a date. As with the fish tails, the lemon butt pistols were also made with brass stocks. A particularly fine example from the Colville Collection in the National Museum, Edinburgh, is illustrated. This example is dated on the barrel 1621 and the makers mark is 'MM' (fig. 182).

The earliest dated brass lemon butt pistol is one which bears the makers mark 'IL' and the date 1614. This example, one of a pair in the R. Gwynne collection, is unusual in that the butt pommels can be unscrewed to extend the stock. It is when we leave the 'standard' lemon butt pistols and move to those which merely bear the courtesy title 'lemon butt' that we come across some of the most splendid examples of the Scottish pistol maker's art. But before we do this, a brief look at an iron lemon butt pistol. In external appearance the iron lemon butt pistols are not dissimilar to the wood-stocked lemon butts or the brass examples

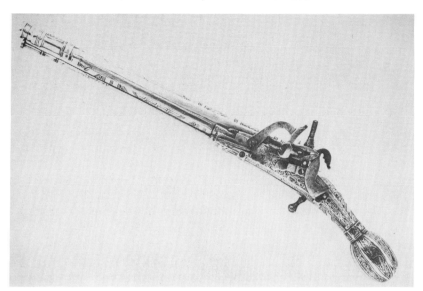

Figure 182. Pistol for the left hand dated 1621. The all-brass lock plate is signed MM and it has a lemon-shaped faceted butt (Colville Collection FA 2). *National Museum of Antiquities of Scotland*

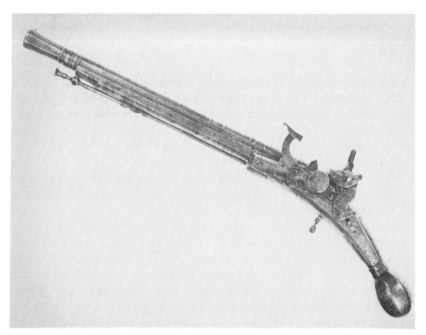

Figure 183. Lemon butt pistol of iron with brass lock plate dated 1634 on the fence. The lock plate is signed IL (40-45ae). *Glasgow Art Gallery and Museum*

which we have already seen. They appear to be conservative in appearance and this is perhaps understandable in view of the more intractable nature of iron as compared with brass. There are few examples, and the only two dated examples known to me are one entirely of iron in the National Museum, Edinburgh marked 'IG' with the date 1627, and another marked with the maker's initials 'IL' and the date 1634 (fig. 183). The latter example is from Glasgow and it has an iron barrel and stock and brass lock plate. Overall length is 0.43 m. The decoration on this pistol is minimal and as with many of the phase I pistols parts of the lock have been replaced at some time in the past.

Compare the rather sober appearance of the iron lemon butt with the magnificence of the pair of all-brass pistols from Aberdeen (fig. 184). We are indeed fortunate that these pistols have survived and that they are in Scotland. Perhaps the most outstanding of all the phase I pistols in this country, they have a flattened lemon-shaped butt terminal decorated with a single central rosette and are quite remarkable (fig. 185). Dated 1634 on the barrels, the lockplates of these pistols bear the initials 'AG' (fig. 186). I know of no other examples of this style of butt, but one brass fish tail pistol signed 'AG' was to be found in the Arsenal, Berlin, before the war; to the best of my knowledge it has yet to be rediscovered. If comparable to the Aberdeen pair of AG's work, then the loss of the Berlin Arsenal pistol is tragic.

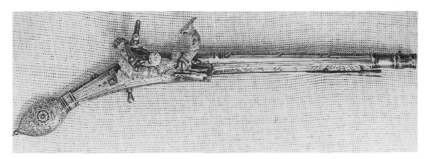

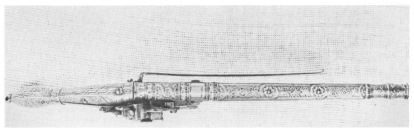

Figure 184. Pair of smaphaunce pistols of brass with lemon butts marked AG on the lock plates and 1634 on the barrels. *Marischal College Museum, Aberdeen*

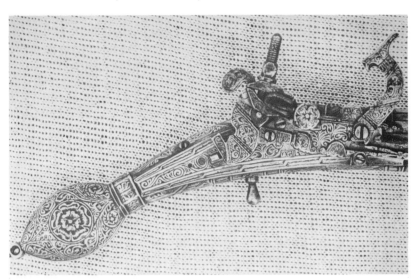

Figure 185. Pistol by AG 1634, detail of decoration on the terminal. *Marischal College Museum, Aberdeen*

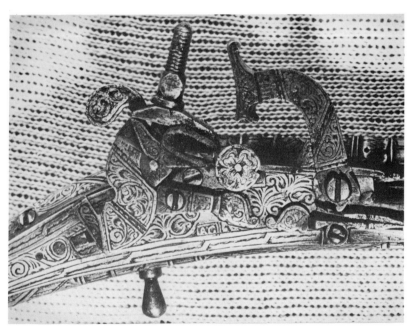

Figure 186. Detail of lock plate of pistol by AG 1634. *Marischal College Museum, Aberdeen*

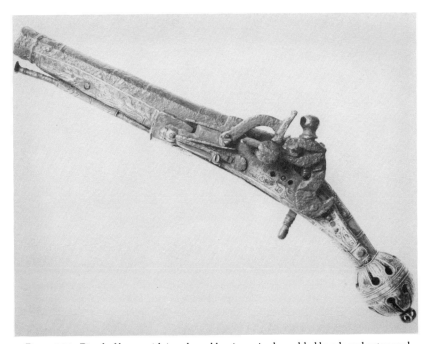

Figure 187. Pistol of brass with iron barrel having raised moulded bands and octagonal muzzle. Lock plate of brass with the initials IC. Globose butt, pierced and provided with a pricker. *People's Palace Museum, Glasgow*

A very interesting brass pistol marked 'IC' was for many years to be seen in the Old Glasgow Museum on Glasgow Green (fig. 187). One of the few phase I pistols with a known provenance, this pistol was excavated near the site of Partick Castle in Glasgow. With brass lockplate and stock, this example illustrates yet another of the variations possible, since the barrel here is iron. Also this pistol at 0.33 m is slightly smaller than the usual and the butt is pierced. This feature brings us to a whole range of extremely interesting pistols, the majority of which are in Scandinavian collections. The first of these are a pair in Stockholm, nos. 5685-6 (figs. 188, 189). Dated 1629, the butt terminals or pommels are octagonal in cross section and again decorated with a pierced design. Like others in this series the butt contains a pricker which can be unscrewed, the head of which is cubical with two transverse holes at right angles to each other. These pistols were presented to the Livrustkammar in 1876, their previous history being unknown. From the collection in the same museum in Stockholm come yet another pair of truly outstanding pistols.[1] These are earlier, 1613, and bear the initials of the maker 'IA' They are of brass, gilt, and we know to whom they belonged — Count

Figure 188. Butt of pistol signed IL. One of a pair with stocks of gilt brass with faceted, pierced butts and steel barrels, part gilt and dated 1629 (nos. 5685-6). *Livrustkammar, Stockholm*

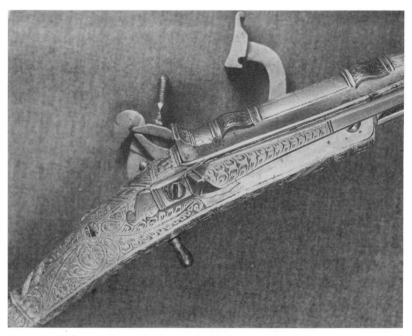

Figure 189. Belt hook of pistol by IL 1629. *Livrustkammar, Stockholm*

Axel Oxenstierna, the famous Swedish Chancellor, and the family coat of arms with the initials 'AOS' is to be found on the central panel of the barrel, a panel all too often left bare. These pistols have unusually long barrels; this seems to have been a feature of what must have been presentation pistols since they are somewhat difficult to hold in the conventional manner. The butt pommel is again of variant design, being flattened — 'barrel butt' is the term that comes to mind.

Yet another variation is to be seen in the same collection on a pistol signed 'IS' and dated on the fence 1633. The pommel is round in cross section and quite plain except for an engraved central band. I must confess to being slightly doubtful about the pommel on this pistol and would not argue with anyone who might be disposed to say that this was a later replacement.

From the foregoing we have established the general features of the fish tail and lemon butt styles. We have seen the variation in length, material of construction and design. One thing does, however, remain constant throughout this period and that is the design of the lock. There would appear to be little or no technical innovation during the period and, except where the lock has been repaired or altered at a later date, the general features remain the same.

So let us have a look at the external appearance of the lock and see how it differs from the later flintlock. The locks fitted to the phase I pistols are not strictly speaking flintlocks although they rely on flint as a means of ignition; they are snaphaunce locks and there are some significant differences which merit discussion.

First of all let us look at the outside of the lock. By lock I mean the whole of the device for giving fire to a small quantity of powder in the pan. The main feature of the lock is the lock plate, the flat piece of metal on which the rest of the lock is mounted. Attached to the plate is the pan. This is quite often a separate piece of metal and it can be replaced if worn by corrosion. On what I call Scottish locks (because that is what they are), the end of the pan has a circular, or at times an octagonal, fence. This is often decorated and, fortunately for us, is also often dated. Sometimes the dates on the fence do not agree with the date on the barrel and this poses some interesting questions. If we now move to the front end of the lock plate we come to the feather spring for the steel. This is attached to the lock plate by a single screw and the steel against which the free limb of the spring bears is hinged so that it can move from the position in which we now see it to a position where the bottom of the steel rests against the pan. Moving rearwards past the pan and fence, we next come to the buffer. This plate, screwed to the lock plate, arrests the forward movement of the cock and appears to have been an effective method of achieving this end. We now come to the cock itself. As with most other aspects of the Scottish phase I pistols, the cock is unusual and unlike the cocks on other locks. First of all, most cocks of this period have a delightful decorative comb. This is not just for decoration since the rear of the moveable top jaw is provided with a slot which engages the comb and so locates the top jaw in relationship to the bottom. The jaws of the cock are different from other locks in their shape and also in the method of tightening the two together to hold the flint. Even here the Scottish practice differs, since the top jaw is tightened by means of a nut running on a captive thread instead of a capstan screw, which was later practice. The tail of the cock is shaped so that when at full cock it is held in that position by the nose of the sear which passes through a slot in the lock plate. Turning now to the inside of the lock we find, at the front, the mainspring, which bears against the tumbler. The tumbler in this lock serves three functions. The first is the means by which the stored energy of the mainspring is converted into rotary movement to drive the cock. The second is that it provides a bearing surface for the cock, the axle of which passes through the lock plate, and the third is that it impels the pan cover forward. This latter function is peculiar to snaphaunce locks and wheel locks. The rod, attached by a pin to the tumbler, can be seen passing forward to the pan cover swivel. This is hinged at the bottom and pinned to the pan cover so that the latter can slide to and fro when the lock is at full cock. It should be noticed that on these early snaphaunce locks there is no provision for a half cock, or 'safe' position, nor indeed, because of the construction of the lock, is there need for one. To fire the pistol, the barrel is loaded with powder and ball. The cock is brought back to full cock, the steel moved forward out of battery and the pan cover opened. The pan is primed with fine powder and the cover slid over to retain the powder in the pan. The pistol is safe to carry in this position providing that the steel is not allowed to fall into battery. With the steel out of battery, even if the cock should be accidentally released, the worst that could happen is that the priming will be lost when the pan cover opens.

When the pistol is to be fired, the steel is brought into battery above the pan. When the trigger is pulled, the cock rotates and the rod inside the lock pushes forward against the pan cover swivel and opens the pan by causing the cover to slide to the front. The flint, held in the jaws of the cock, strikes against the steel, causing small particles of red hot metal to be removed from the face of the steel which fall into the pan and, hopefully, ignite the priming. The fire from this passes through the priming hole in the side of the barrel, igniting the main charge. Quite apart from the unusual features already mentioned, this lock has yet another peculiarity. The sear which holds the cock at full cock against the pressure of the main spring is mounted on a vertical pin. The tail, therefore, when acted upon by the trigger blade, moves to the rear, the trigger itself being mounted inside the butt and hinged on a pin high up in the stock. This is contrary to the practice in the later French lock where the whole arrangement of the sear is quite different. This mounting of the sear and trigger remained a feature of true Scottish locks for the remainder of their life span and it confuses those who try and fit conventional locks to Scottish pistols, since they cannot work without the whole of the trigger mechanism being altered as well. The locks are quite ingenious but are also simple and present no problems in manufacture. Certainly anyone who could mend the town 'knock' could make a phase I Scottish snap-haunce lock.

In most areas where guns have been manufactured, the separate crafts which made the necessary parts of a gun soon became specialised. This specialisation produced barrel makers, lock smiths, stockers and so on. Whether or not the trade was sufficiently advanced in Scotland for such specialisation to appear still remains an area of debate.

The locks are important for one other reason — the lock plate — for on the lock plate of the majority of phase I pistols will be found two initials. We assume with some fair degree of confidence that these initials are those of the gunmaker, and even in the brief survey we have made here we have come up with several of these mysterious initials. The earliest initials are those of the Dresden pair of wooden fish tails, the initials 'IK'. The other pair of wooden-stocked fish tails in Copenhagen are those dated 1602, and these bear the initials 'IL'. Here we have the commonest initials in the whole series. There is a pair of brass fish tails in Glasgow bearing these initials and another pair in Edinburgh dated 1611 with the lock plate marked 'IL'. The lemon butt pistols dated 1634 on the fence are marked 'IL' and a pair in Sweden dated 1629 are marked 'IL'.

If we are to assume that the initials are those of the maker, who then was 'IL'? Certainly he was an important maker of phase I pistols, and we have some clue as to who this remarkable man might have been. The word 'might' has to be used since we have no positive identification, but we believe the man to have been James Low of Dundee. In making this statement we have to make two assumptions. The first is that Dundee was the centre of the craft of gunmaking during the period of the phase I pistols, and there is much to defend this statement. The second assumption is that the initials on the lock plates of the phase I pistols correspond with the names of the gunmakers recorded in the 'Lockit Books' of the Hammerman Craft of Dundee, Edinburgh, Aberdeen, Stirling, Perth, St Andrews and Glasgow.

The Dundee craft, in which we are most interested, possesses one ancient document, the 'Lockit Book', which was begun in 1587. The book has been carefully kept for over three centuries. It contains a list of the brethren of the craft when the book commences, a list of those subsequently admitted and a register of the apprentices who entered with the craft. In addition, the volume also contains a code of laws for the welfare and good government of the craft and other acts and statutes subsequently passed.

In 1587 there were thirty-five masters, and of these eight were gunmakers. The names are of interest to us — James Alysoun, Peter Alysoun, Jhone Alysoun, Andro Alysoun, Robert Alysoun, Hew Ramsay, son of Silvester, Lichtoun and Patrick Ramsay, deacon of the Craft. It is of interest to see that the deacon of the Craft was a gunmaker and that his brother Hew was also a gunmaker. Both were sons of another member of the craft, Silvester.[2]

There were five Alisons, all gunmakers, and from the list we have the following initials, J A, P A, J A, A A, R A, H R, A L and P R the deacon. From the records we find that James Low (initials I L) was admitted freeman when he was described as the son of James Low, lockmaker. This is the lockmaker who signs in the opening list of 1587. In the craft of the hammermen there could be as many as twenty separate trades. Some became extinct, others combined. In 1587 in Dundee we find gunmakers, smiths, goldsmiths, lockmakers, pewterers, cutlers, guardmakers swordslippers, lorimers, sadlers and blacksmiths. One interesting feature of the Dundee incorporation is the use of the term 'gunsmith'. Elsewhere, in Glasgow for example, the term 'dagmaker' was used. The first Glasgow dagmaker recorded was David McBen who was entered in 1621. In 1635 we have James Smithe, in 1647 Ninian Darroch, and in 1671 the first gunsmith, Johne Currie. One of the facts often recorded in the records is the essay or test piece. The gunsmiths' essays were often 'ane gunlock', the 'lock of a gunn', but Patrick Buchanan was asked to provide 'side pistol with ane irone stock' for his 'sey piece' in 1718. No identified examples of the Glasgow dagmakers' art (apart from Buchanan, see below) are known and there are many dagmakers and gunsmiths whose work does not appear to have survived and conversely several examples of gunmaking for which no maker can be identified. The Glasgow records commence in 1616,[3] the Dundee ones, as we have seen, in 1587. The Edinburgh records start in 1582 and we find that the dagmakers are joined with the locksmiths and that, in 1594, their essay was a hackbut and a dag. The dagmaker vanishes from the records in 1676. In his stead is the gunsmith, his essay being 'a pair of sufficient pistols.[4]

The hammerman records are a fascinating window on life in the towns of Scotland at the time of the union of the crowns. Many of the acts and ordinances sound very up-to-date and would be worthy of industrial legislation of today: 'That none be made free without he is sevin years prentiss and that he is qualified the craft'. The period of seven years was to conform to old use and custom and was designed to ensure that the craftsman was fully qualified in his art and vocation. If fully qualified he would be admitted, if not, refused until 'he attain to more knowledge and practice of his craft'.

With the problems of demarcation still causing concern in the twentieth century it is interesting to see that yet another rule was that 'every master work his own work he professes and no other mans'. It is to be regretted that there is nothing in the acts and ordinances of the Dundee craft that tells us anything about the practice of gunmaking or of the gunmakers themselves.

From the lists which have now been carefully examined, and after a rather long delay published,[5] we can get some idea of who the masters were who signed their work with their initials. We lack precise knowledge of the areas where they worked, but it seems likely that Dundee was the foremost gunmaking centre in Scotland. We have looked at the pistols themselves and we are still no nearer to discovering their origin. We have looked at the people who we think are the makers, the craft organisation, and the towns where they were made. We know something about the trade routes of the period and it seems reasonable to state that seaports were convenient places for the manufacture of these rather special pistols to take place.

The main requirements for manufacture are, the men, the material and the market. In the men of the Hammerman Craft we have craftsmen sufficiently skilled to do the sort of work needed. Raw materials, iron and brass, could be imported from Europe, brass from the Low Countries, iron from Sweden and steel made locally in the quantities required by the craft itself. For those pistols with wooden stocks we perhaps have a clue in the shipping records for 1614, where we find 'John Smyth, skipper and master under god of the schip called the Elspeth latlie cum from Flanders containing two hundredweight of brissell'.[6] The quantities of all the materials required were very small compared to the value of the finished product. We are then left with the market. A seaport could export the finished pistols, and in the case of Dundee there was a thriving trade with the Baltic, Germany, the Low Countries, France and Spain.

In addition there were the mercenary soldiers who passed through Dundee on their way to the wars in Europe. Little is known of how and when they purchased arms. It is likely that the common soldier was provided with arms on arrival in Europe. The officers would more likely purchase their arms before they left home, and if my personal opinion is the correct one, they would not leave their native shores without a Scottish pistol or a brace of pistols. I am convinced that the Scottish pistol was not so much a weapon — the broadsword would still be preferred — but a badge of rank. Certainly, the number of Scottish pistols that have found their way into European collections makes it likely that they were taken abroad by their owners, the Scottish soldiers of fortune. Others, there is no doubt, were taken or sent as presents to important and influential men.

One of the few contemporary references to pistols in the phase I period is from entries in *The Compt Buik of David Wedderburne, Merchant of Dundee*. Mentioned is 'my gryt hakbut with the scrow' and 'my uther snap hakbut with my bandaler', and 'my horn flass and the scrow with key'. A 'red puther flass' was borrowed in 1592, and in 1597 he sends to England 'ane pair of pistols to be sold', and in 1608 he sends to Spain with William Renkyn four pistols with other merchandise to be sold there.

Again the historical record is silent about the type of pistol. One can only surmise that it is unlikely that a common pistol would receive special mention and be given special instructions, such as were given to John Scrymgeour in 1597: 'a pair of pistolls, given him commission to sell the same in Ingland or any other port he thinks best to my profit or to barter the same or exchange, if they not be bartered or sold to profit rather bring them home'. In September 1594 Wedderburne of Dundee records that he gave 'Patrick Ramsay a crown of the sun in arrels of a pair of pistols'. Later he gave him another crown of the sun and 3 lbs. of silver. Then a further crown of the sun was given to William his man. This Patrick Ramsay is, of course, the deacon of the Hammermen and also a gunmaker. I have not been able to discover any weapons which could be attributed to any of the Ramsays, but perhaps the clue is somewhere in Spain, a pair of brass fish tails, marked 'Moorish pistols'. It is also of some concern that Wedderburne did not keep a diary, or if he did it is now lost. What a wealth of knowledge we might have been able to garner from a diary such as kept by Pepys. Imagine it: 'This day took me to Hilltown where I bought a fine pair of pistols from Patrik Ramsay. They are mighty fine, of gilt brass and have a most curious shape to the stock like that of a fishes tail. I must have a care when I take home lest my wife see them and complain about the expense'. Alas, such a diary was not kept or has been found.

We know so very little about the gunmaking in Dundee. Did the gunsmiths make other types of pistol as well as the phase I fish tails and lemon butts? Certainly there is little evidence until the early years of the nineteenth century that conventional pistols were made in Scotland. Scottish pistols of all types appear to have been highly prized by those who bought them, and those who received them as presentations. Of the phase I pistols which have survived, few have a known provenance. I have mentioned the brass pistol dug up in Glasgow; then there is the pair of pistols given to Count Oxenstierna.

All of the pistols we have looked at show little sign of what we might call Celtic influence, unlike the later phase II and phase III pistols. The main feature of most of the phase I pistols is the four-petalled rose. One finds very few thistles. The nearest decorative art form to that on the stocks and barrels of our phase I pistols is to be found on the painted ceilings of Scottish houses[7] where once again we find the rose appearing, and also the decoration applied to contemporary silver. The quality of the decorative work varies quite widely and there is no evidence to suggest that the craftsman was a specialist. It seems likely that the makers did their own work, but again we have little knowledge of the organisation of the craft and the degree of specialisation which had taken place.

The phase I pistols vanish from the scene as quickly as they appeared. Certainly by 1650 the fish tails and lemon butts had been replaced by other styles, the heart butt and the scroll. The lock changes also, a snap-haunce lock continuing to be made for a short time, but this is replaced by a variant form of flint lock with combined pan cover and steel although the Scottish flint lock retains its unusual character in that the arrangement of the sear differs from the conventional lock. It would be neat and tidy to find some reason for the disappearance of the phase I pistols. There is some slight evidence that some of the craft skills did manage to survive, but from the early examples of the phase II pistols it seems as though the gunmakers were learning their craft all over again. With the possible exception of one maker only, the gunmaker's art in Dundee appears to have vanished. One likelihood is that the pistol-making craft was destroyed by the sack of Dundee by General Monk in 1650. Five years before, Montrose had attacked and taken Dundee, and recovery from the destruction wrought by the attackers was protracted.

The 'Lockit Book' tells us but little of these hard times but it is perhaps significant that by 1663 the numbers of the brethren had sunk to but twenty, and of these there were but two gunmakers, John Alisone 'I A', possibly another of the Alisons.

This necessarily brief look at the fish tail and lemon butt pistols of Scotland has produced more questions than answers. This is inevitable since so little time and energy have been devoted to a study of the subject. Enigmatic perhaps, fascinating certainly, the pistols of this period are unique examples of the gunmaker's craft. Their survival in the museums and collections of Europe is adequate testimony to the curiosity they continue to arouse in those who see in them part of the Scottish heritage.

Acknowledgments

My thanks are due to the various officials of the museums named for their help in providing illustrations or for facilities for photography. In particular I wish to express my thanks to Mr J. G. Scott, Glasgow Museums & Art Galleries, and Mr S. Maxwell and Mr D. H. Caldwell of the National Museum of Antiquities of Scotland, Edinburgh, for their help and advice.

NOTES

1. A. Hoff, 'Scottish Pistols in Scandinavian Collections', *Journ. Arms & Armour Soc.*, i (1953-5), 203, pl. XXXII.
2. A. J. Warden, *Burgh Laws of Dundee* (London, 1872), 473.
3. See H. Lumsden & P. Aitken, *The History of the Hammermen of Glasgow* (Paisley, 1912).
4. W. C. Little, 'Observations on the Hammermen of Edinburgh', *Archaeologia Scotica*, i (1792), 170-83.
5. C. E. Whitelaw, *Scottish Arms Makers*, ed. S. Barter (London, 1977).
6. *The Compt Buik of David Wedderburne, Merchant of Dundee 1587-1630 (Scot. Hist. Soc.*, 1898), 245.
7. See M. R. Apted, *The Painted Ceilings of Scotland, 1550-1650* (Edinburgh, 1966).

10 Armour in Seventeenth-Century Portraits

Sara Stevenson

In 1680, the artist John Michael Wright painted one of his most striking portraits: the portrait of Sir Neill O'Neill (?1658-1690) (fig. 190) in Irish dress, which was a popular painting in its day and a counterpart to his portrait of an unknown Scottish chieftain (fig. 191). Both paintings are remarkable for the accuracy and affection for detail that charac-terised Wright's work when his interest was engaged. His interests were by no means limited by the bounds of portraiture since he had also been a professional antiquarian at the court of the Archduke Leopold in Antwerp. His private collection was not just confined to paintings and his handsome library, but is known to have included agates, shells and medals. John Evelyn described it as 'an excellent collection, especially that piece of Correggio, Scotus of de la Marca,[1] a design of Paulo; and above all, those ruins of Polydore, with some good agates and medals, especially a Scipio, and a Caesar's head of gold.'[2] Bainbrigge Buckridge commented in 1706 after Wright's death, 'He was likewise well skilled in statuary, and had a considerable collection of antique medals, of which he was an excellent judge.'[3] Michael Wright plainly had a professional and informed eye both for collecting and reproducing antiquities and curiosities. His taste for them is demonstrated in the portrait of Sir Neill O'Neill by the presence in the foreground of a pile of Japanese armour. Casual piles of armour as an index to the warlike nature of the sitter were a common convention in portraits. A casual pile of Japanese armour in the same context is a cultural shock.

This Japanese armour presents two problems: where did it come from and what is it doing in the portrait of a seventeenth-century Irishman? The only known suits of Japanese armour in Britain at the time were two which were presented to James VI and I by Captain Saris who brought them from the Emperor of Japan in 1614. From this date Christianity was banned in Japan and eventually the island was practically sealed off from outside contact. It would seem reasonable to suppose that the armour Wright painted was one of these two in the royal collection, except that there are still two suits of Japanese armour in the Tower and neither resembles his painting. At this stage the possible permutations become considerable and are in no way assisted by the vague use of the term 'Indian' in seventeenth-century writing which was often extended to mean the East as a whole. In 1651, during the Commonwealth, when a

Figure 190.   Sir Neill O'Neill, ?1658-1690, by John Michael Wright. *Tate Gallery, London*

Figure 191. 'The Highland Chieftain', by John Michael Wright. *Scottish National Portrait Gallery*

Figure 192a. Japanese armour presented to James VI and I by the Shogun of Japan.
The Tower of London Armouries

Figure 192b. Japanese armour presented to James VI and I by the Shogun of Japan.
The Tower of London Armouries

large part of the royal collection was sold, one of the items in the sale was described as 'One Indian box wth an Indian Armor in it a head peece a vizard back & brest. 2 sleeves wth gauntletts. one placard for ye brest. & one for ye back. 2 peeces for ye Thyghs & leggs. & 3 small brass plates'.[4] It was sold to Major Edward Bass, a merchant, for ten pounds. Michael Wright is said by George Vertue[5] to have been present at the royal sale but this idea seems likely to have been a simple confusion with another Mr Wright and the artist may well have been abroad at the time. In July 1662 'many persons of quality went to the Armoury in the Tower of London to see that most noble and strong defence for the body, the suit of armour sent from the Emperor Mougul, which suit was presented to His Majesty the King of England'.[6] This description is slightly augmented by the juvenile John Lauder of Fountainhall who visited the Tower in 1665: 'we saw also many coats of maill and among the rest on[e] very conceity all joined like fines of fisches on to another, which they informed me came as a present from the great Mogull who commands over 36 kings'.[7] Since a confusion between 'Shogun' and 'Mogul' is easily made, this might be either of the two suits of Japanese armour (figs. 192a-b), now in the Tower,[8] which were given to King James. I incline to the view that this was the same suit of armour which was sold during the Commonwealth, re-acquired, like many items from the royal collection, after the Restoration, and exhibited because ten years' absence made it once more an impressive novelty. This sequence has also the virtue of neatness, since the alternatives require the Mogul to have sent Charles II a sixteenth-century Japanese suit of armour or the Tower to have lost a very conceity Indian suit of armour. Unfortunately, this still leaves us with Michael Wright's Japanese armour unaccounted for.

It is possible that, during the fifty to sixty years when Japan was open to the West and was encouraging Christianity and cultural contact, a suit of Japanese armour could have found its way to Ireland and into the possession of the O'Neill family. John Evelyn describes in 1676 Lord Wotton's house 'built with vast expense by Mr O'Neale, an Irish gentleman who married Lord Wotton's mother, Lady Stanhope. The furniture is very particular for Indian cabinets, porcelain and other solid and noble moveables.'[9] This *might* just imply a connection between Neill O'Neill and the taste for oriental goods. Moreover, though Japan and Japanese artefacts had theoretically been sealed off by official rule from Western trade since the earlier part of the century, the suit of armour might still have come from Japan since that time. A number of Dutch merchants were still permitted under strictly limited and occasionally humiliating conditions. These limitations presumable made the trade immensely profitable, and where profit is to be made it is extremely hard, if not impossible, to seal off any country from the attentions of smugglers.

These remarks about potential trade with Japan apply as well to anyone else in the West acquiring the Japanese armour. I am prejudiced in favour of the idea that Michael Wright found it when he was working as antiquary for the Archduke Leopold in Brussels. Since he would be known to be interested in distinguished objects, merchants bringing remarkable goods into Antwerp, which was a major centre for the East India trade, might well have taken them to him direct. In this case he might have bought the armour for himself if not for the Archduke and carried it into England when he left his service.

The range of possible explanations for the presence of Japanese armour in the portrait of an Irishman is distinctly bent in the direction of historical fiction. However, its presence tends to obscure the fact that this painting and Wright's Highland Chieftain stand apart from the main run of portraits and were popular in their day as exotic costume pieces rather than as portraits of particular men: 'He also drew a Highland laird in his proper habit, and an Irish Tory in his country dress; both which whole-lengths were in so great repute at the time when they were done, that many copies were made after them.'[10] That the Highlander's identity has been lost and the Irishman's has been confused, when a number of copies were made, implies that it was the image, rather than the personalities, which was admired. The Highland Chieftain is the first major portrait of a man in Highland dress. Irish dress had been depicted once before, but in the portrait of Captain Thomas Lee by Marcus Gheeraerts. This was probably painted for Sir Henry Lee, who organised the Acession Day Tilts in Queen Elizabeth's reign, including one which involved 'wild Irishmen'.[11] The painting is thus a piece of fancy dress comparable to the same artist's portrait of a lady in 'Persian' dress. Wright's two pictures are fairly obviously in the same tradition as these and other pictures like Van Dyck's portrait of the Earl of Denbigh in Indian dress; they are all portraits but they are also all decorative and 'curious'. In this context, the presence of a suit of Japanese armour is merely adding one 'curiosity' to another.

The Japanese armour in the portrait of Sir Neill O'Neill presents in an exaggerated form a similar problem to that of many seventeenth-century armed protraits. For a large part of the seventeenth century and during the early eighteenth century, there was a constant flow of portraits showing men wearing more armour than it was practicable to wear in comtemporary warfare. The same questions arise in relation to this habit: where did the armour come from, and why did so may men wish to be painted wearing obsolete armour?

Cited in articles like Sir James Mann's on Sir John Smythe's armour in portraiture are the entries in account books at Knole for 1642 and at

Ditchley for 1718 noting the sale of large quantities of armour as scrap iron.[12] While I can appreciate that the more basic and commonplace armour may well have been thrown out in large quantities because it was damaged, rusted or obsolete, I find it hard to credit that the major and handsome suits of armour would have been discarded. The big country houses are remarkable for their squirrel-like hoarding and they kept many objects of far less importance. The memory of the cost of a full suit of armour would probably have induced its owners to keep it, with no other encouragement. Certain pieces of armour like breastplates were undoubtedly re-used and were preserved in that way, since the period was never very far from war. The use of armour in decorative schemes like those set up at Windsor and the Tower at the end of the century presumably also preserved some armour which might otherwise have been thrown away.

Although commonly based in the cities, the seventeenth-century portrait painters were generally prepared to travel into the country to undertake large commissions. Here they would, in theory, be able to see what the individual families owned in the way of armour. The practice of Sir Anthony Van Dyck's studio, as reported by Eberhard Jabach, probably also applied to other artists: 'il dessinoit en un quart d'heure sa taille et ses habits qu'il disposoit d'une manière grande et d'un goût exquis. Il donnoit ensuite le dessin à d'habiles gens qu'il avoit chez lui par le peindre d'après les habits mêmes que les personnages avoient envoyés exprès à la prière de Vandeik. Ses Elèves ayant fait d'apres Nature ce qu'ils pourront aux draperies, il repassoit légèrement dessus et y mettoit en très peu de temps, par son intelligence, l'art et la vérité que nous admirons. Pour ce qui est des mains, il avoit chez lui des personnes à ses gages de l'un et de l'autre sexe qui lui servoient de modèle.'[13] Either by visiting the homes of their clients or by requesting that the armour be sent to them, the painters could draw them wearing the suits of armour which belonged to them. On the other hand, the sitters for seventeenth-century portraits were not unduly anxious to appear in their own clothes or with their own possessions. The Countess of Sussex who sent a number of letters of instruction to Van Dyck after she had sat for her portrait on the subject of thinning down her face to make it more attractive and painting her wearing a particular kind of fur wrap which she had plainly seen on someone else, remarked afterwards that he had painted her wearing a diamond brooch far more valuable than any she possessed. She was pleased rather than disconcerted by this and said that it would not hurt posterity to think her richer than she was.[14] This fondness for impressing posterity and presumably also contemporaries joined with a simple practical consideration to reduce the number of full suits of armour that would be painted worn by their owners. For the most part of the century full suits of armour would be in the possession, not of the original owners, but of their descendants. This meant that unless the armour was specially cut down it would not fit its owner. It was not, in any case, common for a sitter to pose at length for the whole portrait, and the costume and background were usually finished off in the sitter's absence. The special models employed by Van Dyck, and the pupils and relatives of other artists who must have served the same purpose, could have been loosely draped or squeezed into the clients' clothes, but armour is less flexible. The only way of being sure that a particular suit of armour was worn for the portrait painter is if it turns up in several paintings in different poses. The armour in several of Van Dyck's portraits of Charles I (fig. 193) is an example of this. In this instance, it would have been worth while, in terms of prestige and the money to be made from the different versions Van Dyck painted, and the many copies produced by his studio, for him to seek out a model of the right proportions.

So far as I know the only reasonably accessible armour set up in a natural pose, as against armour set up on wooden frames, was the Line of Kings in the Tower originally set up in the 1680s and 1690s.[15] It seems likely that this would be a considerable convenience to artists studying the articulation of armour, particularly in the way it related to the horse (such equestrian statues as existed must have been almost useless for practical purposes because they were lofted on pedestals, while the 'Kings' were on ground level). An example of the copying of the actual armour from the line may be the armour of Sir John Smythe which Alan Borg suggests was used for the figure of William III. This armour turns up in portraits by Michael Dahl and portraits attributed to Johann Van Diest (fig. 194).[16]

Some artists may well have owned armour themselves. A suit of armour which could be used for different clients in different poses would justify the searching out of an appropriate model or the cutting down of the armour to fit someone in the artist's household. A very clear case of an artist who owned armour is Michael Wright whose Greenwich armour appeared in a number of portraits seen from different angles and in different poses (fig. 195). He may well have owned more than one suit of armour and could have had in his collection the armour decorated with lions' heads which George Monck, Duke of Albemarle, wears in the three portraits of him by Wright. This suit of armour was apparently incorporated at a later date into the Line of Kings in the Tower and is now in the Tower Armouries.[17] Unfortunately, Michael Wright was rare in his meticulous attention to detail, and few seventeenth-century portraits permit the precise judgment of a suit of armour that is possible in his paintings.

Figure 193.   Charles I and M.de St Antoine, by Sir Anthony Van Dyck. *H.M. the Queen*

Considering the difficulties involved in painting armed portraits, it would hardly be surprising if the late seventeenth century devoted itself to repetitions based on a limited number of standard patterns. During the 1660s and 1670s, the Scougal family did adopt a standard pattern for their head and shoulders portraits in armour. These are all shown from the same angle and wearing the same armour with the same small dent,

Figure 194. Field-Marshall George Wade, 1673-1748, by or after Johann Van Diest. *National Museum of Antiquities of Scotland*

which is seen in the portrait of Patrick Smythe (fig. 196), but this was by no means applied to all their portraits of that nature. In practice, repetitions were not as common as might be expected, even if the sitter plainly did not own the armour he was painted in. When the Countess of Leven was told in a letter in 1693 that John Baptiste Medina was on his way up

Figure 195.   John, Duke of Rothes, 1630-1681, by John Michael Wright. *The Duke of Rothes*

to Scotland with a collection of bodies painted in advance by 'two men' and her correspondent followed this up by saying, 'If there be any men who want there pictors, they could be quite finished here except the face, such being generally done in armour',[18] it might be suspected that his male portraits in Scotland would all fetch up wearing the same suit of armour. Curiously enough, this did not happen and I imagine this may be attributable to the professional integrity of the two men. Artists like

Figure 196. Patrick Smythe, 1655-1674, by John or David Scougal. *Miss Smythe of Methven*

Peter Lely, Godfrey Kneller and Medina employed other artists, some of whom like John Baptist Gaspar were professional drapery painters. Given that their work was paid for by the portrait painters, who would criticise it on a professional level, and that the painting of drapery and armour was their usual employment, which would have been boring if it was repetitious, they had a double interest in varying the armour they painted. The sources of their armour are harder to pin down and I am not qualified to say whether they were painting from a whole series of different suits of armour or whether there was a substantial measure of invention in their work. I illustrate four of Medina's armed portraits as examples of the work of the drapery painters (figs. 197-200). It seems possible that they knew one or two suits of armour which they could sketch on a model from differing angles and that they then imposed a series of details from other suits of armour, seen in private collections, in the Tower or in other paintings, onto the basic drawings. I have, however, no evidence for this.

The repetitions that do occur, when an artist was less anxious to seem original, could have been derived from either engravings or the paintings of other artists. At first sight, it seems reasonable that the common and relatively cheap engraving would be a more obvious source than the less accessible originals. A painting, for example, like the portrait by L. Schuneman of General Thomas Dalyell, which was probably painted in the 1660s, may well have taken its design and armour from an engraving of one of the Van Dyck portraits of the Earl of Strafford (figs. 201, 202).

With engravings, the question of the source of the armour used is confused by the fact that not all engraved portraits came directly from a painted original. Some might be based on a drawing done especially for the engraving but others might well derive from another engraving. Engravers were, naturally, the most likely people to have suitable engravings to hand that they could imitate. This internal plagiarism is further complicated by the altered plate engraving. The elaborate engraved plates — and these include a high proportion of the armed equestrian portraits — involved a considerable amount of work. Should the demand for the engraving have proved less than was expected, a great deal of effort would have been expended for a small profit. Since the armoured portrait showed little that was personal beyond the head and hands and perhaps a title or a coat of arms, it was easily altered by rubbing out these details on the plate and re-engraving it with different features. The most remarkable instance of this kind of alteration is undoubtedly the group of prints all taken from the same plate by Pierre Lombart. This probably started life as a portrait of Oliver Cromwell during the Protectorate, it was altered to a portrait of Charles I after the Restoration, given trial runs as Louis XIV and Gustavus Adolphus and converted back to Cromwell when relics of his time had become rare and of value to collectors (figs. 203, 204).[19] The armour and the main composition in the engraving derive from the Van Dyck portrait of Charles I in the royal collection. Lombart's engraving was probably not, however, drawn directly from the Van Dyck original.

After the sale of the royal pictures in 1651, the painting came into the hands of Remigius Van Leemput, who appears to have been largely em-

Figure 197. George, 1st Earl of Melville, 1636-1707, by Sir John Baptiste de Medina. *Scottish National Portrait Gallery*

ployed as a copyist of Van Dyck's work before the Civil War. Curiously enough, the Commonwealth does not seem to have interfered with his trade in copies of this portrait of Charles I. A letter to Sir Justinian Isham, who was interested in acquiring this equestrian portrait in 1655, presumably refers to Van Leemput as the copyist: 'the King's Picture on horsebake is vallued at a great price 250 pounds, which once might have been bought for 80 pounds. Soe if you desire to have a good coppy thereof it will cost you 50 pounds'.[20] Van Leemput's copies were not all

Figure 198. David, 3rd Earl of Leven, 1660-1728, by Sir John Baptiste de Medina. *Scottish National Portrait Gallery*

strictly faithful to the original, sometimes leaving out the figure of M. de St Antoine, the riding master, or substituting a landscape for the archway. He also apparently used elements of the design for portraits of other men. A painting of an unknown man, called the 1st Duke of Hamilton (fig. 205), is a re-working of Van Dyck's design and is presumably by Van Leemput. The family resemblance between this re-working and Lombart's engraving, in the figure of the page and the lie of

Figure 199. James, 2nd Titular Duke of Perth, 1673-1720, by Sir John Baptiste de Medina. *Scottish National Portrait Gallery*

the landscape, suggests that Lombart was working from one of Van Leemput's versions rather than the original. The engraving thus started life two removes away from reality even before it was altered.

Portrait painters in the seventeenth century undoubtedly owned and studied engravings even if they did not use them directly as a source for borrowing. John Baptiste Medina's will, for example, includes '12 Mazietinto prints in John Medina's custody' and 'Vandyk's postures',

Figure 200. Thomas, 6th Earl of Haddington, 1680-1735, by Sir John Baptiste de Medina. *Scottish National Portrait Gallery*

which I take it were also engravings.[21] Just how far they used engravings in their work is more of a problem. It is certainly true that the portraits of the great and influential men and the more spectacular paintings were liable to be engraved. Both the sitter and the artist, not to mention their admirers, had an interest in this. But we tend to think of a portrait as being a single and a private object, designed for one client, painted for him and hung in his house. In fact, a major painting by a popular artist of an important man would automatically bring a train of demands for copies in its wake. This was accepted by the client. Artists and their

Figure 201. Thomas, 1st Earl of Strafford, 1593-1641, engraving by Wenceslaus Hollar after Van Dyck

Figure 202. General Thomas Dalyell, c.1599-1685, by L. Schuneman. *Scottish National Portrait Gallery*

studio assistants ran a considerable trade in copies which were sold at a far cheaper rate than the originals because they were known to be less good and far quicker to paint. It may well have been an added inducement to produce striking portraits that extra money could be made from them in the form of copies and also in the form of versions for new sitters. Certain of Van Dyck's portraits fell well into this category. The painting of Charles I which is standing full length in armour[22] was copied but also repeated as a pattern for portraits of the Earl of Arundel, the Earl of Kinnoull and others. His painting of the Duke of Hamilton is another case of a painting that his studio copied on a number of occasions (fig. 206). This painting developed a life of its own, independent of Van Dyck, and turns up in several versions by different hands, both before and after the Civil War, as the first Earl of Craven (fig. 207) and also, in a painting by one of the Scougals, as William, 3rd Earl of Lothian (fig. 208).

Copies and versions of portraits with new sitters' heads substituted were by no means foisted on an unknowing public. The number of portrait painters in Britain in the seventeenth century capable of original design, especially in three quarter length or full length portraits, was small. This was well known to the clients. By borrowing from the owner of a handsome painting, a sitter could send a good, highly finished painting to an artist of mediocre or restricted talent as a model and expect in return a reasonable approximation of the original painting at a considerably lower price. An example of this is to be found in the repetitions of the portrait of George, Earl of Dumbarton by Henri Gascars (fig. 209). In a letter from the Duke of Hamilton, the owner of the picture, to the Marquis of Queensberry in 1681 he says, 'It was my fault you got not my brothers picture for I forgot to tell Robt. Kennedy, but now I have ordered him to deliver it to Scugall he is feared your angry wt him so you must tell him you are not'.[23] The Marquis of Queensberry, who was the brother-in-law of the Duke of Hamilton and of the Earl of Dumbarton, was plainly impressed by the original painting and wanted a copy of it. This copy, which is probably by John Scougal, is now in the Buccleuch collection (fig. 210) in the company of another, reversed version of the pattern called General James Douglas who was the brother of the Marquis of Queensberry (fig. 211). It would seem that Queensberry, having paid Scougal to copy the Gascars, then handed the copy over to another and less competent artist, L. Schuneman, and asked him to produce a complementary portrait of Lord James Douglas. Although details like the background and the baton in the hand have been omitted, Schuneman may have actually traced or pricked off Scougal's copy since a minor detail like the cravat has been accurately rendered in reverse. Both Scougal and Schuneman added the design of this portrait to their repertoires and painted a number of other portraits on later occasions in the same armour and costume (fig. 212). The seventeenth-century correspondences are full of references to copies and requests to borrow paintings to have them copied, and the habit of producing versions of portraits with new heads was plainly not merely condoned but encouraged by the sitters. This must have been especially true in the relatively small and interrelated aristocratic society.

Figure 203. The 'Headless Horseman' engraving as Oliver Cromwell, by Pierre Lombart

Figure 204. The 'Headless Horseman' engraving as Charles I, by Pierre Lombart

Figure 205.   Portrait called 'the 1st Duke of Hamilton', presumably by Remigius Van Leemput. *The Marquess of Lothian*

Figure 206. James, 1st Duke of Hamilton, 1606-1649, by unknown artist after Van Dyck. *Scottish National Portrait Gallery*

Figure 207. William, 1st Earl of Craven, 1606-1697, by unknown artist after Van Dyck. *National Portrait Gallery, London*

Figure 208.   William, 3rd Earl of Lothian, ?1605-1675, by David Scougal after Van Dyck.
The Marquess of Lothian

Figure 209. George, Earl of Dumbarton, ?1636-1692, by Henri Gascars. *The Duke of Hamilton*

Figure 210.   George, Earl of Dumbarton, ?1636-1692, probably by John Scougal after
Gascars. *The Duke of Buccleuch*

Figure 211. Portrait called 'General James Douglas', by L. Schuneman after Scougal. *The Duke of Buccleuch*

Figure 212. William Fraser, Lord Saltoun, 1654-1715, by John Scougal. *Lord Saltoun*

In the seventeenth century, portraits were ordered and painted with one eye on posterity. Posthumous portraits painted by artists who had never seen the sitter formed a memorial or monument of the dead man comparable to the funeral monument in a church. In a sense, portraits as a whole were all potential funeral monuments. Robert Kerr, 1st Earl of Ancram, wrote in 1653 explaining the purpose of his portrait by Hercules Sanders: 'I send home . . . to Scotland a picture of mine for you, done by a good hand. I would have it hung up in Ancram on the wall of the hall, just foregainst the door as you come in . . . I think that will be the place, for it will be a monument of my so long being there — and not to show which of the bairns is likest their grandfather.'[24] The concern for historical realism was not pursued beyond the point where it affected dignity. The Countess of Leven's passing remark, quoted above, to the effect that Medina's portraits of men were 'generally done in armour' when full armour had long ceased to be a practical proposition on the battlefield, had more to do with dignity than with reality.

Alan Borg makes the point in his article on the Line of Kings displayed in the Tower from the late seventeenth century that they were intended to impress the bystander with feelings of awe and remind him of the great heroism of the royal line and the monarch's ancient royal lineage.[25] Like the galleries of portraits of great men and aristocratic ancestors, they provided a forceful moral and political example. The anachronism which gave thirteen kings from William the Conqueror to George II suits of armour mostly dating from the sixteenth and early seventeenth century was plainly of little concern to the authors of the Line. The late seventeenth century was not so innocent as to be totally unaware of this anachronism and there must have been plenty of intelligent antiquaries and armourers capable of criticism. The concern for historical accuracy was overridden by the concern to display armoured figures of all the great kings. The argument of the Board of Ordnance in 1761 when the Champion at George III's coronation wanted one of the suits of armour as his fee may reasonably be read as an echo of the seventeenth-century view: 'as it is Customary to mount a Suit of Armour in memory of a deceased King, the Board will not only be at a loss for one of King Charles the 2d, but likewise one for His late Majesty, as it is apprehended that Art is entirely lost'.[26] Custom has fossilised the original reason, but the concern for the dignity and the memorial are still there, regardless of historical logic.

The possession of a full suit of armour was always an impressive sign of status and a visible declaration of wealth. With the decline of the use of armour in the field, the possession of a full suit of armour would be an impressive sign of ancestral status. As suits of armour became obsolete and historical objects, they would become increasingly associated with the dignity of armed funeral monuments; the less real they were as contemporary artefacts, the greater would be their symbolic dignity. A fully armed portrait was thus able to take on an aspect of timeless heroism. The Michael Wright portrait of John, Duke of Rothes (fig. 195), which was painted after the Restoration, shows him carrying a tilting lance and wearing armour for the tilt. In another version of this picture, which used to be at Tong Hall, the lance has been painted out.[27] This second version was one of a formal set of four portraits of the great generals of the period and therefore the equivalent of one of a group of great heroes. I have not seen this second version but it seems reasonable that the painting out of the lance and the substitution of the more conventional baton was done in the seventeenth century because the lance had not developed into a symbolic object like the armour but seemed merely a perverse historical curiosity.

The interrelation between armour and ancestral respectability may have led to its becoming an unofficial family affair comparable with coats of arms. The copies of the portrait of the Earl of Dumbarton, cited above, are possible examples of this interest in declaring a family relationship, and another is to be found in the portraits of William, third Duke of Hamilton and William, first Marquis of Annandale (figs. 213, 214). The original portrait of the Duke was painted in 1682 and was copied by John Scougal with the addition of a new head for Annandale, who was the Duke's nephew. By using the same pattern and the same armour, he emphasised the family connection between the two men rather than their individuality. William, first Earl of Craven, who was a soldier and a wealthy man who could afford to be painted by the best masters, was painted on at least three occasions in a pattern based on the Van Dyck portrait of the Duke of Hamilton (fig. 207). The post-Restoration version of his portrait was engraved for the 1679 edition of John Guillim's *Display of Heraldry*, as one of only two earls to be illustrated. This could indicate an interest in establishing a solid aristocratic status and a desire to ally himself visually with the socially secure Hamiltons.

A later example of a man who made the connection between status and armour was William, Earl Cadogan. He fought as a soldier with Marlborough and later became Master of the Ordnance. Whilst holding this post, he borrowed several suits of armour from the Tower[28] and was painted on three occasions wearing two different suits. The portrait of him in the National Portrait Gallery in London shows him wearing a white and gilt suit of armour from the Tower (fig. 215). The fact that he thought of armour in terms of status and related it to the dignity of funeral monuments in a practical fashion was shown at the death of the Duke of Marlborough. In 1722, Cadogan became Master of the

Figure 213. William, 3rd Duke of Hamilton, 1635-1694, by Sir Godfrey Kneller. *The Duke of Hamilton*

Figure 214.   William, 1st Marquess of Annandale, 1664-1721, by John Scougal after Kneller. *Major Hope Johnstone*

Figure 215. William, 1st Earl Cadogan, 1675-1726, attributed to Louis Laguerre.
National Portrait Gallery, London

Figure 216. Czar Peter the Great, by Sir Godfrey Kneller. *H.M. the Queen*

Ordnance and was presumably responsible for the issue of a fine suit of armour from the Tower which was laid on Marlborough's coffin during the funeral.

The dignity of armed portraits was enhanced still further by an implied connection with the classical heroes. Armed equestrian portraits and equestrian statues were still very consciously associated with their original inspiration, the statue of Marcus Aurelius in Rome. The armed mounted figure was the formal warlike equivalent of the throned judge and appeared on the reverse of the royal seal. Certain seventeenth-century artists and sculptors confused details of classical and modern armour, and both paintings and engravings commonly showed sitters in a classical, allegorical setting wearing contemporary armour. Details of armour, like the scalloped edging to the gorget and the tasset, or the fald appearing below the tasset like the skirt of the tunic worn under the classical breastplate, must have added to the confusion. A newsletter written in 1698 describing Godfrey Kneller's portrait of Peter the Great (fig. 216) shows signs of suffering from just such a confusion of mind: 'drawn to the life at full length in a Roman habit, a Marshall's staff in his hands and the Regalias, lying by him and shipps storming a fort on the Sea Side'.[29]

With all this dubious symbolism and potential double meaning trailing in armour's wake, it is a pleasure to find that armour was also appreciated for its aesthetic and decorative possibilities. When Prince Rupert re-decorated Windsor Castle in 1670, John Evelyn reported that he 'had begun to trim up the keep or high round Tower, and handsomely adorned his hall with furniture of arms, which was very singular, by so disposing the pikes, muskets, pistols, bandoleers, holsters, drums, back, breast, and headpieces, as was very extraordinary. Thus, those huge steep stairs ascending to it had the walls invested with this martial furniture, all new and bright, so disposing the bandoleers, holsters, and drums, as to represent festoons, and that without any confusion, trophy-like'.[30] More remarkable than this display was the work of John Harris, who decorated Whitehall, the Tower and Hampton Court in the 1680s and 1690s with arms and armour arranged to make 'the Witch of Endor, an organ, Medusa's head, a pair of gates, the backbone of a whale, waves of the sea, fans, crescents, pillars and stars'.[31] It is sad that so few of the late seventeenth-century portraits display Mr Harris's imagination and virtuosity in dealing with armour.

NOTES

1. This is presumably the painting of Duns Scotus by Jusepe de Ribera bought for the royal collection from 'Mr Wright's lottery' in 1671, for which, see Sir O. Millar, *The Queen's Pictures* (London, 1977), 81.

2. *The Diary of John Evelyn* (London, 1966), i, 376.

3. B. Buckeridge, *An Essay towards an English School of Painting* (London, 1969), 437. Wright's coins and gemstones are said to have been bought by Sir Hans Sloane and are therefore presumably now in the British Museum.

4. The sales of the royal collection, edited and collated by Sir Oliver Millar in *Walpole Society*, xliii (1970-2), 154.

5. 'Vertue Notebooks' (vol. iv), *Walpole Society*, xxiv (1936), 76.

6. Quoted in C. ffoulkes, *Inventory and Survey of the Armouries of the Tower of London* (London, 1916), i, 44.

7. *Journals of Sir John Lauder Lord Fountainhall*, ed. D. Crawford (Scot. Hist. Soc., 1900), i.

8. I am grateful to Mr Ian Eaves of the Tower of London for telling me about the second suit of Japanese armour which has only recently come to the Tower from Sandringham and is therefore not the one illustrated second in ffoulkes, *Tower of London Armouries*.

9. *The Diary of John Evelyn*, ii, 110.

10. Buckeridge, *An English School of Painting*, 437.

11. R. Strong, *The English Icon* (London, 1969), 279.

12. Sir J. Mann, 'Sir John Smythe's Armour in Portraiture', *Connoisseur* (1932), 88.

13. Quoted in L. Cust, *Anthony Van Dyck* (London, 1905), 139.

14. F. Parthenope, *Lady Verney Memoirs of the Verney Family during the Civil War* (London, 1892), i, 258.

15. A. Borg, 'Two Studies in the History of the Tower Armouries', *Archaeologia*, cv (1976), 317-52.

16. Mann, 'Sir John Smythe's Armour in Portraiture.

17. C. Blair, 'Notes on the History of the Tower of London Armouries; *Journ. Arms & Armour Soc.*, ii (1958), 233-53.

18. Scottish Record Office, Leven and Melville Papers, GD/13/270/3.

19. G. S. Layard, *The Headless Horseman* (London, 1922), discusses and illustrates the full set.

20. Sir O. Millar, *The Tudor, Stuart and Early Georgian Pictures in the Collection of Her Majesty the Queen* (London, 1963), 94.

21. In the Hermitage collection.

22. In the Hermitage collection.

23. Scottish Record Office, Queensberry Transcripts, GD/224/171.

24. Quoted in D. Thomson, *A Virtuous and Noble Education* (Edinburgh, 1971), 26.

25. Borg, 'Two Studies in the History of the Tower Armouries', 328.

26. Quoted in Blair, 'Notes on the History of the Tower of London Armouries', 241.

27. Illustrated in G. Wilson, 'Greenwich Armour in the Portraits of John Michael Wright', *Connoisseur* (1975), 112.

28. ffoulkes, *Tower of London Armouries*, i, 55.

29. Quoted in J. D. Stewart, *Sir Godfrey Kneller* (London, 1971), 77.

30. *The Diary of John Evelyn*, ii, 54.

31. Quoted in ffoulkes, *Tower of London Armouries*, i, 22.

11 The Word Claymore
Claude Blair

The word *claymore*, as has frequently been pointed out, is an anglicisation of the Gaelic *claidheamh-mor*, which is pronounced in much the same way and simply means 'great sword'. It does not seem to occur in Old Scots, and, presumably for this reason, is not included in the *Dictionary of the Older Scottish Tongue*.[1] As a written word it is, strictly speaking, English, and it may be significant in this connection that the earliest recorded example of its use mentioned below dates from after the beginning of the 1715 Rising, and that it came into wider use with the 1745 Rising, when, for the first time, the Scottish Highlands and their inhabitants became of real interest to people in Southern England. Phonetically, 'claymore' is, of course, the same as *claidheamh-mor*, and it is both pointless and confusing to make any distinction between the two words: one is appropriate to the English language and the other to the Gaelic, and that is their only difference.

So far as I am aware, 'claymore' has never been applied to anything other than a sword of Highland type. Because its literal meaning is 'great sword', however, purists, starting apparently with Auguste Demmin in 1869,[2] have maintained that it should be confined exclusively to the characteristic two-hand swords that were used in the Highlands and Islands from probably the end of the fifteenth century to the third quarter of the seventeenth century and which remained in occasional use until as late as the '45,[3] and that it is quite wrong to apply it to the Scottish basket-hilted sword.[4] Sir Guy Laking, with what can only be regarded as considerable effrontery in view of his apparent complete ignorance of Gaelic, even went so far as to coin the name *claybeg* ('small sword') for this last,[5] though, perhaps fortunately, it has never been adopted. In fact, this restricted use of 'claymore' seems to be no more than arms-historians' pedantry, for there is a good deal of readily available evidence to show that, by the early eighteenth century, at least, the word was applied in the Highlands to the basket-hilted broadsword as well as to the old-fashioned two-hander. This has been pointed out before,[6] but I do not think that anyone has ever published any of the supporting evidence. The purpose of this paper is to do so.[7]

The earliest instance of the use of the word *claymore* known to me is found in a rare anonymous pamphlet, written in Dumbarton in 1715, and entitled *The Loch-Lomond Expedition with Some Short Reflections on the PERTH Manifesto*. It is included in the following description of the group of Highlanders who went out to deal with a rising led by

Gregor McGregor, nephew of the famous Rob Roy McGregor:

> . . . fourty or fifty stately fellows in their short hose and belted plaids, arm'd each of 'em with a well fix'd gun on his shoulder, a strong handsome target, with a sharp pointed steel, of above half an ell in length, screw'd into the navel of it, on his left arm, a sturdy claymore by his side, and a pistol or two with a durk and knife on his belt.[8]

The two-hand claymore, so far as I am aware, was never worn at the side, while there is no evidence to suggest that it was still in general use as late as 1715.[9] The strong probability is, therefore, that the 'sturdy claymore' mentioned in the above extract was a basket-hilted one.

The remaining examples of the use of the word 'claymore' that have come to my attention all date from 1745 onwards. The first one is important because it comes from no less a person than Lord George Murray, commander of the Jacobite army under Prince Charles. In his account of an incident in the skirmish at Clifton on 18 December 1745, which took place when he was talking to Cluny MacPherson, he says:

> I immediately drew my sword, and cried CLAYMORE! Cluny did the same, and we ran down to the bottom ditch, clearing the diagonal hedges as we went.[10]

Here again, for reasons already given, there can be little doubt that, at this late date, Lord George's troops, to whom his cry was addressed, would have been armed mainly, if not entirely, with basket-hilted swords.

The next group of references occur in *The Lyon in Mourning*, the manuscript 'Collection (as exactly made as the Iniquity of the Times would permit) of Speeches, Letters, Journals, &c. relative to the Affairs, but more particularly the Dangers & Distresses, of [Prince Charles Edward Stuart]', prepared between 1746 and 1775 by the Reverend Robert Forbes (1708-75), who from 1762 was Bishop of Ross and Caithness.[11] All are contained in accounts of events that took place during 1746, but which were not collected or written down by Forbes until 1747 or 1748. These last must, therefore, be regarded as the dates of first-recorded use, though, since Forbes obtained his information directly from people involved in the events concerned, there is every reason to think that 'claymore' was the word used when they actually took place. The references are as follows, given in the order of the events with the dates when the accounts were written down indicated in brackets: *17 January 1745/6 (1748)*. At the Battle of Falkirk, Major Donald MacDonald of Tiendrish was captured by the English and delivered up his arms to Lord Robert Ker who prevented him from being killed. Forbes comments: 'When the Major at any time spoke to a friend about delivering up his good claymore and his fine pistol, he used to sigh and mention Lord Robert Ker with great affection.' MacDonald was executed at Carlisle on 18 October 1746.

26 April 1746. (August 1747). 'Murdoch MacLeod was then a lad only of 15 years of age . . . When he heard of the appearance of a battle, having got himself provided in a claymore, durk, and pistol, he ran off from the school, and took his chance in the field of Culloden battle.'

30 June 1746 (July 1747). Prince Charles, after his disastrous defeat at Culloden, arrived, a hunted outlaw wearing female dress, at the house of Alexander MacDonald of Kingsburgh. Kingsburgh informed Forbes on 11 July 1747, that he 'was at pains to represent to the Prince the inconveniency and danger of being in a female dress. . . . He advised him therefore to take from him a suite of Highland cloathes with a broadsword in his hand. . . .' Subsequently, 'Agreeable to Kingsburgh's advice they met at the edge of the wood where the Prince laid aside his female rags. . . . After the Prince had got himself equipt in the Highland Cloathes with the claymore in his hand, the mournful parting with Kingsburgh ensued.' In another account of the same events, also recorded in July 1747, Forbes notes that 'When Kingsburgh returned to his own house he told his lady that after the Prince had got on the Highland dress and the claymore in his hand he was a sogerlike man indeed.'[12]

The last of these references makes it clear that 'broadsword' and 'claymore' were regarded as synonymous. 'Broadsword' was the normal term for a sword with a straight, double-edged, broad blade designed for use with one hand, and was the one usually applied to the Scottish basket-hilted sword at this date.[13] On this evidence alone it is clear that this is the sense in which claymore is used here, though one should perhaps draw attention also to the obvious absurdity of Prince Charles as a hunted fugitive being advised, and accepting the advice, to encumber himself with a very large two-hand sword!

The next example of the use of 'claymore' known to me is in John Campbell's rare pamphlet, *A Full and Particular Description of the Highlands of Scotland,* which was published in London in 1752.[14] This contains a description of the Highland dress, which Campbell points out was then proscribed, including the following:

> they have a short Coat made of Plaid, and cross the Shoulders there are two small Straps for securing the Sword Belt. . . . Now to compleat this grand Dress they wear a broad Sword, which they call a Clymore (sic), a Stroke of which, delivered from one of their Hands, would be sufficient to chop off the Head of the strongest Champion that ever lived. . . .

The passage of which this forms part is obviously intended to be a description of typical Highland dress of the period immediately before the Proscription Act of 1746, and there is ample evidence to show that this

normally included a basket-hilted broadsword and not a two-hand
sword,[15] even though some specimens of the latter may have been used
during the '45. Furthermore, a two-hand sword could not easily have
been used to deliver a stroke 'from one of their Hands'.

In the satirical Scots poem, 'Had awa' Frae Me, Donald', first recorded
in a publication of 1760, the apparently Lowland author describes a Highlander's courtship of a Lowland lady, in which he lists
various 'highland rarities' to attract her. Amongst them he mentions his
'pistol and claymore To flie ta lallant lown' (i.e. 'to scare the lowland
loon'), while at the end, when she has pretended to reject him, he says:

> Sae langs claymore pe po my side,
> I'll nefer marry tee, Mattam.[16]

Here again we have someone who was clearly well acquainted with the
Highlanders indicating that 'claymore' was a word normally employed
by them in the mid-eighteenth century for a sword which was worn at
the side, and is not likely, therefore, to have been a two-hand one.

The next reference I have noted comes from Thomas Pennant's
description of his visit to the Island of Raasay in 1772[17] and quite un-
ambiguously describes a two-hand sword:

> In a wood in a snug corner lies Talyskir, inhabited by Mr *Macleod*
> . . . See here a *Cly-more* (sic), or great two-handed sword, probably
> of the same kind with the *ingentes gladii* of the *Caledonians*, men-
> tioned by *Tacitus*: an unwieldy weapon, two inches broad, doubly
> edged; the length of the blade three feet seven inches; of the handle,
> fourteen inches; of a plain transverse guard, one foot; the weight six
> pounds and a half. . . . The same kind of sword . . . was preserved in
> the highlands to this present age: but the enormous length of the
> weapon has been found useless against the firmness of determined
> troops, from the Battle of *Mons Grampius*, to the recent victory of
> *Culloden*. The short swords of the forces of *Agricola*, and the
> bayonets of the *British* regulars, were equally superior.

The passage is interesting in that it shows that 'claymore' was still being
used to describe the two-hand sword in the Highlands at this date, and
that there was at least a tradition that Highlanders had been armed with
such swords as recently as the Battle of Culloden in 1746. The implica-
tion that they were generally armed with them is not, however, supported by other evidence,[18] and one suspects that Pennant may have
preferred not to enter into details that would have spoiled the analogy he
draws between the wars of the ancient Romans and of the modern British
(sic!) against the Scots.

What appears to be conclusive evidence to support the thesis of this
article is provided by a passage in James Boswell's *Journal of a Tour to
the Hebrides with Samuel Johnson*. On 15 September 1773, the two

tourists were at Dunvegan, seat of the Chieftain of the Macleods, and were shown various relics of the early seventeenth-century Sir Roderick Macleod, known as Rorie More. Amongst them were his arms, about which Boswell wrote:

> We also saw his bow, which hardly any man now can bend, and his Glaymore (sic), which was wielded with both hands, and is of a prodigious size. We saw here some old pieces of iron armour, immensely heavy. The broadsword now used, though called the Glaymore, (i.e. the great sword,) is much smaller than that used in Rorie More's time.[19]

After this date, and especially with the development of a romantic interest in the Highlands in the nineteenth century, 'claymore' was gradually accepted into the English vocabulary.[20] Curiously enough, the British War Office, which has been accused of responsibility for its alleged misapplication to the basket-hilted sword, does not seem to have used it officially until the Dress Regulations of 1883: earlier Dress Regulations merely refer to a Highland-hilted or basket-hilted sword as being appropriate for Scottish regiments.[21] At regimental level, however, the word 'claymore' was used. For example, a Regimental Order of the 79th Regiment issued on 10 November 1817 states:

> No. 5. The flank officers, when in Highland uniform, are to wear frog-belts and claymores the same as the other officers.[22]

The regiment in question was the Cameron Highlanders, which was recruited in the Highlands and, at this date, would have been largely Gaelic speaking.[23] It is difficult to escape the conclusion that the reason why 'claymore' was employed in the Order is that it was the word that was familiar to everyone in the Regiment because it was the normal Gaelic one for the basket-hilted sword.

It is not uncommon to find that old technical terms modified or widened their meanings over long periods as the objects for which they were originally the names themselves modified their forms or were replaced by something else that did the same job. In light of the evidence I have put forward in this article, I suggest that there can be no doubt that the word 'claymore' did likewise, and that it is perfectly correct to apply it to both the two-hand and basket-hilted forms of Highland sword. Indeed, it is positively desirable to do so on the grounds that it is foolish for any historical subject to have a modern technical vocabulary that does not conform as closely as possible to the vocabulary found in the contemporary sources. If, for convenience of classification, a distinction has to be made between the two main types of Highland sword, all that is necessary is to call one the *two-hand claymore*[24] and the other the *basket-hilted claymore*.

Postscript
Stuart Maxwell

I suggested to Mr Blair that someone knowledgeable about Gaelic should be consulted about *claidheamh mor* and he agreed.

Kenneth D. MacDonald, Editor of *The Historical Dictionary of Scottish Gaelic* (in production at Glasgow University), replied to my enquiry as follows:

> One must, I think, assume that the collocation *claidheamh mor*, 'large sword', was widely current in Gaelic before it found its way into English, and yet, I'm astonished to discover, on examining our slips, that the only 2 instances we've so far picked up are both from the poetess Mary MacKellar, date 1880. This may suggest that our evidence is somewhat deficient, but I think there may be another explanation. References to swords in earlier Gaelic literature, and they are very numerous, normally occur in the context of panegyric, where the aristocratic warrior is presented conventionally accoutred. The *claidheamh mor* would, presumably, be too unwieldy to fit in here, being used, one supposes, only on special occasions, or only by the less aristocratic fighting men. Certainly the qualifying adjective suggests that the sword was larger than that ordinarily carried by a Highland gentleman. This may account for the absence of literary evidence in Gaelic.

He continues, 'Clearly, we here need to investigate the term more thoroughly.' I think he has said all that can be said at present, and we look forward to the relevant entry when the *Dictionary* is published.

I have been interested in the word 'claymore' for many years and I am grateful to Mr Blair for this article. He puts me further in his debt by allowing me to add a postscript. I would put more stress on the information he relegates to his last Note;[24] in all the pre-1715 references I have collected to weapons, there is a distinction between swords and 'twa handit' swords. Even in a purely Highland context, although the language is Scots or English, the distinction is shown; for example, in the receipt given by Campbell of Inveraw for the Maclean's arms, 10 February 1679, he sums up the total as 'which number of arms extends in all to 185 swords, 95 guns, 3 pistolls, 5 Lochabur axes and ane two handed sword'.[25] I submit that in this and many other records, it is difficult not to believe that if the word 'claymore' had been in general use, for either type, it would have been used. It appears, then, that the 1715 usage[26] is a new one, that it refers as Blair has indicated to the broadsword, and that it was in use with that meaning among Highland and Lowland Scots, until the 1770s when the Englishman, Pennant, and the anglicized lowland Scot, Boswell, began the confusion of their successors by equating a claymore and a two-handed sword.

In conclusion, I draw attention to the list of Highland words John Ray made about 1700, which begins 'A sword (Klaiv) . . .'[27] — again we look forward to Mr Macdonald's *Dictionary,* supplementing the misleading entry in the *Scottish National Dictionary.*

Addendum

Since this article went to press Mr George A. Gordon has kindly drawn my attention to correspondence about the word 'claymore' in the *Scottish Field* for June, July and August 1970. This includes (July, p. 79) a letter from Mr R. I. McAllister drawing attention to an instance of the use of the word in 1678 and an alleged instance of its use in 1707. Mr McAllister has provided me with the sources of these and very generously given me permission to use them here.

The earlier reference comes from the *Memoirs* of William Veitch (1640-1722) and George Brysson (Edinburgh & London, 1825, 518), quoted in J. R. Elder, *The Highland Host of 1678* (Glasgow, 1914, 132-3):

> In the year 1678, there was a great host of Highlanders came down in the middle of the winter to the Western shires. The shire of Air was the centre of their encampment or cantvning, where they pillaged, plundered, theeved, and robbed . . . four of them came to my father's house . . . They pointed to their shoes and said they would have the broge off his foot, and accordingly laid hands on him, but he threw himself out of their grips, and turning to a pitchfork which was used at the stalking of his corn, and they having their broadswords drawn, cryed 'clymore', and made at him; but he quickly drove them out of the kilne and chaseing them all four a space from the house, knocked one of them to the ground.

The later reference was said by Mr McAllister to be in the Jacobite song 'The Broad Swords of Scotland', which was reputedly written after the Act of Union of 1707. The version of this given in James Hogg's *Jacobite Relics of Scotland* (Reprint of 1st Series, Paisley, 1874, pp. 78-79, 260) does not, however, include the word 'claymore'.

NOTES

1. Ed. Sir W. A. Craigie & A. J. Aitken (Chicago & Oxford, 1937- in progress). See also n. 24.
2. A. Demmin, *Guide des Amateurs d'Armes* (Paris, 1869), 390-1.
3. A great deal has been written about the two-hand claymore, but much of it is repetitious. The most useful recent accounts, all of which also give references to earlier publications, are: G. A. Hayes-McCoy, *Sixteenth Century Irish Swords in the National Museum of Ireland* (Dublin, 1959), 26-52; J. Wallace, *Scottish Swords and Dirks* (London, 1970), 10-11; K. A. Steer & J. W. M. Bannerman, *Late Medieval Monumental Sculpture in the West Highlands* (Edinburgh, 1977), 5-6, 167-70. See also: I. Finlay, 'The Claidheamh-Mor', *Connoisseur* Oct., 1937, 188-92; idem, *Scottish Crafts* (London, 1948), 83-85. The date when the two-hand claymore went out of general use is uncertain, but most modern writers suggest that it was in the first half of the seventeenth century. J. T. Dunbar, in his *History of Highland Dress* (Edinburgh & London, 1962), 42-43, however, quotes sources of 1677 and c. 1678 which refer to Highlanders being armed with two-hand swords, while Thomas Pennant writing in 1772 suggests that such swords were used at Culloden in 1746 (see also below p. 381 and n. 18).
4. See, for example, Sir G. F. Laking, *A Record of European Armour and Arms* (London, 1920), ii, 302-4; C. J. ffoulkes & E. C. Hopkinson, *Sword, Lance & Bayonet* (London, 1938; 2nd Edn., 1967), 66; I. Finlay, 'Weapons of the Clans', *S. M. T. Magazine* (Edinburgh), July, 1940, 35; Dunbar, *History of Highland Dress*, 193.
5. Laking, *European Armour & Arms*, ii, 302-4.
6. S. Maxwell & R. Hutchinson, *Scottish Costume* (London, 1958), 148; Hayes-McCoy, *Irish Swords*, 26; C. Blair, *European & American Arms* (London, 1962), 6.
7. I should like to make it clear that I have not attempted to search every possible source of information about the use of the word 'claymore', since the readily available information on the subject seems to me to be sufficient for the purposes of this article.
8. The pamphlet was printed in Glasgow in 1715 and is inscribed and dated at the end 'Dumbarton, October 15, 1715.' It was reprinted by Camis Erskan in 1834 from an apparently unique copy, once owned by the Reverend Robert Woodrow, in the Library of the Faculty of Advocates, Edinburgh: *The Lochlomond Expedition MDCCXV. Reprinted and Illustrated from Original Documents* (Glasgow, Duncan Macvean, 1734). The passage quoted is on p. 8. I am grateful to Mr Stuart Maxwell for drawing my attention to it.
9. See n. 3 and n. 18.
10. From Lord George Murray's own memoir, 'Marches of the Highland Army', quoted in the Rev. R. Forbes's *Jacobite Memoirs of the Rebellion of 1745*, ed. R. Chambers (Edinburgh, 1834), 70. I am grateful to Mr G. A. Gordon for drawing my attention to this reference.
11. Rev. R. Forbes, *The Lyon in Mourning . . . 1746-1775*, ed. H. Paton, 3 vols., (Scot. Hist. Soc., 1895-6).
12. Ibid., ii, 129; i, 163, 75, 76, 122.
13. See Sir W. Hope, *A New, Short and Easy Method of Fencing* (Edinburgh, 1777), passim; F. Grose, *A Treatise on Ancient Armour and Weapons* (London, 1786), 81; ffoulkes and Hopkinson, *Sword, Lance & Bayonet*, 66; H. Angelo & T. Rowlandson, *Hungarian and Highland Broadsword* (London, 1798-9), passim; B. Robson, *Swords of the British Army* (London, 1975), 14ff. In a letter dated 12 Oct. 1745, from a Miss Hepburn to a Miss Pringle, the former describes a visit she has made to the Jacobite camp at Duddingston, near Edinburgh, and records that Prince Charles Edward had

'over his Right Shoulder a very rich Broadsword Belt, his sword had ye finest wrought Basket hilt ever I beheld all silver' (W. Duke, *Prince Charles Edward and the Forty-Five* [London, 1938], 113). The description of the sword, incidentally, suggests that it is the one with a solid silver hilt by the London goldsmith Kaendler now in the National Museum of Antiquities, Edinburgh.

14. P. 8. See also pp. 391-2 here.

15. See, for example: J. Drummond & J. Anderson, *Ancient Scottish Weapons* (London, 1881); C. N. M. North, *The Book of the Club of True Highlanders*, 2 vols. (London, 1892); Lord A. Campbell, *Highland Dress, Arms and Ornament* (Westminster, 1899); Dunbar, *Highland Dress*. All passim.

16. F. W. Fairholt, *Satirical Songs and Poems on Costume* (Percy Society, London, 1849), 227, 230. Fairholt comments (p. 226): 'This excellent sample of Highland courtship, including an inventory of articles then considered as desirable for personal adornment, is given from Herd's *Ancient and Modern Scottish Songs*, vol. ii, p. 161, Edinburgh, 1776. The first edition was published in 1760. the dates of the original composition of the ballads in the volume are not given, but this one is certainly as old as our preceding song [c. 1750] if not older.'

17. T. Pennant, *A Tour in Scotland and Voyage to the Hebrides MDCCLXII* (Chester, 1774), 289.

18. Apart from Pennant's reference, the latest evidence for the use of the two-hand sword by Highlanders comes from a satirical poem written in c. 1678 by William Cleland which describes the members of a Highland army as being armed, amongst other things, 'With a long two-handed sword, As good's the country can affoord' (W. Cleland, *A Collection of Several Verses & Poems* [Edinburgh?, 1697]. In 1716, however, the Inverness armourer Robert Low surrendered a 'two-handed sword' with other arms under the terms of the Disarmament Act of 1716 (C. E. Whitelaw, *Scottish Arms Makers* [London, 1977], 250). All the known eighteenth-century illustrations and descriptions of Highland costume of the period down to the end of the '45 Rising, including David Morier's well-known painting of an incident during the Battle of Culloden, indicate that the basket-hilted broadsword was the main weapon (see the works cited in n. 15). The opinion generally accepted by the authorities cited in this paper, which I share, is that the two-hand sword had gone out of regular use by the third quarter of the seventeenth century.

19. J. Boswell, *The Journal of a Tour to the Hebrides with Samuel Johnson* (3rd edn., London, 1786; Everyman reprint, London, 1931), 170-1. I am grateful to Mr G. A. Gordon for drawing my attention to the fact that the F. A. Pottle & C. H. Bennett edition of the *Journal of a Tour to the Hebrides* (London, 1936, 171), which was produced from the original manuscript, gives the last line of the passage as: 'The broadsword which is now called the *claymore* is much smaller than the sword used in Rorie More's time, and is of modern invention.' For an illustration of Rory Mor's claymore see F. T. MacLeod, 'Notes on the Relics Preserved in Dunvegan Castle, etc.', *Proc. Soc. Antiq. Scot.*, xlvii (1912-13), 119, fig. 10.

20. See the *Oxford English Dictionary*, under *claymore*. The word was used by Walter Scott in *Waverley*, published in 1814, which would have brought it to the attention of a very large number of people.

21. I am grateful to Mr W. F. G. Boag of the Scottish United Services Museum for this information.

22. Robson, *Swords of the British Army*, 125.

23. I am grateful to Mr A. V. B. Norman for this information.

24. The normal sixteenth- and seventeenth-century Scots word for a two-hand sword (in a variety of spellings) was simply 'twa handit sword', which presumably covered both

the Lowland and Highland varieties. See Drummond & Anderson, *Ancient Scottish Weapons*, 19-20; Whitelaw, *Scottish Arms Makers*, 271.

25. *Highland Papers*, ed. J. R. N. Macphail (Scot. Hist. Soc., 1914), i, 317.
26. *The Lochlomond Expedition MDCCXV.*
27. J. L. Campbell & D. Thomson, *Edward Lhuyd in the Scottish Highlands 1699-1700* (Oxford, 1963), 202.

12 A Scroll-Butt Flintlock Pistol by Patrick Buchanan of Glasgow

Jack G. Scott

In the spring of 1978 Glasgow Art Gallery and Museum was fortunate to be able to acquire a fine scroll-butt pistol by Patrick Buchanan, of Glasgow (reg. no. A7829; fig. 217). I am indebted to the Director for permission to publish this note about the pistol, and to Miss Helen C. Adamson, of the Department of Archaeology, Ethnography and History, for facilities to examine it, and also for photographs taken by Mr Rupert R. Roddam, of the Art Gallery and Museum.

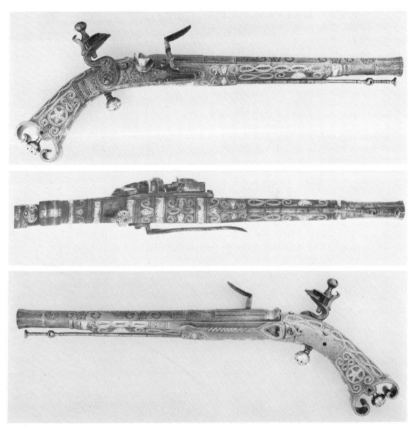

Figure 217. Scroll-butt pistol by Patrick Buchanan of Glasgow. *Glasgow Art Gallery and Museum*

The pistol is of all-metal construction, of iron, engraved and inlaid with silver, 15⅝ inches (0.397 m.) in total length. The barrel length is 10½ inches (0.268 m.) and the muzzle diameter $\frac{9}{16}$ inches (14 mm.). The barrel is fluted at the breech, tapering and swept at the muzzle, which has eight decorated facets. The large transverse flute at the base of the barrel, notched for the backsight, is matched by a similar flute at the fore-end of the stock, which is also faceted. The stock is of stout but subtle construction, the butt and trigger being offset (fig. 217, middle) to suit a right-handed marksman. The scroll terminals are moderately inturned, the butt, rather unusually, pierced between them. The belt-hook, spirally grooved, with heart-shaped terminal, has lost its rear fret: it is not impossible that this was deliberately removed, since it might have made the pistol difficult to draw from the belt. The ramrod is original, as are the silver trigger and pricker, which match in construction and engraved decoration.

The lock is of Scottish type, the steel and pan-cover in one, as in the normal flintlock, but with the sear working horizontally through a hole in the lock-plate (fig. 217, top): part of the top of the steel is missing, probably because of an old break. There is a half-cock safety position. The lock-plate is signed by Patrick Buchanan, and it is amusing to note that the letter C omitted in error from the surname has been added above the Christian name.

The barrel, lock-plate and cock bear engraved ornament only. The stock, by contrast, has profuse silver inlay, mostly in bands emphasised by punched dots. The engraving on the muzzle facets is competent and well worked out; elsewhere it is less so. A debased plant motif, possibly a lotus, engraved on the barrel, appears inlaid with silver on the stock. Other motifs are roundels, both engraved and inlaid, along with inlaid scrolls and borders. It is only too obvious that the decorator's ambition has exceeded his skill. His work does not gain from close scrutiny, yet the overall effect is not unpleasing, and no doubt was in accord with the taste of the time.

Patrick Buchanan is recorded as a Glasgow gunsmith by Charles E. Whitelaw.[1] First mentioned as burgess and gunsmith on 25 September 1717, Patrick Buchanan was admitted to the Incorporation of Hammermen on 24 January 1718. Thereafter there seems to be confusion in the record, inasmuch as he is stated to have been buried on 25 January 1729, yet was a guild brother by purchase on 8 October 1733. There remains therefore the possibility that there were two almost contemporary Buchanan gunsmiths named Patrick, though if so the younger does not seem to have been the son of the elder, since a Patrick Buchanan's eldest son John was admitted hammerman burgess in 1735, followed by his second son Colin in 1750.

It is a curious fact that this is the only all-metal scroll-butt pistol by a Glasgow maker as yet known, though it is difficult to believe that Glasgow's output would have been much less than that of any other Scottish gunmaking centre. It is therefore interesting to compare the pistol stylistically with pistols of the earlier eighteenth century from eastern Scotland, where the heart-butt type predominated, and from Doune, the home of the classic scroll-butt pistol. The Buchanan pistol is unusually large. In this respect, and in its fairly straight butt set at a shallow angle to the stock, it compares better with the larger east Scottish heart-butt pistols. But in barrel style, above all in decoration, and also in the way in which the upper line of the barrel and stock continue in an even curve into the butt, the pistol shows affinities with the Doune style, though far less refined in execution. These affinities are not unexpected, for the Glasgow market, like Doune's, must have been predominantly a Highland one.

Above all, the Buchanan pistol impresses as a practical weapon. It is well balanced, and when grasped comes easily 'to hand'. The degree of offset in the butt, for the benefit of the right-handed marksman, makes one wonder whether it once had a companion left-hand pistol, and if so whether this was correspondingly offset. However this may be, it is indeed fortunate for the study of Scottish firearms that the only known Glasgow pistol of this type should have survived in such good condition, unrestored, with its original component parts.

NOTE

1. C. E. Whitelaw, *Scottish Arms Makers* (London, 1977), 231.

13 A Type of Highland Target
Claude Blair

In 1892 C. N. McIntyre North drew attention, in *The Book of the Club of True Highlanders*, to an account of the Highland dress published in 1752 by John Campbell in his *Description of the Highlands*.[1] Surprisingly, later writers on the subject have ignored it, so, although the present note is concerned with only one of the things mentioned by Campbell, it may be useful to republish the whole passage:[2]

> Their native Dress (called Kiltine) is different from that of the Lowlands of *Scotland*, and so is their Language, seeing it is as unintelligible there, as the *Welsh* is in *England*. Now the Manner of their Cloathing is thus; they have a short Coat made of Plaid, and cross the Shoulders there are two small Straps for securing the Sword Belt; there is another small Belt that they tye round their Middles, in which is secured their Plaid made up in the Form of a Woman's Petticoat, and which hangs down in like Manner, only one Corner thereof they fix at the Top of the Shoulder with an Ivory Pin, or a Fork; they use no Breeches. Now to compleat this grand Dress they wear a broad Sword, which they call a Clymore, a Stroke of which, delivered from one of their Hands, would be sufficient to chop off the Head of the strongest Champion that ever lived; they wear a Pair of Pistols, and a Durk, which resembles a Dagger, intended chiefly for Stabbing; this Weapon hangs before in a Scabbard, along with a Knife and Fork, and a Purse for their Money, which they term a Sparren; next they have a Large Powder Horn, that they sling cross their Shoulders, with a small Belt full of brass Nails; and to finish the Dress, they wear a Target, composed of Leather, Wood and Brass, and which is so strong, that no Ball can penetrate it, and in the Middle of this Target there is a Screw Hole, wherein is fix'd a brass Cup lined within with Horn, which serves them to drink out of upon Occasion; and in the Time of Action it serves for to fix a Bayonet in. Thus accoutered they make a most splendid and glorious Appearance, it being esteemed by all Judges to be the most heroic and majestic Habit ever wore by any Nation, but at present they are prohibited the Use of their antient Cloathing,[3] which may in Time prove hurtful to the Interest of *Great Britain*, seeing this Habit kept up the martial Spirit in them, they always delighting in Feats of War; next it is an active Dress, seeing they have nothing to do when entering upon Action, but to throw off their Plaids, and draw their Swords and Pistols, and as they wear no Breeches, and

tie their Garters below their Knees, they are much more alert than those who are bound up like so many Dolls; and they are not only fitter to pursue the flying Enemy, but likewise to retreat, according as Circumstances require; though it is very well known, that they are commonly the first in the Field, and the last who turn their Backs.

The part of Campbell's account with which I am concerned here is the description of the boss of the target being made as a brass, horn-lined drinking-cup which screwed into a central hole that 'in the Time of action' would take a bayonet. The existence of targets with unscrewable central spikes — kept when not required in a leather sheath attached to the inside of the target — has been well known since Drummond and Anderson's *Ancient Scottish Weapons* appeared in 1881.[4] It seems, however, that the existence also of targets that exactly fit Campbell's description has hitherto gone unnoticed. At the moment I know of only two examples, but I have little doubt that others remain to be discovered.

The finer of the two recorded targets with unscrewable bosses (fig. 218) was acquired by its present owner, Mr R. T. Gwynn, from the collection of the late Lord Glentaner at Christie's on 1 March 1972 (Lot 40). It is described as follows in the sale-catalogue:

A FINE AND RARE SCOTTISH TARGE of wood covered with tooled leather and with applied pierced plates of thin brass, some revealing a red cloth lining, and studded throughout with brass nailheads of different sizes, the five circular bosses also of brass engraved with scrolls and expanded flowers, set over horn liners and pierced with hearts, the central boss with orb finial (the finials to the others missing) — 19½ in. (49.6 cm.), early 18th Century.

This entry does not describe the interior of the target, which is covered with deer(?) skin, fur side outwards, and shows traces of the attachments for the brases by which it was secured to the arm.[5] It is otherwise excellent, except in one very important particular: it makes no reference to the fact that the boss can be unscrewed. I draw attention to this, not to denigrate Christie's standards of cataloguing, which are usually high, but to make the point that the reason why the existence of targets with removable bosses has never been commented on before is certainly that everyone has assumed that all bosses are fixed.

In the case of the target under discussion, it was not until after the sale that Mr Gwynn — to whom credit for the discovery of the whole group is due — found that what appears, at first, to be a fixed boss (fig. 219) is, in fact, a false boss which can be unscrewed. It covers a slightly smaller brass boss — the true boss (fig. 220) — bearing the engraved inscription *INVERNES 1716 W F*,[6] which probably refers to the original owner rather than to the maker. In the middle is a small circular hole through

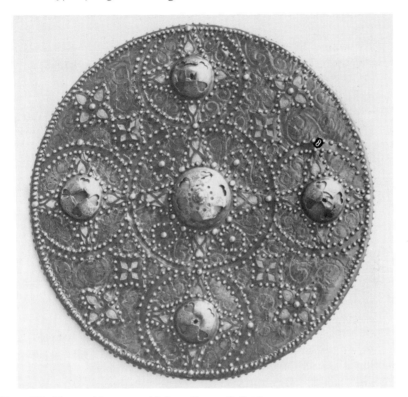

Figure 218. Target with unscrewable boss. *Gwynn Collection*

which a screw on the false boss passes to engage in a corresponding threaded hole in a concealed iron plate. The evidence of the two other targets mentioned below suggests that this plate is probably actually a short iron strip.

The false boss (figs. 219, 221, 222) can be likened to a hollow hemispherical mushroom, with the screw by which it is attached to the target representing the stem. The head of the mushroom, which is $3\frac{1}{4}$ in. (82.6 mm.) in diameter and approximately 1 in. (25.4 mm.) deep, is raised out of thin sheet brass and lined with what is, in effect, a hemispherical cowhorn cup (now slightly damaged), which provides a decorative filling for the ornamental piercings in the brass. Its capacity is approximately one-third that of a normal-sized modern tea-cup, which would have been perfectly adequate for drinking any liquid (water or whisky?) in the field. The central screw, which is also made of brass, would not in any way interfere with the use of the boss as a cup.

The second target with a detachable boss known to me is in the R. L. Scott Collection in the Glasgow Art Gallery and Museum.[7] The con-

Figure 219. Detail of the Gwynn target

Figure 220. True boss on the Gwynn target

Figure 221. False boss on the Gwynn target

Figure 222. Horn-lined interior of false boss on the Gwynn target

struction is similar to that of the Gwynn target, except that, instead of an inner boss there is a small strip of iron with a threaded central hole. A similar arrangement is found on a target in the National Museum of Antiquities illustrated by Drummond and Anderson,[8] from which it may reasonably be inferred that this too was originally fitted with a detachable boss. Neither target is inscribed like that in the Gwynn collection, but roughly scratched inside the horn lining of the boss on the Glasgow one is *A 1769* (?1767),[9] which perhaps stands for *Anno 1769*.

In conclusion, I should like to express my gratitude to Mr R. T. Gwynn for encouraging me to publish his target, and to Mr J. G. Scott, formerly of the Glasgow Art Gallery and Museum, for allowing me to attempt to unscrew the bosses of the targets under his care, with success in the case of the example from the Scott Collection mentioned above.

Postscript

Since the above was written, Mr Stuart Maxwell has kindly drawn my attention to the following letter from Henry Fletcher to his brother, Andrew Fletcher of Saltoun, then staying in Paris:

Saturday 21 Januar 1716

In your last you desired a description of the Highland Targe, which I shal give you according to the best Impersonation I have yet got, but is not perfect. The outward forme of ane Highland Targe is a convex circle, about 2 foot in diameter, but some have them oval; the innermost part of it nixt the man's breast is a skin with the hair upon it, which is only a cover to a steel plate, which is not very thick, for the whole is no great weight; on the inner side of this Steel plate the Handle is fixed, which hath two parts, one that the left arm passes throw till near the elbow, the other that the Hand lays hold on: without the Steel plate there is a Cork which covers the Steel plate exactly, but betwixt the Cork and the Steel plate there is Wooll stuffed in very hard: the Cork is covered with plain well-wrought leather, which is nailed to the Cork with nails that have brass heads, in order round, drawing thicker towards the center. From the center sticks out a Stiletto (I know not the right name of it, but I call it so, because it is a sort of short poignard) which fixes into the Steel plate and wounds the Enemy when they close: about this Stiletto closs to the Targe ther is a peece of Brass in the forme of a Cupelo about 3 inches over and coming half way out on the Stiletto and is fixed upon it. Within this brass there is a peece of Horn of the same forme like a cup, out of which they drink their usquebaugh, but it being pierced in the under part by the Stiletto, when they take it off to use it as a cup, they are obliged to apply the forepart of the end of their finger to the hole to stop it, so that they might drink out of their cup. The leather which has several lines impressed on it, the brass heads of the nails disposed in a regular way, the brass cupelo, and the Stiletto, which make up the outside of the Targe, give it a beautiful aspect. The Cork they make use of is ane excrescence of their Birk-trees, which when green cuts like ane Apple, but afterwards comes to that firmness that a nail can fasten in it. The nails sometimes throw off a ball, especially when it hits the Targe a squint: but tho' a ball came directly upon it and miss the nail heads, piercing betwixt them, yet they reckon that the leather, the cork, the wooll so deaden the ball, that the Steel plate, tho' thin, repells it and lodges it in the wooll. I want yet to know the exact dimensions of the most approved Targe (for they are very various) both as to the largeness and thickness of the Steel plate, and how it is tempered, the thick-ness of the Cork, and of the wool stuffing, and the weight of the whole Targe, which I shal endeavour to get an account of.[10]

NOTES

1. C. N. M. North, *The Book of the Club of True Highlanders*, 2 vols. (London, 1892), ii, 7-8. See also n. 2.
2. J. Campbell, *A Full and Particular Description of the Highlands of Scotland* (London, 1752), 8-9. For an account of Campbell's life see *The Dictionary of National Biography*, s.v. He had a thorough knowledge of the Highlands, and his pamphlet was written with the intention of persuading 'the Brave and worthy Inhabitants of Great Britain and Ireland' that, despite the 1715 and 1745 Risings, something could be made of the Highlands and their inhabitants.
3. This refers to the prohibition on the wearing of Highland dress imposed after the 1745 Rising.
4. J. Drummond & J. Anderson, *Ancient Scottish Weapons* (Edinburgh & London, 1881), 16, pls. I, V, VIII.
5. Unfortunately, it is not clear whether or not these attachments also held a sheath for a spike.
6. A target with a similar inscription and an unscrewable boss, said to be dated 1714, appeared as Lot 125 in the sale of Lord Londesborough's collection at Christie's on 4 July 1888. I am grateful to Mr Gwynn both for drawing my attention to this and for the suggestion that it was, in fact, the same target with its date wrongly given.
7. No. '39-65. It is illustrated at B on the unnumbered plate of Highland targets in the second volume of F. Joubert's *Catalogue of the Collection of European Arms & Armour formed at Greenock by R. L. Scott* (Privately Published, 1924). It was Lot 27 in the Breadalbane (Morgan Granville-Gavin) Sale at Christie's, 5 July 1917.
8. Drummond & Anderson, *Ancient Scottish Weapons*, pl. V, 5.
9. The first digit is scratched twice, so it is unclear whether it represents the number *11769*, or the date *1769* inscribed by an unpractised hand.
10. 'Letters of Andrew Fletcher of Saltoun and his family, 1715-1716', ed. I. J. Murray, *Scot. Hist. Soc. Miscellany*, x (1965), 153-4.

14 A Carpenter's Rule belonging to Thomas Gemmill, Armourer of Glasgow

G. L'E. Turner

In the possession of the Glasgow Museums and Art Galleries there is a jointed rule, signed on a brass extension arm, 'Thomas Gemmil Armowrer in Glasgow' (reg. no. '17-66cl). This is a standard carpenter's rule, such as would have been available on the commercial market, but is of special interest because it bears Gemmill's name. He was admitted a freeman of the Glasgow Incorporation of Hammermen in 1716, and became King's Armourer in Scotland in 1718. The form of the inscription — Armowrer, but not King's Armowrer — suggests that the rule was in Gemmill's possession before 1718. The fleur-de-lis and stellar stamps on the rule are to be found on other instruments of the early eighteenth century, including a backstaff signed by the London instrument-maker, Edmund Culpeper (c. 1666-1738), and suggest a date for the rule between 1700 and 1725.

The rule, made of boxwood and brass, measures eighteen inches opened out, with an additional brass arm to make twenty-four inches; carpenter's rules generally measured twenty-four inches. One side (fig. 223) is marked out in inches divided in eighths, and with two Gunter's lines in series. These lines are logarithmic, and function in the same way as a modern slide rule. Calculations are made with the aid of a pair of dividers. The other side (fig. 224) has a line of board measure (numbered from 9 to 36) and a line of timber (numbered from 11 to 30), with additional tables of figures to extend the scales.

The board measure gives the length of a board to make up a square foot from a given width of board. If the width of a board is measured as nine inches, then 9 is found on the line of board measure, and on the opposite side of the rule — on the inch scale — will be found the number 16. Now 9 x 16 = 144 square inches, or one square foot. At the other end of the line is 36, opposite 4 inches, again giving 144 as product. The table at the left of this scale extends the range from 1 inch to 7 inches, which would be off the scale. The middle row of numbers are feet, and the bottom row inches. Thus, 144 ÷ 7 = 1 ft. 8 in.; 144 ÷ 5 = 2 ft. 4 in.

The line of timber gives the length to make up a cubic foot given the square edge of cross-section. It works assuming the section is square, and you take the edge in inches from the scale. On the opposite side of the rule, the inch scale gives the result. Thus, 11 inches square is opposite 14¼ (nearly) inches, to give 11 x 11 x 14.3 = 1728 cubic inches, or one cubic

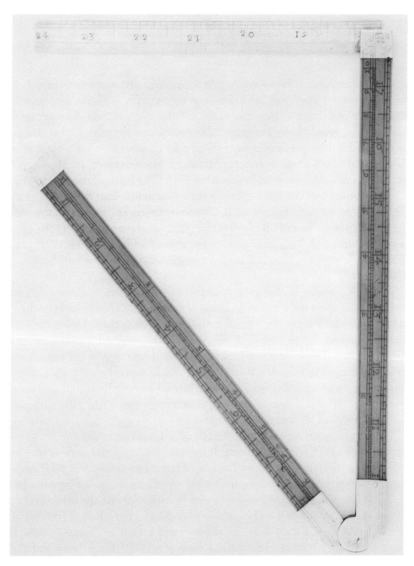

Figure 223. Gemmill's rule, showing the inch measure (0-24) and the two Gunter's lines
(1-10 each line). *Glasgow Art Gallery and Museum*

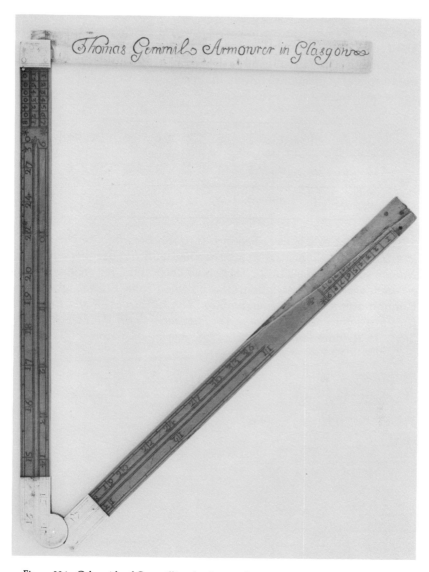

Figure 224. Other side of Gemmill's rule, showing his name on the brass, six-inch extension piece at the top; the line of board measure (9-36) and extension table on the left-hand arm; the line of timber measure (11-30) and the extension table on the right-hand arm. *Glasgow Art Gallery and Museum*

foot. Again, 24 x 24 x 3 = 1728, so 24 is opposite 3 inches. The table to the left is incomplete, because the wood is broken off. As for the previous table dealing with areas, it extends the scale, and reads inches of the edge of a section in the first row, the feet (second row) and inches (third row) to make a cubic foot. Thus, edge 9 inches gives 9 x 9 x 21⅓ = 1728 cubic inches, and 21⅓ in. converts to 1 ft. 9 in., and these figures would appear in the table if it were complete.

The table reconstructs as follows:

1	2	3	4	5	6	7	8	9	[In. Sq.]
144	36	16	9	5	4	2	2	1	[Ft.]
0	0	0	0	9	0	11	3	9	[In.]

This type of rule is described in J. B. [John Brown], *The Description and Use of the Carpenters-Rule: Together with the Use of the Line of Numbers* . . . (London, 1662). There is no illustration, but an illustration, accompanied by a description clearly copied from Brown, appears in Edmund Stone, translator and editor, *The Construction and Principal Uses of Mathematical Instruments. Translated from the French of M. Bion,* . . . (London, 1723; 2nd edn, 1758; reprinted London, 1972).

15 A New-Found Sword by John Simpson

William Reid

Since Charles Whitelaw published his fundamental paper, 'Notes on Swords with signed basket hilts by Glasgow and Stirling Makers', those few short pages have proved to be the richest of lodes for writers on Scottish arms. So much has been written in the intervening years since 1934 that it is difficult to believe that much more can be extracted. However, when from time to time a hitherto unpublished sword comes to light which is not quite like any other it seems justifiable to make it the subject of a brief article for the benefit of those to whom even a fragment of new knowledge is of interest (figs. 225-7).

The basis of Whitelaw's article in the *Transactions of the Glasgow Archaeological Society* (New Series, Vol. VIII. Part IV, Supplement) was the discovery that some of the many Scottish hilts which he had studied were signed below the guard, about halfway between the back edge of the blade and the quillon's scroll terminal. These signatures comprise the two initials of the maker's name above a third initial which Whitelaw identified, rightly as it would seem, as that of the town where the hilt was made. Unfortunately only a handful of makers have been identified in this way, but nonetheless they serve as a key to the place and date of manufacture of many Scottish hilts either directly through the signatures or through the stylistic resemblance of some unsigned hilts to those with initials. A sword that is now in a private collection in England is engraved with the initials ascribed by Whitelaw to John Simpson the younger, referred to by Whitelaw as 'No 2'. He was admitted to the Incorporation of Hammermen of Glasgow as a Freeman on 22 March 1711, his test piece being 'Ane broad Hieland sword with hilt and mounting yrof'. The Burgess Roll records his admission as burgess and guild-brother on 7 June of the same year. He also became Collector of the Incorporation in 1711 then, in 1724 and 1725, Deacon. There is good reason to believe that it was he who was described in a list of subscribers to Isaac Ambrose, *Prima, The First Things*, 1737, as 'John Simpson, Senior, His Majesty's armourer in Glasgow'. His will was recorded on 3 August 1749.

Up to 1934 Whitelaw had examined three hilts by this maker. Since then others by the same man have been published but none, or any known sword by other Glasgow makers, is quite like that now under discussion. The outer side of the guard as it hung at its owner's hip is relatively close in style to several other Glasgow hilts, the nearest being

Figure 225. Basket hilt sword by John Simpson, outer side of guard. *Private Collection*

IX-873 in the Tower Armouries which bears an unidentified monogram which may read *IIW*. It is forged from thick heavy metal, the frettings perhaps lacking the delicacy of some of the finer hilts; the whole varnished black and enriched with gilt ornament of the type often known as 'Japan enamel'. The reverse of the hilt is open but does not have the oval ring found often on what have come to be called 'horsemen's swords'. In this case the roughly rectangular pierced plate which protects

Figure 226. Same basket hilt sword by John Simpson, inner side of guard, showing atypical opening

the distal finger joints in a 'full' basket hilt have been omitted and, instead of the relatively common oval ring, the opening for the reins is strengthened towards the pommel with a stout down-curved, U-shaped bar echoed by another similar bar near the characteristic loops which strengthen the front-lower section of all good Scottish sword-hilts of the eighteenth century. At some time the sword has been dismounted and the

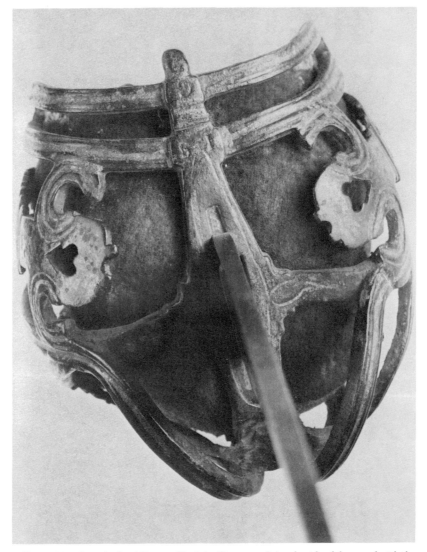

Figure 227. Same basket hilt sword by John Simpson, the underside of the guard with the initials IS/G

pommel-button lost. The typical downward curling quillon terminal has been broken off, probably, but not certainly, by accident.

The grip is covered in fish-skin bound with twisted brass wire, a turk's-head knot at top and bottom. The guard retains a lining of soft leather similar in colour and texture to buff-leather with an outer cover of scarlet worsted which closely resembles the cloth of an eighteenth-century military coat. The edges of the leather and the worsted are stitched to-gether with yellow silk thread which may also have formed a fringe. The lining is not, as is sometimes the case, cut to follow the line of the opening in the guard.

The German blade is undistinguished: 32.3 inches long (0.821 m.) and 1.4 inches wide (35.5 mm.) at the hilt, it is single-edged to within 8 inches (203 mm.) of the point with a double fuller near the back. Close to the hilt is engraved on both faces the spurious signature 'ANDREA FARRARA' in Roman capitals, a leafy-stemmed flower above and below.

It appears that the sword first came on the market some twelve years ago and nothing is known about its earlier history. Without being an object of outstanding beauty or extreme rarity, it does represent an unknown variation of the form of hilt made in Glasgow in the early years of the eighteenth century, probably in the period bracketed by the Jacobite risings of 1715 and 1745.

16 Letters from Walter Allan, Armourer in Stirling, to Colin Mitchell, Goldsmith in Canongate, 1741-1750

Stuart Maxwell

John Simpson, senior, of Glasgow was the first of the Scottish sword-smiths who signed the sword hilts they made. John Allan, senior, was booked apprentice to Simpson in 1702; he is next found in Doune, which he left in 1714 for Stirling at the invitation of that burgh. His eldest son, Walter, born about 1710, became a freeman of the Incorporation of Hammermen of Stirling in 1732. Walter married Janet Allan in 1734, and there are various references to him in the Stirling burgh records until his death in March, 1761, when he was deacon of the Hammermen. Charles Whitelaw wrote of Walter Allan that he was 'the outstanding artist in this line [hilt-making] in the country and a man of wonderful versatility';[1] and William Reid paid him an equally handsome tribute in an article which described known Allan swords, including one owned by Sir Donald Cameron of Locheil,[2] with a hilt thought at that time to be of silvered iron (figs. 228, 229). As well as Allan's mark, 'WA/S', the hilt has the letters 'CM' (twice), a stag's head, and a mark resembling a capital 'L' (figs. 230, 231); Reid identified 'CM' as Colin Mitchell of Canongate. Sir Donald kindly allowed the hilt to be examined in the Research Laboratory of the National Museum of Antiquities of Scotland some years ago, and photographs to be taken; the hilt proved to be of silver, thus rescuing Mitchell from the suspicion that he marked metal other than silver or gold.

Locheil's sword was the only connection between Allan and Mitchell until documents relating to Colin Mitchell were discovered in the Scottish Record Office;[3] Mitchell died in debt in 1753 and the Edinburgh Commissary Court impounded his papers. Among them are fifteen letters from Allan to Mitchell and other relevant letters and papers. These are the subject of this article — but why did Allan send swords and scabbards from Stirling to Edinburgh? There was at least one goldsmith in Stirling in 1745, Patrick Murray, who was 'out' in the '45 and was executed at Carlisle;[4] he was working there in 1737, a few years before the letters begin, but it is probable that there was no other goldsmith in the burgh. That Allan should turn to Edinburgh rather than Glasgow for a partner skilled enough to come up to his own standards was perhaps natural. The capital contained many more goldsmiths than Glasgow and

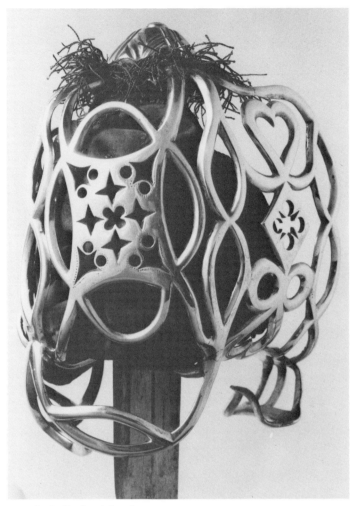

Figure 228. Lochiel's silver hilt, side view

the gentlemen who were Allan's customers were more likely to be there. Mitchell's house, 'at the head of the Canongate', was little more than a stone's throw from the Edinburgh goldsmiths' quarter, round the High Kirk of St Giles, and Canongate itself still retained the town houses of his and Allan's customers. The burgh of Canongate was then owned by Edinburgh, but it still functioned as a burgh, with its own courts and incorporations. Perhaps it was just as important to Allan that the Canongate craftsmen were more free in their interpretation of their incorporation's rules and regulations than were the Edinburgh goldsmiths, who,

Figure 229. Lochiel's silver hilt, front view

indeed, suspected Mitchell on one occasion of using silver of less than the approved standard. There may, however, be a simpler explanation, a relationship or at least a long-standing friendship between the two men. One letter begins 'Dear Cusing', which is not conclusive proof at that time of a blood relationship, but Mitchell was born, in 1699, at Kilbride in the parish of Dunblane, and Allan's birthplace was probably Doune, only a few miles away.

The first letter, the lower part of which is torn, is dated 28 July 1741. Allan asks Mitchell to send him buckles, '. . . for I cannot get lived with

Figure 230. Walter Allan's mark on Lochiel's sword

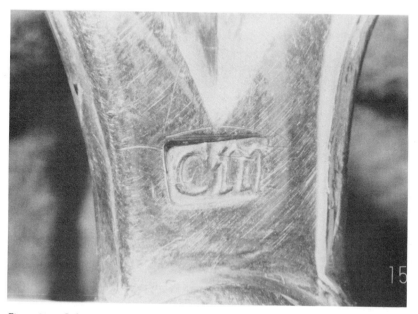

Figure 231. Colin Mitchell's mark on Lochiel's sword

Mr Jaffrey for plaging me every day about them'. The second letter is worth quoting in full, both to give the flavour of the correspondence and because of its importance.

Collin Mitchell
Goldsmith in y^e
Cannogeat head
Ed^r.   Stirling 10 June 1745.

S^r

   I recevd all Clanronalds mounting very right   the bukel is vastly strong but it will lest the longer you remember the misor [measure] I gave you for a Chape to Glenbukies sword I have got orders for two houks and a mouthpiece which you must make in a heast   begin as shoon as this letter comes to you pr post so that you can get it redy against night to give it to the post boy when he comes of with your letter with it derected to me to the cair of ffinlay Mc Kinnin ffalkirk post who will bring them to me very cairfuly   the reson is that I will not go to the Highlands till Wedensday morning after the post Comes so that I have no more to do to that Sword but to put them on and as I go for Ballochallans Glenbukies is no grait way from that for I will mak on Earand of all since I have Clanronalds sword to go with so be shore to send your Charge of Glenbukis huks Chape & mouthpice inClosed and when you give them to the post boy yourself give him a penie or twopene to be Carfull in giving them to ffalkirk post to be given to me and I will pay ffalkirk post myself S^r your heast in this will oblidg me in this since I am desined to go you will be so good as when you write me to lett me know if the Earell of Glan Orchie be comed to the Abie yett for I have 6 broadswords redy waiting him according to h(is) oun order when he went throw Stirling in [the] way to london this is all

yor Most Humbl Sev^tt
Wal^t Allan.

This tells us more about scabbards and sword belts than about swords. An odd page from a daybook of Mitchell's (dating from between June 1745 and June 1746) includes the entry 'To Walter Allan, mounting to a broadsword and a belt buckell £2. 8. 2.', which suggests that Clanranald's 'bukel' was for his sword belt. 'Glenbukie' had ordered a silver chape for his scabbard (the ferrule at the tip); before the sword was ready, it seems, he added a request for two silver belt hooks and a silver 'mouthpiece', the English 'locket', which, according to Whitelaw,[5] was added to Scottish scabbards before the middle of the eighteenth century. In the next letter (below) Allan calls it a 'crampet'.

The names of Allan's customers and his journey to deliver his swords are of great interest. 'Clanronald' was the elderly Macdonald of Clanranald, and Allan would have to go to Moidart, the Clanranald country west of Fort William. 'Balloch Allan' was David Stewart of Ballochallan, near Callander, who was 'out' in the '45 and died about 1768. 'Glenbukie' was Alexander Stewart of Glenbuckie, south of Balquhidder, who was either murdered or committed suicide at Leny when about to join the Prince.[6] The 'Earell of Glan Orchie' was Lord Glenorchy, the Hanoverian son of a Jacobite father, the Campbell Earl of Breadalbane. Throughout the '45 Breadalbane, then in his 'eighties, lodged at Holyrood Palace in Edinburgh, which may explain Allan's expectation that Glenorchy would be visiting [Holyrood] Abbey. Allan therefore supplied weapons to men who fought on both sides during the rising, for, while Glenorchy was no fighting man, Lord Home (mentioned in a later letter) fought on the Hanoverian side at Prestonpans. Allan's visit to Moidart almost coincided with Prince Charles Edward's arrival in Scotland on 25 June. There is, however, no mention whatsoever of civil war in the correspondence, and as the next letter shows, Allan valued his work so highly that after some six months of war he was enraged that a broadsword mounting had been stolen from him! Since it contains the only known description of an eighteenth-century broadsword by its maker, the letter must also be quoted in full.

Mr Colin Mitchell Goldsmith at the Head of the Canonget Edr.
Stirling 11 Decr 1745.

Sr   I beg the ffavour of giving you this troubel to aquant Mr duglass if ther Comes a broad Sword mounting to his hand new finished wanting a pumill it is but a small round wandeed hilt and ther is filed in the two broad sheelds of it 4 harts 4 Clibs and a four poynted Star in the midel of ech of the shelds and it his rather hard new lether to it it was Stolen last week from me and I hop Mr duglass will do me the ffavour as to acquant [h]is Good brother if any such comes to hand to sucure the same to me and I will give you all the marks of it besids what I have given and if any such affairs of this beloning to any of them lay in my way I should do all that lay in my pour to serve them and you may aquant any other tredsman that works in any of that way in mounting of swords and get the saim secured to me and what Charges you ar att Ill pay it Youll receive the misor of a Crampit which you ar to make in all heast the very saim begness and sent it out wtt the Carier this week without ffell for it is to go away a munday first so do not disapoynt me in the

Silver Crampet this is all depending on the Crampet
Sr your Most Obedient Sev^{tt}

Wal^r Allan

PS Sr Mind my kinarie seed this week for the Carier his forgot it
this two weeks bygon.

Allan is so worked up about his loss that it is not until the end of the
letter that he gives instructions about a commission to Mitchell. The
'misor' is presumably in the form of a drawing, a template rather, for
measurements alone could have been given in the letter.

Allan describes the stolen hilt as 'a broadsword mounting'; it is easy
for us to forget that even to the supreme artist it is the sword blade which
is the important part. The pommel would be put on separately and therefore not necessarily available for the thief to steal, but it is interesting
that Allan had already fitted the leather liner. He calls it a 'round wanded
hilt', recalling William Reid's careful observation the 'all three members
of the [Allan] family tended to use round-section bars in conjunction
with flat plates pierced with stars, circles and hearts. Their Glasgow contemporaries favoured ribbed, flat-section bars, such as were preferred by
the Allans of Stirling for the inlaid hilts referred to above.'7 Reid also
commented that Locheil's sword is the only Allan 'fancy' hilt to be built
up of round section bars, but he did not know that it was made
by Mitchell in silver to Allan's design. The pierced, flat plates of the
stolen hilt must have been like those on a 'standard' hilt; they are named
by Allan 'the two broad sheelds of it', and of course he had filed the
piercings in them. He describes these as a 'four poynted Star in the midel'
surrounded by '4 harts and 4 clibs'. Stars are not usually found on
standard hilts, but Allan favoured them; there is a five-pointed star in the
Allan hilt in the Tower of London Armouries,8 and a four-pointed one
on Locheil's sword (fig. 228). Locheil's sword has plain hearts on the side
panels, but the standard basket by Allan in the Dick Institute, Kilmarnock has more complicated hearts, almost like some silver, crowned
heart brooches.9 'Clibs' are presumably clubs, the trefoils familiar from
their use on playing cards, but I have not been able to identify them with
piercings on hilts by Allan or anyone else. 'Mr duglass' is probably John
Douglas, an Edinburgh armourer, active between 1725 and 1758,10 but
there is no clue to the identity of his 'Good brother' [brother-in-law];
Douglas was Mitchell's customer and required the same services as
Allan.

Letters four and five are dated 17 March and 19 March 1746. In four he
begins by asking Mitchell to buy a 'pound of the best Sybow [onion]
seed' for a friend, then gets down to business. 'my Lord Hooms' sword

will be sent by the carrier 'wt the bill', also '6 hilts to Mr Ovit[11] the Cutler and the other hilt to the other Gentleman . . . wt the bils'. On the outside of five is 'wtt a broadsword and 7 rugh hilts w[tt] plumits'. Later in letter four Allan asks Mitchell 'to go to Mr Bren[?d] the Saddlers and get the 6 shagreen skins that you and I secured', and adds, 'if you can hear of any more in toun' he will be glad to have them. Mitchell might use shagreen for covering silver cases or flasks. Allan, it appears, assembled complete swords in some cases, as for Lord Home, presumably those with the finest hilts; he required shagreen for the grips and leather for the liners. He also made rough hilts which he sold to a cutler (and one to a gentleman) who would fit blades to them. Mitchell is to receive 'thirtie shiling' for 'my Lord Hooms', an indication of the current pronunciation of the name, but only '18 pence' each for the rough hilts [letter five]. Allan also asks Mitchell to let him know 'how my Lord plases his sword'. He adds in a postscript to letter five that he has 'got a pound of borox out of Glasgow' and offers Mitchell half, for what he paid; both swordsmith and goldsmith would use borax for soldering. It cannot have been easy for Allan, isolated in Stirling, to obtain many of the things he needed for his craft. Letter six is dated 15 August 1746, five months later; it is entirely concerned, even the postscript, with a request that Mitchell, as he had done in the past, should 'call for Captain Hamiltone and acquaint him that his swords are finished'. Allan is anxious about the transaction, for he asks Mitchell to tell the Captain that 'as I employed workmen to outridd the work and provided all materials', he expects prompt payment and collection of the swords; if not, he 'must come in once errand', i.e. come to Edinburgh. The postscript reads, 'You may show this letter to Captain Hamilton for I am not to keep goods after finished in my hands to be abused.' Unfortunately there is no indication as to which part of swordmaking Allan could farm out to other workers.

There is no indication of the Captain's reaction in Allan's seventh letter (8 September 1746), but he does say that he has been away from home. The main topic is a parcel of goods (unspecified) which he has despatched by ship to Leith; the parcel, he says, is marked 'WA'. The letter is also concerned with silver Allan wants from Mitchell, but mentions an unnamed General who wants silver spurs. He writes again at the end of the month (30 September), from Glasgow, the only letter not from Stirling [eight]. Allan encloses a pound of borax, price six shillings sterling, which he has 'got from Mr. Simpson', who sends his 'kind compliments' to Mitchell; the postscript asks Mitchell to buy 'two pair of Smothing Irons for smoothing Cloase on pair lairger and a pair lesser' and send them to 'Archbald Simpson Hammerman in the Salt Market Glasgow'. Walter, and John Allan his brother, and Archibald Simpson are mentioned in the testament of John Simpson the younger, the

Glasgow swordsmith; 'a parcel of hilts old and new and pummells' were sold to Archibald at the roup of John's goods.[12]

The ninth letter is dated 4 February 1747. It is short and is about cloth one is buying for or from the other; there is also mention of a receipt for an account for swords. On the back is a list of objects, probably wanted by Allan; it includes 'Small bundell fils', along with fishing gear, a powder flask and a 'cheespan'.

Part of the tenth letter (17 March 1747) concerns swords and is worth quoting: '. . . youll recive inclosed a patren and mouth pice it is for a Crucked Shabell for Cragforth so I must have the Crampet and Mouthpice out with the Cairers this week for the Laird is going a fild Mundy first and he must have it alongs with him. I have likeways sent you a silver hilt which you Must make a new Shell and the small pice to go nixt the shell where you se the Eye of hilt brok and the pice you must mend the Eye and a new Shell and what the ads [additional silver] is in the exchange'. The postscript reads, 'the gentleman weghted the hilt it is 20 ozs 13 drops I beg to you make a good shell for it and send me the charges w[tt] it'. The laird's 'Crucked Shabell' must have been a sabre or cutlass; the Scottish National Dictionary gives 'A curved sword, a sabre or cutlass' for 'shabble'. The 'silver hilt' is presumably a small sword, with shell guards; Aylward says that Andrew Mahon, in his English version of a French work (1735), calls the *pas d' ane* of the small sword 'the eyes of the hilt';[13] Mitchell has been sent the broken pieces, but the letter is not explicit (to me at least!) as to what has to be mended and what made anew.

The next letter [eleven] is dated a year later, 23 March 1748, and Allan indeed begins, 'I am a grait stranger . . .'; he continues that he will see Mitchell when he delivers 'sum swords and belts for Lord John Murray's Redgment' and asks for a dozen 'tops for tongs'. He wrote again [twelve] on 20 July 1748, but the only sentence of interest to us is, 'I had a fin Sword to send to a Cap[tt] but cannot get it finished till nixt week.' Letter thirteen (12 December 1748) begins with a complaint that Mitchell has not sent 'Crampits', but Allan realises that Mitchell has had 'some trubell in your ffamelie'. He asks Mitchell to deliver a letter to a 'Mr Mansfild', who, along with Allan, had not received money owing to them by Lord Loudon. He goes on to say 'that work was delivered to the Contraks and within the time as I was under a penaltie of ten pounds if they had not been delivered in time . . .' John Campbell, fourth Earl of Loudon, was a notable soldier, later Commander-in-Chief in North America. That there was a penalty of ten pounds in the contract suggests that this may have been quite a large order for swords for Loudon's troops. We are only tantalised, however, with the further information that Mitchell knows 'how I have been used wt that work first and last and as the work was taken of my hands your faithfulness in this will ever oblidge . . .'

There is another interval until 1 August 1749 [fourteen], when Allan complains that he has not had an answer to a letter about spurs and 'ffrancks' (for letters); he warns Mitchell that he will lose the commission, for 'the Man is to go away this week'; he adds, 'I have wrote to John Hoge to provid me sum open work', which is a puzzling remark. Almost a year later, 7 May 1750 [fifteen], once more Allan writes asking Mitchell to remind someone about an unpaid bill, for which he (Allan) threatens legal action. The remainder of the letter is about a 'gold hart' (probably a heart brooch), the loan of a 'whissel' and teaspoons, and the price of a silver buckle. This is the last letter and in some ways it is typical, for it gives the impression of Allan's rather testy disposition and of Mitchell's slowness in complying with his requests. Colin Mitchell had serious money troubles in the years before his death in May 1753.

Among Mitchell's papers are sheets of what must have been his working day book. One entry referring to Allan has already been quoted; others include 7 June: 'a Crampt 2 Stecks and a Locket 13/3'; 1 September: 'Mounting for three brod Swords £1. 11. 0'. Mitchell also made similar items for Douglas, including 'Crampts', 'a Cutlass' and 'a back warand and Cross' (£1. 2. 11).

After Mitchell's death and the impounding of his papers and goods, Allan petitioned the Lords Commissaries of Edinburgh (28 October 1755) as follows: 'That sometime before the decease of Colin Mitchell Goldsmith in Canongate, I (as I was frequently in use to do) left with the said Colin Mitchell three Broadswords in order to dispose of for me . . . The said Swords . . . were taken into your Clerk's Custody where they still remain.' He offers to prove his statement, which the Commissaries allowed; there are, however, no papers relating to his proof in the collection.

Mitchell's other correspondents in Stirling were also Allans. Henry Allan, whom we have not been able to identify, wrote a furious letter dated 4 May 1753, complaining that Mitchell had neither mounted his shell nor returned it; Mitchell was probably making a cowrie shell into a snuff box by adding a flat silver lid. James Allan, designated here 'Armourer in Stirling', is described in Stirling records as a sword cutler;[14] he was the son of Andrew Allan, journeyman with Walter Allan; he wrote twice in 1746 (21 May and 2 June), and once in 1752, the last letter about the payment of money. The first 1746 letter reminds Mitchell that 'a good while ago I was with you and speaking anent some fyles at which time I left you 6 Shillings str [Sterling] to purchase the same . . . as yet have not received the fyles and have wrote you frequently theranent'. In the second letter he is still asking for the files!

NOTES

1. C. E. Whitelaw, 'Notes on swords with signed basket hilts by Glasgow and Stirling makers', *Trans. Glasgow Archaeol. Soc.*, n.s. VIII, iv, supplement (1934); it has been reprinted in C. E. Whitelaw, *Scottish Arms Makers* (London, 1977).
2. W. Reid, 'Walter Allan, Armourer in Stirling', *Scottish Art Review*, IX, i (1963), 16ff.
3. RH 15/176/1.[2] I am indebted to my wife for this discovery and for help in transcribing the letters.
4. *The Prisoners of the '45*, ed. B. G. Seton & J. G. Arnot (Scot. Hist. Soc., 1929), ii, 218-19.
5. Whitelaw, *Scottish Arms Makers*.
6. Major John Stewart of Ardvorlich has kindly confirmed my identifications of the Stewarts; both were cadets of the Ardvorlich family.
7. Reid, 'Walter Allan, Armourer', 18.
8. Ibid., 18, pl. 4.
9. Ibid., 17, pl. 2, and compare the hilts in the National Museum illustrated in J. Wallace, *Scottish Swords and Dirks* (London, 1970), pl. 27, with central, four-pointed star (LA 128), pl. 28 (LA 129), pl. 33 (LA 22 — by John Allan, senior) and pl. 35 (LA 107 — by John Allan, junior); see also pl. 32 (1965-699 in Royal Scottish Museum — by John Simpson, junior, Glasgow).
10. Whitelaw, *Scottish Arms Makers*, 66.
11. The name appears to be 'Ovit', which is not known in Scotland. If the initial 'Ov' is read as 'Qu', the whole might be a version of 'White' in what would be an archaic form in 1746. There were Whites who were cutlers in Canongate throughout the previous century — see Whitelaw, *Scottish Arms Makers*.
12. Ibid., 303.
13. J. D. Aylward, *The Small-Sword in England* (London, 1945), 10.
14. Whitelaw, *Scottish Arms Makers*, 285.

17 The Return of Mons Meg from London, 1828-1829

Robert B. K. Stevenson

In 1967 Dr Claude Gaier gave us at last the fascinating original documentation of the bombard first (and apparently until the seventeenth century) called *Mons* — now familiarly known as *Mons Meg* — manufactured in 1449 by Jehan Cambier at Mons for Philip, Duke of Burgundy, and gifted and convoyed with an escort of 50 men-at-arms to Scotland to James II in May 1457.[1] She was then, and for centuries later, the heaviest piece of artillery in Britain, 13½ feet long, weighing about 8½ tons, and firing an 18-inch stone ball up to 2,867 yards at 45° elevation, it was said in 1734[2] — a very positive inducement to stiffen the twenty-six-year old king's confrontation with England. Her apparent absence from the siege of Roxburgh in 1460 may be only due to the incompleteness of our records, and to the overshadowing explosion of a smaller bombard, the *Lion,* fatal to the king. Two of the gun's rare moves into action have often enough been described from the Lord Treasurer's Accounts, to Dumbarton in 1489, and to Norham in 1497, and so have the *feux de joie* in 1588, 1660 and 1680, when she finally cracked.[3] (A nineteenth-century estimate, mentioned below,[4] suggests that some two hundredweight of iron was lost on that occasion from the exterior of the base of the barrel, where parts of two 3-inch bars are missing).

The Galloway tradition, recorded in the seventeenth century, that she was forged by a local blacksmith for the siege of Threave Castle in 1455 had long met with scepticism, and had been strongly attacked in Mons in 1894 by M. de Behault, who just missed identifying *Mons Meg* with the gun *Mons.*[5]

As an appendix in 1967 Mr Claude Blair published, from the Board of Ordnance records, amusing correspondence of 1835-6, which included much of the past history, as well as details of the provision of the cast-iron carriage that bore the gun from 1836 until 1935, when replaced in turn by one more 'in period'.[6] That iron carriage, cast under contract by J. Hague, Cable Street, London, was designed and constructed at the Royal Carriage Department at Woolwich. Though not illustrated by Mr Blair, it is well shown, incidentally, in M. de Behault's paper and in that by Sir James Balfour Paul. It replaced the wooden carriage which had come back with the gun from the Tower of London in 1828, and collapsed 'with a great crack' on 9 June 1835. Though the Master General and Board of Ordnance authorised the provision of the new carriage, they did so at the request of the Society of Antiquaries of Scotland, to whom they deferred regarding the non-painting and repositioning of the gun with her new much heavier carriage, for at least the Commanding Officer of Artillery in North Britain was under the impression that she then belonged to the Society.

The return of *Mons Meg* to Edinburgh, for which Sir Walter Scott is usually given the credit, is itself something of a saga, of which there is an unpublished letter-book from the Society's archives.[7] It was a project which many people may well have cherished since *Mons* had been removed from the Castle on 19 April 1754,[8] following an order from the Board of Ordnance that all unserviceable cannon should be sent south, a belated consequence of the '45.[9]

J. G. Lockhart in his *Life* of Scott, writing of George IV's famous visit to Edinburgh in 1822, records that

> When Scott next saw the King after he had displayed his person on the chief bastion of the old fortress, he lamented the absence of Mons Meg on that occasion in language which his Majesty could not resist. There ensued a correspondence with the official guardians of Meg — among others the Duke of Wellington, and though circumstances deferred her restoration, it was never lost sight of and took place finally when the Duke was Prime Minister, which I presume smoothed petty obstacles.[10]

The immediate obstacle is explained in the letters to which Lockhart refers — though one suspects that there was also elsewhere a certain reluctance to co-operate, such as was ultimately evident in the unwillingness to provide any finance for the move. There are two letters, both published in 1894.[11] In the first the Duke of Wellington as Master General of the Ordnance writes to the Rt Honble Robert Peel, the Home Secretary, on 18 September 1822:

> I have omitted to answer you respecting *Mol Meg* (sic). This gun is in the Tower and is one of the principal articles of Singleton's Shew.[12]
>
> But I shall have no objection to its being sent to Edinburgh Castle; nor will Singleton I should think, if he is allowed a Deputy to shew it to the inhabitants of Edinburgh. You may tell Sir Walter Scott that it shall be sent to Edinburgh, but I must get the King's orders to remove it from the Tower, which I will as soon as ever I return to England.

Peel sent this on with his own letter of 22 September:

> My dear Sir Walter
> A wish you expressed for the Restoration of *Old Meg* in the Castle of Edinburgh did not escape me, and on my Return from London I

commenced a Treaty with the Duke of Wellington which was broken off by his abrupt departure for other more complicated negotiations.

He sent me however a parting line from Dover, which I do not send you *officially* but in *confidence,* and rather to allay your private anxieties about the old Lady, than to authorize you positively to announce her intended departure from the Tower. I fear the Shewman more than the King — but great as will be the difficulties in selecting a Trustworthy Deputy, in determining the rate at which Meg shall be shewn in Edinburgh etc etc, I still hope the King and the Duke of Wellington will prevail

Ever most truly / Robert Peel

There is no reference to the subject in Scott's later correspondence with Wellington, nor in his Journal references to their conversations in London in November 1826, though in 1825 he had written (Journal, 10 December):

The Knave demands of me in a postscript to get back the sword of Sir W Wallace carried off from Dumbarton Castle to England . . . It was wrong however to take away that and Mons Meg. If I go to London this spring I will renew my negotiations with the Great Duke for recovery of Mons Meg.[13]

One must assume that the obstacles persisted sufficiently to put him off.

Whatever may have been the situation in 1826, it is clear from the Antiquaries' papers that, contrary to Lockhart's surmise, a completely new initiative was made in 1828, in which apparently there was no reminder to George IV of Scott's past interest, or reference to it at all. Scott's own attitude remained, indeed, curiously lukewarm, and he figures extremely little, though he was a vice-president of the Society; unfortunately he did not write up his Journal between June 8 1828 and January 10 1829.

The new initiative came from Mr. J. Graham Dalyell, later baronet of the Binns, advocate and historian, then a Fellow of the Society of some thirty years' standing, and sometime vice-president. To him, as stated in the minutes of the Society's meeting on 12 May 1828

. . . along with the Duke of Gordon, the public would be mainly indebted, if Mons Meg be restored to her antient 'lair'. Mr Dalyell related his having seen this curious relic of Scottish antiquity not long ago in the Tower of London.

A valuable role as intermediary, at the beginning, was played by Alexander Scot of Trinity, W.S., F.S.A.Scot., apparently man of business for the Duke in Edinburgh. It is also possible that the enterprise might have failed without the pertinacity of the Society's honorary secretary, E. W. A. Drummond Hay, one of the Lyon Court Heralds, who resigned in May 1829 to become H.M. Consul-general in Tangier. Copies of some of his letters fill much of the letter-book, rather verbose and occasionally tactless but obtaining good results. To him Graham Dalyell wrote on 4 April 1828:

> I have been very desirous of submitting to the Society a project for obtaining the restoration of a celebrated piece of artillery *Mons Meg*, now in the Tower to its original Arsenal — Edinburgh Castle. I think we have grounds for claiming it, as by the Articles of Union, our fortresses, consequently, our Artillery, are to be preserved — But as favour often operates more forcibly than right — might this not be a proper season for endeavouring to accomplish this measure through the interference of the Duke of Gordon—?   I am confident many would approve of our design — for antiquities, always interesting to those contemplating fugacious time, lose much of their impressive character when removed from their proper site —
>
> May I solicit you to have the goodness to lay this note before the Council as a preparative for some ulterior proceedings.

Before the Council met, one of its members, Sir Henry Jardine, King's and Lord Treasurer's Remembrancer, was involved as a note of 22 April shows:

> Mrs Scot presents her compliments to Sir Henry Jardine by a letter Mrs S had last night from Mr Scot who is in London she is desired to let Sir Henry know that the Duke of Gordon has got the promise of *Mons Meg* being restored. Mr Scot wishes an application from the Antiquarian Society sent to the Duke of Gordon as soon as possible.

From this resulted a letter to General His Grace the Duke of Gordon, G.C.B., Governor of Edinburgh Castle, signed by E. W. A. Drummond Hay on 25 April:

> In consequence of an urgent desire having been expressed by several members of the Society of Antiquaries of Scotland, that the antient piece of Artillery, called *Mons Meg*, which was removed from Edinburgh to London in the year 1754, should be restored to its antient place in our metropolitan Castle, of which your Grace is the Governor, it was Resolved at a Meeting of the Society's Council held this day, that an application should be made to your Grace by myself, in their name, on the Subject.
>
> I have therefore, my Lord Duke, the honour to request that your Grace would be pleased to make application to the Master General of the Ordnance, or to such other Authorities in the Government as to your Grace may seem fit, for the purpose of this curious relic of our antient fortifications in Edinburgh being replaced, where it is

understood to have been planted at the first introduction of heavy artillery into this northern Kingdom.

The Board of Ordnance papers now in the Record Office[14] show that this was passed on quickly. Mr R. Porrett reported fully on 30 April to the Board for the Principal Storekeeper, stressing the gun's age, size and weight. He also mentioned an enquiry made

> . . . soon after the return of His Majesty from Scotland in 1822 in consequence, as it was understood, of a strong desire expressed by the inhabitants of Stirling to have it returned to that place, they having stated that previously to its removal to Edinburgh it stood on the Castle Green there, [and he suggested] that the rival claims of Edinburgh and Stirling would have to be taken into account.

The successful outcome in the form of a letter of 9 June from the Office of Ordnance signed by General the Viscount ̇ Beresford, the Master General, was forwarded after ten days through Mr Scot:

> I have brought before The King the application which Your Grace transmitted to me from the Society of Antiquaries of Scotland; and I have the satisfaction to inform you that His Majesty has been graciously pleased that the Gun, called Mons Meg, may be removed from His Tower of London to His Castle of Edinburgh.
>
> I will therefore give the necessary Orders for placing the Gun at the disposal of the Antiquarian Society of Scotland for that purpose.

When, after speaking to the Duke in September, the Secretary wrote direct to the Master General, the reply of 22 October from Colonel Lord Downes was less than satisfactory:

> I am directed by The Master General of the Ordnance to acknowledge the receipt of your Letter of the 8th Instant, and to acquaint you that when, in conformity with His Majesty's Commands, He notified to The Duke of Gordon that the Gun Called Mons Meg was placed at the disposal of the Antiquarian Society of Scotland, it was with a view to the Society taking such steps as they might think proper for its removal to Edinburgh. The Ordnance Department have no means for transporting the Gun to that Place, but if the Society should require any assistance in embarking or loading it, His Lordship will be happy to give any aid which the means of the Departmxnt at the Tower and Leith can afford.

However, following an introduction from Mr Scot with a promise of £20 or £25 from the Duke in reserve, the London and Edinburgh Steam Packet Company wrote on 5 November to their Agent in Leith:

> Your letter of 1 inst was this day laid before the Committee, and I am directed to state they most cheerfully accede to the Honble Mr A H (sic) Drummond Hay's request to take the Great Gun, Mons or Munch Meg from this to Edinburgh in the 'City of Edinburgh',

Freight free, on condition that the Antiquarian Society put it on board & land it at their own expence, you are probably not aware that it weighs upwards of Six Tons, and without carriage is 13 feet long, consequently could not be taken on Deck. The 'City' has neither Tackle nor spars to take on board such a weight, but that can be managed here if you have a crane at Leith to which the vessel can go with safety to take it out. I am further directed to request you to inform the Secretary of the Antiquarian Society that the Committee will feel much pleasure in forwarding the views of the Society in this matter, & keeping the expenses as low as possible, which may be accomplished by a little previous arrangement.

He added himself:

It now remains for you to apply to the proper quarter for the use of a Lighter to convey the Great Gun to Blackwall alongside the City of Edinburgh — There is no Crane at Leith that can take out such a Weight, therefore you will have to get one erected, the City of Edinburgh will again leave Blackwall on Saturday the 22d Inst.[15] (fig. 232).

These arrangements were explained in Drummond Hay's reply to Lord Downes, commenting that the Society

had flattered themselves that [the move] would have been effected at public Expence,[16] [and requesting that] a Lighter be sent with the Gun from the Tower [to Blackwall, with hoisting machinery, that the] Crew of the Steamer have the aid of some of the Royal Engineers or Artillery capable of conducting the operation of embarking the Gun; [and also that there should be] some show of military honor [for the final move to the Castle].

There was a favourable reply to the requests, and the Office of Ordnance in the Castle notified the garrison and the Commander of the Artillery at Leith Fort. He, along with Captain G. W. A. Knight of the Royal Navy, made the landing arrangements, doubtless bearing in mind the letters from the shipping company of 24 and 25 November, the latter from 'On Board the City of Edinburgh':

The Great Gun Mons Meg was safely spt [shipt] on Board the City of Edinburgh on Friday morning — she weighs nearer Ten Tons than Six without the carriage.

The Captain of the City of Edinburgh has received instructions not to allow any Spars to be fixed to the Deck, or purchase to be fixed to the Main Mast for the purpose of getting the Gun out in case it should injure the Vessel. I have to intimate to you as the Secretary of the Antiquarian Society that they are liable for all risks and accidents that may arise in Spg & Landing this Great Gun.

I have the pleasure to inform you of the safe arrival of the City of

The **CITY** of **EDINBURGH**, Capt. **DEWAR**,
𝕰legantly fitted up for 𝕻assengers,
WITH MACHINERY AND ENGINES BY Messrs BOULTON, WATT, & CO.
Will sail *FROM LEITH HARBOUR*, for
BLACKWALL, LONDON,
(Calling off Scarborough to land and receive Passengers, Weather permitting,)
On SATURDAY EVENING, the 15th November, at 6 o'clock.

The **TOURIST**, Capt. **BASTARD**,
From LEITH HARBOUR, on SATURDAY Afternoon, 22d Nov. at 2 o'clock.

After which a Packet will sail every Saturday from Leith Harbour at Daylight Tide;
and from Blackwall, London, every Saturday Evening.

FARE TO LONDON.—CABIN, 5 Pounds; STEERAGE, 2½ Guineas.
SCARBOROUGH.—CABIN, 3 Guineas; STEERAGE, 1½ Guineas.

PASSAGE TICKETS to be had at the *Company's Office*, 13, WATERLOO PLACE, EDINBURGH, and
at their *Office*, NEWHAVEN.

CARRIAGES and HORSES on Freight as usual.

Passengers must be on board half-an-hour before the sailing of the Packet.

GOODS for LONDON will be received at the Company's Office, 13, Waterloo Place, EDINBURGH, until
3 o'clock, and at the Office, NEWHAVEN, until 5 o'clock, afternoon, of the day previous to the sailing of the
Packet. After 5 o'clock, Goods can be received at the Packet only.—Care must be taken that Goods sent as
above are regularly booked.

The GLASGOW Carriers, Messrs HOWEY & Co. of Montrose Street, have Post Waggons every day, and
THO. JACKSON, Brunswick Street, has Daily Post Carts.—*Shippers, in order to ensure the shipment of their
Goods, should make an agreement with the Carriers to have them delivered at Leith by 3 o'clock, afternoon,
of the day previous to the sailing of the Packet.*

Mr LYON has Four-Horse Post Vans which start with Goods, from his Coach Office, Dunlop Street, Glasgow,
every Friday Afternoon, at 6 o'clock, and arrive in time for the Packet.—*Goods for Mr LYON's Van must be
delivered at his Office, on Fridays, by 4 o'clock, afternoon, to ensure their arrival in time for the Packet.*

Every information will be given by Mr JAMES CRAWFORD, 77, Miller Street, Glasgow, agent for the Packets.

GOODS from LONDON, for Scotland, will be received at the Company's Office, 35, Leadenhall Street.

The Company will not hold themselves liable for detention caused by casualty or accident, nor be responsible for
loss or damage in respect of the Luggage of Passengers. Nor will they be responsible for loss or damage in respect of any Package containing Goods or Articles above the value of Five Pounds, unless the same shall have
been booked at their Office, and Freight paid according to the value.

London & Edinburgh Steam Packet Co.'s Office, }
    13, Waterloo Place, Edinburgh, 1828.   }

R. W. HAMILTON.

W. Reid & Son, Printers, Leith.

Figure 232. Handbill of the London and Edinburgh Steam Packets, annotated with note
on Mons Meg's length

Edinburgh Steam Packet this morning having on Board the ancient piece of Ordnance Mons Meg. Have the goodness therefore to communicate with Col. Birch at Leith Fort to get her Ladyship safely landed — which I propose should be to morrow about three °Clock.

When the Gun was disembarked 'at a civil cost of £9. 5. 5.,[17] she was placed temporarily in the Old Naval Yard — and remained there over three months. The difficulty seems to have been her carriage. Already before its arrival Drummond Hay had discussed the matter at Leith Fort, and in the Minutes of the Society's Council of 8 December we read:

> The Secretary had conferred with Lt Col Birch . . . regarding the fittest persons from whom instructions may be received as to a proper iron carriage for remounting Mons Meg . . . and reported communications from Sir Walter Scott . . . and other . . . gentlemen willing to subscribe. . . . before the question of raising funds by general subscription . . . it is desirable to ascertain what the expence . . . might amount to . . . either of mounting Mons on an highly finished iron . . . carriage ornamented with emblematic devices in *alto relievo;* or . . . on a plain carriage distinguished only by some short inscription indicating the time of the founding of this ancient piece of ordnance, the year of its carrying away to London, and the period of its restoration to the Castle of Edinburgh.[18]

A scribbled note in the letter-book shows only £4. 9. 0 promised, including £2. 2. 0 by Sir Walter. Later, perhaps in January, Drummond Hay noted that

> Lt. Colonel Miller [Proofmaster of H.M. Ordnance?] recommends that we apply for instruction as to constructing the iron carriage designed for Mons Meg to Mr Sainton principal Proprietor of the Canon (sic) Compy, who may be addressed at Thames St, London.

Possibly in connection with this there was provided by Lt. T. Battersbee R.E., and exhibited to the Society, a hurried drawing 'or rather the geometrical representation' of Mons Meg, for which he apologised, along with measurements which he vouched as 'perfectly correct'[19] (figs. 233, 234). He added some very approximate calculations of weight. The measurements are more detailed than those on the drawing made by Lt. Bingham R.A. in 1836, published in 1853 and reproduced in 1967.[20] There are important differences, not solely where his training gave the engineer an advantage over the artilleryman. Battersbee did not omit to show the low flange that surrounds the mouth, and spaced both sets of windlass holes equally; he also showed the gap properly in the side-view of the break. It is difficult to check his interior measurements, or the real difference between his straight base for the chamber and Bingham's dished and dimpled outline. Bingham gave no figure for the diameter of

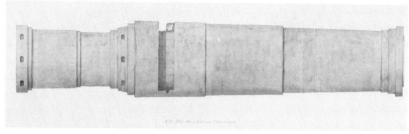

Figure 233. Mons Meg, drawing by Jackson, after Battersbee

the chamber, but drew it as 10¼ inches (0.26 m.) and the barrel as uniformly 20 inches (0.508 m.). Battersbee's figure for the chamber is 8½ inches (0.216 m.) and for the inner end of the barrel 18 inches (0.457 m.). The front portion of the barrel is shown to taper on the outside though less than the central section. All this gives a stronger chamber and breech, and a more sophisticated barrel with the bore tapering 2 inches in the opposite direction from the exterior, over a length of 8 feet 10½ inches (2.705 m.), or according to Bingham ¼ inch less.

It was decided on 20 February 1829 at the Council of the Society to wait no longer:

> Resolved: 2. In consequence of the very considerable delay which may yet continue for several months, before the very difficult arrangements be completed for obtaining a suitable brass or iron carriage for Mons Meg, that the Secretary . . . [arrange with the Artillery and Ordnance to have] the Gun removed from off the *truck carriage* on which it is at present (& which is broken) to such other carriage as may be deemed capable of safely conveying the Gun up to its destination; that it be thereafter and forthwith painted of a dull red resembling its present appearance as rusted iron, & as in some degree according to the color of which it was anciently wont to be painted
>
> 4. . . . the secretary authorised, taking advantage of the very obliging offer of Lt Colonel Birch [Leith Fort] for that effect, to request that officer to lend his intelligent superintendance in causing, as at the Society's expense, the old [wooden carriage, which accompanied the Gun from the Tower of London] (which is much decayed) to be put in as an efficient state as possible; and then painted of the same color used for all gun carriages by the Ordnance Department at this day; . . . to receive the Gun . . . until . . . a metal carriage . . . for its permanent support [is attained].

This was all put in hand promptly, and a very strong waggon was provided free of all charges, other than for painting and perhaps strengthening it, by Mr Wallace, builder.

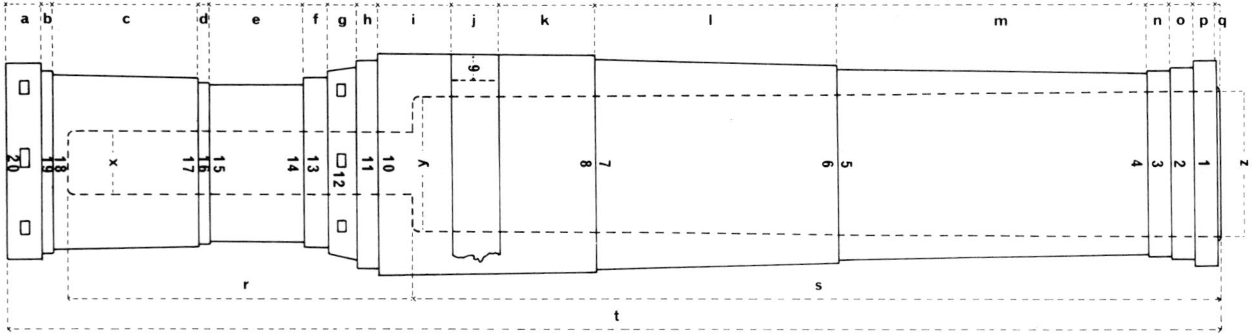

a	$4\frac{1}{2}$ in. /11.4 mm.
b	$1\frac{3}{4}$ in. /4.4 mm.
c	1 ft $6\frac{3}{4}$ in. /0.476 m.
d	$1\frac{1}{2}$ in. /3.8 mm.
e	1 ft $0\frac{1}{2}$ in. /0.318 m.
f	3 in. /7.6 mm.
g	4 in. /10.2 mm.
h	3 in. /7.6 mm.
i	$9\frac{3}{4}$ in. /24.8 mm.
j	$6\frac{1}{4}$ in. /15.9 mm.
k	1 ft $0\frac{1}{2}$ in. /0.318 m.
l	2 ft 8 in. /0.813 m.
m	3 ft $5\frac{3}{4}$ in. /1.06 m.
n	$2\frac{3}{4}$ in. /70 mm.
o	$2\frac{3}{4}$ in. /70 mm.
p	$3\frac{1}{4}$ in. /82.6 mm.
q	$\frac{3}{4}$ in. /19 mm.
r	3 ft 10 in. /1.168 m.
s	8 ft $10\frac{1}{2}$ in. /2.705 m.
t	13 ft $4\frac{3}{4}$ in. /3.778 m.
x	$8\frac{1}{2}$ in. /21.6 mm.
y	18 in. /45.7 mm.
z	20 in. /50.8 mm.

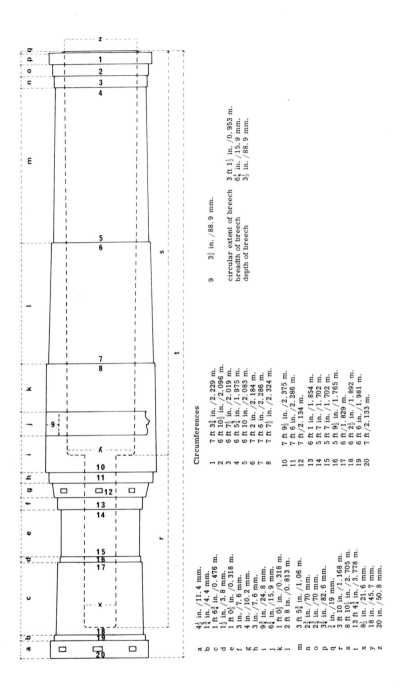

Circumferences

1	7 ft $3\frac{3}{4}$ in. /2.229 m.
2	6 ft $10\frac{1}{2}$ in. /2.096 m.
3	6 ft $7\frac{1}{2}$ in. /2.019 m.
4	6 ft $5\frac{3}{4}$ in. /1.975 m.
5	6 ft 10 in. /2.083 m.
6	7 ft 2 in. /2.184 m.
7	7 ft 6 in. /2.286 m.
8	7 ft $7\frac{1}{2}$ in. /2.324 m.
10	7 ft $9\frac{1}{2}$ in. /2.375 m.
11	7 ft 6 in. /2.286 m.
12	7 ft/2.134 m.
13	6 ft 1 in. /1.854 m.
14	5 ft 7 in. /1.702 m.
15	5 ft 7 in. /1.702 m.
16	5 ft $9\frac{1}{2}$ in. /1.765 m.
17	6 ft/1.829 m.
18	6 ft $2\frac{1}{2}$ in. /1.892 m.
19	6 ft 6 in. /1.981 m.
20	7 ft/2.133 m.

9	$3\frac{1}{2}$ in. /88.9 mm.
circular extent of breech	3 ft $1\frac{1}{2}$ in. /0.953 m.
breadth of breech	$6\frac{1}{4}$ in. /15.9 mm.
depth of breech	$3\frac{1}{2}$ in. /88.9 mm.

Figure 234. Mons Meg, section drawing by Battersbee (re-drawn)

Meantime other matters and misunderstandings were coming to a head. An unfortunate complaint passed on to Lord Beresford on 13 December was followed ten days later by a bill from the Steam Packet Company, and the two got entangled in a series of lengthy letters and reports exchanged between the Society's Secretary, the Company, and the Ordnance. Drummond Hay was prevented from debiting the bill to the Duke of Gordon's promised £20, or even from welcoming support regarding it from an unexpected quarter, by his too Scottish sense of principle and failure to understand Mr Porrett's quizzical humour (which was later shown to better advantage in the disquisition on Mons Meg in 1836, quoted by Mr Blair).[21] Most worth quoting for their matter and manner are the Ordnance's letters. Lord Downes wrote on 14 January:

> I am directed by the Master General to acknowledge the receipt of your Letter of the 13th Ultimo, and to transmit to you the enclosed copy of a Report from the Chief Clerk in the Office of the Principal Storekeeper on the circumstances attending the embarkation of the Gun called Mons Meg, at the Tower.
>
> Lord Beresford thinks that the Antiquarian Society of Scotland, after perusing this Report, will feel that they have been misinformed as to the Department having failed to render any assistance on the occasion in question, and that if all was not done which the Master General & Board and their officers wished, every aid was afforded of which the circumstances would admit.

The enclosure dated 5 January, signed R. Porrett, reads:

> In returning the Board's Order of the 29th Ult? $\frac{M}{1028}$ calling for a report on the Statement made by the Secretary to the Antiquarian Society of Scotland 'that not the slightest aid was afforded by the Ordnance in embarking the Gun called Mons Meg on board the City of Edinburgh Steam Packet at Blackwall in November last.'
>
> I have the Honor to report, that when the Extract from the Board's Minutes of the 17th November reached me on the night of the 18th., it appeared to me impossible that the embarkation of the Gun could take place on the day required the 20th, as the Ordnance had no machinery at Blackwall in readiness for raising the Gun from a Lighter onto the Vessel, and it appears from the enclosed Letter from the Superintendant of Shipping dated the 20th November that he was so entirely of that opinion that he had abandoned all idea of effecting it before the next Voyage of the Steam Packet, and commenced his prospective arrangements accordingly.
>
> Being however very desirous that the immediate removal of the Gun as requested by the Antiquarian Society and agreed to by The Master General and Board should if possible take place, I communicated with Mr Mitchell the Agent in London for the Steam

Packet Company, and stated to him the difficulty respecting the Shipment at Blackwall when he informed me that if I would cause the Gun to be put on board a Lighter off the Tower, and have it conveyed to the Steam Vessel at Blackwall it would be all that would be necessary, as the Crews would have at an adjoining Wharf the use of powerful Cranes, which they occasionally employed when very heavy Weights were to be shipped and which would easily effect the desired object. Mr Mitchell said nothing as to any expense which would attend the use of these Cranes, and I inferred that the Steam Packet Company could and would command their employment for this object.

The principal difficulty being thus removed, the Gun was with much exertion and the employment of a working Party of Artillery, put on board the Lighter, Slings of Rope of great strength (8 inch) were adjusted round the Gun, so that it might be immediately suspended without difficulty to the double hook technically called the Ram Head of the Crane, and these were sent so adjusted, with the Gun to facilitate the embarkation at Blackwall and the disembarkation at Leith: the said embarkation was also superintended by Mr Hayley sent for that purpose from the Office of the Superintendant of Shipping; so that the inforrmation given to Mr Hay that not the slightest aid was furnished by the Ordnance in this operation, is entirely incorrect.

The Gun having been embarked without the slightest accident in the shortest time, and as I conceive in the best way that circumstances would admit, and having also reached its destination in safety with the assistance of the Royal Artillery at Leith; I was at a loss to conceive what could have occasioned the complaint involved in the representation made by the Secretary of the Antiquarian Society of Scotland; until it occurred to me that some little pecuniary charge connected with the restoration of this Ancient relic of Scottish History might have been made upon the Funds of that National Institution; I therefore sent to the Office of the Steam Packet Company to ascertain this point, and received from thence the enclosed Memorandum of Charges made from that Office on the said Society and which have been paid, amounting to £6. 1. 9 thus verifying my suspicion and as this payment may have been considered by the Society as one that should devolve upon the Ordnance under the terms of The Master General's Minute of the 15.th Novr last $\frac{M}{991}$, I have to submit whether the money should not be refunded to the Society in question.

The bill in question reads:

'Antiquarian Society
      To London & Edin: Steam Packet Co
      for charges paid out *at London* for
      Mons-Meg, as follows—

To Shipping	£ 3"14" 3
To Allowance paid Seamen	2" 2 —
To Petty charges	" 5" 6
	£ 6" 1" 9

Newhaven   22 Decr. 1828

This is more fully explained later by the London agent (24 February):

had the labour of the people employed been charged, the amount would have been nearly double — £3-14-3 was paid Messrs Wigrams & Green for the use of their Cranes in Landing the Gun from the Craft & Shipg it on Board the City of Edin^r, for which you may have their rec^t — £2-2/. was for unmooring the City of Edin^r, taking her alongside of the Wharf, assisting with the ships tackles, and remooring the Vessel; 5/6 was *a portion* of Waterage paid to see these things were properly attended to.

The answer to Lord Downes was delayed till 2 March without advantage, while Drummond Hay made belated and tactless enquiries to the Company about the bill; but the outcome was satisfactory, contained in the following letter of 10 March signed W F Johnson:

In the absence of Lord Downes, I have laid before The Master General your Letter of the 2nd Instant, upon perusing which His Lordship cannot but observe that whilst His only object has been to do every thing that depended upon him, consistently with his duty to the Public, to gratify what might be considered a national wish, as regarded the Gun in question, the Society of Antiquaries of Scotland appear to have viewed the subject in a totally different light from that in which it actually stood, and they have through their Secretary commented upon it accordingly.

The Master General desires me to observe to you that the case is as follows —

His Grace The Duke of Gordon applied on the part of the Antiquarian Society of Scotland to the Master General of the Ordnance to have the Gun called "Mons Meg" returned to Edinburgh Castle, upon which The Master General took His Majesty's Pleasure, who was graciously pleased to consent to the Gun being given up to the Society for the object stated. This was communicated to The Duke of Gordon, who was informed that the Gun then in the Tower of London was at "the disposal of the Antiquarian Society". The Master General did not think himself authorised to pay the expences, and this was stated from the beginning. Your Letter of the 2ᵈ Instant says, speaking of this expence of £6‖1‖9, — "which it was distinctly understood here the Ordnance Department were engaged to undertake, for the purpose of carrying into effect His Majesty's most gracious commands to the Master General." — His Lordship is quite ignorant of the grounds on which this distinct understanding existed; — the communication to His Grace The Duke of Gordon, which it is presumed was sent to the Antiquarian Society, and of which a Copy is enclosed, would not authorize such a conclusion; the words being that His Majesty permitted the removal of the Gun, and for that purpose The Master General would place it at the disposal of the Antiquarian Society.

The Master General has been rewarded by complaints against the Department, altho' it was the wish and intention to give every possible assistance. The expence of removing the Gun from Leith to Edinburgh has lately been directed to be paid by the Ordnance; and as His Lordship has now ordered that the charge of £6‖1‖9 for putting it on board the Steam Vessel should also be defrayed by this Department, he trusts that the subject is brought to a conclusion.

The Ordnance's readiness to pay for the move from Leith to Edinburgh is shown in a rather different light in a letter to Drummond Hay from the Storekeeper at Edinburgh Castle, Rob. McKerlie, dated 16 May:

I beg leave to transmit to you herewith enclosed, Mʳ Mortons' Account of Leith Walk, for repairing and painting Mons Megs' Carriage, amount £5. 12. 10.

I regret exceedingly that I cannot venture to submit it for payment, in another quarter, having succeeded, through my own representations, to cover the undermentioned expenses, which are perhaps regarded as not inconsiderable.

Expence of landing and lodging Mons Meg in the Naval Yard..............................	£ 9. 5. 5
For conveying the Gun from the Naval Yard to Edinburgh Castle	5.11. 0
	£14.16. 5

The Society promptly paid the painting bill, which according to the Secretary included painting the gun too.

The Council meeting on 20 February was chaired by Sir Walter Scott, making an exceptional appearance — and remarkably did not receive a mention in his Journal for the day despite the nature and amount of its business. (Several other things he did and did not do were mentioned). Besides dealing with Mons Meg's support and transport, as already described, the Council fixed 'the 9th of next month' for the return to the castle. The Secretary was authorised to write formally to various military authorities, including Major General the Commander of the Forces in North Britain, and provision of tickets for all members of the Society in town and others was approved. Sir Walter offered the services of the Celtic Society, of which he was President, to form part of the gun's escort, and this was warmly welcomed.

The considerable correspondence which followed included the issue of handsomely lithographed invitations to witness the operation within the fortress, distribution of tickets to the Celtic Society and for friends of the garrison, suggestions both for the strength of the military escort and for provision of policemen on the line of Leith Walk, and the arrangement with the civil authorities by Mr Trotter, Old Provost of the city, that the bells of St Giles would play 'Oh! Ye hae been lang a coming — Royal Charlie' when 'our ancient tower of strength comes in view of the Castle.'

Lord Robert Kerr sent:

General Order   Adjutant General's Office
                                                   Edinburgh 6". March 1829

A Troop of the 3rd Dragoon Guards with the Band of the Regiment, the whole of the Depöt 78th Foot off duty, with the Music of the Depöt; and the whole of the Royal Artillery off duty, to Parade at the Naval Yard Leith on Monday the 9th Instant at Eleven o'Clock forenoon for the purpose of Escorting the piece of Ordnance called Mons Meg to Edinburgh Castle — The Troops will be arranged on the spot, by a Staff Officer who will attend for that purpose.

The Adjutant of each Corps to attend at this office on Saturday the 7th Instant at half past Eleven o'Clock

By Order of the Major General
the Honble Sir Robert Wm O'Callagahan K.C.B.
        etc   etc   etc
                  Rt Kerr   /   A A G

One can see how Sir Walter Scott came to escalate his comments on the Secretary, who by now was writing of 'our Castle'.

23 Feb. after breakfast Mr Hay Drummond (sic) came in enchanted about Mons Meg, and roaring as loud as she could have done for her life when she was in perfect order

1 Mar. Mr Hay Drummond had something to say about Mons Meg

4 Mar. Mr Drummond Hay, who has an alertness in making business out of nothing came to call once more about Mons Meg. He is a good humoured gentlemanlike man but I would Meg were in his belly or he in hers.[23]

Almost identical reports of the procession of 9 March were printed in the *Scotsman* and in the *Edinburgh Weekly Journal*, both on 11 March:

After an absence of nearly seventy five years this ponderous mass of antiquarian ordnance was on Monday replaced in our venerable fortress with all due honours. It was on the 24th of April 1754 that this piece of antiquity left the Castle, and was drawn down the Canongate, and thence by the Easter Road to Leith where she was shipped on board the Happy Janet for the Tower of London, where she lay neglected, till the Antiquarian Society interested itself with success to get her restored to her ancient domicile. Some time ago we mentioned her arrival and landing at Leith from the City of Edinburgh steam-packet, whose proprietors gave her a gratuitous passage, since which time she has lain in the Naval Yard. As it was generally known that Monday was the day fixed upon for her removal, a great concourse of spectators assembled. A troop of the Third Dragoon Guards, a party of the Royal Artillery, and a strong detachment of the seventy-eighth Highlanders, all under the direction of Major Broke, Assist. Quarter Mas.-Gen., were in attendance to escort Meg to her old quarters, which at ten minutes past twelve (preceded by some members of the Celtic Society,[24] among whom were General Graham Stirling and Mr. Macdonald of Staffa) left the Naval Yard, drawn by ten horses, decked with ribands and evergreens, the two leading horses being rode by two boys dressed in tartan and carrying broadswords. The line of march was that adopted on the landing of his Most Gracious Majesty, viz. by Leith Walk, York Place and St. Andrew Square, and then by the North Bridge to the Castle, where the Royal Standard was hoisted in honour of the occasion, the gates being closed, and all other ceremonies being duly observed. At half-past one o'clock the advanced guard gave notice of Meg's approach, when she was welcomed by the hearty cheers of a dense multitude of all classes, the band of the Dragoons playing the "Highland Laddie", which on her entering the gate was changed to "God Save the King". She was then drawn to the Argyll Battery, and placed on a carriage prepared for her reception in front of the Main-guard-house. There were a number of carriages on the hill, among which was that of the Countess of Hopetoun, the rest chiefly belonging to military persons. The day was fine, and the bells of St. Giles lent their aid to enliven the gay scene, nor must we omit to state that the flag was displayed from the top of Marshall's Panorama, which also fired guns in honour of the occasion.

Instead of the *Scotsman's* last two sentences as just quoted, the *Weekly* reported:

During the ceremonies of the reception, the Castle had a remarkably lively appearance, every place from whence a view could be obtained being filled by persons of the higher classes. One numerous group had taken their station on the rock a little beyond the Barrier-guard-house unconscious, probably, that they stood on the identical spot occupied by Meg in former times . . . The Celtic Society, to the number of about 100, dined together in the evening in the British Hotel. Sir Walter Scott Bart in the Chair.[25]

The Antiquaries held an ordinary evening meeting, as well apparently as dining together. Thereafter there was correspondence on two further matters to complete the installation, besides numerous letters of thanks a week later, several of which mention Drummond Hay's family anxieties in the past week and the loss of an infant child. Early in April the Stone Shot were placed at the Society's disposal, in accordance with their request in February for

> sanction to and orders for the displacing, from the tops of walls and from doorways or other by-places within the Castle or elsewhere, the seven (or less or more in number of) stone Shot, that are supposed yet to remain of those formerly used in loading *Mons Meg*, in order that these shot be piled upon the Argyle Battery near to the Great Gun.

It may be more than a coincidence that the number of balls officially destroyed in 1754 was also seven.[26] There are still 5 18-inch balls beside the gun in 1978, apparently of granite, and one of limestone as well as an 18-inch hollow iron mortar bomb. They have been stated in the past to be of Galloway granite, but a check on them is necessary. Gaier states that at least twenty-four out of sixty-one 18-inch balls originally provided by Cambier for Mons were quarried at Ecaussines in Belgium, and an unspecified number of stone shot was included in the gift to James II.[27]

The final concern was the protection of the Gun from weather and visitors (still a source of concern to her custodians) — 8 May 1829:

> The Society have a wish to complete the painting of the great Gun and its old wooden carriage, as soon as the weather permit; but they are desirous that, previously to that operation, you would be so obliging as to cause a sufficient quantity of *chevaux de frise* to be delivered from the Ordnance Stores at this Place, for the purpose of their being placed around the Gun at Lt Colonel Birch's direction, and so as to afford additional facility to the sentries, in preventing further injury to both the gun & carriage; which the recent Garrison Orders, issued by the Lt Governor of the Castle, have no doubt checked.

The Argyll Battery, just inside the second of the Castle's present entrance-archways, and even its north-west end, was perhaps too busy a spot but there is no suggestion in the letter-book of a move to the uppermost ramparts. However, Mons' present position there on the Bomb or Mortar Battery was fixed in 1836, as described in Mr Blair's article, despite the additional work required in strengthening the understructure.

Acknowledgments

Much help in finding sources additional to the Letter-book and in interpretation has been mostly kindly given from time to time: by the late Mr M. R. Dobie, Mr J. C. Corson, Mr H. L. Blackmore, Mr I. Brown, Mr I. MacIvor, and Mr D. H. Caldwell.

Figure 235. Carving of pieces of artillery and other equipment, Mons Meg at left. *Edinburgh Castle*

Figure 236. Carving of pieces of artillery and munitions with gunner loading a gun. *Edinburgh Castle*

Postscript
Mons Meg's Original Carriage and the Carvings of Artillery in Edinburgh Castle
David H. Caldwell

Built in to the entrance pend of the modern outer gatehouse of Edinburgh Castle are two carvings in high relief of various guns and pieces of equipment, including Mons Meg, resting on a gun cart (figs. 235, 236). This has massive wooden sides and rests on four spoked and studded wheels solidly bound with iron. Behind is a coign for elevating and depressing the gun, and lying in the muzzle is a gunner's quadrant. The present carriage of Mons Meg, made in 1935, is based upon this carving which dates to the early seventeenth century.

When Mons was taken to the siege of Norham Castle in 1497 she only got as far as St Leonards just outside Edinburgh when she had to have a new 'cradle' made,[28] presumably because her old one had collapsed. It is unlikely, however, that this cradle is the one represented in the carving. By 1501 Mons was lying neglected in Edinburgh Castle, but in that year the earth was cleared away from her and she was turned over so that her touch hole lay uppermost. She was then lifted and laid on trestles, painted with red lead and a shelter made for her and another two guns with forty-nine rafters.[29] It is possible that Mons was the great bombard taken on James V's naval expedition round Scotland in 1540, in order to overawe the Islesmen. If so it may be to that year that the cart shown on the carving dates, for the Treasurer's Accounts for that year include payments to workmen and for materials for 'the stokking of the grete bumbert'.[30] This, incidentally, could have been the last time Mons was taken from her home in the castle until her departure for London in 1754. By that time she was again lying on the ground carriage-less,[31] and the carriage she was mounted on when she returned to Scotland was presumably one made to exhibit her in the Tower of London.

In the accounts of the Duke of Burgundy for 1436 there is mention of a great bombard called *Bourgogne* forged in two pieces for transportation on two separate carts, each pulled by forty-eight horses, and in 1443 two bombards were purchased, each in four parts and firing thirteen-inch stones.[32] Although it seems clear that Mons was manufactured in two pieces which it would have been easier to transport separately (hence the two rows of windlass holes for inserting levers to screw and unscrew chamber and barrel), there is no mention of this fact in early sources or that she was thus moved about. Early manuscript illustrations normally show large bombards without trunnions mounted on trestles or laid on the ground for firing. The cart on which Mons reposes on the carving in Edinburgh Castle is, however, obviously intended for firing the gun from — hence the coign and gunner's quadrant. Apart from its large wheels, it is a suitably enlarged version of the carriages on which guns for service in fortifications and ships were mounted as recently as last century. There are no obvious means of how it might have been drawn by a team of oxen or horses, and in the opinion of the present writer it was not designed for that.

The two carvings of guns are a unique pictorial record of the early Scottish artillery. We are indebted to the pages of Sir Daniel Wilson for the following account of their original situation:

> 'Immediately within the drawbridge [of Edinburgh Castle] there formerly stood an ancient and highly ornamented gateway, near the barrier guard-room. It was adorned with pilasters, and very rich mouldings carried over the arch, and surmounted with a curious piece of sculpture, in basso relief, set in an oblong panel, containing a representation of the famous cannon, Mons Meg, with groups of other ancient artillery and military weapons. This fine old port was only demolished in the beginning of the present century [i.e. the nineteenth], owing to its being found too narrow to give admission to modern carriages and waggons, when the present plain and inelegant gateway was erected on its site. Part of the curious carving alluded to has since been placed over the entrance to the Ordnance Office in the Castle, and the remaining portion is preserved in the Antiquarian Museum [i.e. the National Museum, Edinburgh]'.[33]

Wilson indicates in a footnote that his source for this information was R. McKerlie, Esq., of the Ordnance Office (see above, p. 432). Furthermore, McKerlie was responsible for preserving the two parts of the carving and having them placed in their then homes. The piece without Mons Meg (fig. 236) appears in the catalogue of the National Museum published in 1859 (no. G 40) but not in the catalogue of 1892, by which time the stone had been handed over for inclusion in the new gatehouse of Edinburgh Castle in 1888.

Apart from Mons Meg, the two carvings show in considerable detail a selection of the rest of the equipment in the royal gunhouse. Most prominent are five large cast (bronze) guns mounted on field carriages. One of them has an octagonal chase, a design which was fashionable for much of the sixteenth century, another has the fore-part of its barrel writhened, just like a cannon of Francis I (1515-47) in the Musée de l'Armée, Paris (N.65). It is being loaded by a gunner (fig. 236). All these guns have conical cascabels, which suggests a date for them in the late sixteenth century. Between them is a mortar or small bombard with trunnions, mounted on a stand, and scattered round about are several chambers for breech-loading guns. These have rectangular handles, a clearly defined neck and slightly convex sides, and are remarkably like a wrought-iron chamber in the National Museum, Edinburgh (LH 236). Arranged crosswise in the background are two small unmounted field guns with octagonal barrels and two hagbuts of crok with stocks ending in loops like a wrought-iron gun in the collection of Sir Walter Scott at Abbotsford. An assortment of ladles, sponges and rammers for loading the guns, a powder horn for priming them and a lintstock for firing them are clearly visible behind the guns, while in the foreground are piled up barrels of powder and gunstones. There is a bucket and perhaps either trestles or a set of scales beside the gun nearest to Mons Meg. Behind Mons is a grappling iron for throwing over walls and above the two large guns placed back to back two fire arrows and a bow(?).

The exact date of these carvings is not known. While all the guns and equipment shown could quite happily be dated to the sixteenth century or earlier, the best evidence of date is provided by the clothing of the gunner. He appears to be wearing Venetians (knee-length breeches), and although they became high fashion at least in France and England during the 1570s, the whole outline is much more typical of the early seventeenth century, or even later.[34]

NOTES

1. C. Gaier, 'The origin of Mons Meg', *Journ. Arms & Armour Soc.*, v (1967), 425-31, 450-2.
2. J. B. Paul, 'Ancient Artillery: With Some Notes on Mons Meg', *Proc. Soc. Antiq. Scot.*, l (1915-16), 199.
3. *Treasurer Acct.*, i, 115, 348 for the two sieges and vol. x, 367 for the *feux de joie* in 1558. The contemporary publication, *Mercurius Publicus* (cited by J. Grant, *Memorials of the Castle of Edinburgh* [Edinburgh and London, 1850 edn], 166) is the source for her being fired in 1660, and the account of her bursting in 1680 (sometimes erroneously given as in 1682) is in Sir J. Lauder of Fountainhall, *Historical Observer*, ed. A. Urquhart & D. D. Laing (Bannatyne Club, 1840), 5.
4. Battersbee see p. 426.
5. A. de Behault, 'Le canon d'Edinbourg "Mons Meg" forgé, à Mons, au XVᵉ siècle', *Annales du Cercle Archéologique de Mons*, xxiv (1894), 1-96; cf. W. H. Finlayson, 'Mons Meg', *Scot. Hist Rev.*, xxvii (1948), 124-6, Mons Meg compared with Dulle Griet.
6. C. Blair, 'A New Carriage for Mons Meg', *Journ. Arms & Armour Soc.*, v (1967), 431-50, 452.
7. Antiquaries MSS 533, National Museum, Edinburgh, handsomely bound and indexed sometime after 1841, containing 74 documents, mostly letters and copy letters (wrongly numbered), and some historical notes and extracts.
8. *The Scots Magazine*, xvi (1754), 202 (cited by Drummond Hay).

9. MSS cited by Blair, 'A New Carriage for Mons Meg'. Extract by Drummond Hay from Ordnance Office records in Edinburgh Castle — '24 April 1754 Nr 19. Broke up and destroyed by Order of the Board dated the 28th Feb: Among other articles
Stones for Mons Meg 7
Nr. 20 to Woolwich and there delivered to John Cockburn Esq Ordnance Storekeeper to clear the Stores at Edinburgh Castle — By order of the Board dated 26th February last, by the *Happy Janet* John Dick master'.

10. J. G. Lockhart, *Life of Sir Walter Scott* (Edinburgh, 1902-3 edn), vii, 79-80.

11. *Familiar Letters of Sir Walter Scott*, ed. D. Douglas (Edinburgh, 1894), ii, 155-6; now National Library of Scotland MS 3895, fos. 103-5.

12. From a jocularly disparaging reference in 1836 by a senior subordinate, Mr Porrett, quoted by Blair, 'A New Carriage for Mons Meg', we learn that Mark Singleton Esq. was Principal Storekeeper in the Tower. He remained so till 1829, but there is no sign of his having made any difficulties, or financial arrangements, in 1828.

13. *The Journal of Sir Walter Scott 1825-32*, ed. D. Douglas (Edinburgh, 1890).

14. Public Record Office, WO 44 529: photocopies in the Tower Armouries.

15. *The Scotsman*, 4 Oct. 1828, reported that 'The City of Edinburgh Steam-Packet . . . sails this forenoon from Leith Harbour, being her One Hundredth Voyage betwixt this and London since she started in 1821.' Quoted in the *Scotsman*, 4 Oct. 1978.

16. The papers of the Board (PRO, cited in n. 14) show that Lord Downes had considered this, getting on 20 Oct. a report from the Royal Arsenal's Shipping Superintendent 'that to send the Gun to Leith by any of the Ordnance Vessels the expense cannot be reckoned at less than £25 . . . but might be effected by freight in one of the Leith Traders for about £10 . . . no cranes at Tower Wharf equal to slinging the Gun into a Vessel . . . but I do not suppose there would be any difficulty in removing it by a Devil Carriage from the Tower to Leith Wharf where there is a crane of sufficient power . . .'

17. See above, p. 432.

18. It is interesting that these ideas on ornament and inscriptions approximate to what was carried out in 1836.

19. The coloured drawing and careful ink section, ascribed in the letter-book to Lt. Battersbee, must be the 'beautiful copy' of it given to the Society on 9 Feb. by Adam Jackson Esq., civil engineer. In copying it now the lines and figures have had to be made bolder.

20. J. Hewitt, 'Mons Meg, the Ancient Bombard, preserved at Edinburgh Castle', *Archaeol. Journ.*, x (1853), 25-30; Gaier, 'The Origin of Mons Meg', pl. CIX.

21. Blair, 'A New Carriage for Mons Meg', 436-45.

22. The Superintendant found it necessary to postpone the movement of the gun for a fortnight because 'it will take some time to erect Sheers on the Tower Wharf'. However, on 22 Nov. he reported it had indeed gone as 'Officers at the Tower not conceiving it to weigh more than 5 tons it was shipped on a lighter . . . and . . . by means of a crane at Blackwall' (PRO, cited in n. 14).

23. See however note of a farewell dinner, and appreciative pen-sketches in *Journal*, 25 May 1829 and 13 Nov. 1831 — 'high spirits, a zealous faith, good humour, and enthusiasm'.

24. 'About 30, "in costume"', according to Scott's *Journal*. He himself accompanied the Countess of Hopetoun.

25. Scott's long *Journal* entry about the day includes: 'The style in which the [artillery men] manned and wrought the windlass which raised Old Meg, weight seven or eight tons, from her temporary carriage to that which had been her basis for many years, was singularly beautiful as a combined exhibition of skill and strength. My daughter had what might have proved a frightful accident. Some roquets were let off, one of

which lighted upon her head and set her bonnet on fire. She neither screamed nor ran but quietly permitted Charles Sharpe to extinguish the fire.'

26. See n. 9.

27. Gaier, 'The Origin of Mons Meg' 426-7, 430-1. It is possible that the limestone ball in the castle is from Belgium and it is hoped to put this to the test scientifically. I am grateful to G. H. Collins of the Institute of Geological Sciences for advice about these balls.

28. *Treasurer Acct.* i, 347.

29. Ibid., ii, 24-25.

30. Ibid., vii, 354.

31. W. Maitland, *The History of Edinburgh* (Edinburgh, 1753), 164.

32. Napoleon III & I. Favé, *Études sur le passé et l'avenir de l'artillerie*, 6 vols (Paris, 1846-71), iii, 128-9; see also A. de Behault 'Le canon d'Edimbourg "Mons Meg" forgé, à Mons, ae XVᵉ siècle', *Annales de Cercle Archéologique de Mons*, xxiv (1894), 51; and R. C. Clephan, 'The Ordnance of the fourteenth and fifteenth centuries', *Archaeol. Journ.*, lxviii (1911), 106. These guns would have been screwed together like the large Turkish gun at the Tower of London, presently lying in two pieces.

33. D. Wilson, *Memorials of Edinburgh in the Olden Time* (Edinburgh, 1891 edn), i, 160-1.

34. I am grateful to my colleague, Mrs Helen Bennett of the National Museum, Edinburgh, for advising me on the costume.

Index

(Page numbers in italics indicate illustrations)